*Mike Tyson*

# MIKE TYSON

## *Money, Myth, and Betrayal*

by Montieth M. Illingworth

A Birch Lane Press Book
Published by Carol Publishing Group

For Crystal, the love of my life

A Birch Lane Press Book
Published by Carol Publishing Group
Birch Lane Press is a registered trademark of Carol Communications, Inc.

Editorial Offices: 600 Madison Avenue, New York, N.Y. 10022
Sales & Distributions Offices: 120 Enterprise Avenue, Secaucus, N.J. 07094
In Canada: Musson Book Company, a division of General Publishing Company, Ltd.,
    Don Mills, Ontario M3B 2T6

Queries regarding rights and permission should be addressed to Carol
Publishing Group, 600 Madison Avenue, New York, N.Y. 10022

Carol Publishing Group books are available at special discounts for bulk
purchases, for sales promotions, fund raising, or educational purposes.
Special editions can be created to specifications. For details, contact:
Special Sales Department, Carol Publishing Group, 120 Enterprise Avenue,
Secaucus, N.J. 07094

Excerpt from *Invisible Man* by Ralph Ellison © 1952 Courtesy of Vintage Books.

Manufactured in the United States of America
10  9  8  7  6  5  4  3  2  1

**Library of Congress Cataloging-in-Publication Data**

Illingworth, Montieth M.
    Mike Tyson : money, myth and betrayal / by Montieth Illingworth.
        p.   cm.
    "A Birch Lane Press Book."
    ISBN 1-55972-079-4
    1. Tyson, Mike. 1966-   . 2. Boxers (Sports)—United States—
Biography.  I. Title.
GV1132.T97I45 1991
796.8'3'092—dc20
    [B]

"I am invisible, understand, simply because people refuse to see me. Like the bodiless heads you see sometimes in circus sideshows, it is as though I have been surrounded by mirrors of hard, distorting glass. When they approach me they see only my surroundings, themselves, or figments of their imagination—indeed, everything and anything except me."

*   *   *

"You ache with the need to convince yourself that you do exist in the real world, that you're part of all the sound and anguish and you strike out with your fists, you curse and you swear to make them recognize you. And, alas, it's seldom successful."

—*Invisible Man* by Ralph Ellison

# *Acknowledgments*

I thank my agent, Bernard Kurman, whose support and guidance made this book possible.

I also thank Mike Tyson. I believe that he wants the world to know who he is, and what it's been like to live his life. In some of our discussions, I sensed in him the hope that perhaps I would be the one to convey those thoughts and feelings truthfully. But at the same time I knew that faith in others was a quality of his humanity that Tyson had decided long ago to keep in reserve, and use sparingly. I don't begrudge him. I know he did all that he could.

This book was born in the opinion of an editor at *Vanity Fair* magazine that enough had been said about Mike Tyson. I thank her for being wrong. Steven Schragis and Sandy Richardson were the first people at Carol Publishing Group to believe in my ideas, and the value of the project. The contributions of my editor, Allan Wilson, are deeply appreciated. I also thank David Eichorn, my publicist and the best in the business.

The suggestions and counsel of my friend Michael Zeitlin kept the writing on the right path. The friendship and love of many others helped me through the tough times: Dr. Tom Barnard, Dave Brisbin, Dr. Harold Bursztajn, Corey Copeland, Mitchell Friedman, Corinna Gardner, Bronagh Gibson, Josh Goldin, Dwight Greene, Ruth Greene, Joan Illingworth, Dr. Patricia Illingworth, Laura Innis, Joe Kelly, Laurie Newbound, Jim O'Brien, Joel Parker, Sam Pollard, Cynthia Setchell, Claire Timoney, Kathy Weaver, and Graham Yost.

Tony Fox of HBO introduced me to boxing. Seth Abraham of Time Warner Sports gave me countless hours of his time explaining the business of boxing. Larry Merchant, also of HBO, was always generous with his time. I learned much from his insights. Don King let me be witness to the phenomenon of his person, often from close up. Dorothy Zeil opened her heart and brought emotional focus to the dramatic core of the story. Nick Beck and Steve Lott spoke from the heart as much as the mind. Butch Lewis opened up my eyes to the art of the real deal. James Dupree, a man not afraid to do the right thing, was an inspiration.

The following people all provided important information and insights: Teddy Atlas, Matt Baranski, Phil Berger, Dr. Gene Brody, Bill Cayton, Ernestine Coleman, Dr. Max Day, Camille Ewald, Joe Fariello, Ross Greenberg, Rick Hornung, David S. Mandell, Wally Matthews, Tom Patti, Dr. David S. Rosenthal, Ed Schuyler, Joseph Spinelli, Bobby Stewart, José Torres, Alex Wallah, Brian Hamill, Jay Bright, and Reuben Givens.

Finally, there's Crystal D. Greene, my wife. I took so much from our marriage, and our family, to write this book, and she gave, and gave, with love, patience, and understanding. My biggest debt is to her.

# PART ONE

# The Champion Made

# Chapter One

**N**ot much is known about Lorna Tyson. She was born Lorna Smith in 1930, probably in the South. Like so many other blacks after World War II, she migrated north in search of work and more social freedoms. There is no account of her keeping in touch with or ever seeing her parents, siblings, or any other relatives. Mike Tyson had no recollection of such extended family on his mother's side. He has described Lorna as around five-foot-six with a big, sturdy frame. She had medium-brown skin and dull-gray hair that waved back from her wide face. She wore glasses and had an air of quiet dignity.

At some point during her first years in Brooklyn, New York, she married Percel Tyson, of whom nothing is known. They later divorced. Lorna never remarried. She did fall in love, with Jimmy Kirkpatrick, a heavyset, boisterous roustabout who drove big cars, worked menial construction jobs, and dreamed of owning his own business. Kirkpatrick had sixteen children when he moved in, all of them living with their various mothers. He fathered three more with Lorna. The first was a boy, Rodney, born in 1961. Next came Denise in 1964. Two years later, well into Lorna's third pregnancy, Kirkpatrick moved out. On June 30, 1966, in Cumberland Hospital, Michael Gerard Tyson was born.

Without the help of Kirkpatrick's occasional paycheck, Lorna struggled. She worked off and on, once as a nurse's aide, but made barely enough money to support her family. Another boyfriend, Edward Gillison, moved in. He contributed little. By the time Michael was eight years old, the Tysons had moved four times within Brooklyn. Each move took them deeper into poverty. His last home with Lorna was 178 Amboy Street, Apartment 2A, in the heart of Brownsville, Brooklyn's most destitute section.

The Tyson family lived in perpetual crisis. Lorna began to drink. She and Gillison argued constantly, and when they fought, Lorna took the worst of it, until one day, while boiling water, she chased Gillison around the apartment and seared him. In between jobs she went on welfare. When the heating bill couldn't be paid, they all slept in their clothes. Tyson put cardboard in his shoes to cover up the holes. Food was scarce. Meals at times were made of flour and water.

Even genetics seemed to conspire against the family. By the time Rodney was twelve, he weighed a blubbery 280 pounds. Denise also tended to put on weight. They all suffered, but it seemed that the youngest boy suffered most. "Big Head Mike," as he was known to neighbors in the building, was ridiculed for every little oddity of appearance and character. On the streets, because of his lisp, the other children called Tyson "Little Fairy Boy." He was bigger than most other children his age, but intensely passive. They beat him up for the lisp, for his shoes, and for whatever he had in his pocket. He wore glasses briefly, and they beat him up for that. Tyson became increasingly withdrawn around other children, and that earned more beatings.

His father had stayed in Brooklyn, and he and the Tysons would have chance meetings. "When Mike was seven, he, Denise, and Rodney were walking down the street in Brownsville and saw their father," said Camille Ewald, the woman who would later become his surrogate mother. "He dished out a dollar for each of them. Mike threw his on the ground."

By age nine, Tyson had started keeping pigeons in a coop on the roof of a nearby abandoned building. The family dog, a black Labrador, once killed a half dozen of the birds, piling them up in Tyson's bedroom. Other kids would steal his pigeons, and he would steal theirs. The only taboo was death. You could steal, but not kill.

One day, Tyson found an older boy taking a bird out of the coop. They argued, and the boy ripped off the bird's head with a single, vicious twist of his hand. Tyson went into a blind rage and pounced on the boy, punching and kicking with every ounce of strength he could muster.

For any boy, such a battle would have been a watershed event. For a boy raised in Brownsville, it would yield a sense of victory in the perennial battle against overwhelming feelings of helplessness and poverty. Years later, when Tyson became heavyweight champion of the world, that moment of rage would be constructed into an epiphany. Tyson played along. It fit ever so conveniently into his public persona as some primal force of destruction. Tyson would cavalierly recount that and other seminal events as if he had found not just liberation but, when the urges were tempered into systematic violence, empowerment as well.

When he indulged in that persona, he wanted the world to believe that he was a nine-year-old man-child wreaking havoc without a care for the feelings of his victims—a sociopath. He felt nothing and cared for no one. He wanted no one's love. "I did evil things," he said in early 1988. His sister, Denise, affirmed the self-portrayal. "It became fun for him to beat up kids," she said to a reporter also that year. "Everyone was afraid of him. He stopped being called Mike. It became 'Mike Tyson.'"

The stories tumble out from Tyson. There was the time he and Denise played doctor on a sleeping Rodney. Tyson took a razor blade, sliced his arm, and poured in alcohol into the wound. Tyson stopped going to school. He joined a gang, the Jolly Stompers. He drank cheap liquor and smoked cigarettes. He stole from fruit stands. He beat up other kids without provocation. He would offer to carry a woman's grocery bags, then run off with either the food or her purse. Tyson became an expert pickpocket. He particularly enjoyed ripping gold chains from the necks of women at bus stops. As Tyson once said, he relished a concept of himself as Brownsville's own Artful Dodger.

Whether those stories were true or not didn't seem to matter to him. Tyson's life as champion would reach the point where appearance and reality—what people wanted to believe about him, and who he really was—became hopelessly blurred. He would be raw material to feed cultural curiosity about the nature and origins of sociopathic viciousness. By early 1988, *Sports Illustrated* writer Gary Smith, taking his lead from such stories by Tyson, would succumb to literary romanticism and equate the rage in Tyson with social ethics. "He is justice!" Smith wrote about Tyson after being told about the rooftop battle. "Instincts haven't made him fight. Outraged innocence has."

The idea that Tyson became a fighter in order to right the wrongs done to his person, family, neighborhood, class, and race ignored what was probably the most significant point about what really happened on that rooftop. Tyson reveled in a perverse romanticism about his past, to disguise rather than reveal.

The rage was rooted in feelings of confusion about his life—about where his next meal would come from, what his future might be, who would care for him, and most important, whether his mother, or anyone else, loved him. The rage set in motion a vicious cycle in which rage only pushed farther away the people closest to him. It also alienated Tyson from himself. When rage is your only friend, all the other qualities of human nature—kindness, pity, affection—wither. No human being can live that way for long, and Tyson, if ever he was as far from human as he wanted others to believe, surely didn't. Rage and a life of systematic violence meant death. Within Tyson there was always a whispering voice that sought life. He was a survivor.

By the age of eleven, Tyson was going in and out of juvenile detention centers in Brooklyn. Tyson escaped as often as he could. By the age of twelve, he had graduated to Spofford, a medium-security facility in the Bronx. A dozen times he went there for short stays, until the family courts, and his mother, realized that he had to be sent out of New York. Just thirteen years old, Tyson went to the Tryon School for Boys, two hundred miles upstate in the town of Johnstown. There he would either straighten out or they would keep him until the age of sixteen.

Many of the kids who end up in places like Tryon go on to become adult felons and do a stint or two in prison before making an effort to go straight. Tyson, to the amazement of everyone who knew him then, started his reform early.

In comparison to Spofford, Tryon was a country club. "Instructors" referred to it as a "campus." The boys lived in "cottages." There were no chaotic dormitories, fences, barbed wire, or barred windows. Boys lived one to a room. The food was plain, and starchy, but it came three times a day, 365 days of the year. There were movies, school classes, trade instruction, and sports. It was not unusual for some boys to run away a few days before discharge so that they could enjoy the punishment of staying longer. The alternative, after all, was a return to the streets of New York.

There are two different versions of what happened to Tyson soon after he arrived. In the first one, he got locked up in the "secure" cottage called Elmwood after some violent outburst. While there, he found out that one of the supervisors, Bobby Stewart, was a former professional boxer. He pleaded to see him, begged for a lesson, got it, and was discovered.

The second version makes more sense. Muhammad Ali visited Spofford once. Tyson marveled at the man, but more than that reflected on the living, breathing symbolism of his life. Ali was a cultural icon of the black man making it his way in a white world. The allure of Ali promised the acquisition of money and power without compromise. For the boy who had learned to be alone, the idea of Ali, regardless of the realities, promised that, if he so chose, he would never need anyone else again. All he had to do was learn to box. And Bobby Stewart, Tyson decided, would be his teacher.

Bobby Stewart had a reputation around Tryon as tough and unforgiving, a strict disciplinarian who considered most of the kids incapable of reform. His pessimism came from the disappointments of his own life.

He was born and raised in Amsterdam, New York, a small upstate town that had crumbling nineteenth-century mills and a dim future. Stewart played football in high school, married at seventeen, then began to box in the amateurs. In 1974, he won the National Golden Gloves light heavyweight title. Instead of holding out for the 1976 Olympics, which would produce such future boxing stars as Sugar Ray Leonard, he turned pro. Stewart won thirteen fights and lost three, then burned out. He was a small-town boy with an honest heart and few dreams.

After boxing, Stewart managed a family-owned bar. He worked part-time at Tryon, then went on staff in 1978. By the time Tyson arrived in 1980, Stewart was still fit, and he had trimmed down in weight. He was barely six feet tall and sinewy, and he had a small, boxy head, a flush of red in his cheeks, and pummeled-down pug nose. He had boyish Scotchman's looks but a gruff blue-collar manner and slurred speech, the result of too many blows to the head.

Stewart had been hired to start a boxing program. Several boys wanted to box, but according to Stewart, few had the desire or the discipline to learn more than the basics. Usually, he just laced the gloves on them and let them flail away for a round or two. Tyson would change Stewart's dismal view of human nature. He differed in every respect.

Once he was placed in Elmwood, Tyson asked for Stewart. For two days, Stewart ignored him. Tyson suddenly became a model inmate. Stewart didn't fall for it. One night he waited for Tyson to fall asleep, then banged violently on his door.

"What the fuck do you want?" he yelled.

"Mr. Stewart, I want to be a fighter," Tyson said meekly.

"So do the rest of these scumbags. They wouldn't be here if they were tough and had balls like a fighter. They're losers!" Stewart spit out.

Tyson said it again. "I want to be a fighter."

For two weeks Stewart put Tyson off. With each passing day, Tyson's behavior improved. Finally, Stewart put Tyson in the ring. There Tyson made an incongruous sight. At thirteen years of age he packed almost two hundred pounds of slablike mass into a five-foot, eight-inch frame. Every part of him looked thick. His head appeared large and out of proportion to his body. He didn't so much walk as lumber, as if the mass, and its arrangement, was an insupportable burden. The most obvious anomaly was his voice—too high-pitched to match the menacing physique and with a slight, almost farcical lisp.

Stewart didn't want to take any chances. He dared not let Tyson pummel one of the other boys and become some kind of bully. So into the ring went Stewart himself, and for three rounds he humiliated Tyson.

"After we finished, the first words out of his mouth were, 'Can we do it again tomorrow?'" Stewart recalled later. "I didn't care if he could box—I was amazed with his mind. He wanted to better himself. He knew he wanted that at age thirteen. It almost scared me. None of the other kids were like that."

Tyson became a puzzle to Stewart. If he was such a bad kid, why had he been put in Tryon, a less-then-minimum-security facility? Stewart checked Tyson's file: all the crimes were petty, the worst being the theft of fruit from a grocery store. In an evaluation by the Tryon teachers, Tyson tested as borderline retarded, but as Stewart discovered, he had been in school a total of two days over the previous year. "Of course he tested badly—he could barely read or write!" Stewart remembered.

Stewart began to see the psychological scars. Tyson didn't just have self-esteem problems. They were more fundamental. He had no sense of self-worth at all. It was the affliction of the abandoned personality, the unloved. "He felt bad about his body, being so big, and the kids taunted him for it," Stewart said. "I'd never seen anyone that bad. He was scared of his own shadow. He barely talked, never looked you in the eye. He was a baby."

They trained together every day, boxed every other. Stewart secretly asked one of the other boys to tutor Tyson. He improved both in the ring and the classroom. Tyson went from a fourth- to a seventh-grade reading level in three months. In the gym he improved too, in strength and in skill. Without any practice, he bench-pressed 245 pounds. His punches also started to become accurate. "He broke my nose with a jab. It almost knocked me down. I had never before been hit that hard with a jab. I had the next week off, so I let it heal at home and never told Tyson what he'd done," Stewart said.

Emotionally, Tyson did not heal. His size, his prowess, and the aura of inexplicable power made him almost freakish to the other boys. Special treatment by Stewart created suspicions. "To those kids, someone who's doing well is on the outside," Stewart said. Nor did Tyson have any desire, it seemed, to use boxing to become a leader. "He didn't have the confidence to lead."

Stewart's support and approval counted for something. But it was Lorna's love that Tyson wanted most. The boys got to call home every Sunday. When Tyson first called Lorna, he mumbled a few words, then glumly handed the phone to his mentor. "He wanted me to tell her how good he was doing. 'Tell her, tell her,' he kept saying. His mother said she had trouble believing that he had changed. She sounded drunk. Mike told me she drank a lot," Stewart said.

Not once during Tyson's nine-month stay did Lorna visit the facility, send any Christmas presents, or write a letter.

The boxing gave Tyson purpose and provided a ray of hope about the future. It brought a semblance of order to his feelings, but not resolution—at least not yet. Despite the progress, Stewart sensed the deep-down pain. "I thought his negative self-image could hurt him as a boxer. Everyone always knew he could win, but he convinces himself he can't."

Stewart didn't want Tyson to go back to Brownsville. He could succeed if he had the right help. Stewart knew that Cus D'Amato, a seventy-two-year-old fight manager who lived just outside the town of Catskill, ran an informal boxing camp for boys. Some were from town families. Others, usually the more troubled boys from New York City, stayed in D'Amato's house. Camille Ewald, his companion, served as den mother. D'Amato was tough, he knew boxing, and he provided a familylike environment. For a kid like Tyson, it was a halfway house back into the world.

Stewart called his own former trainer, Matt Baranski, who had worked with D'Amato since the late 1960s. Baranski agreed to set up a meeting. Stewart prepared Tyson every day for a week. D'Amato didn't run a charity. He looked for something special in a boy. Desire and determination to succeed impressed D'Amato more than ring skills. Tyson's glaring emotional problems might put him off. Nonetheless, Stewart gave Tyson a few advanced lessons that he knew would be impressive, like spinning out of a corner and slipping a punch.

For every hour they spent in preparation, Tyson doubled it when alone. He sensed opportunity. "One of the guards went by his room at three in the morning and heard grunting and snorting," Stewart recalled. "He was working on slipping punches."

On a chilly weekend in March 1980 they drove down to Catskill. D'Amato had converted a town meeting hall located above the police station into a gym, plopping a boxing ring in the center of a room maybe a hundred feet long and sixty feet wide. There were no windows. Five round Deco-style lamps provided the only light. As in all boxing gyms, the walls were covered with press clippings boasting of the feats of his boys, some fight posters, and a collection of fading black-and-white still photos of heavyweight notables through the ages—Jack Sharkey, Jack Dempsey, Joe Louis, Rocky Marciano, Sonny Liston. Also on the walls were photos of the two champions D'Amato had managed and helped train during the 1950s and 1960s—Floyd Patterson, a heavyweight, and José Torres, who won crowns in two weight classes.

"Mike started to throw me around," Stewart recalled of the exhibition they gave D'Amato. "He had that incredible speed and power. I caught him with a couple right hands and his nose bled. Cus wanted to stop it. Mike almost cried. 'No, we always go three rounds. We have to go three.'"

Cus had seen enough. His first words to Stewart would become a centerpiece of the Tyson mythology: "That's the heavyweight champion of the world," he said—as if everyone with eyes had to reach the same conclusion.

Afterward, they all went to D'Amato's home for lunch. D'Amato and Ewald lived four miles outside Catskill in the town of Athens. The house was a quarter mile off the main road in a clearing on a hill. A yellow sign on a tree at the driveway entrance reads Children at Play. The house, built at the turn of the century in a late Victorian design, rose up three stories and was covered in white clapboard. Several dormer windows jutted out from the shale-gray roof. A porch wrapped around three-quarters of the section with the river view. Rosebushes hugged one side. Two towering maple trees shaded part of the well-kept lawn. Nestled back at the edge of the forest sat a barn-shaped coach house. It was the sort of spread, ten acres in all, that once would have belonged to the town judge.

Tyson had never seen anything like it. When they pulled up the driveway, a look of awe spread across his face. "I told him that if he wanted to, he could live here," Stewart said. "He couldn't believe it."

They entered the house through the long, narrow kitchen. The dining room table could seat ten or more. But the heart of the fourteen-room house was the mock-Tudor-style living room. Deep, rich mahogany paneling went halfway up the walls. Broad beams crossed the ceiling. There was a fireplace that had been covered up. The couch looked deep and comfortable; the chairs sported rich leather, and solid, heavy, hardwood frames. One entire wall held a collection of hardcover books. A family lived here. To Tyson it seemed warm, secure, and, with the books, slightly mysterious.

For her guests Ewald cooked a hearty meal. D'Amato did all the talking. To Tyson, he must have seemed an odd old man. D'Amato had a large, round, bald head set on a thick neck and broad, square shoulders. His hair, almost snow-white, was cut short around the sides. His eyes were deep brown and set a bit apart. The nose looked strong. Though only five foot eight, and a bit overweight, D'Amato had an imposing presence. He had a barrel chest, thick forearms, and large hands.

D'Amato's voice was gravelly and harsh, a voice from some urban New York place that Tyson couldn't place. The word "champion" came out as "champeen." His eyes was busy. He'd squint, then suddenly his eyebrows would rise up and his eyes would open wide. It made him look alternately skeptical and surprised. He blew air out of his nose in light bursts for no apparent reason and made a "tch" sound with his tongue in the middle of a sentence.

It wasn't easy to follow his thinking. D'Amato frequently meandered off the point, diverted by some inner music into other ideas, anecdotes, and aphorisms, all related to boxing. He seemed to speak about obvious, self-evident things in complex ways—at times getting lost in the web of his own spun-out thought. Often he would stop himself and ask, "What was I talking about?" Ultimately, he'd manage to return to the original point, which he would then complete as if he'd never strayed.

For Tyson, not used to having to sit and listen for so long to one person, let alone an old white man accustomed to a captive audience, D'Amato must have seemed both foreign and annoying. At the same time, he was also mesmerizing.

Ewald remembered the day. As she watched Tyson drive away with Stewart, the car suddenly stopped. Tyson jumped out and ran back to her. "We had all these rosebushes around the house. He asked if he could take some flowers back to Tryon. 'I've never seen roses before,' he said. 'I thought only the very rich people grew roses. I want to show them to the other kids.'"

Ewald found out later that by the time Tyson got back to Tryon, the roses had died.

D'Amato insisted that Stewart provide proof of Tyson's age. He couldn't believe that any boy of thirteen was both that physically developed and mentally focused. Stewart looked in the Tryon records, but he couldn't find a birth certificate. He did, however, get verification of Tyson's birthday from New York City officials.

Stewart took Tyson back to Catskill for three more visits. All during this period at Tryon, Tyson was conforming even more to the role of model student. "When he did something wrong, any little thing, he'd ask me, 'Will you still work with me?' He didn't want to take the chance of losing me or missing out on the opportunity to live with Cus," Stewart said.

D'Amato watched him box but didn't offer much instruction. He spent more time alone with Tyson, talking, but also listening. He was more interested in the boy's mind than in his body. He wanted to see the bends in Tyson's mind and the distortions of his heart. Sometimes the more troubled the boy, the better—it gave D'Amato the chance to completely reorder the psychic furniture. That was the core of his method, on which all the other training depended. He'd knock and bang until the boy opened up, and then he'd stomp about inside, pointing to the disorder to make the boy see the truth about himself. And the truth he was most interested in was human fear. D'Amato believed that a boxer, by confronting fear and using it effectively in the ring, assured his success—the imposition of the will through violence.

Of course, D'Amato's method didn't always make a champion. Sometimes all that D'Amato's mind-work produced was a more confident young man, not a champion boxer. Many of the boys left him because he was too strict about what they did, both in and out of the ring. And D'Amato had yet to see any of his protégés—Patterson and Torres included—execute fully his unique style of boxing, a style that, as far back as the 1950s, his critics had ridiculed. The D'Amato style required almost robotlike training, intense concentration, extreme confidence, and superb emotional control. D'Amato believed that when executed to perfection, especially by a fast-punching heavyweight, the style would produce an unbeatable boxer.

Tyson had the kind of hand speed D'Amato required and certainly, given his size at the age of thirteen, the potential to grow into an imposing natural heavyweight. D'Amato also realized that he had a teenager whose psychic furniture was disposed in a chaotic and entangled clutter of fear and insecurity. Tyson wanted desperately to find order and meaning in his life, but didn't know how. D'Amato did. "After they'd talked for hours, Cus decided Mike had it," said Ewald. "He told me, 'Camille, this is the one I've been waiting for all my life. My third champion.'"

\* \* \*

Transferring Tyson into D'Amato's care wasn't easy. Tyson had been at Tryon only six months when Stewart raised the issue with state officials. There were problems. Tyson was still only thirteen; the mother's approval was needed. A troubled urban teenager would be put in a small-town school, with unforeseeable consequences. And there was the matter of his support. Who would pay? D'Amato?

D'Amato's situation looked far better than it actually was. He had declared bankruptcy in 1971 and still owed hundreds of thousands of dollars to the Internal Revenue Service, a by-product of his turbulent years as a fight manager. Ewald, however, owned the house. And they derived income from a variety of sources. Local and state officials supplied funding for D'Amato and some of his live-in fighters to train local boys in the Catskill gym. Some of the older boys who already lived in the house, and were training to become professionals, worked part-time. And the parents, if they had money, contributed.

One unusual source of funds was Jim Jacobs and Bill Cayton, who had a company in New York that licensed out the rights to their collection of fight films. The two also had experience managing fighters. From them D'Amato got a monthly stipend of one thousand dollars. The money covered expenses for the gym, but mostly paid for the house. For their stipend Jacobs and Cayton expected, some day, to get a promotable fighter, who would repay the investment. It was an unusual arrangement, highly speculative from a business standpoint, and tolerated mostly because of D'Amato's long friendship with Jacobs. So far, the investment hadn't produced a fighter worthy of professional development.

Stewart and D'Amato prevailed with the state. On June 30, the day he turned fourteen, Tyson was released into D'Amato's custody. His life was about to become intimately intertwined, for better or worse, with one of boxing's most unusual personalities.

# Chapter Two

Constantine D'Amato was born January 17, 1908, in a small tenement near the intersection of Southern Boulevard and 149th Street in the area of the Bronx known as Classen Point. His father had come to New York from Italy in 1899 and worked delivering ice and coal. In all, there were eight sons. Three died in infancy. D'Amato was the second youngest. In Italian the first *n* of his name was not pronounced, so it became Costantine, then Coster, Cos, and eventually Cus.

His mother died when D'Amato was four. His father cared for the boys as best he could but lost them, as it were, to the streets. Love alternated with beatings. Many beatings. The boys respected the father, though. He didn't put up with injustice. He was the kind of man who showed respect to those he felt deserved it and hatred for those who didn't.

D'Amato took the beatings with the attitude that he had to accept the consequences of his actions. "I knew I deserved it," D'Amato said in a 1976 interview titled "The Brujo of Gramercy Gym," published in a periodical called *Observations From the Treadmill.* "I knew before I got hit what I was getting hit for, and I knew before I did what I did exactly what was gonna happen, just like day follows darkness. There was nothin' to be resentful about."

His father, a former wrestler, loved boxing. D'Amato's older brother Jerry trained at a gym in the Frog Hollow section of the Bronx. It later became famous as Stillman's. D'Amato carried Jerry's bags and watched. One day, Jerry got in a fight with a policeman—and was shot dead.

D'Amato had his share of scraps. At twelve, in a street fight with an older man, he suffered a blow to the head that partially blinded him in the left eye. A deviated septum caused breathing difficulties (hence the odd blowing). Still, D'Amato never backed down from a good fight— that is, when he could fight for what he believed was right.

In old New York, neighborhoods were highly territorial. You didn't throw your weight around on someone else's block unless you were ready to back it up with force. One day, a man with a reputation for knife fighting came into D'Amato's small patch of the Bronx. He started to push some of D'Amato's friends around. When they pushed back, the man challenged each one to a knife fight. Everyone backed down. The man began to humiliate them, or as D'Amato explained the story to author and friend Norman Mailer, "He said things he shouldn't have." D'Amato challenged him to a fistfight. The man insisted on knives. D'Amato agreed.

They were to meet the next morning, shortly after dawn, in an abandoned building. D'Amato, with good reason, couldn't sleep that night: He had had no experience with knife fighting. He knew boxing, though. At dawn D'Amato taped an ice pick into his left hand and wrapped a coat around his right forearm. He'd fight like that. He arrived at the appointed site a half hour early to check the place out and shadowbox. At seven, the knife fighter wasn't there. D'Amato waited for several more hours, but still no opponent. The knife fighter never appeared again in the neighborhood. D'Amato became a street hero.

He learned soon after that heroism had its limitations. A rival gang invaded his neighborhood, and D'Amato joined a group of boys ready to do battle. When the two gangs met, D'Amato rushed ahead, screaming a war cry. When he looked around, he found himself alone. The other boys had retreated. The rival gang, respecting his courage, let him be and chased the others.

It was from such incidents that D'Amato later developed a practical psychology of fear and made it the foundation for everything else he taught young boxers. D'Amato argued that no essential difference existed between the coward and the hero. The hero can control his emotions; the coward can't. "Fear is like fire," D'Amato said time and again, repeating it like a mantra. "If you don't control it, it will destroy you and everything around you."

From boyhood, D'Amato had what could only be called a warrior's obsessions. He always seemed to be preparing for some battle of life and death. To steel himself against an imaginary enemy who threatened starvation, he would fast for days at a time. Even though the sight in his left eye was poor, he insisted on closing the right eye when reading. That led to a habit of squinting with the bad eye.

He believed deeply in Catholicism. The deterministic concept of heaven held special appeal. As a boy, he would watch funeral processions go by and long for death. If heaven was the ultimate good, D'Amato thought, there was no point of mortal life on Earth.

D'Amato dropped out of Morris High School to hang around boxing gyms. His father got him work in a mill that made iceboxes. D'Amato, then seventeen, couldn't help pointing out to the other men how to do their jobs. That led to a lot of fights. In one, he nearly beat a man to death. D'Amato quit a year later and went back to the gym. Money didn't interest him. "To me, working was a waste of time. It was a bore," he once said. His favorite reading material then was the *National Police Gazette*, a magazine popular among boxing sportsmen since the mid-nineteenth century.

In 1939, D'Amato and two other friends opened a gym at 116 East Fourteenth Street in Manhattan. In 1942, he was drafted into the U.S. Army. The ascetic in him found heaven on Earth. He slept on the floor. At mess hall meals he traded his cake for bread. During bivouac there were always so many flies around the food that D'Amato once promised himself to eat the next mouthful regardless. A spider crawled into it. He hated spiders, but he ate it anyway—with bread.

D'Amato made a perfect soldier. He took orders well and kept his locker neat and spotless. D'Amato's commanding officer put him up for a commission. At the test, he refused to recite the General Orders. D'Amato knew them, he just didn't want to be an officer. He preferred the rigors of the lowly G.I.

D'Amato stayed Stateside during the war and afterward returned to his gym on East Fourteenth. He lived in a back room on a cot with a dog—a boxer—named Cus. He believed that extraterrestrial beings came to Earth on occasion, and he bought a telescope to watch for them. He felt that upon arrival they were likely to seek him out. D'Amato also harbored a deep mistrust of women.

D'Amato told friends that he wanted one day to have three champions. They laughed. Managers and promoters had taken away, by hook or by crook, other men's champions, but no one in the sport of boxing had ever developed and held on to three. D'Amato would train anybody that came up the two flights of stairs and walked through the door. He especially wanted the boys who came alone. The more afraid they were, the better. Fear was always his window into their souls.

"He was so charismatic and persuasive with those ideas about fear," said Joe Fariello, one of those boys. "He understood better than anybody else that all fighters are afraid. And that's good. Otherwise, they'd be walking into punches. He taught you how to control it, make it work. He taught you what would happen in the ring, why and how you could correct it."

Fariello met D'Amato in 1952. They were from the same neighborhood in the Bronx. Fariello didn't know his father. His mother worked occasionally. The family lived on welfare. He got kicked out of high school for fighting. Fariello boxed for a few years, then at age seventeen stopped because of a broken nose and hand. D'Amato asked him to train the other fighters. Fariello moved into D'Amato's apartment on Fifty-third Street. "Cus was the only man I looked up to as a father," said Fariello, now a highly respected New York trainer.

Fariello worked with D'Amato and some of his fighters until 1965, when the two men had a falling-out. He remembered D'Amato as a son would remember a father with whom he battled constantly, or as a disillusioned disciple would remember his master.

"I realized that Cus couldn't control his own emotions. He was afraid to drive; he wouldn't fly; he feared heights, elevators, tunnels, water, thunder and lightning," Fariello said. "That's okay, but he acted like he wasn't contradicting himself. He didn't deal with those fears; he rationalized them away, made things the way he wanted them to be."

But that, in the end, isn't what caused the split. D'Amato was the kind of person someone coming into manhood had to get away from. "His whole philosophy on boxing and on life was a brainwashing. That's why he wanted young kids from the beginning. He could start with a fresh mind," Fariello maintained.

Fariello moved out of D'Amato's apartment, got married, and started to develop his own ideas about boxing. He had wanted to make more money, but D'Amato didn't care much about the size of his fighters' purses, only that they were developing as he wanted them to. And

Fariello had made his mistakes. He had a weakness for gambling. D'Amato could rationalize away his own quirks of character, but couldn't tolerate either Fariello's independence or his faults.

"He always said his whole purpose was to make you independent of him. But he never knew when to cut the cord and let someone go out and make his own mistakes," Fariello said.

D'Amato eventually found the battle he had been preparing for since childhood.

At the outset of 1949, Joe Louis, the heavyweight champion for twelve years, decided to retire. Harry Mendel, a leading press agent in boxing, hatched an idea for an elimination tournament among the top contenders to determine the new champion. The idea, though, needed financial backing and a promoter. Mike Jacobs, who had promoted Louis for the past twelve years, also wanted to retire. Mendel pitched his idea to a Chicago business man named James D. Norris, the son of a wealthy Midwest commodities merchant known as the "Grain King." Norris had used his share of the family fortune to buy several major baseball stadiums, indoor arenas, and the Detroit Red Wings hockey team. He accepted the invitation into boxing.

Norris and his partner, Arthur M. Wirtz, created the International Boxing Club. For $100,000 it bought Jacobs's lease and promotional rights to stage fights at the mecca of boxing, New York's Madison Square Garden. The I.B.C. also cornered boxing rights at the outdoor Polo Grounds, Yankee Stadium, and a few smaller arenas. Joe Louis secured the signatures of the four top contenders for the tournament and sold the contracts to the I.B.C. for $150,000 and a $15,000-per-year salary as vice president. Just to keep a lock on the Garden, Norris and Wirtz bought thirty-nine percent of its public stock.

Every fighter who entered the tournament, including the eventual winner, signed multifight contracts binding them to the I.B.C. Norris used the same tactics in all the major weight classes. Soon, no contender could hope for a shot at any title without also signing up. The I.B.C. dictated purse amounts, rematch terms, the date of the title shot, and in some cases the outcome of the fight. Some managers had to relinquish control of their fighters entirely. The I.B.C. loaned money out to fighters and managers as a means of obligating them in future deals.

Between June 1949 and May 1953, the I.B.C. and its affiliates around the country promoted thirty-six of the forty-four championship bouts that took place in the United States. Champions Ezzard Charles (who won the tournament), Jersey Joe Walcott, Rocky Marciano, Jake LaMotta, Sugar Ray Robinson, and Joey Maxim all did their deals with the devil, as it were, for the money and the fame.

The I.B.C. took on the imprimatur of a big business, but its ethics arose from the underworld. Though raised to be a blueblood, Norris indulged in a prurient taste for the unsavory. As a Chicago college student in the 1920s he befriended Sammy Hunt, one of Al Capone's bodyguards. They remained close up through to the 1940s, when Hunt introduced Norris to a New Yorker named John Paul Carbo, alias "The Uncle," "The Southern Gentleman," "Jerry the Wop," or just plain "Frankie." The moniker "Mr. Gray" stuck because of his understated style of dressing.

Carbo, mild-mannered, polite, soft-spoken, had a long history of murder charges. He once served twenty months for manslaughter. Notoriety came in 1939 when he was indicted and tried for killing Harry ("Big Greenie") Greenberg under contract to the Jewish mob organization, "Murder Inc." The chief witness against Carbo mysteriously fell to his death from a Coney Island hotel. Two of the twelve jurors refused to believe the remaining evidence. A hung jury set Carbo free. Norris relied on Carbo for inspiration, ideas and enforcement. Carbo was always seen sitting just a few feet away from Norris in his office. Several Carbo associates became promoters and managers in I.B.C. fights.

In the 1976 "Brujo" interview, D'Amato said that as soon as the I.B.C. was formed he became passionately determined to break its monopoly, on the grounds of principle. However, he needed the means to achieve that end. "I knew that when I made my move, I had to do it with a certain kind of fighter," D'Amato said. "So I was waiting for the right type of guy, that had the right type of character and personality and loyalty to make a champion. I hadda have a guy who would listen, because the things I'd hafta do would require the complete cooperation of the person I was managing. Patterson was the first guy to have the qualities I'm speaking of."

Floyd Patterson, like Fariello, was a lost boy. D'Amato met Patterson in 1949 when Floyd was only fourteen and going to a "600 School" in New York, a new type of classroom for inner-city children considered emotionally disturbed. Patterson was deeply withdrawn, sensitive, highly impressionable, a scrawny 147 pounds, and, most important for D'Amato, full of fear. D'Amato helped train him for the 1952 Olympics.

Patterson won the middleweight gold medal. D'Amato told the boxing press that he would make Patterson the future heavyweight champion.

For the next four years, Patterson won a series of middleweight fights with non-I.B.C. opponents in small arenas in New York and around the country. On January 4, 1956, Patterson's twenty-first birthday, D'Amato published an open letter challenging all top heavyweights, including undefeated champion Rocky Marciano.

The boxing community did not take the challenge seriously. Marciano had forty-one knockouts to his credit; Patterson had yet to fight beyond eight rounds. At 182 pounds he was similar in weight to Marciano but was not known to have as powerful a punch. Most of all, Patterson's boxing style was odd.

American boxing style had its roots in early-eighteenth-century England. Traditional style, stripped down, put the left foot forward and the left hand out. The left hand jabbed into the opponent's face. It also set up the right, which remained cocked back. Various other types of punches were added onto that basic form: left and right hooks that arched out and then into the side of the head or body, crosses, and uppercuts.

The fundamental problem for all boxers who used that form, no matter what punch they threw, was exposure. Throwing a punch, almost by definition, left one open to a counterpunch. Defenses were concocted—stopping the punch with an open glove, crossing the arms in front of the face, and of course moving back or away—but they didn't help much. In order to inflict pain, a boxer had to take it.

D'Amato didn't accept that premise. He devised a style for Patterson that limited risk yet at the same time delivered maximum punishment. D'Amato called it his "system," and it was described in detail by A. J. Liebling, who wrote on boxing, among other subjects, for the *New Yorker* from 1935 until his death in 1963. In the system, both hands were up around either side of the head, the elbows tucked against the body. That created, in Liebling's words, a defensive "shell." D'Amato then put Patterson in a crouch, with the feet along a horizontal line. Movement looked awkward, off-balance, like "a man going forward carrying a tray of dishes," Liebling observed.

Fariello disputed D'Amato's claim to sole authorship of the "system." D'Amato had taught him to box in the traditional style. Then, as Fariello became a trainer in the late 1950s, one of his fighters, Georgie Colon, said he felt more comfortable putting both hands up around the head. "D'Amato got pissed off with me about using that style," Fariello said. "But it caught on with the other fighters. Even Torres used it." Charlie Goldman, who trained heavyweight champion Rocky Marciano, ridiculed it as the "peek-a-boo" style. When *Life* magazine did a feature on D'Amato and his stable of fighters, and the distinctive peek-a-boo, D'Amato claimed authorship. "It got so much publicity he had to endorse it. That's when Cus started teaching the peek-a-boo to Patterson."

Whatever the origins of the hand placement, D'Amato took the basic idea and made a variety of tactical and strategic additions. He realized that the stance, though awkward, was potent. It baffled opponents. Patterson didn't telegraph his punches. He could shoot out just as easily with a left or a right. Still, there were risks. Patterson found it awkward to move backward in his shell. He had to go forward, and he had to get close enough to deliver.

D'Amato didn't want Patterson to get hit doing either. He drilled Patterson on how, while keeping his hands up around the head, to move the whole upper body from side to side as he went forward to elude the jabs—in other words, to "slip" (the sideways motion) and "weave" (the duck-and-move-forward motion). Once that series of elusive movements brought him in close enough, Patterson attacked. D'Amato taught him to exploit the moment by throwing a combination of two or more punches.

The system had drawbacks. It was a highly mechanical, robotlike technique that required intense training to master. A fighter could go in only one direction, forward, and to do that without getting hit he had to have naturally good reflexes. Combination punching also required fast hand speed. And then there remained the problem of exposure as the combinations were being thrown. That posed a dilemma. Moving back gave up the offensive opportunity, but staying in risked getting hit by straight rights and uppercuts.

In order to resolve that problem, D'Amato insisted that Patterson should attempt the nearly impossible: once in position, to attack and defend in a continuous motion. In almost the same instant that he threw a punch, he had to anticipate the counterpunch and elude. One moment's lapse of concentration and he could get hit, easily and at close range.

D'Amato's most interesting wrinkle had nothing to do with technical training. He believed that training alone, no matter how diligent, wasn't enough to master such a ying-yang synthesis of offense and defense. It had to be instinctual. He tried to teach Patterson to see the counterpunch in his mind before it happened. It was almost a spiritual thing for D'Amato. Years later, he discovered that what he tried to teach Patterson also lay at the foundation of Zen archery.

In the "Brujo" interview, D'Amato described how in the late 1950s he once saw a Texan named Lucky Daniels shoot a BB pellet out of the air with another BB, a seemingly impossible task. Daniels challenged D'Amato to a mock gunfight. D'Amato got to hold his gun pointed and cocked; Daniels's gun stayed in its holster. As D'Amato pulled his trigger, Daniels was able to draw and shoot first. D'Amato picked Daniels's mind and found out that he had been applying the same principles to boxing. When, in the late 1960s, he told the story to Norman Mailer, he was given a book on Zen archery. "I was doing what the guy said in the book!" D'Amato said.

First, then, the concentration. Second, detachment. "Eventually a pro becomes impersonal, detached in his thinking while he's perform-ing. You separate and watch yourself from like the outside the whole time," D'Amato said.

D'Amato believed in out-of-body experiences. "Everything gets calm and I'm outside watching myself. It's me, but not me. It's as if my mind and body aren't connected, but they are connected and I know exactly what to do. I get a picture in my mind what it's gonna be. I can actually see the picture, like a screen," D'Amato said.

He also believed that this gave him immense power over others. "I can take a fighter who's just beginning and I can see exactly how he's gonna end up, what I have to teach him and how he'll respond," he added. "When that happens, I can watch a guy fight and I know everything there is to know about the guy. I can actually see the wheels in his head. It's as if I am the guy. I'm inside him!"

Presumably, that's what D'Amato had in mind for Patterson. He should see the punch coming before it came, through some kind of spiritual detachment. In other words, he was taught, don't look at the man's hand or it will hit you. Instead, see a concept of the fight in which you know all the things your opponent might do and use that knowledge to advantage.

In precisely what terms D'Amato explained those ideas to Patterson, or if he explained them at all, is not known. Clearly, after first reordering Patterson's psychic furniture—via the lessons on fear—he instructed him in the basics of the system. The advanced lessons on spirituality would seem heady stuff for anyone, let alone the young

Patterson. He did well enough with the basics. As a middleweight with naturally quick reflexes, Patterson managed, far better than his peers, to hit without getting hit. But the heavyweight division posed new challenges and increased risk. The added bulk on his own body slowed him down. And a true heavyweight opponent, close to or above 200 pounds, would hit with bigger punches. The question was whether Patterson could make the system work as a heavyweight. Not just with his body, but also with his mind.

D'Amato's public challenge to the heavyweight division was, at most, a thorn in the side of the I.B.C. Norris and Carbo had no reason to put their franchise fighter, Rocky Marciano, at risk, so D'Amato started to play the ends against the middle. Publicly, he bombarded the I.B.C. with accusations about its monopolistic practices. Privately, he borrowed money from Norris: $15,000 on June 7, 1956, and another $5,000 two months later. D'Amato wanted to lull Norris into thinking that he had fallen into line with all the other managers who served their fighters up to the I.B.C. The debts, in other words, would obligate D'Amato to keep Patterson under I.B.C. control should he beat Marciano.

In April 1956, Marciano unexpectedly retired from the ring as an undefeated champion. An elimination tournament was set up by the I.B.C. to fill the vacant title. D'Amato entered Patterson, who beat "Hurricane" Jackson, barely, in a split decision. On November 30, Patterson fought Marciano's last victim, thirty-nine-year-old Archie Moore, and won. At twenty-one he became the youngest heavyweight champion ever.

With the title in his grasp, D'Amato felt no obligations to Norris and the I.B.C. He agreed to a rematch with Jackson in the first defense eight months later, then took Patterson off into a series of independently promoted bouts. That snub, he insisted later, broke the I.B.C. monopoly. Not exactly. The United States government did that.

In 1951, the Justice Department charged the I.B.C. under the Sherman Antitrust Act. The I.B.C. won a ruling that boxing, like baseball, was beyond the limits of the antitrust laws. The government appealed to the Supreme Court and won. After a trial that finally ended on March 8, 1957, Norris and his codefendants were found guilty. They appealed the conviction to the Supreme Court, which upheld it. On January 12, 1959, the I.B.C. was ordered to dissolve and sell its stock in Madison Square Garden. Three justices dissented and called the dissolution "futile." New corporations, they argued, would be formed to attempt similar monopolies.

Soon after, Norris died of a heart attack. Frankie Carbo was convicted on November 30, 1959, on three misdemeanor charges—conspiracy, undercover managing of boxers, and undercover matchmaking—and sentenced to two years in prison. Upon his release, he stood trial in Los Angeles on racketeering charges for attempting through threats and extortion to muscle in on the management and promotion of Don Jordan, a welterweight champion. He was convicted and sentenced to twenty-five years at Alcatraz. Around that same time, a U.S. Senate subcommittee held hearings on mob influence in boxing. The "Kefauver Committee," as it was known, wrenched from middleweight champion Jake LaMotta the admission that he was forced by the I.B.C. to lose to Billy Fox in a 1947 bout as a condition for a title shot.

During the seven years of trials and appeals, not once did D'Amato give testimony for the government's case against the I.B.C.; nor did he appear at the Kefauver hearings. And assuming that he was in fact threatened by Carbo henchmen, he could have, like Jackie Leonard, the manager of Don Jordan, gone to the police and cooperated in phone taps to build an official case. D'Amato did none of that. He fought the I.B.C. his way, which turned out to have little effect. The early Patterson fights he staged at another New York arena were small and insignificant, more a minor annoyance than major competition. At best, his public rantings brought attention to the monopoly, but even then only long after the government had begun its prosecution.

The significant point is that D'Amato wanted to be portrayed as the lone white knight championing the cause of justice. In fact, he was more dedicated to using Patterson to make a play for his own control of the heavyweight division.

He didn't do that for the money but, as was usual with D'Amato, for the fulfillment of an idea. This one, however, got twisted around. The idea, he claimed, was to do everything for the benefit of the fighter. But D'Amato pursued that objective obsessively. He ended up using some of the same tactics as his enemies. The effort drove him into a state of paranoia, and in the end the fighter was not well served. Without his champion, and disgraced by his meddling in the promotion of Patterson's fights, D'Amato was pushed into obscurity—until Mike Tyson came along and D'Amato was rediscovered, repackaged, and made sagelike to a new generation.

Even though the I.B.C. slowly crumbled, D'Amato continued during Patterson's reign to see the enemy in every dark corner. Years later, he told people that someone once tried to push him in front of a subway train. In another story, Rocky Marciano supposedly knocked at his door. When D'Amato opened it, he found the boxer in the company of two mobsters. According to D'Amato, he spun the double-crosser Marciano around, put an ice pick to his throat, and said, "Get outta here or the champ dies."

Perhaps that happened. Perhaps not. To the men who knew him well then, it seemed more likely that D'Amato couldn't stop fighting an imaginary war. Fariello held this view. "It was all because of the I.B.C., he said. They were out to get him, hurt him. I never saw anything that justified those fears."

D'Amato enjoyed food and drink on the town, but he feared that someone would spike his beer, so he stopped going out. He was afraid someone might drop drugs in his pocket, so he sewed the pockets of his jackets. When the phone rang, he never spoke first, choosing instead to listen until he could identify the caller. He kept a hatchet under his bed and an ice pick in his pocket. To anyone riding in an elevator with him, D'Amato, fearing that some I.B.C. hit man was at the controls and waiting with a gun, would say, "If it goes down to the basement, we're dead."

D'Amato went to great lengths to protect Patterson from these imaginary enemies. He assumed that any big-time New York promoter was I.B.C.-connected. D'Amato sought out inexperienced and easily controlled independents. Between July 1957 and June 1959, Patterson defended his title only three times. He fought in Seattle, Los Angeles, and Indianapolis. The opponents, all nearly unknowns, barely tested Patterson's abilities. Pete Rademacher, the 1956 Olympic champion, had his first pro fight with Patterson; not surprisingly, he lost by a knockout in the sixth. A year later, Patterson fought Roy Harris, a schoolteacher and club fighter from Cut and Shoot, Texas. A year after that, he disposed of a British journeyman named Brian London.

D'Amato's paranoia began to destroy the proverbial Golden Goose. The long layoffs and easy matchups dulled Patterson's unique boxing skills. In the Harris and London fights it took Patterson thirteen and eleven rounds, respectively, to do the job. "I couldn't put anything together," Patterson told Liebling of his performance against Harris. "I said to Cus he's got to get me more fights."

The London promotion showcased D'Amato's obsession with total control. When London arrived to complete his training for the fight, he went to D'Amato's gym, where he used a hand-picked D'Amato trainer and Patterson's own sparring partners. D'Amato appointed a U.S. "representative" to co-manage London for a cut of his purse. He barred the press from interviewing London. Those were all tactics used by the I.B.C.

D'Amato eventually fired the first inexperienced promoter. The second, Bill Rosensohn, had only one fight to his credit, the Harris match. Rosensohn was young, eager to please, and, so D'Amato thought, easily controlled. He also worked for TelePrompTer Corporation, recently formed to exploit the relatively new concept of closed-circuit theater television.

Traditionally, promoters made money on the radio broadcast and ticket sales, less fighters' purses and expenses. With the advent of television in the 1950s—at one point fights could be seen three nights a week on the small screen—advertiser revenue expanded the pie. Managers fought bitterly with the I.B.C. and its promoters at Madison Square Garden to get a share of the television revenues. They didn't get very far.

Closed-circuit posed a new opportunity, and D'Amato, as manager of the heavyweight champion, knew he could exploit it. Now he, and not the I.B.C., controlled the promoter. D'Amato dictated the split of the closed-circuit revenues.

Rosensohn, a thirty-eight-year-old, ambitious, heavy-eyed, slim-faced, Princeton-educated dandy, readily accepted D'Amato's terms. In the Harris fight, D'Amato brought in a friend, Charlie Black, to profit from the promotion. D'Amato and Black were boyhood friends, and despite Black's convictions for bookmaking, plus his underworld ties, Cus kept up the friendship. Black, after all, was the kind of man who could come in handy. D'Amato ordered Rosensohn to pay Black 50 percent of the net profits. He paid, but profits were low, and Rosensohn made only a few thousand dollars. D'Amato, in another classic I.B.C. move, also put a lock on Harris should he beat Patterson. He required Harris to sign a managerial contract with Black.

Rosensohn started to get hungry. He tried to initiate his own deal and signed Ingemar Johansson, a capable Swedish heavyweight, to a forty-day option for $10,000. During that time, Rosensohn had to get him a match with Patterson or lose the money. Rosensohn felt he had a tailor-made D'Amato opponent: non-I.B.C., not much of a threat, easily controlled.

D'Amato stonewalled. Perhaps he felt that Johansson, known for having a thunderous right hand, would be no pushover. But it's more likely that D'Amato delayed as a pressuring tactic to keep Rosensohn in line.

Rosensohn gambled heavily and usually lost more than he won. He needed money to finance the promotion, plus some way to make D'Amato cooperate. Rosensohn went to his bookmaker, Gilbert Beckley, for help. Beckley had once introduced him to an East Harlem-based mobster named Anthony ("Fat Tony") Salerno. Rosensohn asked Salerno to finance the promotion in exchange for a share of the profits, adding that there was one problem: he had already promised Charlie Black 50 percent of the net. Not to worry, said Salerno. He knew Black; a deal would be made. Rosensohn ended up with $25,000 for the promotion and a $10,000 loan for himself. He gave Salerno and Black each one-third ownership in his company, Rosensohn Enterprises.

Not long after that, D'Amato delivered Patterson. But he had a new demand. D'Amato wanted 100 percent of all ancillary rights (closed-circuit, radio, and movie) plus half the net from ticket sales. Rosensohn felt he'd been set up in an elaborate plan to trade off the promoter's rights so that D'Amato, Black, Salerno, and Patterson could profit. D'Amato threw in one more zinger. When Johansson arrived, D'Amato assigned another friend, Harry Davidow, as "representative" for a 10 percent purse cut.

The only piece of the pie D'Amato left intact was the option on Johansson's next fight if he should win. Unlike in the deal with Harris, he gave that to Rosensohn. It proved a big mistake.

It drizzled a warm, wet rain on the night of the fight, June 26, 1959. Ticket sales were dismal. Patterson, wrote Liebling, "came out to prove himself." He shot jabs out at Johansson, who merely retreated. Johansson looked patient and held his mysterious right hand—dubbed the "Hammer of Thor" by the press—in reserve. In the third it became clear that for Patterson almost three years of easy opponents and infrequent bouts had taken their toll. Johansson hit him with a straight right that virtually ended the fight. Patterson got up, stunned. Johansson dropped him seven times before the referee called it quits.

The whole, sordid mess blew open a month after the fight. Rosensohn's joy over lucking into promotional control of the new heavyweight champion didn't last long. He lost $40,000 on the fight. He personally owed $10,000 to a gangster. Rosensohn then found out that Salerno and Black, in an effort to hide their roles, had transferred their ownership in his company to a front man, Vincent Velella, a Republican state politician from East Harlem, then also making a bid for a municipal court judgeship. Rosensohn made an unwise power bid. He went public with the story that he'd been forced to sell two-thirds of his company, perhaps to arm-twist Salerno and Black into selling back their interest or risk exposure.

The bid backfired. The New York State Athletic Commission and the attorney general's office both conducted investigations. Rosensohn was stripped of his promoter's license and forced to sell his rights to the rematch. He moved to California, became a salesman, and in 1988 committed suicide. Salerno, Black, and Velella were barred from boxing. Salerno rose in the mob; then, in 1985, old and sick, he was convicted in the infamous "Pizza Connection" heroin-smuggling case and sent to prison for what remained of his life. Finally, the scandal prompted Senator Estes Kefauver to establish the Senate Antimonopoly Subcommittee to investigate boxing.

D'Amato was the only principal who refused to testify. He fled to Puerto Rico during the hearings. Always wary of his enemies, D'Amato traveled under the name Carl Dudley. The Athletic Commission criticized D'Amato for trying to wrest control of the heavyweight division by acting as both manager and promoter, and revoked his manager's license. The state attorney general also began preparing an antitrust action against D'Amato, then dropped the case. D'Amato blamed it all on old enemies at the I.B.C. "They are trying to destroy me," he told Gay Talese, then a reporter for the *New York Times*.

Other reporters were not so gentle with D'Amato. His only diehard supporter among the New York sportswriting community, columnist Jimmy Cannon, was a close friend until he inquired about D'Amato's meddling with Brian London. D'Amato said he "wasn't at liberty to discuss it." Cannon became one of D'Amato's biggest critics. He was "Cus the Mus" from then on in Cannon's column. During the Patterson/Johansson scandal, Harold Weissman, sports columnist for the tabloid *New York Mirror*, dubbed him the "Neurotic Napoleon." Dan Parker, another columnist at the *Mirror*, ridiculed D'Amato's new boxing "system," in which the writer included business practices: "guaranteed to get everyone in trouble and your fighter knocked out."

What did D'Amato know and when did he know it? Perhaps he didn't conspire to drive Rosensohn to Salerno and Black. Maybe Rosensohn was just a loose cannon moved by his own inexperience, bad judgment, and greed. D'Amato apparently never discussed the details of what happened with anyone. It's hard to believe, however, that a man so obsessed with control would not have known about the Salerno-Black connection. "He was too close to Charlie Black not to know," said José Torres, who became D'Amato's next boxing protégé.

And so an observer's proposition: D'Amato at the least knew about Salerno and Black, felt the promotion slip from his grasp, and rationalized the problem away. "He forgot that a shining knight on a white horse was not supposed to do those things," opined Fariello.

Patterson made $600,000 from the purse and ancillary income. The scandal, though, set in motion Patterson's disillusionment with his domineering father figure-mentor-manager. D'Amato won back his manager's license back on a legal technicality. He stayed in Patterson's corner through his next three victories, all against Johansson. Beginning with the first rematch, Patterson eschewed D'Amato's "system" for the conventional style. It was the act of a young man seeking his own identity. Fortunately for Patterson, Johansson proved to be an inconsistent boxer.

A new group of promoters, conniving with and far more savvy than those D'Amato selected, took over Patterson's fights. They sped up his disillusionment with stories about D'Amato's supposed mob ties and paranoiac behavior. Matters came to a head when Patterson, egged on by his new promoters, accepted a fight against a former convict and rising contender, Sonny Liston. D'Amato warned him not to fight Liston. Without the benefit of the "system," D'Amato felt, Patterson offered too easy and too vulnerable a target to a much bigger, harder-punching heavyweight. Patterson fired D'Amato, not to his face but through a lawyer. He was tired, he said, of being "dominated."

Liston knocked Patterson out in the first round. Patterson never again, despite three attempts, won the title. In a final ironic twist, Liston's management group included none other than mobster Frankie Carbo.

After the split with Patterson, the part of D'Amato that lusted for power died. So, too, did his willingness to ever again get emotionally attached to a fighter. "When my feelings are involved I become a chump," he told an interviewer in 1976. "That's why I never trust anything. I just trust that detachment. My feelings got involved with Patterson."

Everything else about D'Amato remained virtually intact, from an unflagging belief in the technical and spiritual merits of his "system" to the wracking paranoia. He also still wanted to develop another champion.

\* \* \*

José Torres was eighteen years old when he won the silver medal as a middleweight in the 1956 Olympics. The second of seven children, he was born and raised in Ponce, Puerto Rico. Torres's father owned a small trucking business. A family friend introduced Torres to D'Amato after the Olympics and D'Amato took him on, reluctantly.

Torres had basic talent but little taste for D'Amato's many disciplines. Though married with children, he frequently bolted camp to carouse or spend a few days with a mistress. Torres then often lied to D'Amato about why he wasn't training. "José wasn't such a bad guy," said Fariello, his trainer. "He got stupid about things. His judgment was dumb."

Besides being distracted with Patterson, D'Amato never had the confidence in Torres's abilities to actively develop his career. That, and the lingering fears about the I.B.C., kept Torres in a perennial backwater. D'Amato's emotional detachment also may have affected his management of Torres. By deciding not to get as intimate with Torres as he had gotten with Patterson, D'Amato didn't mine the deepest parts of Torres's potential. "With Torres everything was done cold, cool, and calculating," admitted D'Amato in a 1965 *Sports Illustrated* article.

For six years Torres fought and won, first as a middleweight and then as a light heavyweight, against a gaggle of lackluster opponents. D'Amato refused to let him fight at Madison Square Garden for the larger purses. Instead, Torres fought at smaller local arenas and in a host of other cities and towns, such as Boston and Toronto, which lacked constituencies of Puerto Ricans to boost ticket sales. During those six years he earned a total of only $60,000. D'Amato, claiming that he had earned enough money from Patterson's career, did not take a manager's cut.

Finally, against D'Amato's wishes, Torres fought champion Willie Pastrano for the light heavyweight title at the Garden in March 1965. Although not favored, he won on a punch to Pastrano's liver. That turned out to be the climax of his career. After a few defenses against unknowns, he lost the title just over a year later to Dick Tiger in a listless performance. Torres tried to win the title back in a May 1967 rematch, but lost again. Puerto Ricans in the audience were so angered with Torres (he was already disliked for favoring the New York literary salons and the company of Norman Mailer over the environs of El Barrio) that they showered the ring with bottles and chairs in a melee that lasted twenty minutes. Torres announced soon afterwards that he would retire to write an "autobiographical novel."

After Torres, D'Amato wallowed. In 1966, he moved upstate to the town of New Paltz to manage Buster Mathis, a journeyman heavyweight prospect who gained some cachet when he beat Joe Frazier in the 1965 U.S. Olympic trials. They met again in 1968, Frazier won (and went on to considerable fame when he defeated Muhammad Ali in 1971, a match generally regarded as one of boxing's greatest displays of ability and courage), and Mathis's career fizzled out.

Even before Mathis finally flagged in the ring, D'Amato's paranoia ended his role as manager. He became convinced that Mathis's backers—four well-heeled New York executives all in their twenties— were out to kill him. At one point, D'Amato, disoriented and fearful, locked himself in a room at the training camp for two days.

In 1971, D'Amato declared personal bankruptcy. He claimed liabilities of $30,276 and, despite purse cuts from Patterson that should have amounted to well over a million dollars, assets of only $500. It was actually much worse. D'Amato owed $200,000 in back taxes to the IRS.

What happened to his money, whether he even got it, and what he did with it were all questions that became shrouded by D'Amato's self-generated hero's lore. He once said that he spent thousands of dollars on a network of spies and informants used to battle the I.B.C.

Sometime during the 1960s, D'Amato also bought a large, white, Victorian house near the town of Catskill. He gave title to the house to Camille Ewald, who also lived there. They had first met in the early 1950s. Ewald's sister had married Tony D'Amato, one of Cus's older brothers. Cus and Camille kept up a relationship, but never lived together for any length of time, nor did they marry or have children.

In 1968, D'Amato finally moved in with Ewald. There he stayed, training young boys, being visited by disciples every now and then, proffering advice to the odd professional boxer who came through (Ali reputedly often called for guidance) and developing the careers of a few, without much result.

It was as if he had decided to sleep for a while, just as Rip Van Winkle had, according to the fable, in the nearby Catskill mountains. Winkle logged a full twenty years. D'Amato did thirteen before being awakened by Mike Tyson. In a sense, D'Amato expected Tyson, or someone like him, a third champion, to one day come calling.

"What do you think about when you think about the future," he was asked in 1976.

"Lately, I began to think...I said I never used power," D'Amato responded. "See, I'm involved over here and my involvements are forms of distraction because these kids involve my undivided attention. How could I give these boys my undivided attention, which constitutes a distraction, and still be able to concentrate this power on getting somebody and doing something? I'd have to quit here and then sit down and you'd call it meditate. If I did that hard enough, and deep enough, I would get a picture and it would happen."

"This picture, it would be for you to manage an important fighter?"

"Yes."

"To make another champion?"

"Yes."

# Chapter Three

When Tyson moved into D'Amato's house, eight other boys lived there, all aspiring boxers, every one of them white, tough, and confident. They lived two to a room. Ewald cooked the dinners and the boys cleaned up. All other meals they cooked for themselves. Food was for the taking, though Ewald expected no one to consume more than his fair share, especially of the cookies and ice cream.

For the first few weeks, Tyson stayed in awe of his new surroundings. He did as he was asked, talked little, and acted shyly. At dinner, he closely watched the other boys to learn table manners. D'Amato, of course, lectured constantly. Most of the time, Tyson could barely follow his train of thought. A week into his stay, D'Amato gave him a book, *Zen and the Art of Archery*. Tyson couldn't get past the first page. He was more interested in reading the books on boxing.

Tyson's feelings of awe gave way to suspicion. Through most of that summer of 1980, D'Amato spent far more time talking with Tyson than training him in the gym. Every night and morning he told him to repeat out loud the words "Day by day in every way, I'm getting better and better." D'Amato came into Tyson's room at night and woke him up to complete a thought from the day's lecture, one of the many that got lost in his meanderings. Remembered Ewald of Tyson: "He was always saying, 'What the white dude want to do with the black kid?'"

D'Amato drilled him on fear those first few months. "Who is your best friend?" D'Amato asked Tyson early on. Before he could answer, D'Amato cut in, "Fear is your best friend."

He'd go on, "Fear is like fire...fear is like a snowball going down a hill—if you don't learn to control it, it will get bigger and out of control...fear is like an ugly friend who smells bad but saves you from drowning.

"Control your emotions. Fatigue in the ring is psychological, the excuse of the man who wants to quit.

"The night before a fight you won't sleep. Don't worry—the other guy didn't either. You'll go to the weigh-in and he looks so much bigger than you, and calmer, like ice, but he's burning up with fear inside. Your imagination is going to credit him with abilities he doesn't have. Remember, motion relieves tension. The moment the bell rings and you come into contact with each other, suddenly the opponent seems like everybody else, because now your imagination is dissipated.

"The fight itself is the only reality that matters. Learn to impose your will and take control over that reality."

It took Tyson a long time to make sense of D'Amato's ideas. The suspicions lingered. Tyson also began to feel claustrophobic around D'Amato, who was always watching him, checking up, and bearing down with another lecture. D'Amato seemed to want a kind of intimacy that Tyson had never experienced: people bonded by a mutual belief in ideas. The laws of the streets he knew, and the rules of prison, but not D'Amato's ways. There was an impulse in Tyson to rebel. As the perennial survivor, he expected to be alone in the end anyway.

At first, it was just little things like not cleaning up after himself, bringing stolen ice cream into his room, swearing at Ewald, or turning his back and walking away as D'Amato started to lecture. "When he first came it was rather difficult because there was a lack of communication," said D'Amato in a 1984 interview.

According to D'Amato's understanding with the state Youth Division, Tyson could train all he wanted as long as he continued with school. In September, Tyson enrolled at Catskill Junior High School. At fourteen, he was the appropriate age for the eighth grade. His academic skills lagged a year behind those of the other students; his body was several years ahead. That, plus the fact that it was the first time in almost three years that he'd been in school, let alone one in a small town, made adjustment difficult.

D'Amato did what he could to prepare the school staff for Tyson. "He would be forceful and effective in trying to explain Mike's background to us," said Lee A. Bordick, then the principal at Catskill JHS and now the superintendent of schools in Troy, New York. "Mike was special, he said. Allowances had to be made for him. Cus didn't want us to dislike Mike because he had problems. He wanted us to understand how, with work, Mike had so much to gain. We worked with him. I personally did constant reality checks for Mike to make sure he understood what was expected of him."

During the first few months, Tyson could barely sit through an entire forty-five-minute class. Many times he would walk out. He took as much interest in the academics as was required to placate D'Amato and the social worker from the Youth Division assigned to watch over him, Ernestine Coleman. His passion was boxing and only boxing. "Michael and I had arguments all the time about his not applying himself in school," Coleman recalled. "He knew that I had the power to take him away from Cus and send him back to Tryon, so I won."

Almost won. Tyson attended school every day, but ignored his homework. D'Amato didn't tell Coleman, and neither did he force Tyson to do the homework. He was far more interested in Tyson's aptitude for training than for academics.

Instead of taking the morning bus, Tyson would run the three miles to school. The teachers finally told him to stop because of the smell from the sweat. So Tyson took the bus there, then ran home in the afternoons. At five o'clock, every weekday, he went to the gym for two hours. In the evenings, he talked to D'Amato, watched television, or read boxing books. On weekends, he'd be up at five in the morning, run a few miles, make his own breakfast, nap, then get to the gym again at twelve sharp. Tyson didn't join any school team or make any "civilian" friends. His friends were the other boys in the house, all of whom boxed.

That year there were racial tensions between the black and white students in the adjoining high school. School officials were concerned that Tyson might become some kind of leader among the black students. But he did not get involved. "I used to take some of the kids to baseball games down in New York on weekends," said junior high principal Bordick. "I asked Mike to come and he never did. I got the feeling that he had this block about his past, being a black kid from the slums. This was his break, boxing, and he wanted to do that and nothing else."

The other students made him pay for being different. They ridiculed his size, his lisping voice, and his desire to be a boxer. The black students were particularly cruel. For living with D'Amato and Ewald, they accused him of hating black people, including his own mother. "Three black girls were teasing him in the hallway about his mother," remembered Bordick. "He got angry, they ran into the bathroom, and he followed them. He punched the paper towel holder off the wall, screamed a lot, nothing else. I had them all in the office and one of the girls kicked him. He held back; I could see he was seething with anger, but he kept it in. I took him outside. I remember it was November. A cold rain drizzled down. We stood there and I told him he couldn't lash out at people, he had to learn control."

Bordick realized that Tyson might never be fully socialized into so-called normal society. It was as if everything, and everyone, conspired to keep him different, all of which pushed Tyson further into boxing. "There was more pressure on Michael to behave because he was Mike the boxer with this difficult background. He felt put-upon because the expectations to conform were greater on him than on other students."

During the second half of the school year, Tyson seemed better able to cope with the taunts of the other students. He also tried to use charm rather than rebellion with his teachers. "He was streetwise," said Bordick. "He could play with you almost like a con artist. Mike had this ability to deal with adults on their own level."

Bordick accepted these realities about Tyson. They represented distortions of what boys his age were usually like, but for that matter everything about Tyson seemed distorted. Even the people who cared for him did so for ulterior reasons. D'Amato certainly cared for Tyson, and wanted him to get through school, but Bordick wasn't blind to the motives involved. Nor did he think Tyson was. "Michael was smart enough to realize that others have their own con. He must have known that Cus wouldn't have been interested in him if he wasn't a boxer. Everyone who lived with Cus at the house boxed. Ever since he was a child, Mike got pushed around. The boxing was an escape. The train was going by and he decided to catch it. I think he expected Cus would benefit too."

Bordick, of course, was right. D'Amato and Tyson were using each other, initially in harmless ways. D'Amato wouldn't have let Tyson into the house unless he had held some promise as a boxer. Tyson in turn used boxing, D'Amato, his teachers, anyone, to avoid going back to the reformatory. Beneath the surface, however, in the growing subtext to their relationship, another dynamic was taking shape. D'Amato was tending to a boy's needs, but mostly he was building a champion. The task became an obsession.

\*     \*     \*

D'Amato generally wouldn't spend long hours in the gym working with his stable of young fighters. In the early months, that included Tyson. He would go in only on occasion to refine the instruction given by a trainer he'd been grooming for the previous few years: Teddy Atlas.

Atlas fit the mold of the D'Amato protégé: young, tough, troubled, highly impressionable, and consumed by a desire to box. The two met in 1975. Atlas, then twenty-one years old, was about to go to trial in Staten Island on an assault charge. A neighborhood friend, Kevin Rooney, had been training with D'Amato for a few months. Rooney convinced D'Amato that with help and guidance, Atlas could become a fine boxer. D'Amato appeared before the judge and promised to take in and train Atlas, who got off with five years' probation.

Atlas, however, got no further than the gym. A congenital spinal problem ended his career. D'Amato saw his potential as a trainer, but Atlas, deeply discouraged, returned to New York. Over the next year, he kicked around Staten Island getting into trouble. One street brawl landed Atlas in the hospital with a knife gash down the entire length of his face. That's when he decided to return to D'Amato.

The first few months back weren't easy. "I was a selfish kid, with no direction," recalled Atlas, who at thirty-four has a ruffled, boyish appearance, even with the scar on his face and the flattened nose. There's a lot of rough vowels in his Staten Island voice. He also tends to slur, as so many boxers do. "Cus wanted me to help these kids with the boxing, but I could barely help myself." Twice, Atlas attempted suicide—first with pills, then by breathing in car exhaust fumes. D'Amato saved his life both times. That fact was the turning point for Atlas. "Cus taught me principles of life, how to have purpose and do the right thing, and I gave him my loyalty."

By the time Tyson arrived in 1980, Atlas was training all of the younger fighters who lived in the house. He also ran D'Amato's boxing program for the local boys. "I did everything for those kids—took them to boxing tournaments, picnics, hand-holding, you name it."

Tyson began to occupy the majority of Atlas's time. The trainer knew well D'Amato's unique boxing system. In fact, he had the benefit of several refinements D'Amato had made over the years.

While Torres trained for his title fight against Willie Pastrano in early 1965, a pudgy man claiming to be a horse trainer from France came into the gym and boasted that he could double the speed of a fighter's punches. He had devised a numbering system. There were six steps. In the first, the fighter punched a heavy bag once. In the second, he punched twice, and so on through to the last step of six punches thrown in combination. It was simple yet effective. It systematized the process of acquiring punching speed.

The other trainers and boxers scoffed at the Frenchman's ideas. But D'Amato was impressed. Combination punching played an important role in his much-ridiculed "system." Anything that could increase punching speed was an improvement. D'Amato's system, though, used offense and defense in equal portions. The idea was to move into position without getting hit, then punch and defend in one continuous motion. But that was difficult for a fighter to do. D'Amato knew that more speed could help tremendously.

A natural tinkerer, D'Amato took the six steps and added defensive movement. Step one: punch, then move. Step two: punch, move, punch, and move again. By the sixth step, the fighter unleashed a combination of six punches and defensive movements.

The increase in speed on both offense and defense played into other new ideas D'Amato had been working on over the years. D'Amato argued that the most damaging punch, physically and psychologically, was the one a fighter couldn't see coming. He'd lose that split second of response time needed to try and move away from the blow or to steel himself against the impact. Furthermore, D'Amato believed that a fighter would punch where he last saw the target. To punch and miss was also intensely discouraging. Taking punches that couldn't be seen and trying to hit a target that wasn't there—that's the impact D'Amato wanted his fighters to have on an opponent. Besides wreaking physical damage, it sapped the will.

Just to be sure, D'Amato added a few more advanced refinements. In Torres's training for the Willie Pastrano fight, D'Amato wrapped two mattresses around a pole. He then numbered the main types of punches, 1 through 7, and wrote those numbers on the makeshift bag. Torres set up in front of the bag and D'Amato called out the combinations.

A "5-4" was a left hook to the body to weaken the opponent, followed by a right uppercut to the chin. The "7-2-3" was a left jab to the head that set up a straight right to the head and a left uppercut. Punch "6" was a straight right to the body and "1" a straight left to the head. Every combination included the requisite defensive movements.

Such numbering increased punching accuracy and created an economical verbal shorthand to use in training and in an actual fight. D'Amato put a series of such numbered combinations on an audiotape that Torres, and many fighters after him, would train to. "Punch and move, punch and move. Cus trained you to fight by habit and instinct," remembered Torres. "You shouldn't have to think for half a second." Torres gave the mattress a name, the "Willie Bag," after his upcoming opponent, Willie Pastrano.

Boxing people looked skeptically at D'Amato's system when it was used by Patterson. When he took the title, they began to tolerate it. With Patterson's defeat and slow demise, the system was all but rejected. Even though it was Patterson who abandoned the system in the second half of his career—he earned the distinction of being knocked down in title bouts more times, sixteen in all, than any other fighter in history—D'Amato's system, rightly or wrongly, still took partial blame. Torres's brief success did little to earn it new respect. Torres lacked the interest and the discipline to be consistently evasive in the ring. As he said: "I thought too much. It wasn't instinctual enough for me."

The boxing world gave up on D'Amato's ideas about boxing technique, but he remained stalwart. He continued to tinker with his system, as an inventor would a device he expected to work someday when the right partner came along to help realize its potential. That partner, it turned out, was Mike Tyson.

D'Amato knew that speed, power, and elusiveness in a 200-pound-plus natural heavyweight would have the force of an atomic bomb in the ring. That's what he saw, or dreamed of, on the day Stewart brought Tyson down from Tryon: the potential to create the most devastating heavyweight in history. He also knew that being thirteen and coming from a boy's prison, Tyson was eminently pliable. "Mentally, he had no other choices in life because of his background," said Atlas of his and D'Amato's thinking at the time. "He was a perfect piece of clay."

Atlas taught Tyson the basics. The boy already had the speed and power, but virtually no defense. They worked first on avoiding the left jab, the punch commonly used to keep an opponent at bay and to set up combinations. For the first few months, Atlas spent several hours a week throwing jabs at Tyson's head, requiring him to "slip" to his right. Once Tyson could no longer be hit by a jab, Atlas tried other simple punches. The rule was that Tyson could only elude, not counterpunch.

D'Amato believed that fighters were hit easily by straight right hands because they had a tendency to remain stationary and hold their gloves low. When Tyson slipped to his right, he was taught to keep his left up, but more important, he learned to immediately move again. He'd slip right in a sideways motion, then weave left and slightly forward. In the weave, he was taught not to use the standard "bob" or up-and-down motion. Instead, he moved his head and shoulders in a *U* shape. The slip took him laterally away from the first punch, then the *U*-shaped weave moved under the second—whether or not it was delivered.

D'Amato had a bias against the "weave and bob," a mainstay for the conventionally trained fighter. The weaving he liked; the bobbing, he believed, tended to fix the fighter's position. To D'Amato's mind, it created the illusion that by standing still and moving up and down along a vertical plane he could avoid the punches, whereas in fact, the opposite was the case. All the other fighter had to do was time his punch, D'Amato insisted; it was like hitting a jack-in-the-box.

The idea with Tyson was never to let him "hang" on either the outside or the inside. He had to be constantly moving sideways and forward in a seamless sequence. The goal was to get position and once there to deliver a combination of punches—all without getting hit.

That would seem self-evident, but few boxers could, or knew how to, do it. Slipping away made sense, but constantly moving in seemed counterintuitive. It increased the danger of getting hit. Punch and you were doubly exposed to counterpunches. Those were articles of faith to boxers, but only because they never knew how to do otherwise.

"When his defense started working, his offense did, too, because then he was in position to throw combinations of punches that the opponent couldn't see coming," said Atlas.

The offense: slip to the right, away from a jab, then throw a left hook to the body and another to the head. Or slip right and weave left under the next jab to get positioning on the opponent's exposed side, and execute the same combination. Or weave to either side, hook to the body, and uppercut through the gloves. Tyson was in front, on both sides, high and low. He was taught to punch from every conceivable angle.

"We practiced those punches so much that we used to say he couldn't do it wrong even if he wanted to," said Atlas. Doing it right meant hitting specific targets. D'Amato laid them out: the liver on the right side, the jawbone just below the ear, the point of the chin, and the floating left-side rib.

In the advanced lessons, Atlas added a unique D'Amato-inspired wrinkle. All fighters were at the least taught to slip jabs by moving to their right. Tyson learned how to also slip a jab by moving left. An opponent expected the slip right; Tyson's slip left would come as a small but important tactical surprise.

The training completely exploited Tyson's natural speed and punching power. It also converted into an asset his only potential physical drawback: at five-foot-nine with a reach of a mere seventy-one inches, he was short all around. Since the reign of Jack Johnson in early 1900s, there had been seventeen widely recognized heavyweight champions, and a half dozen or so lesser ones, and in that entire group only two—Rocky Marciano and Joe Frazier—had measured under six feet. Some champions were taller (Jess Willard, the "Pottawatomie Giant" who defeated Jack Johnson in 1914, was six-foot-six-and-one-quarter with a reach of eighty-three inches), and some average (Jack Dempsey, who reigned in the early 1920s, was six-foot-one and seventy-seven inches). Marciano measured five-foot-eleven with a reach of only sixty-eight inches. Frazier was similar in his proportions to Tyson.

Height and reach didn't determine boxing styles, but they did influence them. When tall fighters confronted shorter opponents, they tended to let their hands drop, which exposed the head. The assumption was that the shorter fighters didn't have the reach to hit them there.

D'Amato's techniques to obtain positioning took advantage of that erroneous assumption. Not only would Tyson be able to get within reach, but he would also receive less, and do far more, damage than presumed. D'Amato knew that Tyson's crouching style would make the taller opponent punch downward. That would feel awkward and so tend to throw the fighter off. In body mechanics, a downward punch also has less force than one made along a horizontal plane. More importantly, a punch angled slightly upward from a crouch carried the greatest amount of force.

Tyson was trained to maximize that force. D'Amato eschewed the orthodox punching stance of putting the left foot slightly forward. Once he gained position, Tyson brought both feet up together, knees slightly bent. That way he could leverage his punches off a combined springing and turning motion of his massive thighs and upper body. His arms, shoulders, back, waist, buttocks, and legs were all moving in concert. At the point of contact Tyson actually ended up leaning forward on the tips of his toes.

Most trainers ridiculed D'Amato's theories on the positioning of the feet. They argued that it put a shorter fighter off-balance. They were right, but only if the fighter stopped moving—the opposite of what Tyson was trained to do.

When it all came together, Tyson was a rare, and exciting, sight in the ring: he could win a fight with a single knockout punch. And that, in practical terms, was all D'Amato cared about. Just as with Patterson and, to a degree, Torres, he didn't expect the boxing world, or the casual fan, to be interested in or capable of appreciating the flow, the elegance, of Tyson's defensive skills. But a knockout punch they couldn't ignore.

\*　　\*　　\*

Theory and practice, as D'Amato preached, often differed. He and Atlas trained Tyson to fight as a professional. But in the practical development of his career, Tyson would first have to work his way up through the amateur tournaments toward an ultimate victory in the Olympics. Tyson's boxing style wouldn't go over well in the amateurs, and D'Amato knew it. The crouching, which lowered the head, was against the rules. Amateur officials felt it led to head butts. Without such defensive movement, the shorter Tyson would be far easier to hit. That disadvantage would be compounded by amateur scoring rules. Tyson could knock a foe down, but if the man got up and landed four or five soft jabs, he could win the round on points. In the professionals, a knockdown automatically won the round.

Tyson's skill with body-and-head combination punches also served little purpose. Amateur fights were only three rounds; there wasn't time to waste with a lot of body blows. Headgear was also used in amateur fights, which D'Amato vociferously opposed. Headgear, he argued, created a false sense of security that in turn limited a fighter's confrontation with his own fear.

D'Amato never hid his disdain for amateur rules. He considered them useless in preparing for a professional career. That did not endear him to the amateur boxing establishment. As a result, D'Amato expected Tyson to take a lot of criticism in amateur matches. Fortunately, he had the ability to knock opponents out with a single punch—which made troublesome rules entirely moot.

That left only one major obstacle: Tyson had not yet been tested psychologically. D'Amato and Atlas soon discovered that even with his natural advantages, superior training, and the shortcomings of his opponents, Tyson could be easily, and inexplicably, overwhelmed by his own emotions.

Tyson's earliest fights were "smokers." These were held in small boxing clubs in the tough neighborhoods of Brooklyn and the Bronx. The beer ran free; people gambled, ate heartily, and cared only for the local favorite. No amateur body sanctioned the fights. They were unofficial and unruly, but were a good way for a young fighter to get experience without his mistakes ever showing up in a record book. It was the old method for bringing a fighter along. D'Amato put Tyson in to test his abilities, but more so, his nerves.

At his first smoker, in the South Bronx, Tyson disappeared a few hours before the fight. He sat two blocks away on a curb in view of a subway station entrance. A few years later he would admit to Tom Patti, a young fighter who moved into the upstate house in 1981, that he struggled desperately over whether to take the half-hour subway ride back to nearby Brownsville and never see Catskill again. Atlas found him before the decision could be made.

Tyson did well in the smokers. He'd knock out grown men in the first and second rounds. "One look at Mike and guys didn't want to fight him," said Atlas. "I had to make deals, give the trainers $50 on the side." A few local tournaments followed and Tyson kept up his streak. By early 1981, D'Amato decided to venture out. Kevin Rooney was by then fighting regularly as a professional. He had a bout in Scranton, Pennsylvania. D'Amato got Tyson a three-round preliminary, or under-card, amateur bout.

The opponent was a young, white, marginally talented fighter. Tyson dropped him twice in the first round. Each time, to Tyson's amazement, he got up. After the round, Tyson told Atlas that he was tired. "I told him that he couldn't possibly be tired after one round," remembered Atlas. "His emotions were taking over." Tyson knocked his opponent down again in the second, to no great effect. Back in the corner he complained about a broken hand. He couldn't look Atlas in the eye. Tyson seemed drained of energy, dazed, defeated. Atlas didn't believe the broken-hand story. He grabbed Tyson's head and lifted it up. "If you want to become heavyweight champion of the world, this is it, the title," barked Atlas. "All these dreams end here if you don't beat this guy."

In the third and final round, Tyson stopped punching. He let himself be grabbed and easily hit. He punched back, but without the same snap, or, as D'Amato liked to say, "bad intentions." Atlas had never seen him so passive before, and neither had D'Amato, who sat nearby watching his future champion fizzle. At one point, after taking a straight right and then clinching, Tyson got backed up into the corner and it seemed to Atlas that within seconds he would fall to the canvas and simply give up. "Don't do it!" he yelled. Tyson stayed on his feet, the round ended, and he won on points.

"We talked afterwards down in a hallway in the arena," remembered Atlas. "He was thanking me, he couldn't stop saying it. I told him we made a breakthrough. He knew he wanted to lose. I told him he should never let himself get to that point again." Atlas made one more crucial point. "What counted, I said, was not that he had those feelings; all fighters do. It's that he didn't give in to them."

The Scranton fight exposed a serious flaw that neutralized every one of Tyson's natural and acquired advantages. He fell into an intensively passive, trancelike state in which the will to fight and elude punches drained away. When the group got back to Catskill, D'Amato didn't add much to Atlas's comments. He went over the same ground about fear, and how will overcomes skill, but he made minimal effort to determine what lay at the heart of Tyson's sudden passivity. Sometime later, though, he did send Tyson to a hypnotist. D'Amato had done that with other fighters. He felt that it helped them concentrate better in the ring.

D'Amato had decided to remain emotionally detached from Tyson, just as he had done with Torres. It was as if he chose to commit himself to an idea of what Tyson could become rather than grapple with the full reality of all the chaos in the youth's heart, which would have been more demanding. That, at least, is what Atlas began to see. "Cus was in a hurry with Mike," said Atlas. "He was so set on getting another world champion, a heavyweight, that he didn't want to see what Mike was."

D'Amato may have also been driven by a desire for vindication. It was the rationalization of the egoist. "He knew that no matter what he'd failed to do in the past with Patterson or Torres or whatever, he'd be remembered forever for that one last champion," said Atlas.

Shortly after the Scranton incident, Tyson went to the National Junior Olympics Tournament in Colorado Springs, Colorado. This time only Atlas accompanied Tyson, who stood out from the other fifteen-year-olds. Their muscles had barely begun to form through the layer of adolescent baby fat; Tyson's bulged. He also kept to himself mostly, which soon created a mystique about his background. In his first fight, Tyson scored a first-round knockout of a 265-pound Hawaiian boy with a textbook left hook to the liver. Some boys intentionally lost their fights just to avoid meeting Tyson and possibly suffering permanent physical damage. Tyson won the Junior Olympic heavyweight title, his first major victory.

Tyson's success got big play in the Catskill newspaper. It made him a minor celebrity and, to officials at the junior high school who watched him attend dutifully but learn little, a greater distraction. They decided to matriculate Tyson into the high school without testing. When Tyson's caseworker, Ernestine Coleman, found out, she was enraged. "They wanted Michael out of their hair and he knew it," she said. "I think that hurt him, which caused Michael to act out more. He was feeling that if that's the way they wanted to be, he didn't need school anyway; he'd be a boxer."

The principal at Catskill High, Richard Stickles, was far less patient with Tyson than his counterpart at the junior high school, Lee Bordick. The teachers there also decided from the outset to cut Tyson down to size. The racial tensions of the previous year had persisted and they were concerned that he might become a lightning rod for the black students.

Tyson began to be victimized by some of the other boys in the house. "They baited him," said Tom Patti, who was seventeen years old when he moved into the house that fall to train with D'Amato. "Mike talked back in class, sure. Once a teacher threw a book at him, called him intolerable. He misbehaved. He was never intolerable." Atlas, however, felt that Tyson exploited the fact that others—namely D'Amato—considered him special. "Cus told Mike he'd be world champion. Mike didn't believe it, but he knew that whatever he had was letting him do things other people couldn't do," said Atlas.

The situation fed on itself. Labeled a miscreant, Tyson increasingly acted like one. He was still being taunted by the black students for living with white people, which led to a few schoolyard scuffles. One day, he asked for milk in the cafeteria just as it closed. He was refused and threw his tray against the wall. He was suspended for a few days. It was the first of several suspensions.

During those suspensions Tyson would disappear from Catskill. D'Amato figured that he had gone back to Brownsville, which was exactly right. D'Amato would ask José Torres to bring him back. "He wasn't at home. He'd be out on the streets, stealing, mugging people, screwing around," remembered Torres. When he returned to the house, Tyson would be meek and apologetic. Yet, without provocation, he could turn nasty. Once housemother Ewald asked Tyson to try and shower more often and to keep his gym clothes clean. Tyson angrily called her "a piece of shit." Another time, in an argument over one of his Brownsville trips, Tyson spit at D'Amato.

Atlas understood how someone with Tyson's background—which after all was similar to his own—could have difficulties in a small-town school. But he believed in the principles D'Amato preached in such situations: rise above the other man and control your emotions. Tyson wasn't doing that. As the conflicts worsened, Atlas realized that D'Amato preferred to contradict his own principles rather than under-mine Tyson's focus on boxing. "I told Cus that if we teach Mike to control himself in the ring, but not out of it, he won't develop into a responsible person," said Atlas. "That's what Cus always taught me: develop a boxer in ways that make him successful in life, whether he becomes a champion or not. With Mike, Cus wanted a champion first, a good person last."

When other boys in the gym got in trouble at school, Atlas barred them from training for a few days. He did the same to Tyson. D'Amato vetoed that by bringing Tyson in himself. Atlas relented. "I was loyal to Cus. I didn't want to see what was happening."

By late fall of 1981, the school administration decided to expel Tyson. D'Amato didn't protest this time. He contacted Coleman and convinced her that Tyson had been victimized at school, that boxing was still his best form of therapy. He sent her newspaper clippings of his successes in the ring. Clearly, D'Amato knew that Coleman had the power to take Tyson back into state care. He couldn't risk losing his future champion. D'Amato asked if she would find a tutor. Coleman agreed, and in January 1982, Tyson left the high school.

The tutoring failed. Again, Tyson sat down for the instruction but didn't apply himself. D'Amato promised the tutor that Tyson would work harder, but he never did. The 1982 National Junior Olympics Tournament was coming up and Tyson had to defend his title.

The mystique about Tyson built. Professional fight promoters who stalked the amateur tournaments looking for prospects talked about Tyson as a sure bet to win the gold at the upcoming Olympic Games in Los Angeles. One manager, Shelly Finkel, had already approached

Tyson about his future plans. D'Amato refused to even discuss the matter with Finkel.

At the 1982 Juniors, Tyson again kept mostly to himself, or with Atlas, instead of mixing with the other boys. He knocked out his first four opponents with ease. On the night of the final, as he waited to enter the ring, Tyson broke down in tears. "I'm 'Mike Tyson,' everyone likes me now," he uttered. Atlas did what he could to buttress Tyson's will and took him to the ring. Tyson let loose a flurry of punches that sent his opponent into a corner, trying desperately to cover up. The referee stopped the fight. Tyson won by a technical knockout.

Tyson's flaw, his passivity, seemed in control—barely. Atlas didn't know it, but what had happened at Scranton was only the symptom. Before the Junior Olympic finals, the *cause* of Tyson's passivity, of the flaw that drained his willingness to fight, had once again peeked out.

In Scranton, it was not just the prospect of losing the fight that had paralyzed Tyson. It was that in defeat the emotional attachments with D'Amato, Ewald, the other boys in the house, and Atlas would be severed. Fighting, and winning fights, made those bonds possible. Losing confirmed the fear he had lived with since childhood: that he was alone, unloved, and quite possibly unlovable.

So much of Tyson's behavior from the day he entered Tryon and wanted to see ex-boxer Bobby Stewart sprang from that fear. Boxing was his only way of controlling the intense feelings of isolation, helplessness, and rage. What D'Amato tried to do was make boxing an all-encompassing gestalt: a way for Tyson to recognize and then order his emotions, to use his body as an instrument of his will, and ultimately to situate himself in the world.

The problem for Tyson was that the world—from Tryon to D'Amato's house, the gym, tournaments, and the Junior Olympics—kept getting bigger and more foreign. It was certainly far different from what he came from and where he expected to end up. It was like being cast in a dramatic narrative as the lead player; they were writing as they went along and Tyson never knew what would happen next, only that one day the climax was supposed to be his coronation as heavyweight champion of the world.

It was a difficult role to play, especially when the leading man felt hollow. Tyson could never see himself becoming champion, because he couldn't make purchase on his own core identity. That is the affliction of the unloved: without the basic human attachment of love, one comes to doubt that a self exists, and comes to believe that even if it does, it's probably not worthy of being attached to anyone else. The impulse is toward self-annihilation; the "I" doesn't exist and so it's willfully converted to an "it." The "it," as Tyson demonstrated during his Brownsville childhood, robs, steals, fights, and ends up in prison. The "it" dies an early death.

Of course, Tyson had already demonstrated the will to survive. He didn't want to be an "it." He knew almost instinctually that boxing offered the logical possibility of finding a self. D'Amato, Ewald, and Atlas were all part of the effort. And so, in a sense, what choice did he have but to participate in their drama of making a champion? It was box or be alone. Box or perish.

The stakes, then, were high, and to Tyson they seemed to get higher each day. As he started to win fights, he felt the gap widen between the hope others had invested in him and his own deep, riveting fear of what failure would mean. Emotionally, that sent him bouncing back and fourth between two states. In the one, he believed that the hope of D'Amato, Ewald, and Atlas was grounded in authentic caring, even love. That belief dulled the fear, kept it under control. In the other, however, the fear leapt out like a flame. What if D'Amato's attentions had nothing to do with Tyson the person, only with Tyson the future heavyweight champion?

The gap widened and Tyson began to live a paradox. He cooperated and then rebelled. He progressed in his boxing abilities, to a seemingly perfect degree, and then radically regressed in the blink of an eye. He'd behave as if he belonged, felt wanted, even loved, and then would act rejected, abandoned, and alone. During the positive phases people saw Tyson as kind, gentle, ambitious, determined, and hardworking; in the negative ones, selfish, conniving, deceptive, and at times inexplicably vicious. He alternated, in other words, between being an "I" and being an "it."

D'Amato, for all his preaching on the psychology of fear, did not understand Tyson in those terms. After getting into Tyson's psyche and bringing order to the most obvious confusions, D'Amato realized there were doors in Tyson he didn't want to open and rooms he refused to enter. After Floyd Patterson, he vowed never again to open those doors in a fighter. Besides, D'Amato didn't have the time with this one. He might die before the goal could be reached, and he knew it.

Perhaps D'Amato sensed that whatever caused Tyson's will to fail in Scranton formed the opposite side of that which also made him so devastating. Perhaps that was what lurked behind one of those doors. It created a tension, and an intensity, that won fights. It was as if he entered the ring so emotionally coiled that a psychic energy built up that was desperate for release, and the only place it could go, the only relief for Tyson, was to destroy the other man.

With those forces powering Tyson, he didn't need Zen. Tyson's concentration was already so intense that he didn't need to detach himself, to look down at the task from some spiritually removed place in order to control himself and the opponent. He could win a fight before control became an issue. And so perhaps D'Amato thought to himself, why should I go into one of those dark rooms, reorder and resolve? If I did, I wouldn't have a champion anymore.

*    *    *

Tyson's problems at school, his battle with Atlas, the lack of interest in education, his bolting back to Brownsville, his rudeness toward Ewald—D'Amato rationalized them all away as the price he, and Tyson, had to pay for winning the heavyweight championship of the world.

"Cus took Mike's selfishness and said fuck it, fuck principles, I see a guy that is going to be a world champion," said Atlas. "Cus was manipulative, too, but he could use it better. Tyson did it by instinct; Cus knew exactly what he was doing, how to do it, and who it affected."

Soon after the Junior Olympic tournament, Atlas's disillusionment with D'Amato increased. "Cus had the greatest tunnel vision, so great he didn't even care about himself. He'd let Mike spit on him. When I met him, before Mike came along, he wouldn't put up with that."

In the spring, Tyson boasted around the gym that he didn't need a trainer anymore, that he could win without Atlas, or D'Amato. In June, Tyson's tutor quit. She was frustrated both with his lack of interest and with D'Amato's lack of support. It was no coincidence that on June 30, Tyson turned sixteen and was thus legally no longer obligated to attend school. Moreover, he left the authority of the Youth Division. D'Amato still had to answer to Coleman, however, until Tyson was formally released. He continued to give Coleman rosy reports of Tyson's progress, despite contrary accounts from the tutor. Coleman believed D'Amato.

Over the summer, Atlas continued to bump heads with Tyson and D'Amato. Atlas found out that in the late 1970s, D'Amato had secured a $25,000 grant from a federal agency to fund the boxing club—a portion of which was supposed to pay him a salary. Atlas never saw the money.

He heard rumors that D'Amato gave certain town officials cash payments for their support and influence, especially on those occasions that Tyson had scrapes with the local law. In one instance, a woman complained to the police that Mike had been having sex with her twelve-year-old daughter. The matter stopped there. Atlas suspected that she'd been paid off. D'Amato also no longer seemed to care about the other boys in the club. Atlas watched D'Amato spend freely to cover Tyson's expenses for tournaments, but complain when the other boys needed money for new equipment.

That attitude seemed all the more outrageous to Atlas because he knew that D'Amato had another major source of money to fund his efforts with Tyson. D'Amato had convinced his silent benefactors, Jim Jacobs and Bill Cayton, that Tyson was the prospect they'd all been waiting for: a champion fighter they could develop from scratch and control completely. Cayton was skeptical. But Jacobs shared D'Amato's passion, and he had the same obsessive tendencies. He persuaded Cayton to help pay for the additional expenses of bringing Tyson along. The travel, lodging, and other costs of sending everyone, including Jacobs, to a single tournament reached $6,000. With Tyson's size, speed, and ability, he needed professional sparring, and that was expensive, upwards of $500 a week. They also paid $250 for each pair of Tyson's custom-made gloves. Extra padding was needed to protect his sparring partners. Jacobs and Cayton even paid for gold fillings in Tyson's two front teeth.

They had a verbal agreement on taking Tyson professional. D'Amato would decide whom he would fight and for which promoters. He would not, however, be manager of record. That meant showing income, which he would then have to pay in back taxes to the IRS, which D'Amato had no intention of doing. Jacobs would therefore become manager. Cayton at the time was considering retirement. His role remained uncertain, although he had expertise in advertising, marketing, and television, and expected to share in any profits from Tyson's purses.

In August, Ernestine Coleman discovered that Tyson's mother had been diagnosed as having inoperable cancer. She told Tyson and D'Amato. Despite all the money available for Tyson's boxing career, D'Amato spared none for Lorna's care. Nor had he ever paid for her to visit Tyson in Catskill. Over the past two years, D'Amato had spoken to her only a few times, and then briefly. He didn't want to reveal her son's problems in case the information got back to Coleman. D'Amato deemed his obligations as being only to the officials at the Youth Division.

In September, D'Amato paid for Tyson's one train trip to visit Lorna in the hospital. He went alone. When he came back a few days later, Tyson refused to discuss what he saw, or felt. When his mother died in October, at the age of fifty-two, Tyson again went to New York alone. The trip turned out to be a watershed experience.

When Tyson arrived at his old apartment on Amboy Street in Brownsville, no one was there. Rodney long ago had moved away and had left no new address. When Denise returned home she said that there was no money to bury Lorna. The city would put her in Potter's Field, a cemetery for the poor on an island northeast of Manhattan in the East River. Convicts from Rikers Island prison dug the graves.

Tyson couldn't bring himself to go to the burial. He stayed in the apartment for three days. The phone rang several times but he didn't answer. When he did, finally, it was D'Amato. Tyson said he wasn't coming back to Catskill and hung up.

The next day, Ernestine Coleman came to the door. He wouldn't let her into the apartment. They talked in the hallway. "I told Michael that he had to come back to Catskill," recalled Coleman. "He refused. He was going to stay in Brownsville. I was convinced of that."

Coleman explained that her own mother had died of cancer; she could empathize with what he felt. Tyson wasn't moved. He was stuck in his grief and perhaps weighed down by the guilt he felt for letting his mother down all those years. There was also the shame. At Tryon, he tried to tell her how much he was changing, but maybe he hadn't tried hard enough. If he had called more, cared more, tried harder, as hard as he boxed, maybe he could have earned back her love.

"This was a boy who had more rage than I'd ever seen before, and now he was falling, going into a deep depression. The boxing was a positive direction for him. It was either that or the streets, where he would have ended up dead for sure," said Coleman.

She wasn't prepared to let Tyson commit suicide in this manner. So she lied. "I said that if he wanted to stay I'd have to do the paperwork, the police would pick him up, and I'd place him somewhere in New York."

At sixteen, Tyson was no longer under the authority of the Youth

Division. He could do as he pleased. D'Amato had never told him that, and now, when the information would have perhaps determined his future, neither did Coleman. Perhaps, then, it was the prospect of the police, or just the shock value of the ultimatum, that made Tyson see through his own grief to the stark realities of his situation. He returned to Catskill that very day with Coleman.

According to Ewald, Tyson refused to discuss his mother's death when he returned. But he started to change, radically. "Not long after he got back, Michael told me that he thought he could become the heavyweight champion of the world. Cus had always said that about him before and he knew it. That was the first time Mike said it."

Coleman detected a shift as well. "Until his mother died, he never saw that house as home. Catskill just amounted to a place where he was and a thing he was doing. Suddenly, Cus, Camille, the house, and boxing was all he had left."

Soon after Lorna's death, D'Amato made a move to become Tyson's legal guardian. When Tyson went to New York on the day of his mother's funeral and refused to come back, D'Amato realized that his dream of having another champion could be easily stolen. The only control D'Amato could have was legal guardianship. Up until the age of eighteen, Tyson required the approval of a parent, or guardian, to sign a contract.

D'Amato's duplicity ate away at Atlas like an acid. Every time he tried to discipline Tyson, D'Amato vetoed it. It reached the point where D'Amato had to take over Tyson's training, while Atlas worked solely with the other boys in the boxing club. In November, matters came to a head. Atlas had gotten married over the previous summer. His wife had a twelve-year-old sister who on occasion came to the gym. The girl told Atlas that Tyson had fondled her. Atlas flew into a rage, got a gun, and confronted Tyson at the gym. Tyson ran out and hid in D'Amato's house. D'Amato sent him to stay with Bobby Stewart at Tryon until he could sort things out. That consisted of firing Atlas.

Two weeks later, D'Amato used an old friend to expedite his bid to control Tyson. Bill Hagan was the supervisor of Greene County, in which Catskill was located. Hagan had used his Washington connections to secure the $25,000 federal grant for D'Amato years before. D'Amato told him now that some promoters were trying to weasel in on Tyson. The next day, D'Amato went to a local court with his lawyers and a set of already-completed guardianship papers. The judge approved the request without delay.

Atlas believed that D'Amato had intentionally let his dispute with Tyson boil over. "He let the conflict between me and Mike be brought to a climax so I had to leave and he could take Mike over," said Atlas.

With Atlas gone the issue of who would work in Tyson's corner arose. Baranski would be tapped to organize the sparring partners and work as cutman during fights. Kevin Rooney just months before lost a fight to Alexis Arguello, and lost so badly that it snuffed out any hope of his earning a shot at the welterweight title. When Atlas left, Rooney, his boyhood friend, took over as Tyson's trainer.

Atlas was determined to continue working with the other boys in the boxing club. Some of their parents confronted D'Amato about his dismissal. D'Amato lied. He told them that Atlas had quit in order to work with professionals in New York. The parents knew that Atlas hadn't left Catskill at all. Desperate to cover himself, D'Amato launched a smear campaign against Atlas. He spread rumors among the town officials who supported the club with funding that Atlas had taken up with the Mafia. He recounted tales of Atlas's troubled youth—the street fights, the suicide attempts, and a score of other factual, and not so factual, stories. Atlas was forced to leave Catskill, but the rumors followed. He couldn't get work at any of the New York gyms. Eventually, one of the parents, who was also a member of the Catskill Town Recreation Board and an executive at IBM, got the word to one of D'Amato's supporters that he would have the gym closed if the rumors didn't stop. They did, and Atlas slowly started to get work training professionals at Gleason's Gym in Brooklyn, New York.

Looking back on those days with the benefit of hindsight, Atlas didn't sound angry or bitter. After training professionals on his own for almost ten years, he has learned that some young men can't be changed, that they are coded somehow to turn out a certain way. When that behavior is enforced by others, there's not much anyone could do. "We didn't do everything we could have for Mike. But maybe it wouldn't have made any difference. We could have just been given what was always going to be there," he said, and then added: "Maybe Cus was right. If we did it my way, Tyson might never have become champion."

Atlas paused a moment, as if trying to decide whether his next thought would be taken for sour grapes. He didn't care anymore; for Atlas it was the truth. "This syndrome about Mike when he turned pro, that he was superhuman, Iron Mike, was bullshit. You know, I never thought he'd be a durable champion."

\* \* \*

After his mother's death, Tyson became more devoted to D'Amato as a trainer and mentor, and also as a surrogate father. Tyson spoke for the first time of one day being heavyweight champion. He poured himself into boxing to a degree no one involved in his life then—D'Amato, Ewald, Matt Baranski, Kevin Rooney, or Jim Jacobs—had yet seen in him, or in any other boxer past and present.

"Cus would be sitting in one chair, and Mike across from him in the other, both of them reading fight books. For hours Mike would sit there reading and then asking Cus questions," recalled Ewald.

All the boys in the house had some claim on D'Amato's attention and his role as mentor. D'Amato never hid his special feelings for Tyson. Tyson, for the first time, seemed to feel the same way. "Mike got very angry if one of the other boys made fun of Cus," said Ewald.

At the dinner table lectures, Tyson played chief supplicant. "Hey, Cus, was Joe Gans a good fighter?" he would ask, feigning lack of knowledge, because it was likely that Tyson had spent that whole afternoon reading about Gans, a turn-of-the-century lightweight champion known for his courage. Tyson got the bare facts from the books, and could remember them in detail, but D'Amato explained the significance of a fighter's achievements: the skills he had, or lacked, the mental battles he fought, how he was situated in the great big canvas of the sport. "Mike mastered the facts; he had a photographic memory," said Ewald.

At that time as well, Tyson asked Jimmy Jacobs to send up old boxing films for him to watch. Every week a shipment would arrive of a half-dozen films or more and Tyson would sit with D'Amato and examine them in detail. Tyson was interested in the boxing, of course, but more so in the personas of the great champions. It was not that important to him how Jack Dempsey, for example, fought. Tyson watched the films to find signs of the champion's identity. As someone who had trouble establishing his own sense of self, it was a natural impulse to search and borrow from others.

Tyson marveled at the bravado of Jack Johnson, the most famous of black heavyweight champions, who caught punches with his open glove, talked to people in the stands during the fight, and laughed in the faces

of his hapless opponents. He liked the Spartan, warrior look of Jack
Dempsey. He found out that among the fighters of the 1920s gold teeth
were a status symbol, and had two of his upper front teeth capped in
gold.

D'Amato also told him the story of how early twentieth-century black
fighter Sam Langford, the "Boston Tar Baby," used to wear a lot of
jewelry until he was approached one day on a train by an elderly and
distinguished-looking man. "I want to congratulate you on a fine
career," the older man said in a respectful tone, then left. Langford's
manager asked if he recognized the man. He hadn't. It was steel tycoon
Andrew Carnegie. "But he wasn't wearing any jewelry, or nothing
fancy," Langford was reputed to have said. The manager replied, "He
doesn't need to. He knows who he is." After hearing that story, Tyson
vowed never to wear the heavy gold chains and pendants then
fashionable among some young blacks.

The departure of Atlas also appeared to make Tyson more determined
about his training. It was as if he refused to give in to the thought that
the absence of the person who had helped him through so many
emotional crises in the ring could stop his rise. Tom Patti remembered
the advent of that new intensity. "My room was below Mike's. At night
when we were supposed to be asleep, Mike was up shadowboxing for
hours. I could hear the thumping and grunting."

This new Tyson was devoted to D'Amato and boxing, and more
believing in the dream of his future. He lived the role of surrogate son
and disciplined fighter, and of course continued to win fights with a
single knockout punch. With Lorna dead, and D'Amato and Catskill
and becoming champion his only other recourse, Tyson moved himself
onto the center stage of the drama. He would believe that the paradox
was solved—that D'Amato did truly love him—even if the evidence,
the proof, wasn't in yet. He would live that little fiction. Tyson played
the role well, as did D'Amato and everyone else who obtained a stake in
his growing career. Tyson would have his lapses, he'd bounce between
the light and dark of his personality, but in general he tried to follow the
script.

The first big lapse occurred at the 1982 U.S. National Championships.
The flaw, the overwhelming passivity, struck again. The opponent, Al
Evans, had far more experience, yet not enough to make Tyson look as
bad as he did. Evans pummeled Tyson to the canvas three times and
won the bout by technical knockout. The same thing happened at the
1983 National Golden Gloves Tournament. Tyson lost to Craig Payne in

the final. D'Amato and Rooney would claim that the referees and judges unfairly penalized Tyson for using a professional style. But it was the flaw. Tyson gave in to the opponent's game plan. He stopped punching, which made him easy to hit, or at least easy enough that in three rounds of boxing his opponent racked up the most points.

When Tyson fought well, he functioned like an efficient machine of destruction. When he fought badly, he picked up some bad habits. Before a fight, in the dressing room, he would work himself up into a fevered intensity, which he would then unleash in the first round. If the opponent didn't go down under the initial barrage, Tyson would get frustrated. In that state he'd forget D'Amato's defensive and offensive techniques and look like a fighter out of control. Sometimes that's as far as the regression went. In those cases Tyson's natural strength and speed were usually more than adequate for victory. But if he regressed more, into the passivity, he tended to hug his opponent and lock arms—to "clinch." D'Amato's excuse was that he clinched in order to rest. The reality was that his will to fight had drained away.

Matt Baranski, who started in Tyson's corner as cut man right after Atlas left, remembered the first time he witnessed Tyson's self-defeating tendencies. "Mike was a wild man in the locker room before a fight. He'd shadowbox as hard as he could for an hour. Once when Mike was sixteen, he fought this kid in Boston. The kid was only seventeen; he didn't have a lot of experience. Mike dropped him in the second round and the kid came back and boxed and boxed. Mike started to get tired. If it had gone another round, he would have lost. I warned Cus about that and he said not to worry about it, Mike's in great shape."

Baranski soon saw other problems in Tyson. He knew Tyson was capable of affection and attachment, especially toward D'Amato. He also saw the exact opposite. "He had this dog and once I saw him kick it hard. I told him that if he wasn't so big I'd punch him out for doing that. He denied it to my face. I was standing right there and he denied it.

"He got pigeons, too, put them in a coop behind the house. Maybe he liked them, but he never cared for them. He'd let them freeze in the winter. It didn't bother him a bit," added Baranski.

Baranski doubted the depth of feeling Tyson and D'Amato had for each other. At times, they seemed to be bound by mutual self-interest. "Tyson didn't care for anything or anybody. Mike had it in his head from the beginning that I got to look out for Mike and that's all there is to it. He lied to Cus all the time. Once, after a fight, he disappeared for three days. Cus asked me to go find him. He showed up with two pigeons in the backseat of the car, told Cus he'd been gone just that one day. Cus knew it was three days. Everyone did.

"I'd ask Cus why he put up with that shit—the lies, Mike screaming at him, spitting on him even, incredible stuff. He told me he was ready to give up on him. He couldn't stand Mike acting like an animal."

Baranski felt that this wasn't the normal feuding between a mentor and protégé, or even a father and son. There's no doubt that they felt close, but more in the way of Siamese twins. It was as if they had to be with each other in order to exist. The necessity of the attachment created resentment.

"Cus disregarded a lot of things about Mike because it came with making a champion," said Baranski. "Like Mike's burning out in a fight. Cus knew that most of the time he'd knock the other guy out before that fatigue set in. I also thought it was like a way to control Mike and get the best results from him. If he's fighting, he's not getting in trouble. And if he's fighting with bad intentions, which was most of the time, he's winning."

In 1983, D'Amato had to start preparing Tyson for the Olympic trials. He put him on what for some fighters would be a punishing schedule. For Tyson, though, maintaining a constant level of intensity suited his desperate urge for psychic release. On August 12, Tyson entered the Ohio State Fair National Tournament. On the first day, he knocked out his opponent in forty-two seconds of the first round. On the second day, Tyson punched out the two front teeth of his foe and left him unconscious for ten minutes. On the third day, for the tournament championship, his adversary, the young man who had won the National Golden Gloves title that year, quit before the fight with a bad hand.

The day after Tyson won the Ohio State Fair competition by default, he flew to Colorado Springs for the 1983 U.S. National Championships. Six other fighters had entered the heavyweight division. When Tyson arrived, four dropped out. He automatically advanced to the semifinals. Two victories later—both first-round knockouts—he had another amateur title. In early 1984, he won the National Golden Gloves. All that remained was to get through the Olympic trials, then go onto the games in Los Angeles. With the stiffest competition boycotting—Cuba, East Germany, and the Soviet Union—D'Amato felt that a gold medal was certain. Olympic victory, as it had for so many fighters (Floyd Patterson, Muhammad Ali, George Foreman, and Sugar Ray Leonard, among others), would launch Tyson's pro career. D'Amato believed that in two years, three at most, Tyson could capture the heavyweight champion-ship of the world.

Preparations for Tyson's pro debut had to be made. Jim Jacobs and Bill Cayton had by 1984 invested more than $200,000 in Tyson's develop-ment. That included paying $1,000 a week at one point for a single sparring partner, Marvin Stinson, who at the time was working with heavyweight champion Larry Holmes. As soon as the Olympics were over, they planned to sign Tyson to a management contract and start the march to the title. They had handled two other fighters before, and with some success: Wilfred Benitez and Edwin Rosario, both in the lower weight classes. A heavyweight could become a cultural icon. More mass-market appeal meant larger fight purses, product endorsements, and commercials. Tyson's stunning first-round knockout victories had already garnered him a great deal of attention in regional markets among fight fans. But now that he was about to cross over into the national consciousness at the Olympics, Jacobs and Cayton realized that for publicity purposes they needed a story to tell. That Tyson won fights with a single punch wasn't enough. They needed something more humanizing.

Jacobs talked to Alex Wallau, a boxing analyst with ABC Sports and a friend since the mid-1970s. Wallau agreed to tape an interview with D'Amato and Tyson at the house. The idea was to televise a profile of the two during the Olympics. A look at the unedited version of the tape revealed the rough outlines of a story line that Jacobs and Cayton hoped to use as a publicity device at the Olympics.

Wallau's questions focused on the obvious human-interest news hook: the unique relationship between an old Italian-American fight guru living in the country and a young, black boxing protégé from the bowels of the New York slums.

D'Amato first extolled the virtues of his fighter.

"He's able to throw a punch, like lightning right next to you, and any punch he throws hits where he was and not where he is and in that position he can let a bomb go without any inhibition whatsoever," said D'Amato. "I've never seen a fighter who can make the adjustment on so little so rapidly and do so much with it. I've never seen a fighter like Mike."

"How would you say that Cus has helped you change your life?" Wallau asked Tyson.

"He's changed my life by helping me deal with people. Before I couldn't talk to people. I just wanted to be alone." Then later Tyson added: "He's like my father. I never look at it like he's my trainer or my manager. I go by the way he feels about me and it's like a father-son relationship."

Wallau posed the same question to D'Amato.

"I never let my feelings get involved, no matter how much affection I have," D'Amato said. Then, as if realizing he'd made a mistake, he corrected himself. "Having watched him come from what he was to where he is, I can say honestly I have a very deep affection for him."

On the subject of his future, Tyson downplayed the hoopla over his prospects as champion. Something in him resisted hype. "Dreams are just when you're starting off, that's the image, you have the dream to push the motivation. I just want to be alive ten years from now. People say I'm going to be a million-dollar fighter... well, I know what I am and that's what counts more than anything else, because the people don't know what I go through. They think I'm born this way. They don't know what it took to get this way."

D'Amato wanted to get back to his feelings for Tyson. The core of it turned out to be a soft-pedaled admission of self-interest. "If he weren't here, I probably wouldn't be alive today. I believe that a person dies when he no longer wants to live.... But I have a reason with Mike here. He gives me the motivation. And I will stay alive and I will watch him become a success. I will not leave until that happens."

D'Amato then gave the whole team—Tyson, himself, Jacobs, and Cayton—a plug. "When I leave he will not only know how to fight. He will not only understand many things, but he will also know how to take care of himself, because I have good friends like Jim Jacobs and Bill Cayton who are thoroughly and completely honest and competent in every area, who I know will continue doing what I have done, and probably a lot better than I've done."

Tyson ended the interview in the contradictory posture of the cool, calculating professional detached from all other concerns beyond winning—except that he also wanted to please his mentors.

"We just do our jobs and that's it. I just want to hold up my part of the team. And that's to succeed and make everybody happy."

"What will it take to make everybody happy?" asked Wallau.

"Do my job inside the ring, and they do their job outside the ring."

All the elements of a compelling narrative were there. Here was the fighter with the almost inexplicable abilities ("hits where he was, not where he is") who could destroy an opponent without "inhibition," which was as if to say without remorse or pity. Such a persona was frowned on in the amateurs as too much the product of professional training. In the pro ranks, however, the persona of the Ring Destroyer would play well to national television audiences. The one-punch knockout fighter was the stuff of spectacle.

But those were hardly humanizing qualities. What made for good commerce did little to create basic, personal empathy for Tyson. Fortunately, Jacobs and Cayton could serve up his relationship with D'Amato. That would humanize him: D'Amato had saved Tyson from sure self-destruction in the ghetto, had given him a new life, a ready-made family, and a father's love. In return, Tyson had given D'Amato a purpose for living.

Finally, the narrative needed practical expression. Who would take this man-child fighter driven by primal forces and introduce him to the world? Who would convert into reality the Old Sage's dream to make another champion before his death? Of course, the capable and honest Jacobs and Cayton.

In June, Tyson left for Las Vegas to compete in the Olympic trials. D'Amato and Jacobs considered the trials a mere formality. To everyone's shock, Tyson lost twice to Henry Tillman, a six-foot-three, 195-pound former gang member from South Central Los Angeles. He would not compete in the Olympics. Tyson later accused Tillman of trying to stick thumbs in his eye. D'Amato blamed the amateur boxing establishment for taking out on Tyson their dislike for him. But a look at the fight proved that although it was close, Tillman won by scoring more points. He simply fought smarter.

That's how Alex Wallau read the fight. "Mike didn't fight a very smart fight. He let himself get frustrated and I sensed that he was in conflict about what style he was supposed to use, professional or amateur. He couldn't make the adjustment to amateur style."

Tillman's trainer put it more bluntly. "Tyson boxed like a robot and when Henry started to pick him off with jabs, it was like pulling out a fuse."

D'Amato and Jacobs were stunned by the loss. All of the promise that had built up around Tyson over the last four years seemed in question. He was capable of spectacular successes, and stunning, inexplicable defeats. Despite all the psychological reordering, the work in the gym, battles with teachers, social workers, and tutors, and all the abuse D'Amato took from Tyson, despite the strings pulled and lies told, the cover-ups and the loss of friends, with all that had been expended, Tyson remained an enigma. For that D'Amato disliked Tyson, deeply. He vented those feelings to a boxing promoter at the trials: "He said that Mike was a piece of shit and an animal and that if he had his way, he'd throw Mike out onto the street," said the promoter.

But of course D'Amato didn't have the choice. More than anything, he wanted that third champion. He was obsessed. Just before leaving Las Vegas, he hatched a backup plan to get Tyson the gold medal. Tyson had been selected as an alternate to the team. He'd be permitted to work out at the training camp with the other boys until the competition began. At first, D'Amato was so bitter about the loss that he didn't want Tyson to go. Then he remembered the rule that if any team member was knocked out in sparring he'd have to rest for several weeks, with the alternate taking his place. "Cus told Mike to go out there to the camp and knock out anybody he could," said Baranski. "Mike stayed in the camp exactly one day. The other trainers knew what he was up to and didn't want him around."

After the Olympics (Tillman won the heavyweight gold medal), D'Amato and Jacobs altered their plan for Tyson's pro career. They could never be sure which Tyson would step into the ring, the knockout machine or the passive little boy. It seemed that the flaw could strike with almost any opponent. Still, there was a type they had to avoid matching Tyson with. A fighter who combined basic boxing skills with good movement, confidence, and poise—someone who could easily frustrate Tyson—was the riskiest.

Without the fanfare of an Olympic gold medal, promoting Tyson would also be difficult. The television, newspaper, and magazine exposure that came with a gold medal would have sent him into the national consciousness in a ready-made, prepackaged form. His greatness as a fighter would have been largely assumed. Now they had to build his reputation from the bottom up. That posed a whole different series of management and marketing challenges. Jim Jacobs would dive into the task with the same obsession that D'Amato had the training.

# Chapter Four

**J**ames Leslie Jacobs was born on February 18, 1930, in St. Louis, Missouri. He had one sibling—a sister, Dorothy, who was five years older. Both of his parents descended from German—Jewish immigrants, the first of whom arrived in the United States in the mid-1800s. The families plodded along through the generations. Jacobs's maternal grandfather owned a small wholesale grocery business. His paternal grandfather was a salesman. During the Depression, Jacobs's father sold women's ready-to-wear clothing at a retail outlet in St. Louis. He did well and rose to manager. In 1935, the family moved to Atlanta, where he managed a department store. Within a year, they were back in St. Louis starting over. In 1936, Jacobs's father went alone to Los Angeles to work as a liquor salesman for the Al Hart distillery. The family joined him a year later.

They lived in a three-bedroom apartment in the then largely Jewish Fairfax district. The Jewish holidays were not observed. Dorothy went to Sunday school. "We were Jewish only because we were born Jewish," said Dorothy, who still lives in the Fairfax area under the name of Zeil, the first of her three husbands. The family did not prosper. "My father rose no further than salesman and he spent every nickel he had on the family," she added.

For four years, the children were close. In their fantasy games, Jacobs was the hero. "There was a radio show, Little Beaver and Red Rider. Jimmy always got to play Beaver; he solved all the problems. He also played Robin and I was Batman," remembered Dorothy. "If he had a problem, of any kind, he'd fantasize it away by saying, "What would Robin do?"

When Jacobs was eleven, his parents divorced. The family dynamics shifted dramatically. The mother, also named Dorothy, aligned with her son and purged the daughter. "There was a photo of Jimmy and me taken in St. Louis. I was eight and Jimmy was three. After the divorce, she cut me out and put it back on the wall," said Zeil, a small, thin woman of sixty-five whom years of chain-smoking had left with emphysema and a thin, raspy voice. She mustered just enough wind for one sentence at a time, then had to stop and breathe in deeply. "After the divorce it became his house and my mother's house. She kept us apart. My mother hated me. She told me that. She got pregnant with me on her honeymoon and she said because of me she was unable to get a divorce. What you have to know is that she never got close to anyone, ever, except Jimmy. He was the only man she loved."

And Jacobs loved mother, deeply. "He defended her always. I could never say how I felt about her, " said Zeil. "It was incredible, just incredible how cruel he was able to be if anyone even attempted to say anything critical about her. And it was always 'my mother,' never 'our mother.'"

At about the same time Zeil moved out to join the Navy during World War II, Jacobs discovered a passion for sports. He was thirteen, physically strong, and highly coordinated. Jacobs could play virtually any type of game—basketball, football, baseball—and he did it with a relentless determination not just to win but to dominate. Handball was a favorite. Boxing too. His mother, though, refused to let him box. To fulfill that passion, Jacobs turned to fantasy.

Nick Beck was twelve and Jacobs fourteen when they met. Beck remembered seeing Jacobs around the Hollywood YMCA, strutting around in tank tops, wearing his various medals on a watch chain. "I had a very strange experience with him the first time we met," said Beck. "I used to punch the heavy bag at the "Y". Jimmy came up one day to work out and we started talking. He told me that his father was a famous fighter. I was a big fight fan so I asked who. He said that his father was

Buddy Baer, the brother of Max Baer, a former heavyweight. I challenged him on that. He stuck with the story and eventually we just agreed not to talk about it anymore. Jimmy could do that. He told some outrageous lies."

The friendship continued. Both boys started collecting old fight films, Jacobs in 16 mm and Beck in 8 mm. In the mid-1940s, before television, vintage fight films sat around in attics. People were glad to get any money for them at all. "We'd lend films to each other every now and then to show to other people. Whenever Jimmy didn't want to do that he'd say that his film was in a secret vault in Santa Monica and there was only one key, which his father had. I didn't believe him. He couldn't afford a vault. Jimmy rarely had any money as a kid."

Jacobs quit high school to pursue his other ambition: handball. By the late 1940s he could beat easily any member of the Hollywood YMCA. In 1950, he met Robert Kendler, a millionaire Chicago builder and patron of the sport. Kendler hired young handball champions to work for his company, live together, and teach each other. Jacobs stayed a year, learned from the masters of that time, and then got drafted into the Army. After the Army, he returned to Los Angeles, worked as a business machine salesman, and in his spare time rose slowly through the national handball ranks. In 1955, Jacobs won his first national singles championship. He reigned as the king of handball for the next ten years. Five other singles titles followed, plus six doubles titles. Jacobs never lost a championship tournament. The years he didn't win were those in which, because of injuries, he didn't compete. Jacobs became known as the "Babe Ruth of Handball." A 1966 *Sports Illustrated* profile claimed that "there is no athlete in the world who dominates his sport with the supremacy [of] Jimmy Jacobs."

In handball circles, Jacobs was dubbed "The Los Angeles Strongboy." He brought more than strength to the game. His tactics and strategies, combined with an unshakable will, were so refined, so well planned and executed, that he rarely lost. As the *Sports Illustrated* story pointed out, "He leaves absolutely nothing to chance."

Jacobs's style of play set the pattern for how he pursued everything else in life, particularly the management of fighters. He sought the position on court that afforded the most control over his opponent. Jacobs also didn't so much win a game as force the other man to lose. There were men who hated that aspect of Jim Jacobs. He played to emasculate.

"Everyone else played haphazardly compared to Jimmy," said Steve

Lott, who first met Jacobs in 1965 at the 92nd St. "Y" in New York. Lott was then eighteen. Jacobs would become his mentor in handball and later in almost every other aspect of his life as well. "He'd have an opportunity to take a shot which at that moment would score a point and look good. But he wouldn't do it. He'd make three good defensive shots first to set up the one that put you away without any doubt about the outcome," said Lott. "Jimmy knew his best shots and your greatest weaknesses. He had his game, and yours, figured out. That way, he'd give you shots that you had to take the greatest risk returning. It's like making you lose before he had to win."

Jacobs's inner game stressed strict self-control. He referred to "Mr. Emotion" as predictable, someone that he wouldn't let interfere with winning. He explained that concept in the 1966 *Sports Illustrated* story: "[Mr. Emotion] acts as a reminder to me that the application of the physical talent that I have is under the complete dominance of what I call my control system, my brain." The brain ordered "Mr. Emotion" as one would "some small child."

He went into a match confident that he was prepared for every contingency. "I plan how I'm going to win, meaning the type of play I'm going to employ in order to get the desired result," said Jacobs.

All through the 1950s, Jacobs and Beck continued to build their separate fight film collections. They devised a radical thesis: the great fighters of the turn of the century, contrary to the conventional wisdom, were technical dullards. They grabbed, pushed, tripped, postured, and showed minimal boxing skills. In 1960, Jacobs and Beck put together a mini-documentary to prove their point with old footage from the fights of James J. Corbett, John L. Sullivan, Bob Fitzsimmons, James J. Jeffries, and Jack Johnson. "We showed it at the Hollywood 'Y' to the boxing press," said Beck. "No one had seen these guys before. They groaned. Some of these fighters were just horrible."

Word of the revolutionary footage spread. They got telegrams from all over the world to show the film. Jacobs and Beck decided to show it next in New York. They intended to use the opportunity as an entry into a fight film business. They'd combine their collections, move to New York, rent the library out, and produce fight films for television. While Beck was on vacation in Mexico, Jacobs went to New York to discuss a showing.

The film was to turn Jacobs, already a well-known sports figure, into a celebrity. He soon met two men who would change the course of his life. The first was Bill Cayton, and the other was Cus D'Amato.

Cayton produced a television series called "Greatest Fights of the Century" using footage from his own extensive fight film collection. Jacobs decided to work for Cayton instead of with Beck, and moved to New York. "I felt that he betrayed me, but you know, that was Jimmy," said Beck. "No one could stand in his way."

Beck had seen him do it to other people too. In 1959, while still in Los Angeles, Jacobs met John Patrick, a local fight film collector. Patrick was a close friend of Jess Willard, who in a 1915 Havana match defeated black champion Jack Johnson. Only ten film prints of the fight were known to exist. The negative had long ago disappeared. Patrick and Willard found one of the prints in Australia. They offered to pay Jacobs, then just twenty-nine years old, to go there and buy the film on their behalf. Instead, Jacobs borrowed the money and bought it for himself. Patrick and Willard sued, unsuccessfully.

Cayton was surprised that Jacobs managed to avoid more legal trouble. "Jimmy was never a very sophisticated businessman," said Cayton. "He came to me and wanted prints of some of my fights. He showed me his but I found out he didn't own any of the rights. He just showed them to friends. He was likable, very engaging. I hired him as a film editor."

William D'Arcy Cayton was born in Brooklyn in 1918, the son of a prosperous stockbroker. He did well in school and eschewed sports. After graduating from university, Cayton wrote technical reports for Du Pont. He switched to advertising and in the mid-1940s started his own firm. Cayton Inc. remained a small operation with a few highly profitable national accounts. With the advent of television, he recognized the need for sports programming. Cayton started buying up fight films from retired promoters. "They were the wise guys, the Jewish and Irish mafia from the twenties and thirties," said Cayton. "By then they'd become wealthy gentlemen. They had all these films of Dempsey and Tunney and Louis gathering dust. They were happy to get anything for them. I paid around twenty-five hundred dollars a fight." Cayton also bought the film rights from current fights. He made his first of many such deals with none other than Jim Norris of the I.B.C.

Gillette sponsored a series of live fights on television every Friday night. Cayton's program came on afterwards—and often got better ratings. By the time he met Jacobs, Cayton owned 450 films. Jacobs worked as an editor, then started filming some of the fights himself. He also went around the world buying, with Cayton's money, more old footage. Eventually, he created and produced his own television programs. One of his first ran on CBS in 1962: the Willard-Johnson fight.

The business prospered. The two men produced a new television series called "Knockout." Jacobs became an expert on boxing. Cayton invested in fight films. He bought the entire library collection of Madison Square Garden. They set up new companies, such as Big Fights Inc., to handle the growing demand for sports television programming. By the mid-1960s, Cayton cut Jacobs in for one-sixth of the profits from Big Fights. A few years later, that became one-third. Cayton, however, maintained full ownership control. The money rolled in. By the early 1970s, the ABC network was paying $2 million a year for the exclusive use of the Big Fights 17,000-fight film library. "Big Fights made Jim a wealthy man," said Cayton.

Cus D'Amato also believed that the so-called great heavyweights of the turn of the century were anything but. He sought out Jacobs to see the evidence. They became instant friends. Jacobs moved into D'Amato's small, cluttered, one-bedroom apartment on Fifty-seventh Street in New York and stayed there ten years until D'Amato, bankrupt and finished as an active manager, moved to Catskill.

It seemed like an "Odd Couple" relationship. D'Amato's career as a manager had peaked, and fizzled, with the Patterson/Johansson scandal. Once a powerful iconoclast, he became a tolerated oddity, a fringe player in the world of boxing espousing arcane ideas of little seeming relevance. That a young, athletic, popular, and outgoing man like Jacobs would live for so long with the paranoiac D'Amato puzzled a lot of people.

Their differences, however, were more of style than substance. Unlike D'Amato, Jacobs's thinking processes never wandered. He had a deep and resonant voice, and he spoke in a precise, direct fashion. Jacobs affected the formal, stilted manner of an English professor when he discoursed on boxing. He used such phrases as "Oh, yes, I daresay," and "My dear friend, you must realize." The effect, when combined with his dark eyes, strong jaw, and bull-like physique, was, to say the least, imposing.

Like D'Amato, Jacobs respected the views of very few people. He never allowed anyone else to be the expert. D'Amato's cacophony of thoughts and aphorisms enveloped a person like a dense cloud. Jacobs bore down on, and into, his listener like a jackhammer. They were both impassioned about the rightness of their own ideas, both capable of obsessive tunnel vision. They were egoists focused only on their own ambitions.

D'Amato also found in Jacobs someone who fully understood, could practice and intellectually articulate, the psychology of fear. "Jimmy is one of the few people who have a good grasp of fear," D'Amato was quoted as saying in the 1966 *Sports Illustrated* profile. "He is extraordinary. He not only has an excellent mind, but a tremendous physique and stamina. I have never met an athlete like him."

There were rumors about the pair. It seemed like a simple mentor-protégé bond, but some people suspected a homosexual tie. That's unlikely. It had more to do with the fact that Jacobs perceived his own father as a fallen man, a failure in business and in marriage, symbolically impotent and made all the more so by a domineering wife. D'Amato had also fallen, of course, but in a great battle, and he had emerged with the power of his ideas intact. His demise was unjust. Jacobs found in D'Amato both a wounded father to rehabilitate and a stronger one to be guided by.

Still, Jacobs's sexual identity didn't seem to mature past boyhood. He frequently dated women but had no long-standing relationship and no interest in either marriage or children. He lived for work and he strove to please his mother. Intimacy with her was about all that he seemed to want from the opposite sex. "They'd hold hands, he'd kiss her all the time, and call several times a week," remembered sister Dorothy Zeil. "They used the same pet name for each other, 'Doll,' and signed letters the same way, 'Hugs.' Once, when Jimmy found out she'd been dating a younger man he went into a jealous rage and insisted that the relationship end."

Mother and son became prisoners of their own idealized, inviolate bond. Neither could err in the eyes of the other. Each was perfect. To Zeil it was all an elaborate dance of denial. "My mother was a drug addict. Demerol, barbiturates, everything she could get her hands on," said Zeil. "And Jimmy kept giving her the money to buy them. I told him to stop but he wouldn't talk about it. Money solved his problems, but it was me who had to deal with her. When she started having accidents from the drugs, I had to take her to the hospital."

Jacobs couldn't even bury his own father, who died in 1965 at the age of sixty-five after a five-year bout with lung cancer. "Mother promised she and Jimmy would come to the funeral," said Zeil. "I went to pick her up and she came to the door in her robe and said, 'I'm not going and Jimmy isn't coming home.'"

When D'Amato retired to Catskill in 1971, Jacobs stayed in the apartment for a few more years. He grew much closer to handball protégé Steve Lott and in 1972 hired him to work at Big Fights. In 1974, Jacobs and Lott moved into different apartments in a building on East Forty-fifth Street. They were inseparable. They walked back and forth to work together each day, and frequently traveled overseas with each other to buy fight films. "Jimmy always referred to Steve as his 'clone,'" said Zeil.

In 1975, Jacobs became friendly with a neighbor, Loraine Atter. Slowly, she replaced Lott as Jacobs's primary companion. Loraine was forty-five years old, of Italian descent, and originally from Florida. She worked as an executive at a paper manufacturing company. She was known as an emotionally reserved, fastidious woman, and, according to Zeil, she "worshiped Jimmy." She was the sort of woman who "took care" of her man. Loraine bought his clothes, arranged his social life, decorated his apartment, indeed did everything but cook. They ate out in restaurants every night. And most important, perhaps, was that she met the approval of Jacobs's mother. Said childhood friend Nick Beck: "His mother didn't think any of Jim's girlfriends were suitable, until Loraine."

Still, no one who knew Jacobs well expected him to marry her. They did, secretly, in 1981. Beck was shocked. So was Zeil. She suspected that her brother was talked into it. But what neither Zeil nor Beck nor anyone else except Jacobs, his mother, and Loraine knew was that in 1980 Jacobs had been diagnosed with chronic lymphoid leukemia. Death, he was told, could come within seven to eight years. No doubt they married because they were in love. But Jacobs may have also wanted the experience of marriage for its own sake before he died.

Jacobs wasn't content just collecting and producing fight films, no matter how much money he made. He wanted to manage a boxer, preferably a champion and ideally a heavyweight. One early flirtation came in the late 1970s when he worked as a booking agent for white South African heavyweight Kallie Knoetze. He had D'Amato assert in the boxing press that Knoetze would, without doubt, become champion. Despite D'Amato's training tips, Knoetze did not advance beyond journeyman status.

Jacobs turned to the lower weight classes where there were far greater numbers of available prospects. In 1978, he used $75,000 of Big Fights Inc. money to buy the managerial contract of Wilfred Benitez, a promising young welterweight. Jacobs and Cayton guided Benitez to a championship title in 1979. Soon after, Jacobs and Benitez split up over a contract dispute, and Benitez's career fizzled.

As a team, Jacobs and Cayton earned a reputation for being tenacious about getting their boxer the easiest matches for the most money—and being honest about purse cuts. They tried to maintain a unified front, as if there were no really significant division of labor and no personal tensions existed. Jacobs functioned as manager of record. He initiated negotiations for fights, dealt with other managers, selected opponents, and schmoozed with the sports media. Steve Lott worked as his assistant in charge of the day-to-day business of the training camp. That included getting sparring partners, making travel arrangements, and generally catering to the fighter's daily needs. Cayton preferred to work in the background on the contract negotiations with television networks and promoters. Jacobs and Cayton split the manager's purse fifty-fifty.

Jacobs strutted about as the boxing expert, fight film nabob, and historian. Whenever news stories were done on their fight film ventures, Jacobs the former handball champion took center stage. He claimed that according to a boxing encyclopedia, he was the world's leading expert on the sport. Jacobs failed to mention the fact that he wrote the entry himself. Privately, to friends, he derided Cayton as a boxing dilettante. "Jim wouldn't come out and say anything overtly critical of Bill," said Nick Beck. "He was more insidious about it. He told me that Bill didn't know much about boxing and didn't care about it either. It was just a business to him."

Jacobs also overstated his status in the team. He told people that he had come to Cayton with an enormous film library and plenty of his own money, and that they had pooled their resources and, as equal partners, made boxing film history. One of the first people in boxing to see through that fiction was Larry Merchant, a boxing analyst for HBO Sports. In 1980, Jacobs came to Merchant with an idea to do a comprehensive fight documentary series on videotape. It required transferring thousands of images from film and using advanced video technologies to create special effects such as slow motion and stop-action replays. Jacobs envisaged selling the series to television, then renting out videocassettes. Merchant would narrate, for which he'd get a fee plus a share in the gross rentals. "When I mentioned to Bill [Cayton] what the deal was, he was shocked. Jimmy never told him about it," said Merchant. After that, Jacobs never brought it up again.

Jacobs also claimed to Merchant, among others, that his father owned a chain of department stores in St. Louis. In other variations, his father owned a construction business. When his father died, Jacobs claimed to have inherited millions of dollars. "Jimmy talked about all his money. He told me that his father gave him fifty thousand dollars in 1960 to stake him in the fight film business," said Merchant.

Cayton was aware of Jacobs's public posturing and outright lies but never confronted him with it. "I found the stories about his supposed wealth very amusing," said Cayton. "First he told people he had ten million dollars, and when he got away with that the figure went to twenty million, then thirty million." In Cayton's value system, they were in business together and as long as they prospered, he didn't care about Jacobs's idiosyncrasies. "Essentially, Jim was my employee. I did all the business deals with the fight films and all the boxers. Jim was the front man, the public image. Every deal was made right here, at my desk."

In fact, Jacobs did have a higher opinion of himself than did his associates in the boxing world. "I liked Jimmy. I was curious about his insights on boxing. So were a lot of other people. But he wasn't liked as a businessperson. He had a code in a deal. He gave you his idea of what it was worth and that was it—no other opinion was valid. He didn't negotiate. He said, this is it, take it or leave it," Merchant added.

According to Cayton, on more than one occasion he had to temper Jacobs in a contract negotiation. "Early on, he was a bit too blunt," said Cayton. "I taught him everything he knew."

Perhaps he did. Jacobs was a quick study and a man, once he learned the basics, determined to do it his way to the end. By claiming such high ground, Cayton tried to disguise a measure of envy. Merchant was aware of that: "The ever-popular Jimmy, the astute manager and boxing expert liked by everybody: that's how Bill perceived Jimmy, and he [Bill] resented him for it."

Cayton had an almost mirror-opposite existence to that of Jacobs. Besides not ever being athletic, he suffered from recurring back problems and endocarditis, an inflammation of the heart valves. He was lean, and tall, but frail-looking. His personal manner was stiff, formal, unengaging, dispassionate, almost cold. He tried to offset that with frequent smiling, but to no avail. The smile looked forced and far too self-consciously affected. It had a Cheshire cat aspect, as if Cayton were pleased with himself in advance with whatever was about to transpire—probably at the listener's expense. "Bill was a taker, not a giver," said Camille Ewald. He avoided social outings, except when it concerned business. Not a single person in boxing claimed him as a friend. "Money and business. He's all business," added Ewald.

Not entirely. Cayton had one other abiding interest that may explain part of the reason for his emotional reserve. Every night Cayton would take the 6:40 commuter train to his house in Larchmont, just north of the city. Every weekend is spent at home. One of his three children, a daughter, was born premature in 1947, and then mistakenly given too much oxygen in the incubator, causing blindness and severe retardation. Cayton and his wife, Doris, raised her by themselves at home. "Nothing, no one, could help. Doris devoted herself to her," said Cayton. Apparently, the younger woman will not eat dinner, or go to bed, until he returns home each night. Whatever Cayton is in business, there must be another, far different man at home. Cayton diligently protected that aspect of his life. He rarely gave out his home telephone number, and he never invited business associates to his house.

# Chapter Five

Mike Tyson's professional career began on March 6, 1985. One year, eight months, and sixteen days later, he would capture the heavyweight championship of the world. The list of firsts which led up to that event in sports history is, by all appearances, mind-boggling.

He would win the title at the age of twenty, younger than any other heavyweight. At that age, Joe Louis and Rocky Marciano were still in the amateurs. No other heavyweight ever captured the title in so short a span of time. No other heavyweight ever achieved as high a percentage of first-round knockouts as Tyson—40.5 percent, or fifteen in twenty-seven fights—in his career leading up to the crown.

It wasn't victory just by brute force. Tyson acquired the subtler though far less recognized distinction of defensive excellence. Due to his training in the D'Amato "system," he would be hit far fewer times moving forward than had any other notable heavyweight moving in any direction in the ring.

What won't go into the statistical record books, or the sports lore, is the degree to which those achievements were the product of design. No boxer becomes champion by serendipity. But the careers of some boxers are more intently, and successfully, manipulated than others. In the hands of D'Amato, Jacobs, and Cayton, that manipulation almost reached the level of conspiracy. Recognizing this fact doesn't severely diminish Tyson's achievement. But it does put it in proper perspective.

Informing the whole effort was a single, unspoken motive. None of the men could waste any time getting Tyson a shot at the title. Each of them was on borrowed time.

D'Amato was seventy-seven years old. He had little energy to travel long distances, let alone keep up with the punishing regimen of watching over a rising contender. Tyson was his last hurrah.

In 1985, Jacobs entered the fifth year of his leukemia. According to Dr. Gene Brody, the New York specialist who diagnosed and treated Jacobs, in the early years he managed fairly well. Starting in 1982, Jacobs received occasional doses of two drugs—Leukeran and Prednisone—that kept the disease under control. By 1985, the distorting effect of the cancer on his blood cell count made Jacobs increasingly prone to simple infections. He also suffered enlargement of the lymph nodes in his neck. As Jacobs well knew, chronic lymphoid leukemia, or CLL, is incurable. It's also capricious. He could die with only a few months' warning.

Cayton, of course, also knew that. Jacobs told him of the disease, and his prognosis, in 1981. Since then Tyson's success as an amateur, and the prospect of making him champion, had given Cayton a new interest in his business career. He delayed plans for retirement despite recurring attacks of endocarditis, which had been treated successfully with massive doses of antibiotics. Still, Cayton was a sixty-nine-year-old man. He'd probably outlive D'Amato, but it was a toss-up with Jacobs. No doubt, somewhere in the back of his mind, Cayton wondered if he'd be left having to finish (and profit from) the job himself.

With their collectively fragile mortalities as the background, they devised three basic guidelines for developing Tyson's career.

First and foremost, they could not risk another defeat in the ring. For an amateur losing was excusable. For a professional it would severely diminish the aura they wanted to build around Tyson as an indestructible force in the ring and an inevitable champion of the heavyweight division. Opponents had to be selected carefully, with all factors—such as fight duration, ring size, and glove weight—stacked in Tyson's favor.

Second, they hoped to schedule a fight at least once a month. That served several purposes. It fit in with the mortality factor. It was also a way of maintaining control over Tyson and sustaining his burning intensity. And as long as he could be kept at that upper level of performance, Tyson's tendency to fall into a passive state in the ring might just be avoided.

Third, just as D'Amato had with Floyd Patterson, they had to find promoters willing to let them make most of the decisions. That was the best way to retain absolute control over Tyson's career.

In this first stage of Tyson's career, they needed a completely malleable promoter. Matt Baranski suggested a husband-and-wife team based in Troy, New York, an hour north of Catskill. The Millers ran a true mom-and-pop promoting business. They rarely made much money and certainly couldn't afford to lose any. Jacobs and Cayton would finance the whole promotion. The Millers would be paid out of profits from ticket sales, if any. Jacobs and Cayton also promised to cover all losses.

Tyson's professional debut came against a club fighter named Hector Mercedes on March 6, 1985, in Albany, New York. Tyson's hair was cropped short at the sides in a homage to the Spartan macho aesthetic of Jack Dempsey. Tyson swarmed over the taller, slower Mercedes, who must have felt as if he were fighting two opponents: one who only punched and another who eluded. Tyson then settled down into a more fluid expression of his unique style. He'd revised the "peek-a-boo" by holding his gloves on either side of the chin instead of the temple. That way his punches got off more quickly. He knocked out Mercedes in the first round.

As expected, the fight did not turn a profit. Jacobs and Cayton paid Tyson a purse of five hundred dollars. D'Amato paid Rooney 10 percent of that, gave Tyson one hundred dollars, and put the remainder away.

Tyson's second fight came on April 10 against Trent Singleton. This time he looked more studied. He charged straight in, feinted with his head, slipped and weaved, all the while not getting hit. Then, suddenly, Tyson popped up in close range and let go a series of left and right hooks to the body and head. Singleton went down twice within seconds. When he got up, Tyson reverted to a more conventional offense. He pinned Singleton against the ropes and threw a series of punches, displaying textbook "finishing" abilities. Singelton crumbled. Tyson lunged down to hit his prone opponent again—a serious infraction of the rules—but was stopped by the referee. He turned to his cornermen, Kevin Rooney and Matt Baranski, and smirked.

In his third fight, five weeks later, Tyson regressed. His first two opponents had been tall and black. This one, Don Halpin, was the same height as Tyson and white. From the moment the bell rang, Tyson looked sluggish. There was little head and upper body movement. At times, he let his gloves drop.

Halpin made things worse by standing up to Tyson's punches. He also tended to crouch, which may have confused Tyson. From early in the amateurs, Tyson was always more effective with a taller opponent. It gave him the chance to use his smaller size to advantage. By the second round, he had started to get lazy on the inside, which enabled Halpin to connect with a few straight rights.

By the fourth round, Tyson began to look like any other conventionally trained fighter. Fortunately, because of his superior hand speed and power, he was better at being average than Halpin. Tyson won by a knockout in the fourth, and tried to hit Halpin as he fell. This time the referee openly rebuked him.

It wasn't Tyson's foul play—and there would be much more of it to come—that worried D'Amato and Jacobs afterwards. The passivity had struck their prospect once again, and this time with a handpicked, mediocre opponent. They had no idea what to do about it. "They didn't know Mike," Baranski said. "He was out of control most of the time."

For the next fight Jacobs arranged to get Tyson on ESPN, the sports cable station that stages a weekly fightnight to showcase up-and-coming contenders. These events were organized by top Rank Boxing, owned by Bob Arum. Arum was one of the country's two top promoters, the other being Don King. Jacobs ran a risk letting Tyson come within Arum's grasp. Like King, he was notorious for spiriting away other people's fighters with promises of big money. Jacobs had had one such battle with Arum over Wilfred Benitez.

But Arum had something that Jacobs desperately wanted. Due to his losses at the Olympic trials, Tyson had no chance yet of getting on one of the big three broadcast networks. He had to start with cable. Jacobs made an appeal to Arum's appetite for power. For several years Arum had been battling with King over turf. Arum ended up doing most of the major middleweight fights, and King the heavyweights. Jacobs knew that Arum had always wanted to get his hands on a major heavyweight contender and challenge King for control of that division.

Tyson's first fight under Arum was against Ricardo Spain on June 20 in Atlantic City at the Resorts International hotel-casino. D'Amato and Jacobs didn't want to take any chances with Spain. His height, six-foot-two, didn't worry them, and neither did his record of seven wins, five by knockout. It was his weight, a mere 184¼ pounds, or around thirty pounds under the average for a heavyweight. "They were really afraid that because he was so much lighter than Mike, Spain would run," said Nick Beck, who was at the fight. "Chasing him around the ring would have made Mike look bad."

The fight was scheduled for four rounds. They decided the night before to try increasing it to six, which would give Tyson plenty of time to score a knockout. Jacobs called Spain's manager. He didn't want to do it. Jacobs demanded to talk to Spain. "He offered Spain a few hundred dollars on top of his purse for two more rounds," said Beck. Spain took the money.

Tyson knocked him out in thirty-nine seconds of the first round. Spain, whose *nom de pug* was "The Ram," had unwisely decided to stand and fight, a mistake with Tyson, as many other fighters would soon discover. Ironically, Jacobs's offer may have also made Spain overconfident. If they were that worried about their man's chances, Spain may have reasoned, maybe he wasn't such a threat. No doubt that was the conclusion they hoped Spain would reach.

A few weeks later, Tyson went on ESPN again, this time to fight six-foot-four, 226½ pound John Alderson, a twenty-one-year-old former West Virginia coal miner. Alderson was four victories into his return from a three-year layoff from the ring. He made the perfect victim for Tyson. He had the tall heavyweight's habit of leaning away from a punch. That might have worked against Tyson if Alderson also had good hand speed and leg work, plus punch accuracy, but he didn't. Tyson easily eluded the punches. He then chopped away with combinations at the body and head as if trying to fell an old red oak, bloodying Alderson's nose and eye, and dropping him twice until the referee called the fight over in the second round.

The ESPN commentator noted that Tyson switched to being a southpaw, or a left-hander, midway through the first round. He had indeed been taught—perhaps after a suggestion by Jacobs, who was lethal with both hands on the handball court—to fight as a right- and left-hander. That confused opponents. They couldn't figure out which side of Tyson was the bigger threat. The answer, of course, was both.

Jacobs felt that Tyson had proven himself enough to deserve a regular schedule on ESPN. Arum, in one of the biggest blunders of his promoting career, disagreed. Incredibly, he told Jacobs that his match-makers considered Tyson an average talent. Arum refused to give Jacobs the dates. Jacobs made contact with a promoter in Houston, Jeff Levine, who would go on to handle eight Tyson fights. Jacobs and Cayton, with their long, bitter memories, never forgave Arum his lack of insight. They did one more fight with Arum, then never again let him within a foot of Tyson's career.

In Tyson's next fight, against Larry Sims in Poughkeepsie, New York, he faltered. That is, after an unsuccessful initial barrage, he seemed to get frustrated and lose the seamless union of defensive and offensive movement. It took three rounds to knock Sims out. As with all his fights, this one was taped on video. But Jacobs and Cayton would later deny that a tape had been made. The Sims tape was destroyed. They wanted a record of first-round knockouts and nothing less.

Tyson's next five fights were on average three weeks apart. Every opponent was tall, slow, and used little head or lateral movement—in other words, tailor-made for Tyson. Some of them didn't deserve to be in the ring against a fighter of Tyson's caliber. Not surprisingly, he set off on binge of first-round knockouts.

In pro fight number seven, the slow hands of six-foot-two Lorenzo Canady proved his downfall. Tyson simply ducked underneath, dipped to his left, and let go a concussive left hook to the head. Next was Mike ("Jack") Johnson, fighting his first bout in more than two years. He sank to the canvas after Tyson slipped, then ripped into him with a left hook to the ribs. Johnson got up and Tyson delivered a straight right through the gloves that dislodged two front teeth, which remained stuck in the hard, rubber mouth guard. Tyson turned to Rooney and pointed at Johnson with a gleeful look that said, "Look at that! Did you see what I just did!"

Donnie Long was dubbed "The Master of Disaster." He, too, had recently come back after a two-year layoff. Long had a tendency to hold his gloves out as if displaying a sign. That left a big space, through which Tyson drove a straight right. A few more punches and Long was out. Back in his corner, Tyson blew a kiss at the camera.

"Big Bob" Colay, another tall opponent, came on a platter. He held his hands low and tried to dance, but he lacked the leg speed to move out of Tyson's way. He pawed with left jabs that Tyson easily slipped—to both the right and left, to Colay's amazement. His trademark left hook to the head put Colay out in thirty-seven seconds of the first round.

After knocking out Sterling Benjamin with another left hook, Tyson didn't bother to wait for the count to make sure he stayed down. He walked over to Rooney and Baranski and thrust his hands through the ropes, saying nothing, just demanding with the gesture that the gloves be removed. He'd finished. Job done. As they were about to cut the tape away and undo the strings, Tyson glanced over his shoulder to make sure Benjamin remained prone. After all, the unexpected could happen.

It did. Three days later—November 4, 1985—D'Amato died of pneumonia. Through most of October, D'Amato had battled the illness at home. Always distrustful of doctors, he wouldn't go to the hospital. Finally, he had no choice. By then it was too late. D'Amato spent a week in a nearby local hospital but didn't respond to the drugs. He moved down to Mount Sinai in New York, and died a few days later.

The only person with him during those last days was not Jacobs or Tyson or Torres, but Tom Patti, who still lived in the house even though he'd given up boxing. "I don't know why Mike didn't come," said Patti. "Maybe he didn't want to see Cus like that. Cus looked bad, all bloated up." Patti paused a moment. "Jimmy Jacobs should have been there. I learnt something about Jimmy after that."

D'Amato was buried in a Catholic cemetery on the outskirts of Catskill. The gravestone is a simple pink granite slab, a few feet high, a few feet wide. Chiseled on it are D'Amato's own words: "A boy comes to me with a spark of interest. I feed the spark and it becomes a flame. I feed the flame and it becomes a fire. I feed the fire and it becomes a roaring blaze." And then beneath, "Cus." The day after the funeral, Tyson returned by himself and poured a bottle of champagne over the grave.

It was Jacobs's idea to put those words on the gravestone. They focused on a small part of what D'Amato's life represented. But they were more apt in describing Jacobs's primary commercial ambition: promoting heavyweight contender Mike Tyson. Patterson was at most a flickering flame, Torres a mere glow. Only Tyson blazed.

Jacobs didn't overtly exploit the event of D'Amato's death to advance his interest with Tyson. He did, however, subtly leverage from it as Patti noticed at the November 19 memorial service that Jacobs organized at D'Amato's former gym, the Gramercy, on Fourteenth Street. Dozens of people came; old fighters long forgotten, boys whom D'Amato had helped, and friends from his childhood. Jacobs asked only authors Norman Mailer, Gay Talese, and Budd Schulberg, among others, to give eulogies—which he then videotaped.

"He wanted to have segments just in case they came in handy promoting Mike," said Tom Patti. "Jimmy was using Mike's relationship with Cus. He wrote a program for the memorial service and quoted Cus about fighting and what makes a great fighter. Beneath the quote he wrote in things like 'and Mike Tyson is what Cus meant.' That was true, but what Jimmy did wasn't right. He was thinking about himself, not Cus or Mike."

With D'Amato gone, Jacobs could think about the opportunity of Mike Tyson in different terms. He no longer had the benefit of D'Amato's wisdom on managing a fighter. But he'd listened to D'Amato for years on the principles of the job, and had practiced them with other lesser fighters. "Cus had gone over the plan for Mike endlessly with Jimmy: how often he should fight, who the best opponents would be, when he'd probably be ready for the title, how to handle promoters— everything you could think of," said Baranski. "Then he told Jimmy what Mike was probably going to be like after he won the title. How he'd change, what to look for to head off problems, guys muscling in on him. Cus had the plan, and all Jimmy had to do was follow it."

Without D'Amato around, Jacobs knew that the management of Tyson had become greatly simplified. "It would have eventually come to a head between Jimmy and Cus," continued Baranski. "The bigger Mike got, the more say Cus would have wanted. That would have drove Jimmy nuts. Bill, too. With Cus gone they breathed a lot easier."

Maybe so. But it's almost a moot point, because if conflicts had arisen over management issues, D'Amato wouldn't have had much legal recourse. Once Tyson turned eighteen, D'Amato's guardianship approval wasn't needed anymore on documents. Jacobs and Cayton had tied Tyson into a series of agreements that gave them control over every aspect of his career.

They stuck to the plan of Jacobs as manager and Cayton working behind the scenes on contract negotiations. That suited their temperaments and abilities. They also didn't have any choice. According to the rules and regulations of the New York State Athletic Commission, a body that oversees boxing and wrestling, a boxer is permitted to have only one manager of record.

Still, Cayton had solidified his background role. On September 28, 1984, he obtained Tyson's signature on a contract that made him "exclusive personal manager" for the extraordinary long term of seven years. He would represent Tyson for commercial appearances, product endorsements, and all entertainment activities under the corporate name of Reel Sports, Inc.

Cayton was sole owner of Reel Sports. He also had a private agreement with Jacobs to share evenly the personal manager's commission. That was the other unusual aspect of the contract besides the lengthy term. Personal service agents for athletes usually claim a commission of from 10 to 15 percent. Cayton took 33⅓ percent.

D'Amato, who for so long had prided himself on working in the fighter's interests, did not object to either the term of the Reel Sports agreement or the commission. Nor did he advise Tyson to get a lawyer to review the contract.. Perhaps D'Amato felt that his review was sufficient. He signed the agreement. Under his name it read "Cus D'Amato, Adviser to Michael Tyson, who shall have final approval of all decisions involving Michael Tyson." D'Amato's legal position was shaky. He didn't have a separate contract with Tyson making him exclusive adviser.

A few weeks after the Reel Sports agreement was signed, Jacobs officially contracted with Tyson to become manager. That agreement used the standard Athletic Commission boxer-manager form. Nothing in the specified term (four years) or purse split (two-thirds for Tyson, one-third for Jacobs) was unusual. That same day, Jacobs and Cayton used another Athletic Commission form to put their division of Tyson's purses in writing. The "assignment of manager's contract" enabled Jacobs to legally give Cayton 50 percent of his earnings from Tyson.

*    *    *

Ever since doing the Alex Wallau interview with ABC, Jacobs and Cayton had looked for new media opportunities to push the narrative of the relationship between D'Amato and Tyson. They knew that every great fighter, if he was going to cross over into the mainstream audience, needed a story. The more empathetic the tale, the better. In other words, the more Tyson could be defined through a device America understood, the more likely he'd achieve general acceptance and popularity. Given Tyson's continued bent for the wild side—all through 1985 he continued to disappear for days at a time in Albany and New York, and on one occasion mugged a man in an elevator for his wallet— that story had to move center stage. It would popularize, sanitize, and create the ever-ready, all-purpose rationalization.

Soon after Tyson turned professional, Jacobs pitched a documentary profile of D'Amato and Tyson to the producers of CBS "Sunday Morning," hosted by the avuncular Charles Kuralt. On June 2, 1985, the piece aired. Narrative had been refined into the fable of Cus and the Kid.

The initial image showed Kuralt and D'Amato strolling across the lawn of the house. Kuralt's voice-over cut in: "Cus D'Amato lived a full, rich, embattled life in the big cities. He managed Floyd Patterson to the heavyweight championship of the world almost thirty years ago. But boxing passed him by. And left him in exile in the country."

The image cut to D'Amato in the Catskill gym.

"He considered himself a teacher, a shaper of character... and then suddenly Cus D'Amato is handling fire again. Michael Tyson, a wild, angry teenager from a nearby reform school. Cus, who never married, adopted Michael, took him into his home, taught him about jabbing through fear."

Kuralt talked about each giving the other the same gift, "a future." The piece flashed back to D'Amato's time with Patterson and their eventual estrangement. Kuralt then dug up Patterson and asked if he had any advice for Tyson: "Have faith, confidence in the man you trust. In Cus."

D'Amato claimed, rather incredibly, for Tyson had had only three pro fights up to that point, that he could "go down in history as the greatest fighter of all time."

Kuralt then all but sainted D'Amato. "Cus D'Amato is more than a manager of champions. He's a savior of souls. He saved Floyd Patterson and he is saving Mike Tyson."

D'Amato struck the self-sacrificing pose of a man more interested in souls than the dictates of his own ego: "I succeed when he becomes champion of the world and independent of me."

Kuralt's final remarks tried to strike an ominous note, as if we had only seen the prologue: "But they need each other now. Because someday soon they will be coming out of the country, coming hard and coming fast for the lights of the city."

The following September, an Albany television station added its own flourishes to the fable. The voice-over described Tyson as "a very quiet and gentle man outside the ring," a fighter who didn't want to be the "boss," a "boxing historian" whose "gentle side shows with his pigeons." Tyson claimed that D'Amato never had to worry about where he was because at "nighttime I'm at my coop looking after my birds."

A month after D'Amato's death, Jacobs and Cayton managed to get Tyson on NBC's "Today Show with Bryant Gumbel. "Once a thief, and a thief headed for a life in prison, mind you, Mike Tyson joins us this morning as a young man headed for a heavyweight crown," said Gumbel in introducing Tyson. The interview ran the standard course through the fable until near the end when Gumbel asked Tyson, "Did D'Amato basically save your life?" The answer: "Yes."

Dan Rather, anchorman for "CBS Evening News," chimed in to take his turn with the fable later that December. He introduced a segment on Tyson that hit all the high notes and then some. "He's just nineteen years old, tending his pigeons in the Catskills. A big, strong, country kid..." began the CBS reporter. "His teacher was Cus D'Amato, dead now but living on in his masterpiece... Mike Tyson, age nineteen, has the skills and is determined to win the heavyweight boxing champion-ship of the world. And he has a secret weapon: he wants to do it for Cus."

Cus and the Kid could be viewed as a human-interest story that celebrated universal values. The implicit messages, however, endorsed two abiding myths of American culture: charity is better then funda-mental social change, and love, combined with the human will, conquers all. Cus and the Kid became a paradigm for social reform, but of the most passive variety. It was television fare, after all; pure entertainment. People could watch the problems of the black urban underclass being solved for them in the comfort of their living rooms.

The historical parallels with how other black boxers were packaged are striking. Tyson was made into a black stereotype of the post-civil rights era in which equal political and social rights had supposedly been obtained; economic freedom came to those who were willing to work for it. By that logic, Tyson, with the guidance and love of D'Amato, had fought his way out of poverty toward a certain future of wealth and fame. Heavyweight champion Joe Louis was also made into a stereotype of his era. In the 1930s, equal rights for blacks were a minor issue to most Americans, and yet blacks were still expected to feel empowered by the myth of individual salvation. If only they would "uplift" themselves, the thinking went, their problems would be over. And yet, blacks had to "behave," especially when they obtained a measure of success that placed them in the public spotlight.

Newspaper and magazine profiles of Louis often described him as "nonpretentious," "self-effacing," "Godfearing," and a "credit to his race." Ironically, Louis's manager was also named Jacobs and he, too, was a manipulator of the media. He hired someone to write Louis's biography, *Joe Louis's Own Story*, in which the fighter acknowledged his "duty" not to throw his "race down by abusing my position as a heavyweight challenger."

In the marketing of Tyson, Jacobs and Cayton had the Joe Louis model in mind. They definitely wanted to avoid the Muhammad Ali and Sonny Liston experiences. "Jimmy always believed that Louis represented the right mix of great boxer and astute management," said Nick Beck. "Ali was uncontrollable in public, and too much his own man. Jimmy also wanted to avoid what he called the 'Liston syndrome.' He didn't want people looking at Mike like he was some barely reformed thug."

Of course, with Cus and the Kid the medium was also the message. It was a story that could be told in pictures and words within a few minutes. Jacobs and Cayton took that symmetry between form and content the next logical step. In 1983, the VHS format cassette videotape for home and office use was a novel publicity device already being used to sell financial services, travel, and residential real estate. Jacobs and Cayton were the first to apply it to boxing. They made more than five hundred tapes showing all of Tyson's first-round knockouts and sent them to boxing reporters and the editors of the major sports magazines. Follow-up letters and phone calls were made to set up interviews. In the sports journalism community it came to be known as "The Tape," a must-see and a status symbol for those who had a VCR.

The knockout tape made an appropriate companion piece to presentations of Cus and the Kid. As communications theorist Marshall McLuhan argued, the means of conveying information often has more influence on people than the information itself. On the "cool medium" of television, Tyson's knockouts were fast and efficient, like a blast of numbing arctic air that instantly paralyzed an opponent. There was little sweat, minimal struggle, and only occasional blood; nothing, in other words, to suggest that sentient, and suffering, human beings were involved. If you weren't a boxing fan, you could certainly watch a Tyson fight.

"It wasn't that Jimmy and Bill did anything new or revolutionary in marketing Tyson," pointed out boxing analyst Larry Merchant. "They just knew how to use television better than anybody in boxing had ever done before."

\* \* \*

Nine days after D'Amato died, Tyson went to Houston to fight "Fast" Eddie Richardson. Asked by reporters if the death of D'Amato would adversely affect his performance, he responded like the emotionally detached professional that both D'Amato and Jacobs valued so highly: "I have certain objectives, and I'm going to fulfill them," said Tyson.

At six-foot-six, Richardson was taller than his average opponent. Tyson came out slipping and weaving and in the first punch of the bout plowed Richardson with a straight right that he couldn't react swiftly enough to avoid. Richardson stayed on his feet, though not for long. Tyson eluded a right and countered with a left hook to the head that literally lifted Richardson off his feet and sent him to the canvas like a toppled tower.

The television announcers struggled to make historical comparisons to explain what they'd witnessed. They appreciated only half the phenomenon. One announcer said that Tyson threw a left hook from the same crouch as Joe Frazier and that he had the power of Rocky Marciano. In fact, a lot of heavyweights threw hooks from a crouch: not only Frazier, but Max Schmeling, Marciano, and Liston. What Tyson did better than all of them was make the crouch a single component in a complex defensive and offensive ballet. His body mechanics flowed in a poetic motion that delivered the maximum quantity of physical force.

Marciano punched hard from his crouch, but he had comparatively inferior body mechanics. He was more plodding and didn't blend in as many different types of movements. At a fighting weight of only around 189 pounds, he also had a weaker punch than Tyson, plus nowhere near the same defensive skills. That's why Archie Moore, in their September 21, 1955, bout, was able to knock Marciano down. Moore had the hand speed to exploit the many openings in his crouch. Marciano did, though, have something that Tyson the boxing historian valued very highly. Tyson felt empathy with Marciano because they both found ways to beat taller opponents. Marciano didn't do it as well, technically, but he fought much bigger opponents with courage. "He broke their will," Tyson said of Marciano in a November 1985 *Village Voice* feature profile.

Just over a week later, Tyson arrived in Latham, New York, to meet Conroy Nelson, the stereotypical opponent. Nelson had done some homework on fighting Tyson and had decided to run rather than stand and trade punches. Tyson stalked relentlessly, eventually caught Nelson, and used him as a punching bag. Nelson had no choice but to throw something back, which was like opening the cookie jar. Tyson's left hook took him out with ease.

On December 6, Tyson made his debut in the Felt Forum, an auxiliary arena at the famed Madison Square Garden. This would be his first exposure to the New York sports media.

Kuralt and Gumbel had been useful in creating a consumable, living room persona for Tyson. Still, Jacobs and Cayton wanted something more: for the boxing reporters at the influential New York news-papers—*Newsday,* the *Daily News,* the *New York Post* and the *New York*

*Times*—to anoint Tyson the next great, and inevitable, heavyweight champion. That would be a slow process. They would want to see Tyson undergo several key tests, particularly the all-important "gut check" of his courage against a tough, unrelenting opponent.

That wouldn't come with "Slamming" Sam Scaff, a white six-foot-six, 250-pound, overweight, lumbering, club fighter from Kentucky. He had had thirteen fights, many of them losses. Partway through the first round, Tyson broke Scaff's nose. It made a bloody mess of his face, sent ringlets of crimson red down Tyson's broad brown back, and finished the fight. Scaff, who had once sparred with two world champions, later muttered: "I've never been hit that hard in my life."

Wally Matthews, the boxing reporter for *New York Newsday*, recalled his thoughts at the time: "I got the tape of Tyson's knockouts Jacobs and Cayton were sending around. One after the other. They did a masterful job at convincing people that Tyson had incredible punching power. I bought it. I was skeptical, but I bought it. I think back now and I realize they'd proven only that Tyson was a good one-round fighter because he came out like a maniac. And the guys he was knocking out, everyone else did too. Tyson hadn't been tested yet."

The test quickly approached. Sticking to the schedule of a fight every two weeks, Tyson met Mark Young and knocked him out in one round. Then, to kick off 1986, he put on a remarkable display of his full range of abilities against David Jaco. That brought Tyson to sixteen wins, all by knockout, twelve in the first round. In the process, Tyson picked up a *nom de pug:* "Catskill Thunder," coined by Randy Gordon, an announcer for a sports cable station. In a January cover story, *Sports Illustrated* came up with "Kid Dynamite."

Jacobs and Cayton didn't embrace either name. In fact, they had decided early on to stick with the simplicity of "Mike Tyson." D'Amato had once suggested "The Tanned Terror," as a nod to Joe Louis's "Brown Bomber," but that wasn't taken on. As the children of Brownsville had discovered when Tyson started marauding the streets, his mere name, when combined with the menace evoked by his smoldering manner, the almost animal-like physique, and his performance in the ring, was more than suitable.

The *Sports Illustrated* cover, a slew of new television news segments, more morning show appearances, and talk of his becoming champion—it was a remarkable amount of hype over a nineteen-year-old prospect who had yet to fight anyone ranked near the top ten. What was even more remarkable is that Jacobs began to suggest, in confident asides to reporters, that Tyson would become the savior of the heavyweight division. Its one-time glory, as symbolized in the achievements of Dempsey, Louis, Marciano, and Ali, had been tarnished by the splintering of the title in 1978 into three separate crowns, each awarded by a different sanctioning body. The world had no idea who was the real champion. Tyson, claimed Jacobs, would unify the title, restore its meaning, bring back the public's faith in boxing, and in so doing join the ranks of the great ones.

"Jacobs's pitch made for great copy, whether you agreed with him or not," said Matthews of *Newsday*. "He knew that. Jacobs figured out what everyone most wanted to hear. They wanted a new myth for boxing."

Jacobs buttressed that myth by taking every opportunity to identify Tyson with the great fighters. Starting with the Scaff fight, Jacobs asked Tyson to wear only black trunks and sockless black shoes. Up to then, he'd worn white or blue trunks with a different color trim. The idea was to evoke the classic, austere asceticism of Jack Dempsey. Assistant camp manager Steve Lott then came up with the idea of putting a small badge of the American flag on one leg of the trunks. "I felt that the flag would have a subliminal effect on the press," said Lott. "They'd find it more difficult to write negatively about Mike."

Without question, Tyson was far better than the men he'd fought so far. They were, after all, professional opponents, statistical cannon fodder for the real contenders. Tyson was also likely to prove himself technically superior to the next level of competition he would meet—including most if not all of the fighters in the top ten rankings. But the savior of boxing? In the same tradition as Ali, Marciano, and Louis? That was stretching it.

In technical terms, and on a strict comparison of achievement at equivalent age and level of experience, Tyson was in some respects better than past greats. Certainly he was more elusive. The power of his punch, especially when combined with the speed with which he delivered it, was also in a class by itself. In practical terms, however, Tyson had not yet shown his character. That would emerge from a test of wills: his against an opponent who didn't go down in one or two rounds.

At that point in Tyson's development, such issues didn't press on Jacobs and Cayton. They were in a hurry to get him the title shot. It didn't matter to them if the hype surpassed the reality of the performance. They felt that Tyson, if watched carefully, worked on constantly, packaged, and sanitized, would at the least keep the hype valid, even if he couldn't yet prove it true. He hadn't faltered in the ring for a long time. The mysterious flaw remained in check.

But not for long. That was the flip side of a string of easy opponents. It created a false sense of security for everyone, Tyson included. And that was the sober truth of the man-child within the hype, of the person behind the dual personas of the well-behaved, pigeon-loving surrogate son and the Ring Destroyer, the champion of destiny: nothing could prevent Tyson from bouncing between the opposite terms of his own paradox. It was far easier to control an image of a man than the man himself.

*   *   *

On January 24, 1986, Tyson stepped in the ring to box opponent number seventeen, "Irish" Mike Jameson. He looked like all the others Tyson had dispatched, though less muscular and more bulky. Jameson stood six-foot-four and weighed 236 pounds to Tyson's 215. His record, seventeen wins and nine losses, implied something less than journeyman status. Jameson was also an aged fighter—thirty-one years old. He lived in Cupertino, California, and had never fought east of Chicago. It was expected, and hoped, that Tyson would do away with Jameson rapidly. There was a lot at stake. For the past several weeks, Jacobs and Cayton had been negotiating a multifight deal with ABC Sports. It would be Tyson's first exposure on a national network television, and the first big purse money.

Jameson was no fool. He knew he didn't have a chance slugging it out with Tyson, so he used his height, reach, and weight advantage to lean on Tyson and tie him up. After the two were pulled apart by the referee, Tyson would get off a few punches, but they seemed to have little effect. He'd then end up in a clinch again. It seemed that Tyson was letting himself be held. He was acquiescing to the other man's unwillingness to fight. Tyson looked worse in the second round. He got hit easily by a few left jabs and straight rights, a clear sign that after getting position on the inside, he wasn't moving enough on defense. In the third, Jameson kept getting his punches off first, then clinching to avoid Tyson's blows.

By the fourth, Tyson seemed to wake up as if from a trance. He started connecting with more punches. Jameson, older and less fit, ran out of steam. One flurry of five blows in combination—remarkable for a heavyweight—sent Jameson down, but not out. Early in the fifth, Tyson scored a punishing knockdown, and the referee stopped the fight.

The announcers made an astute point about Tyson's performance:

"What happens when this young kid who can punch so hard hits someone and they're still standing there and comes back and hits him back? Is he going to get discouraged or what?" Apparently, the answer was yes, at least to a degree. That's what happened with Jameson in the first three rounds. Had Jameson been more fit, and skilled, he could have perhaps exploited that weakness in Tyson and lasted a few more rounds. Instead, Tyson won the fight on his natural gifts of superior punching power and hand speed. Fortunately, that was all he needed to beat Jameson. Tyson would, however, need much more in the next phase of his career. He would soon debut on ABC in the first of a four-match, million-dollar deal. The stakes were rising.

Financially, the Tyson team had come a long way in just over eleven months. In the first three fights Jacobs and Cayton had covered all the expenses—$30,417—including Tyson's purses of a few hundred dollars. They'd made a profit of only $166.80. Expenses for the remaining fourteen fights, plus a 10 percent fee for trainer Kevin Rooney, were taken out of the gross purses paid by the promoters, $69,955. That left a total net purse of $57,095, of which Tyson earned two-thirds. In other words, $38,063 for about twenty-eight rounds, or one hour and twenty-four minutes of actual boxing. Jacobs and Cayton earned the remainder, or $19,032, from which they paid a 10 percent fee to Steve Lott.

With the $1 million ABC deal, an unheard-of sum of money for a fighter with only seventeen victories, the economics of Mike Tyson were about to change radically. For the first fight he'd earn a purse of $90,000. As Tyson continued to win, the purses increased in size until the $1 million was used up. Futhermore, with convincing victories, Jacobs and Cayton would acquire a significant amount of negotiating leverage with HBO Sports, a division of the pay-cable service owned by communications giant Time Inc.

In March 1986, HBO would launch a series of fights to unify the fractured heavyweight title. It had most, but not all, of the top-ranked contenders and champions signed up. With the hype surrounding Tyson's rise, HBO became nervous. It faced the nightmare prospect of spending millions of dollars to determine the unified champion only for Tyson to emerge independently as the one true contender, the heir presumptive; the spoiler.

Jacobs and Cayton weren't yet prepared to sign Tyson up. He didn't have the experience to deal with the level of competition in the HBO series. They also had other ideas on how to earn a title shot. In one scenario, they'd match Tyson against old but well-known fighters such as former champion Larry Holmes and even Gerry Cooney, the lone white heavyweight of any reputation. That would establish Tyson's credibility and earn him the right to then match up against the eventual winner of the HBO series.

Both sides of the issue faced a dilemma. HBO couldn't risk letting Tyson go off on a separate track. And yet with only seventeen victories he didn't have the credentials, or the national following, to be justifiably included in the unification series. For their part, Jacobs and Cayton were reluctant to trail off on their own in pursuit of the title. There was no way of knowing if the eventual winner of the HBO series would agree to fight Tyson. They would have done several years' work only to be denied the ultimate prize.

The solution, for both parties, was to get Tyson on a separate but parallel track. In January, Jacobs and Cayton starting discussing with HBO the terms of a three-fight deal. Combined with the ABC fights, they would gain Tyson national television exposure and experience and, if it could be agreed upon, the basis for entry into the HBO series.

There were risks. They had to give up some say over the selection of opponents. ABC and HBO were interested in good ratings, and that meant competitive matchups. It was unlikely Tyson would be scoring many more first-round knockouts. Jacobs and Cayton wondered how well he would stand up under the emotional stress of fighting more seasoned opponents on national television.

First Tyson had to beat Jesse Ferguson in his ABC debut. Ferguson was a young, strong, quick-handed prospect ranked, like Tyson, in the second tier of heavyweights. The more convincing Tyson's victory, the greater his value to ABC and HBO.

Aware of those stakes, Jacobs stacked the deck in Tyson's favor. The fight took place in Troy, New York, the heart of Tyson country. Some seven thousand local supporters would be rooting for a knockout. Jacobs also insisted that the fighters wear eight-ounce gloves rather than the more standard ten-ounce versions. That clearly favored Tyson. His fast hands would be even faster with the lighter gloves. Jacobs obtained another advantage by getting Ferguson's manager to agree to a sixteen-foot, eight-inch ring, smaller by a few feet than standard ring sizes. That way if Ferguson decided to run instead of stand and fight, he wouldn't have as much room.

Tyson came out in black trunks and black shoes, no socks, and no robe. As he climbed into the ring and the crowd cheered, Tyson held up his arms at a low angle and turned the palms up in the manner of a

Roman gladiator—strong, confident, but humbled by both the adulation and his own greatness. His face was expressionless. He paced back and forth, twitching his neck as if trying to remove a kink.

To the relief of the growing group involved in his career, Tyson rose to the occasion. As usual, he came out slipping, weaving, and slugging. He hit Ferguson on both sides with vicious hooks. He doubled up on body shots, going to the ribs first, then coming through the middle with an uppercut. But Ferguson could take a punch. With his own hand speed and sense of timing, he was also able to exploit those few occasions when Tyson stopped moving. He caught Tyson on the inside with a few right uppercuts. Tyson hardly flinched. That answered an important question about his future: he had a tough chin.

Tyson kept connecting through the second, third, and fourth rounds. Ferguson still didn't go down, but Tyson didn't get discouraged. He kept up his intensity and maintained nearly perfect stylistic form. It was by far the highest he had yet taken D'Amato's "system." Twice he hit Ferguson with low blows, and at the end of the fourth he threw a punch after the bell rang. As the referee pulled them apart, Tyson stuck his tongue out at Ferguson. He was enjoying this.

Ferguson came out in the fifth trying to keep Tyson at bay with a pesky poking of his left jab. Tyson easily slipped away. He then backed Ferguson up against the ropes. Ferguson tried to clinch, but Tyson fought through with a series of body shots and right and left uppercuts. Ferguson still didn't fall. In the sixth, finally, he had taken enough. He had only the energy to clinch. The referee warned him several times, but Ferguson continued to hold. He was disqualified.

At first, Alex Wallau, the ABC boxing analyst doing the broadcast, thought that meant Tyson would be denied the knockout, thus breaking his streak. Then the referee, perhaps aware of what his decision meant, clarified the decision. He called it a technical knockout. Steve Lott climbed into the ring and kissed Tyson on the cheek. Afterwards, in a postfight interview, Tyson said to the gathering of reporters: "I tried to punch him and drive the bone of his nose back into his brain."

The New York papers covering the fight quoted Tyson's remarks with relish. It was as if they'd finally seen the real Mike Tyson behind the hype and it was not a pretty sight. Maybe he was, after all, just another thug like Liston. Jacobs was flooded with calls from reporters eager to unpack this dark, new Tyson that he had obviously kept a secret. One boxing reporter even dug up Ernestine Coleman, Tyson's Youth Division caseworker. He cited a letter she wrote to Tyson after reading his comment. Coleman advised Tyson "to be a man, not an animal."

Jacobs's first reaction was to blame someone other than Tyson. He fired the publicity agent he'd retained for the fights, Mike Cohen. He also impressed on Lott, who was living with Tyson at the time, the importance of baby-sitting: "I had to watch him constantly, remind him how to behave after a fight and rehearse what he should say," Lott recalled.

A few days later Jacobs invited a group of boxing reporters to have dinner with Tyson at Jake's, then a New York steak restaurant: Ed Schuyler of the Associated Press, Michael Katz and Bill Gallo from the *Daily News* and Phil Berger of the *New York Times*. Two who were shunned—Wallace Matthews and Mike Marley of the *New York Post*—dubbed it the "Bootlicker's Ball." Schuyler remembered the evening: "No notes, no interviews, just talking. Jimmy was very conscious of trying to make Mike likable, to make him seem like a decent person so that if he got in trouble we'd all say, 'Oh, well, he's just a kid and that's how kids are.'"

Thinking back, Schuyler recalled how strained it all was. "There was a desperation about it all. Like, 'Let's get this guy a title before he gets into serious trouble. Let's keep him busy.' I believe that Jimmy and Bill thought that Mike was really not a nice person, that he wasn't responsible to anyone but himself. He gives you that little-boy voice, but he's capable of doing anything. He's a creature of impulse."

Sure enough, on February 23, the *Albany Knickerbocker News* reported on an incident in the Crossgates Mall. Tyson had entered Filene's department store and come on to a white salesgirl. She declined. Tyson got angry, threw some clothes around, knocked over racks, and insulted the girl and anyone else who came by. That same day, Jacobs denied to the New York reporters that Tyson had done anything wrong. A reporter from the *Times Union* in Albany went back to the mall a few days later to find out the real story. The salesgirl, her managers, and the mall security personnel all refused to comment. The salesgirl implied that if she did, she'd be fired. Rumors circulated that Jacobs and Cayton had paid off people at the mall to stay mum on the incident. They no doubt also relied on the local police to turn a blind eye. "The Albany police commissioner was valuable in taking care of Mike Tyson in many ways," admitted Cayton. "Steps were taken with the help of the police to put lids on things." In return, Cayton made sure that the commissioner of police got ringside tickets to Tyson's upstate fights. Moreover, twice a year he bought advertisements in the Albany Police Department's newspaper.

*Newsday's* Matthews confronted Jacobs about the mall incident, fruitlessly. "He lied to me. You'd call him on it in stories and later he'd admit that he lied to protect Tyson. That was Jacobs for you. He held the press up to very high standards of truthfulness and accuracy—his versions of both—but he never stood up to them himself."

Up to the Ferguson fight, Jacobs handled all questions from the press in his role as manager and front man. That would now change. Cayton had to step forward. They would both be needed to handle Tyson's public image.

For the New York boxing reporters, dealing with Cayton wasn't exactly a breath of fresh air. Yet, compared to Jacobs, almost anybody was preferable. "Jimmy was a propagandist. If he approached anything that made him uneasy, he just closed down on you," said Phil Berger of the *New York Times.* "Sometimes it was innocent things. I once asked him what his father did. He got very uptight and said, 'I don't see what that has to do with anything.' Then he called me back and lied, told me that his father was in the office supplies business." Berger took advantage of Cayton's sudden availability. "I only had perfunctory conversations with Jacobs after Ferguson. When I needed to find out something important, I talked to Cayton."

Matthews had similar dealings with Jacobs—namely, pointless ones. "If he didn't like your question, he'd ridicule you. He'd play word games with your head. I'd ask a simple question and Jacobs would say things like, 'Wally, that's like saying is it colder in the mountains or colder in the winter' or 'Wally, that's like asking me if I'm going to paint the fence green.' After a half hour of that, I'd forget my question!"

Although Cayton was more likely to give straight answers, he could also be trying. "Everything Jimmy said was right and you were supposed to accept it," recalled the AP's Ed Schuyler. "But I could argue with Jimmy if I wanted to. Cayton treated me like I was on the payroll. Cayton I wanted to hit."

Jacobs and Cayton attempted to keep the boxing reporters, and any other inquiring journalist, devoted to what they deemed the key issues: Tyson's indomitable ring prowess, the inevitability of his becoming champion, and whether he would go for the title via the HBO series or by some other independent route. For the most part, they were extremely successful. That was the news, after all, the stuff of sports page headlines. It was also presumably what people wanted to read about at that stage of Tyson's career. And reporters who had to meet the pressure of deadlines two or three days a week might well not have the time or the appetite to delve into the subtler aspects of the Tyson story—especially when getting the basic news from Jacobs and Cayton was such a task.

But the fact remains that the subtleties were missed. One in particular, the issue of just who managed Tyson would later surface as a central drama of his career.

Starting in late 1985, and more frequently at the outset of 1986, Jacobs and Cayton asserted that they were comanagers. No such status existed in the boxing rules and regulations of New York State boxing and they knew it. Jacobs was sole manager, and Cayton a partner sharing in the manager's purse cut. Still, the boxing reporters parroted and endorsed that fictitious label—even though no major boxer in memory ever had more than one manager.

"Boxing being the business it is, what do they call it, an assignee? That's how they did it to become comanagers," said Berger of the *New York Times*. Ed Schuyler also recalled having dismissed the subject of precisely who managed Tyson. "I believe the [New York State Athletic] Commission said Jacobs had a legitimate managerial contract. It never questioned the contract, so I never questioned it. It's such a shady business. I mean, who manages who? There are so many people who have pieces of fighters, so many conflicts of interest. Doesn't make it right, but that's the way the game is."

Taking a lead from the New York State Athletic Commission was not a good idea, especially when the chairman was José Torres.

Torres retired from boxing in 1969. He did do that promised book, not a novel, but a biography, *Sting Like a Bee: The Muhammad Ali Story*, published in 1971. Torres spent the 1970s writing for the *New York Post*. On the side he dabbled in politics. He campaigned in the New York Latino community for John Lindsay's mayoral campaign and for Jimmy Carter. For a brief period of time in the late 1970s, he became an ombudsman for the New York City Council. Four years later, in 1983, Torres was appointed a commissioner of the New York State Athletic Commission by the office of Governor Mario Cuomo. By 1985, just as Tyson turned professional, Torres had been elevated to chairman.

That was the official version of his career outside the ring. On paper it looked impressive. Torres was the first chairman ever to have been a boxing champion. He promised to represent the needs of the fighters, not the managers or promoters. For Torres, that wouldn't be easy. He had a penchant for letting himself be compromised.

As Athletic Commission chairman, Torres had an implicit obligation to act impartially, When it came to Tyson he did precisely the opposite. Torres frequently visited the Catskill gym to offer him boxing advice. He also went to almost all of Tyson's early upstate fights, at the taxpayer's expense. That in itself wasn't improper, but his ringside behavior was. Torres always cheered wildly for Tyson and derided his opponent. At fight's end, Torres often jumped into the ring to embrace and congratulate him. On a few occasions, he would still be sent by Jacobs to track down Tyson in Brownsville during his many disappearances. Torres provided other unofficial services as well. "He used to introduce Mike to Puerto Rican girls all the time," said Tom Patti. "I think he wanted to quit the commission and get involved managing Mike."

That seemed unrealistic. He was, though, at the least willing to see things from the point of view of Tyson's management. And that was a clear conflict of interest. Starting in 1985, he went on record several times stating that Jacobs and Cayton were both the managers of Tyson.

The boxing reporters knew of Torres's partiality, of his incestuous ties to the Tyson camp. They talked about it in cynical asides among themselves. Rarely was it revealed in their news stories. It seemed that a news judgment had been made—perhaps, put in the context of the times, a fairly understandable one.

Recording the emergence of Mike Tyson, the next great heavyweight, was like being swept along by the tides of history. Reporters had the feeling that they weren't just observing, but also participating somehow. They saw the gaps, the rough edges, the inconsistencies, and the conflicts of interest, but they were apparently overwhelmed by the phenomenon. Both the persona of Mike Tyson, and the process by which he emerged in the national consciousness, became extremely seductive. "Tyson wasn't just another boxing story," Matthews admitted. "He was 'the story.' We all got caught up in it."

*　　*　　*

By late February, Jacobs and Cayton had reached agreement with HBO on the three-fight deal. Tyson would earn $1.35 million, or $450,000 per fight. Once again, he broke all records of financial reward for a fighter of his age and experience.

Tyson's next fight was set for March 10 against Steve Zouski at Nassau Coliseum on Long Island. It was designed as a breather fight, an easy victory to bolster Tyson for the subsequent series of tougher matches on ABC and HBO.

Zouski was another appropriate opponent for the purposes of the business plan. He looked better than he actually was. Zouski claimed never to have been knocked down, let alone out, in a record of twenty-five wins and nine losses. The problem was that eight of those losses had occurred in his last ten bouts, putting Zouski on the downward slope of his career arc. Whatever muscle he had seemed to have softened up in large, billowing puffs around an ordinary frame. For two rounds, Tyson used Zouski to showcase his combination-punching abilities. It was over in the third—by a knockout.

Tyson was to meet James ("Quick") Tillis three weeks later. He developed an ear infection and the bout was put off until May 3. That was the longest layoff of his professional career, just over three months. In a sense, it was fortuitous. Tillis was expected to be a watershed fight. Although twenty-eight years old and near the end of his career, Tillis was still considered a fringe contender for the title. In his prime, he'd fought hard-nosed veterans like Earnie Shavers and Gerrie Coetzee. He had also matched up against some of the better fighters of his own peer group, such as Carl Williams and Pinklon Thomas. He had a tough chin, came to a fight in good condition, could employ a full arsenal of boxing skills, and moved well in the ring. Beating Tillis would gain Tyson a measure of confidence, prepare him for the emotional pressures of the next stage in his pursuit of the heavyweight championship.

A crowd of eight thousand people jammed into the Glens Falls Civic Center in upstate New York, and every one of them seemed to be a Tyson fan. When he entered the arena, Tyson got a standing ovation. He had won all nineteen of his fights by knockout. That's what people expected to see, but it was not what he was prepared to deliver. "After coming off the ear injury, he needed one easy fight before Tillis to get into it," Steve Lott recalled. "The pressure of fighting someone as experienced as Tillis made him nervous, and that reduced him to a one-dimensional fighter."

Tillis became a problem that Tyson had trouble solving. Tillis moved well in both directions, which made him a difficult target. And as he moved, he jabbed to keep Tyson at bay. When Tyson did get into punching proximity, Tillis blocked the blows or tied him up. By the second round much of Tyson's aggression seemed to have drained away. He was racking up points, but many of his punches didn't connect solidly. He worked the body, but rarely followed in combination with a blow to the head. And he took punches, too—jabs, uppercuts, and a few left hooks.

Tillis fought far better than expected. He came into the bout seven pounds lighter than usual, which helped his movement, and improved his hand speed. When he took a punch, he struck back, usually in combination. He looked tight, measured, confident, and determined not to get knocked out. But he made one costly error. Near the end of the fourth, Tillis threw a wide, off-balance left hook that turned him around. Before he could turn back, Tyson looped in a hook that sent Tillis down. He got up quickly, though, and fought hard in the fifth, knowing that Tyson would try and end it. To his amazement, and everyone else's, Tyson didn't capitalize on the knockdown. He kept throwing single punches, and in clinches didn't ram blows into Tillis's body. He was still winning rounds, but barely. In rounds six through nine, he gave up trying to capture the inside positioning so essential for his ballet of defense and offense to work effectively. Tyson let himself be pushed back and tied up, and at times just followed Tillis around the ring in a passive, acquiescent state. In the latter half of the tenth and final round Tillis, no doubt thinking that if he scored heavily he could win the fight, stood toe to toe with Tyson. They exchanged blows for a spirited finale. As it turned out, Tillis was close to being right. The judges scored the fight for Tyson, but without the knockdown in the fourth, it would have ended in a draw. The judges gave all the middle rounds to Tillis.

The Tillis fight made Jacobs and Cayton, for the first time, nervous about Tyson's prospects. Did he come away from Tillis feeling that he'd passed a test or failed it? He'd won, but what had Tyson discovered about himself? Did he think that he was the future champion? Or did he see in his feeling of failure an irrepressible urge to give in?

The match with Mitch ("Blood") Green took place seventeen days after the Tillis bout in the 20,000-seat-plus main arena of Madison Square Garden. It was Tyson's first fight on HBO and the first under the promotional banner of Don King. Green had a respectable record of sixteen wins, one loss, and one draw. Ten of his victories had came by knockout. He was not a contender for the title. Still, he was ranked seventh in the estimation of the World Boxing Council. Green was also big (six-foot-five and 225 pounds of sculpted muscle), and he fought with a lot of macho pride in a wide-open, undisciplined style.

The first round set the pattern for the entire fight. Green had been told by his trainer to punch and move out of harm's way, and if he did get caught inside to tie Tyson up. The plan, like Tillis's, was to take Tyson into the later rounds, where he'd not often been and would perhaps be vulnerable. But this time, it didn't work. Tyson had come to fight.

Green, a former leader of the Black Spades gang of the Bronx, was overcome by his own recklessness. He tried to grab, but Tyson punched his way out. Instead of continuing with that tactic, or at least to punch, move, and then grab, Green decided every now and then to stand and trade blows. He took the worst of it. Tyson kept eluding Green's best punch—his left jab—then crowding in and delivering. As Green backed up for room to swing, he only gave Tyson more space to get his punches in first, which he did, repeatedly.

Tyson put on a boxing clinic as he scored with left and right hooks, body shots, and uppercuts, almost all in combination. One of his jabs knocked Green's mouthpiece onto the ring apron—embedded in it were a bridge and two false teeth. By the end of the fourth round, Tyson had thrown 109 body punches alone, 70 (or 64 percent) of which connected. That was an unheard-of statistic for most heavyweights, who usually aren't fast or well conditioned enough to do anything else but headhunt.

In the fifth, Tyson evoked one of Teddy Atlas's training techniques. As Green swung away, Tyson feinted, slipped, weaved, dipped, and bobbed in a series of eighteen separate defensive movements. He avoided every one of Green's punches without countering with a blow of his own. It was a display of pride in his superior abilities, and a bit of arrogance.

The fight went the full ten rounds. Tyson didn't seem to care whether he could knock Green down, or out. He was taking pleasure in the process of chopping Green up, like a cleaver against a side of beef. He sometimes smiled through his mouthpiece at Green and at other times sneered. In the corner before the ninth, while trainer Kevin Rooney yammered away, he leaned over and kissed him on the cheek.

On the judge's scorecards, Tyson won all but one round. Afterwards, at a press conference, Tyson spoke about the win in cool, professional terms. He had been well coached by Jacobs on his postfight posturing since the Ferguson incident. There was no Ali-style histrionics, none of Liston's glum bluntness. "Not to be egotistical, but I won this fight so easy. I refuse to be beaten in there. I refuse to let anybody get in my way."

Tyson had clearly recovered from the Tillis fight. His technical prowess returned in fine form. More important he didn't get frustrated with being unable to win by knockout. Tyson's remarks afterwards also displayed a measure of confidence that Jacobs and Cayton wanted to bolster, and a maturity they had to protect. There would be no more risks like Tillis. They'd set up a string of breather fights until the final approach to the title could be determined.

Still on his breakneck schedule, Tyson fought Reggie Gross about three weeks later (June 13, 1986), also at the Garden and under the promotional banner of Don King. Gross, with an eighteen-and-four record, had long arms but a lazy, inaccurate left jab that dangled out like a heavy salami. Near the end of the first round, Gross moved into the center of the ring and opened up with a series of five punches that Tyson easily avoided as he looked patiently for an opening. He put Gross down twice before the referee called it over. Gross protested. Tyson tried to console him.

Fourteen days passed. Tyson traveled up to Troy to fight William Hosea. Hosea seemed like a fighter who could do a little bit of everything in the ring with a little bit of proficiency: except take a punch. It was over within two minutes and three seconds. Lorenzo Boyd came next—on July 11. A combination right hook to the body and a right uppercut on the chin ended the fight halfway through the second. Tyson was beginning to look bored.

On July 26, Tyson met Marvis Frazier, the son of former champion Joe Frazier. Father was both manager and trainer. That was more a liability than an asset against the technically superior Tyson. Marvis was molded in his father's image. He too bobbed and weaved. Tyson and trainer Kevin Rooney studied tapes of Marvis's fights and noticed that when he crouched, he didn't so much bend at the knees as he did at the waist. In the dressing room before the fight, Tyson announced his fight strategy. "As Frazier bent over, Tyson would time a right uppercut," said Baranski.

In the first round, Tyson launched at Frazier, backed him up into the corner, and, as per plan, sent in the right uppercut at the appropriate moment. That was enough to do the job, but Tyson added a left hook and another right. Frazier crumpled to the canvas thirty seconds into the round. It was Tyson's quickest knockout. He tried to help the fallen fighter up, but by then Frazier's mother and father had swarmed in. Tyson turned away, leapt up, and punched the air in a war dance. Jacobs rushed over and whispered something in his ear and Tyson calmed. "By then, we had him coached on what to say afterwards," Steve Lott remembered. "With a name fighter like Frazier, we didn't want Mike to be disrespectful. People liked Joe Frazier. I sat Mike down before the fight and told him what to say, word for word."

On August 17, in Atlantic City, the betting line against José Ribalta beating Mike Tyson was 7 to 1. Ribalta had a respectable record of twenty-two wins, three losses, and one draw. Sixteen of the wins had come by knockout. The problem was that about a year earlier Ribalta had been knocked out in one round by Marvis Frazier. He was expected to go no more than a few rounds, if that, with Tyson.

What the experts didn't expect, however, was that Tyson, coming off a series of easy fights, had lost some of his intensity and concentration. Gone were the elaborate slip-and-weave movements. He tried to win the fight the lazy heavyweight's way—that is, on a single punch.

In the first round, Ribalta easily saw the punches coming and used a combination of leaning away, covering up, and putting Tyson in a clinch to avoid them. In the second round, realizing that he had to be technically sharper, Tyson doubled up with a right hook to the body and a right uppercut that knocked Ribalta down. The look on Ribalta's face showed more shock than pain. He clearly hadn't seen the uppercut coming. He got up and fought gamely for several more rounds. Tyson fell back into more of a conventional style, connecting often but without effect. He didn't get frustrated; it seemed more like boredom. He wanted to win, but he'd lost interest in scoring a knockout. He appeared comfortable just being a good conventional fighter rather than a unique and spectacular one. The conclusion, at any rate, was foregone. Tyson wore Ribalta down with a total of 328 punches, 68 percent of which landed. A moment's inspiration in the tenth sent in a flurry of punches that solidly connected. The referee ended the fight on a technical knockout.

Asked later if he was disappointed by his performance, a nonchalant Tyson opined: "What can I say? This happens. You don't knock everybody out."

Jacobs was also interviewed after the fight. He claimed not to be disappointed either. He talked about deciding within the week about whether to enter Tyson into the HBO series and to then, within a few months, fight for the title. He had the smug air of someone confident that all was proceeding by plan.

In a sense, he and Cayton had reason to be content. They had achieved the near miraculous. In twenty-six fights over nineteen months, Tyson had been steered to a top ten ranking. Although not yet ranked as a number one contender, he was being perceived by boxing and mainstream audiences alike as the next great heavyweight. He had been sold to America, via the fable of Cus and the Kid, as inoffensive outside the ring and indestructible within it. People believed that it was not a matter of whether he became heavyweight champion, but when.

Privately, however, Jacobs was still nagged by doubts about Tyson's ability to perform at the higher levels of psychological pressure. Fighting for the championship would pit him against the most seasoned and capable fighters. And there could be no more breather bouts with which to protect his sometimes fragile emotional profits from the fights that did test Tyson's character.

He had passed several important tests in the ring, both of his skills and his character. Still, as the Halpin, Sims, Jameson, and Tillis fights demonstrated, he remained completely unpredictable. It didn't seem like a matter of choice for Tyson; it was not as if in those fights he had decided to win in some other way besides by knockout, to take control of the fight, box, try new things, manipulate the opponent, pick his punches, and add up the victory points in his head.

Tyson was capable of a small degree of such control, or "ring generalship," as it is termed. He displayed it with Ferguson and Green. But that wasn't a reliable quality in him as far as Jacobs was concerned. Nor was it the style of boxing he'd been trained in. D'Amato had honed Tyson to be a knockout artist. He'd always believed that was the best use of Tyson's burning, rage-filled, psychic intensity. Jacobs agreed with D'Amato. He, too, feared that if Tyson didn't knock his man out as soon as possible, the chances were high that he'd burn out and regress into a passive, acquiescent state. And so, despite the fact that Jacobs had everyone convinced Tyson would be champion, when it came down to it, he feared that he quite possibly possessed the dark, troubled heart of a loser.

That was the hole at the center of the entire elaborate and emerging spectacle of Tyson's life. In retrospect, it seems incredible that more people didn't recognize the problem at the time. Everything about Tyson was paradoxical.

The problem went beyond almost diametrically opposed performances in the ring. The Albany mall incident offered a glimpse into a counterlife vastly different from the one served up by Cus and the Kid. It just didn't make sense that Tyson was the sum of his dual personas: surrogate son to D'Amato and robotic Ring Destroyer. How could those two beings exist in one, barely grown-up man? "It was very eerie to see

Tyson break people's faces in the ring, then sit down with him and hear that sweet little boy's voice," recalled *Newsday's* Matthews. "I felt there was something I wasn't seeing, but I couldn't put my finger on it."

Nor could Tyson. He remained a mystery to himself. Despite the years with D'Amato, the twenty-six victories, and all the elaborate packaging as the greatest fighter of his time, Tyson was still unable to get any purchase on a self, on the core of his identity. "When people started to recognize Mike on the streets in New York, he used to tell me that he felt they were thinking he wasn't really a good boxer," Lott recalled. "Mike always felt like a fake."

Tyson knew that D'Amato's attentions were, in part, motivated by self-interest. But while D'Amato lived, the role of surrogate son could be played. His religion of the fists, as an all-encompassing gestalt, provided emotional order. It put Tyson in the leading role of his own unique drama of both the inner life and the practical world. With D'Amato around, even if he was a fake, it almost didn't matter. D'Amato made him feel that some kind of self existed. At the least, Tyson felt that he wasn't hollow.

When D'Amato died, Tyson had to play the role without a director. Soon, the persona of surrogate son no longer seemed to hold any validity. He may have never really believed in the veracity of D'Amato's love, or if he did, it was perhaps on a leap of faith for the lack of any other choice when, as a boy of thirteen, he was presented with the option of life with D'Amato and all his eccentricities, or going back to the Tryon reformatory. However Tyson came to terms with D'Amato's attentions, if he did feel loved, the experience left him with no permanent emotional structure. He had, in other words, come full circle. It was like having to go back to the first act of the drama and play it all over again. As Tyson told *Sports Illustrated* in the January 1986 "Kid Dynamite" feature: "I miss him terribly. The many years we worked over things, and worked over things. He was my backbone. All the things we worked on, they're starting to come out so well...God, I'm doing so well, but when it comes down to it, who really cares? I like doing my job, but I'm not happy being victorious. I fight my heart out and give it my best, but when it's over, there's no Cus to tell me how I did, no mother to show my clippings to."

Tyson was alone again and second-guessing the motivations of his supposed intimates. The same nagging paradox remained: Did they want him faults and all, or did they want only the future heavyweight champion of the world?

At first it seemed they only wanted the champion. In the months immediately following D'Amato's death, Jacobs and Cayton were more focused on the business of Mike Tyson than the person. Remembered Camille Ewald: "After every victory, Cus used to have some kind of celebration for Mike. A cake or something. It gave him prestige. Jimmy and Bill didn't do that. They were losing contact with Mike."

Cayton didn't want intimate contact with Tyson. In the four years of Tyson's amateur career, he visited Catskill only once. His only gesture of intimacy with Tyson after he turned professional was to give him a book on raising pigeons. Tyson threw it in the garbage. "Mike knew he was just a business to Cayton," said Jay Bright, another of the boys living in the house during the 1980s.

Jacobs didn't want that kind of intimacy with Tyson, either, but he knew that someone had to step into D'Amato's role. It was that or run a much higher risk that Tyson would self-destruct, either in or out of the ring. Jacobs revealed those views to Nick Beck: "To Jim, Mike became a business. I think that, despite what he wanted everyone to believe, was what motivated Jim in the relationship."

Matt Baranski put it more bluntly: "I had my doubts about Jimmy. I saw the change in him after Cus died, playing up to Mike. Jimmy did it for money and the power."

Perhaps one revealing indication of Jacobs's intentions was how he seemed to be keeping his promises to D'Amato. Over the years, D'Amato secured from Jacobs three, and only three, lifetime promises. The first, that when he started making money off of Tyson, Jacobs should help support D'Amato's brother, Tony. Over the years D'Amato had borrowed several thousand dollars from Tony to cover expenses at the house and to keep the gym going. Tony, who was almost ninety years old when D'Amato died, lived in the town of Catskill in a run-down house in utter poverty. "Jacobs never gave him a cent," said Tom Patti, who lived in the house.

D'Amato also asked Jacobs to help Ewald with the house expenses from his and Cayton's cut of the purses. According to Jay Bright, who still lives with Ewald, the money came, but from the wrong source. "Jimmy and Bill took it out of Mike's end, not theirs," he said. "Cus had a saying," Bright added. "It's not what a man says he's going to do that matters. It's what he does in the end that he meant to do all along."

The third promise was for Jacobs to pay some money to Bobby Stewart, the Tryon instructor who first brought Tyson to D'Amato. Jacobs had yet to fulfill that promise either.

By all appearances Tyson embraced Jacobs, but not so much as a father figure as an older brother. There's also a sense in which Tyson didn't have much choice in the matter. To Tyson the perennial survivor, it boiled down to a simple reality: he needed Jacobs, for practical and emotional purposes, in precisely the way he needed Bobby Stewart at the Tryon school to get him into boxing and D'Amato to keep him there. He needed Jacobs to help him become heavyweight champion of the world.

Jacobs began to forge a more intimate relationship with Tyson immediately after the death of D'Amato. His first move was to get Tyson into closer physical proximity. Jacobs asked Steve Lott, who has an apartment in the building he and Loraine lived in, to let Tyson stay there during visits to New York. "On weekends Mike usually didn't train," Lott recalled. "Jim would invite him up to his apartment. They'd watch fight films, talk about the old boxers, and discuss Mike's future. Loraine was part of it. The three of them spent hours and hours together.

Within a few months, Tyson began to espouse Jacobs's ideas and to speak like him, just as he had done with D'Amato. Jacobs's stilted, professorial phrases were juxtaposed with Tyson's far rougher street lingo. It only added to the many other incongruities between Tyson's appearance and behavior (his solid size and his little boy's lisping voice). It made him seem even more out of sync.

Tyson was either unaware or uninterested in how others perceived his relationship with Jacobs. He saw Jacobs as the closest living connection to D'Amato. It was like tapping into D'Amato's spiritual aura. After all, Jacobs, besides parroting D'Amato on almost every subject connected with boxing, possessed the same oversize ego. Like D'Amato, Jacobs also knew how to make Tyson feel in control of the strange drama of his life. D'Amato did that mostly with Tyson's inner life by helping him take control over his emotions. Jacobs made him feel more connected to the outside world, which, as he got closer to fighting for the championship, was always changing, becoming larger and more foreign. As AP reporter Ed Schuyler observed: "Jimmy was able to talk to him. He was able to make Mike think that he was involved in making the decisions. Jimmy was a clever guy. He knew what he had here. And Tyson felt safe with Jimmy, he felt like one of the team, not an employee."

Their body language when together also added to the many in-congruities about Tyson. Several times before, and after, a fight, Jacobs would kiss Tyson. After Tyson demolished Marvis Frazier, he kissed

Jacobs full on the lips. At the weigh-in ceremony for his fight against José Ribalta, he suddenly bent down and playfully bit Jacobs on the stomach. "Mike never told me how he felt about Jimmy, but I know that at the very least he trusted and respected him," said Steve Lott. "That's what his affection was about. He's affectionate with the people he likes the most."

Oddly, however, not once did they ever buy each other a personal gift for either a birthday or Christmas. A gap existed in their intimacy, one that neither man wanted to acknowledge.

Murad Muhammad, a former security guard for Ali who went on to become a promoter, recounted this story: "It was late at night in New York during the summer of 1986. I saw Tyson walking along by himself, his head down low, like he was depressed or something. He was a pathetic sight. Like no one in the world cared a damn about him. The next day I called Jimmy. I knew Jimmy; we'd worked together. I thought he'd respect my opinion. I said, 'Jimmy, I'm a black man, I know the problems of the black man, and I want you to listen to me on this subject. Mike is a young black lion. He needs other black men in his life. That's where he came from; those are his roots, his experience. You can't breed that out of a man. Jimmy, you need a black man in Mike's life to ground him to his roots."

Jacobs's response was polite but firm: "We have Mike under control," he said. "You don't need to worry for us."

Jacobs probably suspected that Muhammad was trying to insinuate himself as Tyson's promoter. Perhaps he was. But it would turn out that Murad Muhammad had made a prescient point. "Jacobs didn't realize that his young lion would one day hear the roar of another lion, a black man, and he'd wake up."

# Chapter Six

The business of Mike Tyson began to grow at exponential rates. His first seventeen fights over eleven months grossed $69,955. With the addition of the ABC and HBO deals, the second set of nine bouts over six months brought in a total of $2,060,334. In other words, Tyson grossed twenty-nine times more money in roughly half the time. No heavyweight contender had ever before made so much money, so quickly, at that state in his career.

Jacobs and Cayton knew they had seen only a small portion of the money Tyson's career could generate. Once he became champion, there was almost no limit on how large the purses could become. Licensing fees from the television networks and cable stations would increase, as would site fees from casino-hotels, stadiums, and arenas. Other sources of licensing revenue would open up, such as theater closed-circuit television and the expanding base of home pay-per-view. Millions of dollars more would come in from foreign television sales, which would then create a global audience for Tyson allowing him to fight around the world, just as Ali had done in his heyday. They could also sell videocassettes of Tyson's fights to the retail market, produce television specials on his career, earn commissions on commercial appearances and product endorsements, and merchandise his image and likeness on clothing and children's toys.

The business of Mike Tyson could expand into a small industry—if he kept winning fights, if the matchups were compelling to a broad cross-section of a mainstream global audience, and if they were promoted correctly. That was the proverbial rub. Under the laws and regulations of most state boxing authorities, Jacobs and Cayton were not permitted to be both the management team and the promoters of Mike Tyson. That was a restriction they could never quite accept.

Most fighters were lucky to have one or two promoters involved in their early careers. Tyson had so far been involved with a total of seven, three on a recurring basis. That part of the business plan worked out well. Jacobs and Cayton acquired the right kinds of promoters precisely when they were needed. Bob and Lorraine Miller in Albany were used for the small, easy fights. The Houston-based Jeff Levine came in handy when they had to move up a step in both exposure and level of competition. Then, with the three-fight HBO deal, they turned to the most seasoned promoter in the business of boxing, Don King. King was also the principal gatekeeper to the heavyweight title. Along with Butch Lewis, he promoted the HBO Unification Series.

So far, Jacobs and Cayton had had no trouble controlling their promoters. The Millers, Levine, and King were convinced, like everyone else, that Tyson would one day be champion. They each expected to cash in on that inevitability. Jacobs and Cayton exploited those expectations to gain maximum control over Tyson's career. "They promised you everything when Mike was coming up, and once he arrived, they took it away," said Bob Miller.

Traditionally, a promoter pays a boxer a flat sum of money in return for all the various rights to a fight-site fee, live gate, and television, domestic and foreign. In certain cases, the promoter may also offer the boxer a percentage of the ticket sales, or what is termed "the gate." The manager takes his cut from the promoter's payment to the boxer.

That division of responsibility and revenue among promoter, boxer, and manager had prevailed from the advent of modern prizefighting. Since the fiasco of the 1959 Floyd Patterson-Ingemar Johansson promotion, New York state boxing officials had tried to be more vigilant about policing that tradition. Rule 208.21 of the New York State Athletic Commission clearly states that no "promoting corporation" can in any way be "commercially connected" with a boxer. The Nevada State Athletic Commission, where most major prizefights are now staged, has a similar rule. The idea was to protect the fighter by maintaining a balance of power between promoter and manager.

Jacobs and Cayton, like D'Amato before them, did everything they could to bend those rules and regulations. By paying all the expenses of Tyson's first two fights, they functioned like promoters. They also dictated to the Millers a fixed fee for each fight. Jacobs and Cayton then retained the film, video, and television rights for themselves. In both the Hosea and Boyd fights, for instance, Jacobs and Cayton sold foreign television rights for a total of $62,500. (To their credit, Tyson got two-thirds of that money. Fighters usually don't profit from such rights at all.) In each case, the Millers lost money on the promotion because ticket sales did not cover their expenses. Had they been able to share in the television revenue that wouldn't have happened.

When Loraine Miller confronted Jacobs, reminding him of the promise to cover losses, he balked. "We lost twenty-two thousand dollars on those fights. Jacobs gave me a check for only four thousand dollars, and reminded me that as a promoter I should have known there were risks," said Miller. "And then I found out about the television money he'd gotten. I trusted them, and they were greedy and ungrateful."

Jeff Levine didn't fare much better. Fortunately for him, all his Tyson fights made enough money at the gate to pay his expenses. But Jacobs and Cayton drove a hard bargain. Levine did the ABC fights, for which he received a flat fee. In the Ferguson and Tillis fights, Levine was required to share the net profits from the gate. His last fight for Jacobs and Cayton was Tyson-Frazier. It brought in $54,400 of foreign television revenue, from which Levine got nothing.

The Millers and Levine were both told by Jacobs that they would profit from Tyson's eventual big-time fights. But when that time came, Jacobs and Cayton reneged. They had moved on. Their promises now were being made to Don King, and they were of a different kind.

For the most part, King got to play traditional promoter. But in setting those more favorable terms, Jacobs and Cayton had an ulterior motive. As the copromoter of the HBO Unification Series, King had under long-term contract two of the current heavyweight champions and many of the top-ranked contenders. Whether they entered the series now or waited until it was over and fought the unified champion, it was more than likely they'd have to deal with King eventually. They both accepted and dreaded that possibility. Don King was the only man in boxing with a greater appetite for money and power than theirs. King had also demonstrated time and again the willingness to do anything—including commit murder—to get what he wanted. He was the biggest, meanest, most powerful black lion that boxing had ever seen.

*  *  *

Donald King was born on August 20, 1931, in Cleveland, Ohio. He was the fifth of seven children, five boys and two girls. His father, Clarence King, worked in Cleveland's Jones & Laughlin steel mill. On December 7, 1941, as Japanese planes bombed Pearl Harbor, a ladle carrying molten steel broke from its aerial track and fell on Clarence, killing him instantly. The family received a $10,000 insurance settlement. King's mother, Hattie, used the money to buy a house in Mount Pleasant, a neighborhood in Cleveland for the more prosperous black families.

The family struggled to make ends meet. Young Don, perhaps eager to please his mother, was by far the most enterprising. Hattie cooked pies and roasted peanuts that he then sold in the black "policy houses," where people gambled, illegally, on the numbers. During high school King worked part-time at two all-white country clubs shining shoes. He did well in school and planned eventually to study law at Kent State. "I knew I could have been a great lawyer," said King. Upon graduating King continued to hustle. He worked the country clubs on the weekends, then during the week from 3:00 P.M. to 11:00 P.M. at Midland Steel. He also did the graveyard shift at another steel plant as a floor sweeper, but spent most of that time sleeping.

King never made it to law school. His heart, as it were, stayed in the policy houses. King became a runner for a numbers man call Daniel Boone. He wasn't content being another man's gofer. In the Cleveland policy game, each day's numbers were derived from the closing quotations at the New York Stock Exchange. King would call a stockbroker in New York just before the end of trading and get his own exclusive list. "I did the math, that's all, worked them out right, and hit, big time," said King proudly.

Within a few years, King had become a partner with Boone and three other men, and together as the "Big Five" they formed a numbers monopoly. King, known as "The Kid," drove a Cadillac, smoked cigars, and carried a gun. By the time he was twenty-five, the operation was pulling in upwards of $300,000 a week. "I found myself on another path, and on this path things looked like it was going to be peaches and honey," King was quoted as saying in a profile published by the *Cleveland Plain Dealer Magazine* on October 23, 1988. "I was handling a lot of cash and dealing and wheeling and whatnot, and I made a irrational rationalization: "Why should I go to school to learn to earn, since I was earning without learning?"

King began to lead a curious double life—in the one as a policy boss in the Cleveland black underworld, and in the other as a churchgoing family man. It suggested an inner struggle between an unquenchable urge to amass money, and the power, real and imagined, it promised, and a desire for both a quiet home life and social acceptance.

In the early 1950s, King married Luvenia Mitchell and adopted her son, Eric. The Kings attended Sunday services and gave generously to various church-sponsored charity programs. Meanwhile, the numbers business, and King, were getting nasty. In 1954, King shot and killed a man who he claimed was trying to rob one of his policy houses. Prosecutors decided that it was a justifiable homicide. In 1956, the police started cracking down on the Big Five's operations. The high-profile King was being arrested regularly for traffic violations and anything else that the police could harass him with. Tensions began to arise among the five bosses. It all began to fall apart when Alex ("Shondor") Birns, a low-ranking member of a Detroit-based Jewish mob group, tried to extract tribute payments. Birns demanded $1,000 a week, in return for which he promised protection from the police and peace within the monopoly.

King refused to pay. On May 20, 1957, a bomb planted under his house blew off the front porch. King, and his family, survived. He decided to testify for the state against Birns. Four weeks before Birn's trial, as King was leaving his house, he was hit in the back by a shotgun. He survived to testify against Birns but the trial ended in an eleven-to-one hung jury. It was believed that Birns had bought off that one juror.

After the trial, King's life changed for the worse. The Big Five, of course, broke up. King was ostracized by the Cleveland underworld for testifying against one of its own. His new name was "The Mouth." But the most damaging blow came from Luvenia. She had had enough of the violence, and left him, taking her son. From then on it was as if King, without the key ingredient for a respectable life, drove himself to the opposite extreme.

King continued to run his own numbers operation, but it was much harder to be both boss and enforcer. He began to get arrested for more serious crimes, such as narcotics possession and assault. Then, on April 20, 1966, King went over the edge. He had placed a numbers bet with a man named Samuel Lee Garrett. King won the bet and wanted his money, $600. Garrett didn't have it, and so King beat him viciously right there on the street. According to the police report of the incident, Garrett pleaded with King to stop; he promised to pay the money, but King, brandishing a .357 magnum revolver, kicked and punched and pistol-whipped without mercy. Garrett died a few days later. "He was touch-hog," said King about Garrett, a term of "the ghetto," he added, which meant that Garrett was being unnecessarily argumentative. The implication is that king felt that Garrett deserved what he got.

King stood trial for second-degree murder. He pleaded self-defense but was found guilty as charged. The conviction carried a sentence of life imprisonment. King appealed and won a suspended sentence. The appeals judge later ruled that the jury's verdict contradicted the evidence. The conviction was lowered to the lesser crime of manslaughter. In October 1967, King was sentenced to serve from one to twenty years at the Marion Correctional Institute.

"I'll tell you what happened," bellowed King on the subject of his conviction. "I was a black man with money, a successful nigger, and they couldn't live with that, oh no, not a nigger in a Cadillac," and then King affected the voice of a redneck Southern sheriff: "'We got's to get that boy. Ain't no good reason having a nigger boy with money.'"

That had become King's ethical posture about his life as a policy boss. He'd admit that the numbers were illegal, but he wouldn't apologize for who he was or what he did. Instead, King turned the whole scene inside out. He would argue vociferously that the real and true and only crime committed was against him; everything was going along just fine, he'd assert, until racism interfered.

There's something Orwellian to King's reasoning. It's as if he one day discovered that a believable lie is sometimes far more useful than the truth. No matter how wrong his actions may appear, King has always tried to cast himself as either the innocent victim or the gracious hero in the Phoenix-like dialectic of his incredible life story. Everything he has done is woven into a tireless effort to create and re-create himself along those lines. He is the author of his own myth, and also leading player and applauding audience. Regardless of how many people come forward—and there have been dozens—laden with evidence, legal papers, and accusations to contradict the myth, King endures.

Soon after King entered Marion, his mother died. "I can attribute so much to her, because I was so embarrassed at being in prison and not by her side," King once claimed. He used prison for rebirth. " I lived in books. I escaped confinement in my mind: *A Tale of Two Cities*, *Meditations* by Marcus Aurelius, Tom Paine, the *Critique of Pure Reason*, Kant, Hegel, Mill, Machiavelli, Gibran, W.E.B. Du Bois, Marcus Garvey, Freud, Shakespeare, Frederick Douglass, and the Holy Bible. I've tried to emulate Douglass. He fought slavery and extolled his country, America."

King was paroled after serving only four years. According to the legend, the one he later spun out, King started in boxing with the purest of motives. Within less than a year of being released, he persuaded Muhammad Ali to give a boxing exhibition in Cleveland to raise money for the Forest City Hospital. That was in August 1972. A year and a half later, he promoted the George Foreman-Ken Norton fight in Caracas, Venezuela; then, in October 1974, Ali-Foreman in Kinshasa, Zaire. With "The Rumble in the Jungle," as King billed the bout, he broke all purse records by paying each fighter $5 million. Eleven months after that came "The Thrilla in Manila": Ali–Joe Frazier in the Philippines.

*Sports Illustrated* ran a cover story dubbing King "Boxing's New Barnum." He was listed by *New York Magazine* as one of the city's most powerful black men. In 1976, he received the Urban Justice Award. The other recipients were Betty Ford and Supreme Court Justice William O. Douglas. "I spent a lifetime on the streets with the real folk who knew what it is to sweat, bleed, and cry. My magic lies in my ghetto ties," King said at the time. "People are my most important asset. Faith in the Supreme Being, trust, credibility, and performance are the things that have brought me to the top. My understanding and love for people, along with my performance, is what has kept me there."

King spun the legend, building, via his "people assets," greater reserves of apparent credibility. Past biographies handed out by his publicity staff list the 1977 ABC United States Championship boxing tournament, an award from the Cleveland City Council as a leading native son, a 1983 pardon from Governor James A. Rhodes for the

manslaughter conviction, more awards for recognition of his contributions to a dozen charities, audiences with royalty, and the 1984 Jackson
Victory Tour, which brought in $150 million.

King would go on to promote more than 250 title fights. In the
process, he amassed a multimillion-dollar fortune that bought two
thousand acres of farmland in the hamlet of Windsor in Ashtabula
County just east of Cleveland. On one modest parcel of 179 acres he
built a thirty-room mansion with a greenhouse and tennis courts. On a
hill overlooking two man-made lakes, in what King calls his "Liberty
Garden," there are three flags—the Stars and Stripes, another that
reads "Liberty," and a third, his own logo: "Don" in gold letters
underneath a crown, and below that the motto "Only in America."

In the nearby town of Orwell, King also built a training camp for his
stable of boxers, which over the years included Earnie Shavers, Larry
Holmes, Greg Page, and Tim Witherspoon, among many others. He
purchased a five-story townhouse on East Sixty-ninth Street in New
York near Park Avenue, making it the home of Don King Productions,
plus a Spanish-style villa on Star Island in Miami Beach, Florida, and
condos in Los Angeles and Las Vegas.

He even hired his own film producer, whose sole job is to record the
spectacle of Don King. There are literally hundreds of thousands of feet
of footage waiting one day to be cut into some epic tale. And a
Falstaffian figure he'd make: six-foot-four, with a barrel chest heaving
over a bulging stomach, and a puffy face on which explodes an ivory-
white toothy grin and a loud, chopping haw, haw, haw of a laugh. He's
the visage of the happy squire who always looks as if he's about to eat or
has just finished a meal. With that great bellowing voice, every word is
an announcement presuming its own importance. The rhetoric comes
out in an unrelenting, stream-of-consciousness blast of images, quotations, mixed metaphors, mispronounced words, aphorisms, and macho
street lingo. Surely, as in some vaudeville routine, in the filmed epic
King would also be asked to explain the hair. In King's version, it's as if
he got zapped by some force of energy that blasted out all the kinks and
infused him with an inexhaustible positive life force. "I can't explain it.
One day, ping, ping, ping, and there it is, like God reached down and
touched me," he said.

Actually, there is an explanation. In the early 1970s, King kept his hair
short. In 1974, when he promoted the Ali-Forman fight in Zaire, he
came across a newspaper photo of Zambian President Kenneth Kaunda,

who had wild-looking, stand-up hair. King affected the same look by simply growing out his hair and brushing out the kinks with a pick-comb.

The effect, if not the purpose, of King's mythmaking has been to sell, but also to conceal. There is another Don King behind the artifice. But it is rarely seen, and then only in glimpses. Such is the peep-show aspect of his life. It reveals much about how King became a powerful and wealthy boxing promoter. Jacobs and Cayton, along with many other people in boxing who have witnessed his incredible rise, saw enough to know *that* King, and if at all possible, to avoid him.

While a policy boss, King had a licentious streak that ran pure and strong and ultimately full of rage. In prison he got a book education, and lessons on how to reform his methods, but the streak remained. If King's legion of critics can be believed, and none yet have been able to prove their accusations beyond a shadow of a doubt, boxing also revealed his penchant for larceny.

In early 1972, Richie Giachetti was a thirty-two-year-old small-time figure on the Cleveland boxing scene. He had some experience as an amateur fighter, but no professional record. He made money as he could. Giachetti was known by federal law enforcement officials as "Richie the Torch," for his talents at arson.

Giachetti was introduced to King through a mutual friend and lawyer, Clarence Rogers. King, who knew nothing about boxing, wanted someone to help organize the Forest City Hospital Muhammad Ali exhibition. Giachetti joined up. Afterwards, he worked with King as a trainer, and for ten years developed a variety of boxers, most notably heavyweight champion Larry Holmes. In 1982 Giachetti sued Holmes and King for breach of contract. He later settled, but not before offering in depositions a rare first hand account of King's business practices.

According to Giachetti, King promised the Forest City Hospital all the money from the Ali exhibition. In fact, he kept the largest share. The gate brought in $85,000. King gave the hospital $15,000, kept $30,000 for himself, and used the rest to pay the fighters on the card.

King searched for new boxing prospects whom he could exclusively control. In Scranton, Pennsylvania, in 1973, he came upon a young and promising Larry Holmes, who was already being managed by Ernie Butler. King had the contract declared invalid on the ground that Butler had failed to register his agreement with the state boxing commission. He then signed up Holmes. As Holmes would later assert: "Don King buys whoever he has to buy. He takes a young fighter that doesn't have any money, and he puts a thousand dollars or maybe twenty thousand dollars on the table. Boy, then you do anything. Only later do you realize he bought you, he owns you, and it wasn't the right thing to do."

King also used the issue of race to woo Holmes. "Don said to me, 'Why give money to the white man? Don't you want to help your brother?' Don King doesn't care about black or white. He just cares about green."

King got Holmes the fights, Giachetti was the trainer, and on the surface it looked like a masterful career development. In June 1978, Holmes defeated Ken Norton to win the World Boxing Council heavyweight title. As a promoter of the fight, King earned a substantial fee. Despite the rule against his also taking a manager's cut, that's exactly what King did.

"After the first title fight, Larry Holmes was complaining that he was getting less than fifty percent of the money, and Larry Holmes was absolutely right," said Giachetti in his deposition. "He did get less, because Don King got twenty-five percent of Larry Holmes and Richie Giachetti got twenty percent and Charles Spaziani [Holmes's lawyer] got ten percent. He only got forty-five percent. He was cheated.... It was illegal." Giachetti claimed that King divided up Holmes's purses that way for six to eight years. "Don King's word was no good," added Giachetti. "He would never give you a contract binding where you could go to court. He wanted a contract. He always made you sign. But you're not allowed to have one. Those tactics were proved later with many people."

King used whatever tactics he deemed necessary to get what he wanted. When he started out buying up boxers, he was obviously cash-poor from having spent four years in prison. He tapped some of his policy friends. That was revealed in a 1978 investigation into the numbers rackets by the Organized Crime Task Force of the U.S. Department of Justice.

In testimony before a Cleveland grand jury on March 13, 1978, King denied having had any business dealings or relationships with a reputed numbers boss, Virgil Ogletree, since 1970. He also claimed not to have had any bank accounts at Quincy Savings & Loan. More than a year later, King appeared before the grand jury to "correct" that testimony. He testified that in 1972, he referred all his former numbers business to Ogletree, who in turn paid King 25 percent of his take. King also acted as a "controller" for Ogletree's cash flow. He collected and deposited the weekly bets in three separate accounts at Quincy Savings & Loan under the company name of K&G enterprises. King used the alias of Kenneth Donaldson, and Ogletree that of James Woods. When someone won a number, King would direct the money to be paid out to Ogletree.

It was a money-laundering scheme. The choice of Quincy Savings & Loan was intentional. Quincy was owned by Charles V. Carr, a Cleveland city councilman and lawyer. Carr and King were associated during his policy-boss days. King, in fact, gave Carr several thousand dollars for his election campaign. When King went to prison, Carr purchased forty acres of farmland in Ashtabula County for $19,800. By the time King was paroled, Carr had sold it to a fourteen-year-old boy, John Carl Renwick, for the paltry sum of $1,000. The boy's mother was Henrietta Renwick, King's companion and later his wife. The farm formed the first parcel of his sprawling two-thousand-acre estate. The implication was that Carr bought the farm with King's policy earnings. The elaborate transaction was designed both to hide the money from the Internal Revenue Service and to take care of Henrietta.

The IRS alerted the Justice Department to the laundering scheme. It found that King claimed gross earnings of only $39,300 in 1972 and 1973, and did not report any of the money on account at Quincy. It also found that in June 1974, after King had already become a major promoter, he withdrew $50,000 of unreported money from the accounts for personal use. Obviously, King did not leave his policy life behind. Like everything else, both the people and the practices from those days were woven into his new life. Although there's no account of King physically assaulting anyone to enforce a deal, he did use threats. In one early effort to coerce a fighter to break his management contract, King was up against a mob-connected manager. The story of their exchange has been told many times in boxing circles. The effect is always bone-chilling. "You can pick up that phone and get me killed in half an hour," King was reputed to have said to the manager, "but I can make a call and have you killed in fifteen minutes." King got the fighter.

It wasn't the only time he used such tactics. Ernie Butler, the erstwhile manager of Holmes, also received threats when he started to make accusations about King. In his 1986 deposition, Giachetti claimed that "Larry was scared of Don King; he threatened to kill Larry." Giachetti has also admitted in private interviews that King once threatened to kill him. "Don will do anything in the world. He gets up, waves the American flag, he loves everyone, but I understand it's not true."

Presumably, King loves John Carl Renwick, the boy he became stepfather to upon marrying Henrietta. But there are many substantiated accounts of King also using his adopted son (who became Carl King) as a front in schemes to bilk fighters. Starting around 1980, Carl King, under the name of Monarch Boxing Inc., became a fight manager. The fighters he had under contract signed long-term agreements to be promoted by Don King. In those agreements, King required the fighter to give him options on the right to promote a given number of future fights, usually three to five.

Father-son teams in boxing are not unheard of. Getting hooked up with the Kings, however, was rarely all that profitable. Carl King regularly took 50 percent of the boxer's purses, which in most states is illegal; managers are limited to 33⅓ percent. In many cases, Carl King also didn't seem to be making any of the decisions about matchups or purse amounts. Don King did all the negotiating.

Whenever Carl was confronted by fighters on such issues, he deferred to his father. And when King was confronted, he told the fighters to stay with his son or they wouldn't get fights. In some cases, it would turn out that Carl King was managing both fighters in a bout, another infraction of the rules.

King had a similar impact on the managers of other fighters. In 1982, he signed heavyweight Randall ("Tex") Cobb to a title fight with Larry Holmes. King negotiated with manager Joe Gramby to pay Cobb the greater amount of $700,000 or 30 percent of all the revenues from the promotion, an amount estimated to be $1.3 million. A week before the fight, Gramby told Cobb that the bout would be canceled unless the fighter agreed to receive a flat fee of only $500,000. Cobb gave in, then found out later that Gramby had received the difference of $200,000 from King for "consultant services." That transaction was recorded in a letter from King to Gramby. It became the key evidence in a suit Cobb filed against both men.

Apparently, what King did was overpromise on the money to Cobb to lure him into the bout agreement. He then changed his mind, or discovered that the promotion wasn't going to do as well as he expected. The point, according to the allegation, was that King was able to conscript a fighter's own manager into the scheme. "King divides and conquers, isolates and controls." said Mark Risman, a Las Vegas attorney who has negotiated with King on behalf of several boxers.

He was not above conscripting parents too. In 1982, promoter Butch Lewis sued King for inducing one of his promising heavyweights, Greg Page, into breaking their contract. Lewis had been developing Page from the day of his first professional fight in 1978. In 1981, as Page approached a title shot, King showed up in the fighter's hometown and started spreading tens of thousands of dollars around to Page's father, mother and friends. Page, on his father's urging, signed with King. "Don steals a fighter, and if the manager sues, he pays him off. It's a business expense for him," said Lewis.

King's dealings with boxer Tim Witherspoon offered another classic case study. In 1982, Witherspoon was in the third year of a promising heavyweight career. He was set to fight James ("Quick") Tillis in a King promotion but pulled out because of an ear infection. A year earlier, King had secretly bought a part interest in Witherspoon from his manager. King used Witherspoon's withdrawal from the fight to exert total control. He lobbied the Cleveland Boxing and Wrestling Commission to have Witherspoon suspended from fighting. King then told him that if he accepted Carl King as new manager, the suspension would be lifted. Witherspoon agreed, and the suspension was lifted.

Witherspoon signed four different contracts with the Kings. The first was an exclusive, long-term promotional contract with Don; the second, a managerial agreement with Carl in which as manager he would earn 33⅓ percent of all earnings. The third was also a managerial contract, but it gave Carl 50 percent of Witherspoon's earnings. The fourth contract was left blank.

King filed only the second contract with boxing authorities. That gave the appearance of propriety. But when it came time to split purses, the third contract, in which Witherspoon gave up 50 percent of his earnings, was used. As to the last agreement: King frequently required fighters to sign blank contracts so that he could fill in whatever terms, including the names of opponents, he pleased.

Witherspoon fought for the title against Greg Page (another King fighter) in March 1984. He was promised a purse of $240,000. Witherspoon beat Page and became World Boxing Council champion, but got only $41,498. Carl King, as manager, earned $125,000. Witherspoon lost the WBC title in his first defense. In January of 1986, he took the World Boxing Association title from Tony Tubbs. A few months later, Witherspoon defended against British challenger Frank Bruno. HBO paid King $1.7 million to telecast the bout in the U.S. Ticket sales at Wembley Stadium brought in $2 million. British and foreign television sales, plus ring advertising, brought the total to $5 million. Witherspoon was promised only $550,000.

Witherspoon defeated Bruno in a punishing bout that left both men swollen and bloody. He received a net purse of only $90,000. Carl King took $250,000; Don King took the liberty of deducting (but not proving that he paid) the British tax of $75,000. Despite a regulation requiring the deduction of Witherspoon's training expenses from the gross earnings, King took it out of the boxer's net. In other words, expenses are a burden that everyone shares—except King.

King, of course, has always denied any and all wrongdoing. He has accused his adversaries of racism, envy, greed, and lies. "You can't believe anything anyone tells you in boxing," once said King. "The business is predicated on lies. You are dealing with people who very rarely tell the truth." In order to support that claim, King has pointed out that everyone who sues him ultimately settles, and even does business with him again.

Richie Giachetti, for instance, took $50,000 from King in his 1982 suit, only to later resurface as Holmes's trainer again. When Holmes temporarily stopped boxing in 1985, Giachetti remained an employee in King's promoting company. Butch Lewis won a jury decision against King but relented in the settlement talks and took $200,000, far less than he would have made handling Page himself. Lewis later joined up with King to copromote the HBO Unification Series. Holmes sued King, settled, then came out of retirement to fight for him again.

In all, since 1972, there have been twenty-five civil suits brought against King by boxers, managers, and promoters, and almost all have been settled, with almost every litigant later doing business with King. Those who haven't were usually boxers who were too old, or beaten up, to fight anymore. But most returned, because a deal couldn't be made for a title fight in the heavyweight division without King. As promoter Cedric Kushner once said: "I would do business with Don in thirty seconds if the offer was good. I have to give the devil his due—he hasn't cheated me *every* time we've done business. And I learn from my mistakes."

Therein lies the proverbial rub: whatever the merits of those cases against King, the plaintiffs couldn't afford *not* to settle. From 1979 to

1986, King promoted thirty-two out of a total of thirty-nine heavyweight championship bouts—including one in South Africa for a fee of $1 million. During that time, he controlled under exclusive promotional contracts almost every heavyweight champion: Mike Weaver, Michael Dokes, Gerrie Coetzee, Greg Page, Tony Tubbs, Tim Witherspoon, Pinklon Thomas, James ("Bonecrusher") Smith, and Trevor Berbick. In each case, every time one of those boxers won the title, it was from a King fighter. And when they lost it, usually in the first or second defense, it was also to a King fighter.

(The only exception would seem to be Muhammad Ali. King promoted eight of his fights and a dispute about money arose over only one. The explanation is that in each case neither Ali nor his opponent was under King's direct control—that is, caught in his web of multiple, long-term contracts. Only Larry Holmes, when he fought Ali in October 1980, had a close King connection. That was the fight in which Ali sued King for shortchanging him on his purse by more than $1 million. King paid him off in a settlement. The other reason King seemed on such good behavior with Ali was, quite simply, fear. Ali was managed by Herbert Muhammad, who was the son of Elijah Muhammad, leader of the Black Muslims. "Don didn't want to mess with the Muslims," said Seth Abraham, an executive at HBO who has worked closely with King since the late 1970s.)

King's claim that all the civil suits against him are mere subterfuge became another one of his believable lies. The more doubt he can cast on everyone else's motives and integrity, the more he can get away with. And that provides the key to understanding the madness to King's methods. He has worked the deal at the most viscerally emotional level.

When King lays out the contracts for a fighter to sign, he's not concerned with offering a fair deal. He knows that the fighter must accept the terms because so often the fighters' ambitions, and the absence of an alternative, dictate it. He preys on a fighter's dreams, exploits his weaknesses—a thirst for money, or women, a sensitivity to racial issues, or identity problems resulting from the absence of a father—and does anything else it takes to gain leverage. "I was a father figure to Larry Holmes, the only man he ever looked up to," said King. Retorted Holmes: "Did Don say that? He doesn't stop. He won't quit."

Perhaps some of King's adversaries do lie and cheat. But if so, then in many cases King probably created the necessary and sufficient conditions for their corruption. In the final analysis, it's not what King has done to people's bank accounts that matters, but how he has distorted their hearts and minds. To King, everyone else is a Faustus, and he is their Mephistopheles.

Ironically, during King's years of control over the heavyweight division, his crowning achievement of emotional bargaining was not with a boxer; it was with a woman, Connie Harper. Harper was thirty-two years old when she joined King's New York operation as his personal secretary in 1974. In 1978, King advanced her to corporate vice president. Over the next several years she worked intimately with King on many of his boxing-related financial deals. On December 13, 1984, the U.S. government indicted King and Harper on twenty-three counts of willful tax evasion. They were tried the next year. On November 13, 1985, the jury found King innocent of all charges, but Harper guilty. She was sentenced to one year in prison, and served the full term.

The U.S. government had been keeping a close eye on King since questioning him in 1978 and 1979 about maintaining secret bank accounts to disguise income. They were far more interested in convicting King than Harper. Prior to the trial, prosecutors promised leniency if Harper agreed to testify against King. She declined the offer. Even after her conviction, when it was clear that she'd taken the fall for things in which King was if not the instigator at least a party, Harper refused another offer to testify about his activities in boxing.

Connie Harper was born and raised in Cleveland as the youngest of five children. Her parents were middle-class blacks. The children did well for themselves. One of Harper's older sisters became a judge in a Cleveland municipal court. Harper earned a bachelor's degree in English, then went on to work as an editor at the *Call & Post*, a Cleveland newspaper. In 1967, she received a fellowship to the University of Chicago to do research on the problems of urban youth. She went on to a staff job at the Institute for Community Development in Washington, D.C., and stayed there until 1974. Harper then did a brief stint at Africare, a private peace organization that donated money to Africa, but quit abruptly to work for Don King.

King and Harper met through a network of common friends and associates in Cleveland. In 1967, Harper worked on the reelection campaign of black mayor Carl B. Stokes. During his policy-boss days, King made contributions to Stokes's campaign. In 1971, Stokes, no longer mayor, purchased land in the same area of Ashtabula County as did councilman Charles Carr. In fact, Stokes got a mortgage for the purchase from Carr's bank, Quincy Savings & Loan. Stokes eventually sold the land to King.

It seemed baffling to many people that Harper would leave a civic-minded career for such a close association with King and the world of boxing. They were a true odd couple. Harper was five-foot-two, and tended to put on weight. She had a studious manner and dressed in a dowdy fashion. The loud, garish, outgoing King somehow appealed to her.

In Harper's sentencing report, a psychologist concluded that she had an addictive personality that led her to obsessive eating, sleeping, and shopping. She also felt a need "to see herself as a little girl." The report ended with this: "[Harper was] either swept away by the excitement and glamour of Don King's world, or for other reasons still unknown, Harper does appear to have behaved in an uncharacteristic and self-destructive manner."

In the trial of King and Harper, the government stated that between 1978 and 1981 King had diverted for personal use nearly $1 million in money that was due his promoting company. In effect, he skimmed off monies so that they wouldn't show as income on the books. The method was simple. During those years King promoted numerous fights at Caesars Palace in Las Vegas. Caesars paid him a site fee that was due at the completion of each fight. But King couldn't wait for the money. Several times he went to the casino cage window and took advances, sometimes in cash, sometimes in betting chips. Harper, who was with King in Las Vegas, was responsible for passing on records of each advance to the company accountant. She didn't do that. Harper kept those records in her own files. The amount of money so skimmed reached $850,000.

What was King's accountant doing about it? According to King's defense, nothing. There were obvious and glaring discrepancies between money due by contract from Caesars and the net amount, less King's advances, actually paid. But the accountant claimed that he never saw the documents. The government established that besides being withheld by Harper, other such documents were mysteriously removed from company files, were placed for no apparent reason in King's home outside Cleveland, or had simply disappeared.

The government easily proved that income had gone unreported. But it had to show also that King and Harper willfully conspired, in a meeting of minds, to do that. King's defense put the blame on his employees, who supposedly acted "without his knowledge or consent."

Here was a man who started his business career juggling hundreds of thousands of dollars every week—in cash—from dozens of people, a process for which he must have kept meticulous books; here was a man who deftly set up and juggled three secret bank accounts; and, suddenly, he couldn't keep track of a one-man accounting department. It seemed like a hollow defense.

"The point of it is that this is not a smooth ship that's being run here, and we all recognize that King is the captain of that ship, and perhaps can be criticized for not being a more aggressive administrator," said King's defense lawyer in his closing arguments. "But there is no evidence to support that Mr. King has the skills to do that, that he is educated or trained to run that kind of massive ship."

King didn't overtly blame employee Harper for the screwups, but the jury obviously felt she was at fault. King's whole defense was based on pointing the finger at the only person who didn't have an alibi. Roanne L. Mann, who prosecuted the case, put it this way: "She couldn't blame it on her accountant because she didn't have one. Don King could."

The evidence against Harper was her individual tax returns and spending habits. Between 1978 and 1980, she reported income of $70,464. Her actual income was $265,464, which created a discrepancy of $195,000. The fact that King understated his income for those years by $422,000 didn't seem to bother the jury nearly as much. Instead, the jurors fixated on the jewelry, clothes, and savings bonds Harper purchased for herself. That she made many of those purchases days after King withdrew large sums of money from Caesars—implying that he gave the money to her as a gift, or perhaps a bribe—was taken lightly.

In fact, all of Harper's unreported income came from King in the form of gifts, bonuses, and participation in his various deals. When King skimmed money for himself, he made sure that it was Harper who endorsed and deposited the checks. Some of that money went directly into King's private account. Harper would then transfer it to her own account. Other amounts went into a joint private savings account that King and Harper had established.

The picture, then, was of King and Harper handling all that money together, and of the intimacy required between two people in order to conceive and execute such an effort. But mostly, there emerged a picture of a short, overweight, unmarried, and dowdy woman quietly reveling in the attentions of a tall, garrulous, charismatic celebrity. And in that picture there was Harper buying herself a $65,000 diamond solitaire ring, and $15,000 gold and diamond bracelets, all perhaps to beautify herself for a real or desired romance with King. "She loved Don. I doubt that he really loved her," said one former King employee.

The jury didn't see romance in Harper's motives. It decided that Harper was moved only by her own ambition and avarice. The jury missed, or was not clearly presented with, two important points. First, it would seem impossible for Harper to have handled all that money without King's knowledge, approval, and expert advice. The second point, far more compelling but perhaps also difficult to prove, was that there was not a "meeting of minds" but a hooking of the heart: King's wily, conspiratorial mind stole into Harper's heart. Mephistopheles was doing his work.

King seemed to have a similar effect on the jury. He didn't testify in his trial but did take every opportunity to entertain the courtroom in blustering asides. When the verdicts were announced, the entire jury went over to congratulate King, and to ask for his autograph. He then took them all out for dinner. "I underestimated his effect on the jury," admitted prosecutor Roanne Mann.

Mann had one other regret. She had attempted to enter into evidence the fact that King perjured himself in testimony given to the Cleveland grand jury in 1978 and 1979. That would have done much to establish King's "criminal state of mind" with respect to his penchant for money laundering, tax evasion, and the setting up of secret bank accounts. The judge disallowed the testimony.

\* \* \*

As copromoter of the HBO Unification Series, King and his corrupting opportunities seemed legion. It wasn't his first such tournament. The last time King had tried it was with ABC Sports in 1976–1977, and that proved to be one of boxing's biggest scandals—although nothing was ever done about it—since D'Amato's bungling of the 1959 Patterson-Johansson promotion.

In May of 1976, King approached CBS Sports about holding a tournament that would crown champions in the eight major weight classes. CBS declined the offer. King then took the idea to ABC, which readily agreed. The United States Boxing Championship would include sixteen telecasts over five months at a cost to ABC of $2.2 million. The first telecast took place on January 16, 1977. About a month later it all began to fall apart. The tournament appeared to be an elaborate scheme by King to monopolize all of boxing.

For any such tournament to have credibility, there must be quality competition. King, however, wasn't interested in getting good fighters, and certainly not the best, but rather only those he could control. Every fighter who entered had to sign a contract giving King three options on future fights if he won the tournament. A lot of the top-ranked fighters, including the best middleweight at the time, Marvin Hagler, refused to enter on those terms. That created a problem for King. ABC wanted fighters within the top twelve rankings. The higher the ranking, the more it would pay in purses. The solution, and one which King denied ever resorting to, was to fabricate the rankings. Of course, as always, King managed to put other people between himself and all the acts of arm-twisting, deception, and outright fraud.

Incredibly, ABC did not require King to obtain the formal blessing of the two sanctioning bodies of boxing—the World Boxing Council and the World Boxing Association—for the tournament. Both bodies were known to be easily manipulated by promoters, and yet to rank fighters was one of their basic functions. ABC agreed, on King's suggestion, to pay the monthly boxing magazine, *Ring*, the sum of $70,000 to rank the competitors. That was left up to John Ort, a *Ring* editor.

When allegations started to be made that some fighters didn't deserve to be in the tournament, ABC attempted to verify Ort's rankings. That research, and other work done later by a team of outside lawyers, uncovered several fabrications. Overall, thirty-one of the fifty-six invited fighters were not qualified to participate. Some twenty-five fights in *Ring*'s records hadn't even taken place. The authenticity of another eighty-two was highly suspicious.

One manager, Henry Groomes, got seven of his fighters invited, six of whom were highly ranked by *Ring*. Five had phony records, with sixteen fictitious fights in total. Moreover, five of Groomes's fighters were profiled in *Ring* magazine during 1976 and 1977.

Groomes, it turned out, plus at least three other managers (including Richie Giachetti and Joe Gramby) worked closely with King. Indeed, 39 percent of the fighters—almost all of whom had questionable records—were managed by people with similar ties to King.

Ort also turned out to be highly compromised. He had part interests in the management of some of the fighters—including those of Henry Groomes—with false and questionable rankings. In April 1976, and then again months later, Ort received $5,000 in cash from King for unspecified consulting services. He had also received monies for "consulting" over the previous two years from other promoters and managers whose fighters were to participate in the tournament.

The investigation also uncovered allegations that to be included in the tournament, fighters had to kick back part of their purses to either King, his employees and associates, or Ort; and that in order to get invited, fighters had to accept new, King-connected managers.

ABC canceled the tournament in April 1977. When ABC announced that an investigation would be done by a team of outside lawyers, King accused ABC of racial persecution. King had little to worry about. ABC was not about to pay hundreds of thousands of dollars to hang itself. The story had already been covered by every major newspaper, and one rival network, CBS, to the considerable embarrassment of top ABC brass. The two executives responsible for the tournament—Jim Spence, the vice president of program planning, and Bob Greenway, the manager of program planning—were first made aware of the ranking problems from an internal report written in early December 1976. It took them months to verify, let alone act on the allegations. That suggested a greater interest in avoiding personal embarrassment, and career death, than in establishing the truth.

The final report was a hefty 450 pages long. It was a sincere but flaccid effort which was perhaps to be expected given that it resulted from a corporation investigating itself. Moreover, because it was not a government-led criminal investigation, the attorneys had no power to subpoena, no immunity to offer, and thus no deals to make. Most of the principals involved in the worst infractions, plus seven fighters with fabricated records, refused to cooperate. John Ort, obviously the key to revealing King's degree of conspiratorial involvement, was interviewed only once.

Not surprisingly, the report found that King was essentially blame-less. As to ABC, it was conveniently determined that executives "should have acted sooner" but that their not doing so was a "business judgment" and one "beyond the scope of our investigation."

ABC did not give the report wide public release. Reporters were invited to read it in one day at ABC's offices. But King got the jump on everybody. He sent in his own group of readers early in the morning before any journalist had arrived. He held a press conference that afternoon celebrating his innocence. "King co-opted the publicity," said Michael Armstrong, the attorney who headed the investigation. Armstrong was formerly chief counsel to the Knapp Commission, which uncovered corruption in the New York Police Department (upon which the movie *Serpico* was based). He seemed strangely charmed by King—as almost everyone can be. "He's got wit, guts, and bullshit, and he's one of the smartest guys I ever met."

It was the scandal that could have been. In the months and years that followed, examples of King's corrupting influence popped to the surface like so many sunken corpses that wouldn't stay down. Jim Farley, chairman of the New York State Athletic Commission, resigned when it was revealed that he had accepted favors from King. Mark Kram, a boxing writer, was fired by *Sports Illustrated*. In late 1977, Jim Spence and other ABC executives would testify, by invitation, to a congressional subcommittee looking into network sports practices.

In late 1979, ABC would finally get around to taking a sober look at Jim Spence's relationship with King. That occurred after Richie Giachetti, then training Holmes for King, let it slip to ABC boxing analyst Alex Wallau that "King is taking care of Spence"—meaning, paying him off. ABC's outside law firm investigated Spence and found no such payments.

The whole mess over the ABC tournament did, however, bring King to the attention of the U.S. government—hence, King's 1978 and 1979 Cleveland grand jury testimony on the numbers rackets. King also caught the eye of Joseph Spinelli, a special agent for the FBI who had just come off the infamous "Abscam" case in Washington, D. C.. Spinelli, a young, tough, native New Yorker with a hockey player's build, persuaded his superiors to let him investigate the murky world of boxing. He dubbed the investigation "Crown Royal," for no other reason than it was the name of a brand of whiskey. "I love the sport, and it made me sick how corrupt it was," said Spinelli. His team interviewed dozens of people over four years and compiled thousands of pages of notes and tapes and boxes of supporting documents.

In 1980, Jacobs and D'Amato agreed to be interviewed by Spinelli. "I spent four hours with them," Spinelli said. "D'Amato gave us a dissertation on the history of the mob in boxing, from the beginning of the sport until the present. When I asked D'Amato about his connections with Charlie Black and Fat Tony Salerno back in the 1950s, he stonewalled." On the subject of Don King, Spinelli suspected an ulterior motive. They went on and on about King but they didn't have any hard evidence, just leads," Spinelli added. "I knew what they were up to. They wanted to get rid of King and take over the heavyweight division themselves."

Spinelli's work ended up being shelved. When it came time for witnesses to be brought before the grand jury in order to get indictments, many of them got cold feet. The fighters in particular feared reprisals from the promoters. Some witnesses suddenly changed their stories or pleaded the Fifth Amendment to avoid self-incrimination. To get indictments, Spinelli would have had to set up sting operations, which his superiors apparently didn't want to do. "We found some great stuff, like that the first Michael Dokes vs. Mike Weaver fight was probably fixed," said Spinelli. That fight, on December 10, 1982, was promoted by Don King. His fighter, Michael Dokes, won.

Spinelli had reason to believe that a late 1970s bout between Ken Norton and Jimmy Young was also fixed when the judge was paid off. He claimed to have proof that Bob Lee, the head of the International Boxing Federation, received payoffs. 'He should have been indicted," asserted Spinelli. Finally there were witnesses involved in the ABC U.S. Boxing Championships who claimed that at least one fight had been fixed. Devoid of willing witnesses, Crown Royal was ended in 1984. The records remain in the custody of the FBI. Despite several requests made under the Freedom of Information laws, the FBI has refused to release them. "It's all there sitting in a bunch of boxes," said a wincing Spinelli, who later left the FBI to accept an appointment from New York Governor Mario Cuomo to become the state inspector general. "Boxing is a chaotic mess," he concluded. "There is no regulatory body setting and enforcing the rules. Don King persists because he exploits the chaos."

# Chapter Seven

In the business of boxing, the champion fighter is one part in an equation that begins and ends with money.

From the turn of the century, the primary source of money in boxing, or prizefighting as it was then called, was from ticket sales. Sizable sums could be made from a well-promoted bout. The November 1899 James J. Jeffries-Tom Sharkey heavyweight match on Coney Island brought in $67,000, an enormous amount of money at the time for an afternoon's entertainment. As boxing grew in significance in the public's mind, so did the receipts. In the early 1900s, America was looking for what the press had dubbed a "Great White Hope" to defeat outspoken black champion Jack Johnson. The July 4, 1910, bout between Johnson and Jeffries in Reno, Nevada, grossed a whopping $270,775. The most expensive ticket, of which 1,258 were sold, cost $50. In all, thirty-five different promoters from as many cities bid a total of $3 million for the right to stage that fight. Johnson won the fight, proving beyond a doubt both that he was still the best heavyweight in the world and that boxing was a gold mine for the men who controlled the promotion.

In the 1920s, the mass appeal of Jack Dempsey moved the major fights into larger-scale sites such as New York's Yankee Stadium and the Polo Grounds. That raised gate receipts considerably. So did the advent of radio broadcasting of fights in 1922 and the proliferation of movie houses. Fights had been filmed since the invention of motion picture photography in the 1880s. Johnson's prowess over white opponents caused great public alarm, and that led the U.S. government to make it illegal for films of his victories to be sold. The law was repealed after Johnson's demise in 1915. The great matchups of the 1920s—especially the two Dempsey-Tunney fights—earned large fees for movie rights.

The British were the first to televise a fight, in 1933 at a private screening, then in 1939 for public view. Madison Square Garden televised its first bout in 1941. By 1944, Mike Jacobs, the promoter of Joe Louis, had cut a deal with the Gillette Safety Razor Co. to sponsor fifty fight telecasts. At around the same time theater telecasts, or what would be termed closed-circuit, began as well.

The Gillette broadcasts ushered in what became known as the "Fight of the Week" era of boxing. In the first of those broadcasts, main-event fighters earned $186.60 from the sale of the TV rights. By 1964, when the Gillette contract with Madison Square Garden expired, TV rights brought fighters as much as $4,000. The Garden raked in $15 million from television sponsorship over those twenty years.

By the late 1950s, promoters were taking their biggest fights to closed-circuit television. New technologies were able to hook up dozens of theater sites around the country. The June 1959 Floyd Patterson-Ingemar Johansson fight grossed $1 million from closed-circuit with many more sites added on, Sonny Liston-Floyd Patterson brought in $5.5 million.

Television technology made the business equation of boxing more complex. Promoters still ruled the relationship between money and event, but television opened up the field to a lot more players. Almost anyone with the rights to a main-event boxer capable of attracting a national following was in a position to cut a television deal. To that extent, television dispersed power.

To a degree, this had a beneficial effect on boxing. The dispersal of power made entry into the national spotlight far easier for many fighters. They no longer had to deal with one or two dominant promoters to get matches. But eventually the dispersal also undermined the sport. In the age of Dempsey and Louis and Marciano, there was no question in the public's mind about who was undisputed champion. During the reign of Muhammad Ali, the icon of the heavyweight championship also remained intact. With the end of the Ali era, it all began to fall apart. That is, the appetites of the competing promoters, and the eagerness of the television networks for sports programming, reduced the heavyweight title to a near-meaningless state.

In February 1978, Ali lost a split decision to Leon Spinks, the 1976 Olympic gold medalist. Spinks was then required under the rules of the World Boxing Council to fight the number one ranked contender. He decided instead to fight a rematch with Ali, for which he was promised several million dollars from the closed-circuit broadcast. The W.B.C. refused to sanction the fight. Its rival sanctioning body, the World Boxing Association, did. Ali defeated Spinks to become W.B.A. champion. The W.B.C., meanwhile, sanctioned the Larry Holmes-Ken Norton bout and crowned winner Holmes its new champion. The heavyweight title had split into two.

To boxing experts, Holmes ruled as Ali's heir. In the eyes of the wider public, though, Holmes's ascension soon became diminished. Ali all but retired after the second Spinks fight. Between 1978 and 1984, four different champions held the W.B.A. crown. In 1984, Holmes got in a dispute with the W.B.C. and relinquished his title. He was tired of signing blank contracts with Don King. The head of the W.B.C., Jose Sulaiman, sided with King, as he had done for years, against the interests of numerous boxers, managers, and rival promoters, all of which prompted considerable speculation as to what—love or money?—kept them such diehard allies.

Holmes was readily recognized and crowned by the much smaller and upstart International Boxing Federation. That split the heavyweight title into three. During 1984 and 1985, a half-dozen champions came and went. In September 1985, Holmes finally lost. He was beaten by Michael Spinks, younger brother of Leon. Michael, though as good as the rest of the heavyweight crop, was a slightly less than credible heir to the line: he was the first light heavyweight to ever dethrone a heavyweight.

The television networks loved, and hated, the situation. On the one hand, they always had a champion on tap to serve up to audiences. But with the constant churn of dubious champions, the ratings slid. The broader public wasn't interested in a boxing division that in the words of boxing gadfly Bert R. Sugar, resembled a three-legged potato race with each leg going in a different direction. Heavyweight boxing, indeed boxing in general, was shuttled off to the backwater of Saturday afternoon telecasts. ABC's U.S. Boxing Championships converted lack of interest into cynicism about a sport seemingly in decline.

Such chaos wasn't authored solely by the sanctioning bodies. And the W.B.A., W.B.C., and I.B.F. did serve the important function of creating rules of safety in the ring. They also mandated before- and after-fight medical testing, besides other health measures, to protect fighters. But for the most part, they were often tools of the promoters.

Into this mess waded Seth Abraham, senior vice president of sports for HBO. Abraham had been in charge of sports programming at HBO since 1978. He'd come out of a publicity job in the office of the commissioner of baseball. Unknown to Abraham, he was hired to disassemble a failing division. A few weeks after he arrived, HBO's senior executives voted 6–1 to drop sports programming. Michael Fuchs, the head of original programming, cast the one dissenting vote. Fuchs believed that Abraham should be given a chance to make the sports division work.

At that time, HBO was showing more than a hundred different sports, from bowling to Australian-rules football. Abraham quickly pared it down to one: boxing. For several years he played the same game as the broadcast networks—he televised numerous heavyweight title fights, thereby increasing the public's confusion over the real and true champion.

But Abraham brought more imagination to the job than did his counterparts at ABC, NBC, and CBS. He surmised that the networks were missing an opportunity by putting boxing in a time-slot backwater. Abraham looked at boxing like any other form of entertainment programming: stars with marquee value will sell. The problem was how to turn a boxer into a star.

Abraham started with presentation. He put the fights on Friday and Saturday mid-evening prime time. The announcers wore tuxedos. Large sums of money were spent on improving production values, from shooting a fight with six different cameras to generating boxing statistics and doing documentary-style prefight segments that tried to show the human side of every fighter. Abraham also convinced corporate parent Time Inc. to pay top dollar for the best boxing talent. "I looked for an emerging star, a single fighter, that could sell both the event and HBO," Abraham said.

Although Abraham televised several heavyweight title bouts in the early 1980s, the disorganized division never produced his star. The middleweights did. In 1980, he signed Marvin Hagler to a three-fight, $1 million deal. The networks scoffed at spending such a sum, but it paid off. Hagler ruled the middleweights for seven years. His fights on HBO averaged a 26 share in the Nielsen ratings, compared to a 19 share average for its second-run movies. HBO became identified as the cable station of the middleweight champion. Every other major middleweight, plus the top welterweights and lightweights of the early 1980s, ended up fighting on HBO.

The early 1980s were HBO's salad days. Its subscriber base went from four million in 1979 to fourteen and a half million in 1984. The number of local cable affiliates carrying HBO increased from three thousand to nearly seven. Granted, Abraham's sports programming was only one component of that success—but it contributed significantly to public awareness of HBO. By that point, Michael Fuchs had also become chairman of HBO, a job he got in part because of the success of Abraham's boxing. Not surprisingly, he presided as Abraham's principal benefactor within the corporate behemoth of Time Inc.

By 1985, however, growth in HBO's subscriber base had stalled at fifteen million. The number of affiliates began to decline. The issue was not a shrinking market. Hundreds of thousands of new homes around the country were being hooked up every month. HBO's problem was competition. As new cable stations, and new programming, were made available, the pie was getting divided up into smaller pieces.

HBO's programming mix had also become stale. Abraham's sports programming began to flag. Resting on his laurels, Hagler fought only once on HBO in 1985. Sugar Ray Leonard, the only threat to Hagler's dominance, was in retirement. The heavyweight picture worsened when Michael Spinks beat Larry Holmes. The showing of second-run movies lost appeal with the advent of the home VCR. People preferred to rent the movies they wanted to watch than pay HBO up to $15 per month for its choices. Many of the movies HBO produced also became monumental ratings flops.

Fortunately for HBO, Abraham's imagination and ambition were working overtime. He came upon an old idea that had taken on a new currency: "If we could find that one man, the person who could say, 'I can beat anyone in the world,' we would have the Big Story," Abraham recalled thinking. In other words, it was time for a tournament.

To anyone with knowledge of the history of the boxing business, tournaments were bad news. James Norris and Frankie Carbo had used their 1949 tournament to monopolize boxing under the I.B.C. King's fiasco on ABC underlined what had already been proven amply by Norris and Carbo: that tournaments were merely the means for a promoter to assert monopolistic control.

Abraham's tournament would be different, or so it seemed. The heavyweight division desperately needed to be unified again. It was something boxing, and the public, would benefit from. But that's as far as he could take the concept and keep it noble. In 1985, King ruled the heavyweight division. He had two of the three champions, and several of the leading contenders, under contract. No tournament was possible without him. The ultimate undisputed champion would almost certainly come under King's control. It was naïve of Abraham to think otherwise. Ambitious men are rarely naïve, although they do possess the unique ability for self-serving rationalization.

"We were all aware of what happened with the ABC U.S. Championships," one senior staffer at HBO Sports said. "You give a lot of money to a guy like King and he'll use it to tie up as many fighters as he can. But King controlled most of the heavyweights anyway. We knew he'd probably end up with the tournament champion. It was academic. Our concern was whether he'd pay the fighters what he owed them; if King would act fairly and justly, in the context of boxing."

There's reason to doubt that HBO was all that concerned with King's business ethics. Since 1979, almost all of King's heavyweights, and several of his other fighters in the lower weight classes, had fought on HBO: Holmes, Mike Weaver, Greg Page, Michael Dokes, Pinklon Thomas, and Tim Witherspoon. (HBO broadcast the 1982 Dokes-Weaver fight that was suspected by the FBI of being fixed.) For years King applied his shady practices right under Abraham's nose.

In their defense, HBO executives have claimed only to televise fights, not to regulate them. They know that an underworld exists in boxing and that King steps in and out of that place as if it were his own private bordello. But as the self-serving rationalization goes, that's the real world of boxing which, as Abraham has said many times, is "a strange prism for ethics." Not being able to change that world doesn't exclude him from profiting by it.

"Abraham's sole interest in doing business with King was to advance his career and the corporate objectives of HBO," one boxing promoter said. "He didn't give a shit what King did to the boxers, or anyone else. As long as King had plausible deniability on his side, which kept up the appearance of innocence, and if he did nothing overt to damage HBO's corporate image, Abraham stuck by him."

The same logic was applied to the idea for the Unification Series. That's how it seemed to HBO's and King's critics. "The Unification Series was like giving King a license to steal," the promoter added. "You got to understand what their relationship has been about. Abraham did business with King when all the other television guys were scared to. He helped King legitimize himself. Abraham saw that if he helped King, then King would return the favor by bringing him fights. It was pure horse-trading, or Abraham pimping for King, whichever way you look at it."

From that point of view, Abraham's heavyweight tournament was the ultimate trade. King was likely to win control over the fighter who could unify the division. In gratitude, he'd keep that fighter on HBO, and bring along as many others into the deal-making as he could. That might not create a monopoly in the heavyweight division à la Norris, Carbo, and the I.B.C., but it might come close.

\* \* \*

Seth Abraham, like Don King, has indulged in the game of auto-biographical illusion. "I was a Brooklyn street kid who learned about life the hard way," Abraham has said. "Street kid" is stretching it. He was born August 20, 1947, in Brooklyn, New York. Both of Abraham's parents worked as lawyers. He grew up an only child not far from Ebbets Field, home of the Brooklyn Dodgers. Watching the Dodgers was his passion, but the streets were not his life. Abraham completed grades seven, eight, and nine in two years. This enabled him to start college at the early age of fifteen. He earned a BA and an MA in journalism, then in 1969 worked as a stringer for the *New York Times's* Boston bureau. Abraham went on staff at Facts on File and later at *Ski* magazine. But he didn't want to report the news so much as be part of it. In 1971, he moved into a publicity job at the New York PR house Hill & Knowlton, then in 1975 jumped over to work for the Major League Baseball Promotional Corporation to create campaigns with national advertisers.

Physically, Abraham and King couldn't be any different. Abraham is five-foot-ten in thick-heeled shoes, and has a trim, compact, tennis-player's physique. His heart-shaped face is grounded by a bold, jutting jaw. His taste in clothes runs to the prissy: brightly colored suspenders, patterned ties, and textured sports jackets, often with a rose in the lapel and offset by a silk handkerchief in the chest pocket. His voice is crisp to the point of being strident. Conversation is a matter mostly of waiting his turn. "You get this feeling with Seth that the conversation is over when he's lost interest in it," said one boxing reporter who has interviewed him several times over the years. "He leans back with a self-satisfied expression that says, 'Well, I'm finished and so are you.'"

King and Abraham would at first seem strange deal-fellows: Falstaff meets *Pygmalion's* Henry Higgins. But there's much that they share. Foremost is a capacity to make a relationship that is based on mutual self-interest seem like an intimate personal bond. A cynic would say that they were merely conning each other in different ways but to equal, and offsetting, degrees.

A case in point is how both men described their first deal together. It was early 1979. According to Abraham, King was shopping a Holmes-Mike Weaver championship fight to ABC for $1 million. ABC wanted to pay only $750,000. Abraham called up and offered what his budget allowed: $125,000. King literally laughed in his face, but gave the fight to Abraham to spite ABC. "ABC could afford it." King said. "It was busting me. Anyway, I liked the way Seth talked." Added Abraham to the tale: "I was determined to get the deal."

As the relationship grew over the years—long meetings over sumptuous meals that stretched into the morning hours, fiery exchanges over deal points, the annual exchange of gifts because they share the same birthday—it began to take on the proportions of a mythic marriage. Said Abraham: "Fundamentally, I trust him. We have the same birthday, and Don's superstitious about those things. He thinks he can't screw me, that we have karma." Added King, with a touch of what must be the equivalent of boxing burlesque: "The friendship between us means more to me sometimes than the money."

Such a portrait has made for good copy in *Sports Illustrated*. An obsequiously flattering 1990 profile of Abraham set out the legend in all its glory—including the story about the Holmes-Weaver fight. (*Sports Illustrated*, as the story acknowledged, is owned by Time Inc., parent of HBO.) Conveniently left out of that story was the one detail that gets to the heart of their relationship. In early 1979, King was still the pariah of boxing to ABC and every other television network. As one former ABC executive explained: "After the U.S. Championships we looked long and hard at anything King brought to us. We wanted that fight but we didn't want to get deeply involved with King again. That's why HBO got the fight."

It was a union born of necessity. King needed an alternative television venue for his fights, and Abraham needed matches with marquee value in order to save his job. But mostly after the ABC tournament fiasco and the F.B.I. investigation, King was desperate for a public cleansing. By selling more than twenty-seven fights to HBO between 1979 and 1985, that's exactly what he got. "I'm one of Don's respectable allies," Abraham said.

The most legitimizing of acts came when King was indicted for tax evasion in December 1984. A new generation of programming executives at ABC had started to do fights with King again. King, with Abraham's help, had made a comeback. With the indictment, ABC and one other network immediately announced that they wouldn't deal with King while he was under indictment. Abraham was the only television executive to state publicly—for himself, for HBO, and indirectly for staid Time Inc. as well—that he believed King innocent until proven guilty. To prove it, Abraham signed a deal with King for a new fight. It was a risky move. King's conviction would have sullied Abraham's stature at HBO and perhaps brought down the wrath of Time Inc. The future shape of the heavyweight division might also have been vastly different.

But King was found innocent of the tax evasion charges, and another of Abraham's gambles paid off. That's when he decided to take his biggest gamble yet: to launch the HBO Heavyweight Unification Series. He first suggested the idea for the series to King in late October 1985. It obviously appealed to King. The only hitch was that he would have to settle his differences with Butch Lewis, the promoter of I.B.F. champion Michael Spinks and an archenemy even before King signed Greg Page away from Lewis. Abraham created the necessary incentive. HBO, through the generosity of parent Time Inc., would be prepared to spend up to $16 million on the tournament. For $16 million, King and Lewis were willing to become partners. They formed Dynamic Duo, Inc. to copromote the HBO series.

Even before the series began, Abraham's luck seemed to change for the worse. Both of King's so-called champions, plus some of his contenders, started to look rather shabby. Tim Witherspoon, King's most financially gouged fighter, defeated Tony Tubbs in January 17, 1986, for the W.B.A. title. His urine test revealed traces of marijuana. A rematch was mandated.

In the first fight of the series, on March 23, 1986, the aging and unpredictable Trevor Berbick captured the title from W.B.A. champion

Pinklon Thomas. In the second fight, on April 19, Michael Spinks defeated Larry Holmes—again—to retain his I.B.F. title. Meanwhile, on July 19, the questionable Witherspoon successfully defended against England's Frank Bruno.

To American audiences, it still looked like a three-legged potato race. Yes, everyone was going in the one direction this time, but who cared? It was the same old fighters they'd been watching slug it out for the last five years. The Nielsen ratings for the series began to plummet. Abraham had neglected to abide by the very principle that had made boxing on HBO such a success. He didn't have a star. There was no Big Story to tell. He needed Mike Tyson. "Tyson was the only one who could save Seth Abraham's ass," said one senior HBO sports staffer.

Fortunately for Abraham, with the three-fight deal signed the previous winter, he had Tyson on a separate and parallel track. By June, with only the first of those fights completed (even Tyson-Green got higher ratings than the HBO series bouts), Abraham feared that he would have unified the heavyweight title only to see the real heir to the line, Tyson, ultimately do battle on some venue other than HBO. The HBO champion vs. Mike Tyson would most certainly be a closed-circuit pay-per-view event.

Abraham tried to initiate serious negotiations with Jacobs and Cayton in late June. His interests were obvious. He needed Tyson to save the company's $16 million investment. But King took an opposite negotiating posture from Abraham. He contended that letting Tyson into the series amounted to career suicide. King said he feared that if Tyson won the series, Jacobs and Cayton wouldn't give him any options on Tyson's future fights. For the first time in a dozen years, he'd be without a heavyweight champion. "Jacobs told me that King had made it clear in so many words that he didn't want Tyson in the HBO series," said one HBO sports insider.

There's reason to speculate, however, that Abraham and King's conflicting positions were a contrivance. In fact, they both desperately wanted to bring Tyson into the HBO series. And they could only do that together. Abraham with his money, and King with control over two of the three heavyweight champions.

The problem was that Jacobs and Cayton were likely to make similar amounts of money fighting Gerry Cooney, and then Holmes, outside the series. Going that route, they also didn't need, for the time being at least, King's dubious champions. More important, Jacobs and Cayton had made it clear since the beginning of Tyson's career that they didn't want to be committed on a long-term basis to any one promoter, and certainly not to one who practiced the business of boxing like King.

Abraham and King, therefore, tried to turn a liability into an asset: King pretended to stand in the way of Tyson being able to capture all three heavyweight titles, and Abraham posed as the mediator, the voice of reason, the one person who could persuade King to relent, and who could act as a force of respectability to curb King's appetite for subterfuge. He also reminded Jacobs and Cayton that the HBO series was their one and only chance to get all three titles in a single campaign.

Whether Abraham and King actually overtly worked that strategy out together, or after six years of doing business together surmised independently how to best play their respective parts in concert, the result was still the same. The message got through. "Seth Abraham acknowledged to us Don's concerns about losing control of the division if Tyson entered the series," Cayton admitted. "He posed as the mediator between us."

But the real proof of their complicity was an admission by Abraham several years later implying that King's position had been purposely misrepresented: "Don always wanted Tyson in the series. It meant that he could get close to Jimmy and Bill, who were managers only. They didn't have a promoter yet, and Don felt this was his only chance to become Tyson's primary promoter," Abraham revealed.

Watching the Abraham-King act with bemusement was Butch Lewis, the promoter of Michael Spinks. He was aware that when push came to shove, both he and Spinks were of secondary importance to the interests of Abraham and King. "Around those two guys, you sleep with one eye open," said Lewis.

Ronald ("Butch") Lewis came out of a prosperous middle-class black family that lived near Philadelphia. After high school he worked at his father's used-car business, and within a few years rose to star salesman. His father was one of the original investors in the syndicate that developed Joe Frazier. Lewis befriended Frazier and traveled in his entourage as a hanger-on through the late 1960s and early 1970s.

Lewis decided to try his hand at promoting a fight—no ordinary match, but one with Muhammad Ali. He pursued Ali and his manager, Herbert Muhammad, for two years, trying to get their signatures on a deal. They didn't want to get involved with an inexperienced upstart. When he finally managed to secure a meeting with Muhammad, King intervened. He didn't want the competition. Undaunted, Lewis eventually made his deal: Ali–Richard Dunn in Munich, May 25, 1976.

Bob Arum then hired Lewis as a vice president of his promoting outfit, Top Rank. Arum at the time was handling heavyweight contender Leon Spinks. Lewis was assigned to be Spink's full-time handler. In 1978, the year Spinks won and lost the heavyweight title, Lewis left Top Rank to promote on his own. His first fighter was Michael Spinks, the younger brother of Leon.

The older Spinks didn't have much interest in his professional and personal responsibilities. Michael was the exact opposite. He trained diligently, fought hard in every bout, and most of all remained loyal to Lewis despite offers from other promoters. Spinks also stuck with his career despite personal tragedy. In 1983, his common-law wife and mother of their baby daughter died in a car accident. Spinks got the news when his sister appeared in his dressing room with the baby in her arms hours before a fight. He took the baby, turned his back, and cried. "Michael is a special human being," said Lewis.

Spinks was a puzzling type of fighter. Throughout the early 1980s, he dominated the light heavyweight division with a boxing style that was effective yet highly unorthodox. There was nothing fluid in his motions. He was well over six feet tall, and gangly, but oddly stiff in his movements. He could burst at an opponent with a series of quick punches coming from all angles, or play a run-and-gun game where he'd jerkily elude, then suddenly stop and shoot out a right hand. Spinks was unpredictable, off-balance, and seemingly out of control, but he kept winning. He put his success down to "the Spinks Jinx."

When Spinks beat Larry Holmes to capture the I.B.F. title in September, 1985, a whole new world opened up. Lewis scanned the competition at the W.B.A. and W.B.C. and determined that his fighter was as good as, or better than, all of them. He put aside his disdain for King and entered Spinks into the HBO Unification Series. "Michael beat Larry Holmes!" said Lewis. "None of the other guys in the series did. We had a shot at taking it all."

Lewis's optimism was well founded. Since 1981, Holmes had beaten Trevor Berbick, Tim Witherspoon, and James "Bonecrusher" Smith— all entrants in the HBO series—plus many other so-called contenders still hanging around: Renaldo Snipes, David Bey, Carl Williams, and the lone white fighter, Gerry Cooney. By beating Holmes the first time,

Spinks had a shot at unifying the title. When he beat him again in April 1986, his chances seemed even stronger. Now, five months after the contract had been signed, Abraham, whose sole interest was in improving HBO's ratings, wanted to change the deal by bringing Tyson into the series. Suddenly, Spinks's title hopes looked much dimmer.

In July, Jacobs and Cayton failed to make a deal to fight Gerry Cooney on closed-circuit pay-per-view. Dennis Rappaport, Cooney's promoter, turned down their demand to split the revenues on a fifty-fifty basis. Rappaport believed, and perhaps rightly so, that his fighter was a greater audience draw than Tyson. Cooney may never have been a champion, and was long past his prime, but people would be primarily interested in seeing a once-competent white fighter lose to the next great black champion. In other words, it was more Cooney's demise than Tyson's victory that would sell the fight. Moveover, it was likely to be Cooney's last major payday; Tyson could go on to many more big-money fights. By insisting on the fifty-fifty split, Rappaport maintained, Jacobs and Cayton were simply being greedy.

Jacobs and Cayton then tried to do a deal outside the HBO series with Larry Holmes. But Holmes was in much the same position as Cooney. The younger, stronger, and quicker Tyson would probably end his career. Every time they talked with Holmes, his asking price rose. First he wanted $1.5 million, then $1.7 million, then $1.9 million. Finally, promoter Bob Arum intervened. He convinced Holmes to fight Tyson that summer in Las Vegas for $2.2 million.

Jacobs and Cayton had never forgiven Arum for refusing to get them more dates on his weekly ESPN show to help build up Tyson's early career. They argued that Holmes didn't deserve to get $2.2 million of the revenue pie, but what really irked them was that Arum would be involved in the promotion.

As the alternatives outside the HBO series disappeared, Abraham pushed his agenda. King supposedly remained the obstacle to Tyson's entry. Abraham the mediator told Jacobs and Cayton that King could be placated with money. In turn, he would give them assurances that King would be kept at arm's length from Tyson. "Jimmy and Bill eventually came to believe that Don wouldn't dare try and screw them with Seth around," said an executive at one Las Vegas hotel-casino that staged several Tyson fights.

The basics of the deal were worked out in an August 14 meeting. Tyson would get $5.5 million for three title fights, the first being against W.B.C. champion Trevor Berbick. King and Lewis got the entire multimillion-dollar site fees from the Las Vegas Hilton, plus some additional monies from HBO.

The last sticking point were the options on Tyson's future fights when, and if, he won the series. Abraham came up with a compromise to satisfy Jacobs and Cayton. He devised wording that made it seem as if HBO was getting the options, and not King. He also limited the number of options to two fights. "We gave them to HBO, through Don King," said Cayton. "HBO was entitled to the options because it was paying most of the money. We never intended King or Lewis to have direct control over these fights."

On August 20, Abraham presented a memorandum of agreement for all parties to sign. At the last minute, Lewis almost walked out of the meeting, but then reluctantly signed. It wouldn't be his last word on the subject.

*       *       *

Tyson's impact on the HBO series was felt almost instantly. His first fight was on the undercard of the Spinks-Steffen Tangstad bout on September 6. Several weeks before the bout, the Las Vegas Hilton had sold only $180,000 worth of tickets. When Tyson was added to the evening's entertainment, the Hilton sold out in two hours, to the tune of $1.1 million.

Alfonzo ("The Troubleshooter") Ratliff was thirty years old, and had a record of twenty-one wins and three losses, which earned him a number twenty ranking by the W.B.C. At 201 pounds, he was a beefed-up cruiserweight with little or no chance against the now 221-pound Tyson. Ratliff fought to survive. His entire strategy seemed to be jab and run. Tyson waited for the right moment to catch him with a few good punches, which he did midway through the second round, ending the fight.

The victory confirmed the hype about Tyson. Still, there were concerns about whether he could handle the emotional pressures of the HBO series. On the first day of training for the Ratliff fight in Las Vegas, Tyson almost gave in to his deepest fears. When Tyson arrived at Johnny Tocco's Gym, he told trainer Kevin Rooney that he wanted to go home. Rooney called assistant manager Steve Lott.

"He said, 'I don't like it here, I want to go home,'" Lott remembered. "Jim was in New York. He would have been the one to handle things like this. I did what Jim would have done. I told Mike that it was an honor for him to be here, not a sentence. I went through all of his watershed fights, each test he'd gone through in the ring, and in every case I showed to Mike that he'd done well. Mike had suffered a momentary sense of fear that he'd fail."

By mid-September, Jacobs and Cayton finally embraced a *nom de pug* for Tyson. It was suggested by the publicity people at the Las Vegas Hilton: "Iron Mike Tyson." A poster was being done up featuring an illustration of Tyson made to look robotlike, with his face, head, neck, and shoulders a cluster of angled chunks of solid metal colored a dark blue-black hue. It was the first visual realization of Tyson's persona as the Ring Destroyer.

After the Ratliff fight, Jacobs and Cayton arranged a series of television appearances as a buildup to Tyson's title fight against Trevor Berbick on November 22. He was coached to affect an earnest but also humble, deserving, and emotionally dispassionate attitude about the bit of history that was soon to be made. They wanted to keep reminding people that inside the robot was a human being, yet one able to control his emotions; Tyson as the consummate professional. The portrait wasn't always coherent, but that didn't seem to matter in the climate of the times. The Tyson about to fulfill his destiny as laid out in the fable of Cus and the Kid remained a darling of popular culture.

When asked on "The George Michael Sports Machine," a syndicated sports television show, if he might "burn out" before taking the title, Tyson said: "There's no way you're going to burn out when you love what you're doing. The only way people get burned out is because of loss of interest. It's like someone loving sex: you never get burnt out; you want to do it all the time."

On "CBS This Morning" with Faith Daniels, he was made out to be the "Great Hope" of heavyweight boxing, the young man who would "put the glamour back into the sport." When asked if that put pressure on him, Tyson responded, "When I first started boxing it did, but now I'm just going to do my job, to do my best." An October 6 appearance on comedian David Brenner's late-night talk show had Tyson claiming to "love dearly" his old haunt, Brownsville. With Joan Rivers on November 5, he admitted that as a boy he was beaten up constantly. "It's just that I was so frightened at that particular time," he told Rivers. She asked why he didn't have a large entourage. "I only have three people in my entourage. Basically, I'm just a loner," he explained. "I prefer to be by myself at all times and I'm not comfortable around a great deal of people. I feel, like, when you need all those people you're not particularly sure of yourself. I'm a hundred percent confident of myself and I don't need anyone."

Rivers wondered whether Tyson tried to psych out his opponents in the ring. His repetitive answer struck the pose of the ultimate D'Amato-Jacobs-style professional: "I'm very professional and confident and to get angry, that's emotion, and when you're a professional you have to be emotionless and have no emotions at all, because that's a sign of nonprofessionalism and everything's business and when it's business you have no friends, no feelings, and everything's number one."

Television, of course, was the preferred medium for Jacobs and Cayton when they had an innocuous message to get out about Tyson. With few exceptions, they kept him away from the newspaper press, especially the New York boxing reporters. Phil Berger of the *New York Times* was one of the main exceptions. Berger was an invitee at the "Bootlicker's Ball," the private dinner Jacobs had held the previous March to win over the press after Tyson's comment about driving Jesse Ferguson's nose bone into his brain.

In Berger's version, Jacobs and Cayton were not so much Tyson's professional counterparts outside the ring as, quoting Tyson, just "real good friends." Jacobs portrayed himself as an older-brother figure, Tyson's one true intimate. "When Mike comes over for dinner, then he's a kid who talks about Dwight Gooden, girls, and music," Jacobs told the *Times*. Jacobs then talked about buying Tyson a pigeon coop, getting him subscriptions to bird-raising magazines, plus an apartment in Albany, and advising Tyson on his social responsibilities as a rising contender. The idea was to enforce the concept of Tyson as still the growing boy of Cus and the Kid, the orphan whom Jacobs had taken under his mentor's wing.

*Newsday*'s Wally Matthews—one of the reporters they often snubbed—got down to the more relevant issues. In a story published the day before the Berbick fight, Matthews said that what had changed most about Tyson in the past year was not his fighting abilities but "the packaging of the man and the perpetuating of the myth." He tried to get down to the real Tyson, whoever that was. He reminded readers of Tyson's amateur losses, then recounted a story Tyson once told about getting beat up by two girls when he was a boy. "They kept taking my punches, and there was nothing I could do. Then one of them bit me, and I panicked," Tyson said. That, Matthews speculated, was a Tyson that still lived, only now because of all the hype and the mythmaking, "we just see him differently."

\*   \*   \*

Jacobs and Cayton may have wanted to be portrayed as friends to the future champion, but their primary interest was always the business that had to be done. Before Tyson left for Las Vegas to begin training for Berbick, Jacobs secured his signature on a new management contract, although the first, signed in November 1984, still had two years left. Jacobs wanted another four years, which was the standard term. It was better, after all, to have four years of the new heavyweight champion's services than two. It was a perfectly legal means by which to acquire six-year control over a fighter. Tyson signed.

The renewal was also a hedge against the risks of doing extended business with Don King. Now that they were in the HBO series, Jacobs and Cayton were keeping a close eye on King. The first warning sign had appeared with the Tyson-Green fight the previous May. The agreement with HBO and King called for Green to get paid $50,000. The day before the fight, however, Carl and Don King summoned Green to their East Side offices and told him he would accept $30,000 or not fight at all. In the dressing room before the fight, Green threatened to pull out. In marched New York State Athletic Commission Chairman José Torres. "If you don't fight," Torres said sternly, "I'll suspend you and you'll never fight in this country again." Green fought, and didn't even end up with the full $30,000. The Kings cut it down to $7,500, a fact that surfaced when Green later sued the Kings.

Jacobs didn't want such problems to arise with Berbick. Nothing could be allowed to sully Tyson's first title victory. He didn't have to worry. King knew what was at stake. According to Marc Risman, Berbick's attorney, King was a model of propriety. "If Trevor Berbick had been fighting anyone other than Tyson, he would have given him the smallest possible purse, and then cut it with all his tricks. But because Mike Tyson was involved, and King wanted to be his promoter, he was on his best behavior. He was uncharacteristically fair and open."

Before Tyson formally entered the series, Berbick was supposed to get $750,000 for the November date. That was half of Tyson's purse of $1.5 million. When Tyson's entry looked certain, Berbick and Risman tried to negotiate a deal to fight Gerry Cooney outside the HBO series. By early September, they had secured a verbal guarantee of $3 million. King got wind of the effort and upped Berbick's purse to $1.6 million. Berbick's negotiator, Lucien Chen, managed in the course of a single afternoon to work King up to $2.1 million (of which Carl King, Berbick's manager got the standard 33⅓ percent—not his usual 50 percent). King's largess was made possible by Abraham. He was given carte blanche to make sure Berbick stayed in the series.

Berbick was persuaded by Chen, and Risman, not to risk litigation with King and HBO by pulling out of the series. Just to make sure this new and improved King was not a mirage, Berbick pleaded with Abraham to make sure his purse wouldn't be unfairly cut. As it turned out, it wasn't.

Trevor Berbick had grown up in Port Antonio, Jamaica, free, so he often said, to live a pastoral life and to praise the Lord. He started boxing at the age of twenty-three, but despite ten years of experience against all levels of competition (he beat an aging Muhammad Ali in 1981 and a young, tough Greg Page in 1982), Berbick didn't seem to have learned much in the ring. His skills were at best rudimentary. But he was unpredictable, too, a man few of the experts picked to beat Pinklon Thomas in the first round of the series to become W.B.C. champion. That, perhaps, is why the oddsmakers made him only a 3-to-1 underdog. Berbick's lazy jab and lumbering style might find a way to beat the unbeatable Tyson.

Berbick's chances were in fact slim. He was simply too slow to defend himself effectively or hit the constantly moving target that Tyson was likely to be. Tyson figured that out six weeks prior to the fight. He went to Jacobs's office in New York the day before leaving for training camp in Las Vegas. Jacobs gave Tyson a videotape of Berbick's fight against Thomas. Steve Lott, who was with Tyson, remembered his reaction: "I left him alone to study the tape. A few minutes later, I checked back and he was staring at the screen without blinking. Then he nodded to himself as if he'd seen something important. Mike asked Jimmy, 'Was that in slow motion?'"

Tyson trained for six weeks without incident. The day of the fight, while driving to the indoor arena at the Las Vegas Hilton, Lott wanted to make sure Tyson had kept Berbick in perspective. "Mike, what do you think Cus would have said about Berbick?" he asked, breaking the silent tension of the drive. As Tyson pondered the answer it was as if everything had suddenly come into focus. "This guy's a tomato can!" he blurted.

Berbick didn't intend to fight like a tomato can, an old boxing term for someone big and slow and mentally thick. Berbick had a plan: that is, his trainer, Angelo Dundee, had one. Dundee had made his career training Muhammad Ali for several years, and then middleweight champion Sugar Ray Leonard. He opined that there was only one way to fight Tyson: don't act like you're afraid of his punches. By moving away from Tyson, Dundee argued, a fighter only gave him more room to slug. He told Berbick to crowd Tyson with jabs, then try and back him up. "The great Angelo Dundee!" quipped Tyson cornerman Matt Baranski. "He didn't realize that Mike had trouble chasing guys. It got him frustrated. So coming in at Mike just got Berbick knocked out."

At first Berbick followed Dundee's instructions. His jab hung out like a large salami, and Tyson hooked to the left and right of it with impunity. It took thirty seconds or so for him to hit Berbick's head flush on. Tyson landed a sequence of four hooks that sent Berbick down. He got up to complete the round, barely.

Tyson came out in the second round eager to finish the fight. He was all offense. Berbick appeared to have forgotten how to punch and how to protect himself. Tyson kept landing to the body and head. Standing close inside, he connected with a short, chopping left hook that struck just above Berbick's right eye. He froze in place as if time had suddenly stopped, then fell straight back and down. He tried to get up again, but had lost all sense of balance. Berbick careered around the canvas, fell again, got up, then tumbled down a third time. When he rose, the referee called the fight over.

Tyson went over to his corner and pointed at Jacobs as he started to climb into the ring. It was a gesture that said, "See, I told you he was slow." Then he kissed Jacobs quickly, full on the mouth. By that time, two dozen other people had jumped into the ring, including José Torres, who, disregarding all appearances of a conflict of interest, congratulated Tyson repeatedly. King's gesture came later that night. He tried to give Tyson a $50,000 gold Rolex watch. When Jacobs found out, he tersely ordered Tyson to return it.

In the postfight interviews, Tyson gushed on the subject of becoming, at twenty, the youngest heavyweight champion ever. "This is the moment I waited for all my life since I started boxing," he said, adding

later, "My record will last for immortality" and "I want to live forever."
He paid homage to the fable. "I'd like to dedicate my fight to my great
guardian Cus D'Amato. I'm sure he's up there and he's looking down
and he's talking to all the great fighters and he's saying his boy did
it. . . . Everything he said would happen, happened."

After the fight, Jacobs decided to fulfill some of his promises to
D'Amato—sort of. In the accounting documents for the fight, $10,000
was listed as having been given to Camille Ewald. The money came
from the gross purse—in other words, from his, Cayton's, and Tyson's
end. D'Amato had asked for Ewald to be taken care of out of the
manager's end only. Another $5,000 went to Tyson's old Youth Division
social worker, Ernestine Coleman. Presumably, that was a gesture of
thanks for having let Tyson stay with D'Amato despite his school
problems. But it also had the appearance of a payment for the little lie
she told Tyson when his mother died about having to go back to Catskill
or face Tryon again.

A few days after the fight, Jacobs contacted Bobby Stewart, the Tryon
supervisor who had introduced Tyson to boxing and to D'Amato. Jacobs
told Stewart that D'Amato wanted him to be "taken care of" when Tyson
won the title. Stewart drove down to New York with his wife to Jacobs's
office. He was given a check for $10,000. "Jacobs told me not to say
anything about it to anyone," recalled Stewart. "I didn't, and then
someone in the Tyson camp said Cus told them to pay me $100,000.
That's why Jacobs wanted me to shut up about it."

After payments to Rooney and to the manager, Tyson netted
$831,958. He spent several thousand dollars to have his mother's grave
removed from Potter's Field and placed in a proper cemetery with a
headstone. He didn't tell anyone where that was.

# PART TWO

# The Champion Betrayed

# Chapter Eight

The Tyson camp celebrated Christmas of 1986 as it had every other in years past. No one exchanged gifts or cards. Tyson went up to Catskill to have Christmas dinner with surrogate mother Camille Ewald. Jacobs, as he did every year, returned home alone to Los Angeles to visit his mother. His wife, Loraine, joined her relatives in Florida.

Before boarding the plane for Los Angeles, Jacobs called back to the office for messages. His sister, Dorothy Zeil, had called with news that their mother, in a drugged state, had fallen and broken her hip. She needed an operation. When Jacobs arrived at the hospital that night, Zeil was at her bedside. Four days later, on Christmas Eve, doctors operated. It appeared a success. Just as she and Jacobs were about to leave the hospital for dinner, Zeil heard a "code blue" over the paging system. A trained nurse, she knew that meant someone in post-op recovery was in trouble. She called the recovery room. Their mother, eighty-four years old, a drug abuser for decades, had died.

"Jimmy did something that night which at the time was perfectly normal for him, and yet it wasn't until after he died that I realized why he did it." Zeil put another cigarette in her mouth. Her voice was low,

thin, the lungs barely generating a sound. "He pretended that he didn't
know how to make any arrangements. He said to the doctor, 'Who do I
call? What do I do?' and I immediately spoke up, 'I know who to call.'
And I glared at him because I did this alone with our father. He
wouldn't even come to the funeral. Then Jimmy said to the doctor,
'Dorothy knows what to do.'"

Zeil didn't expect her brother to face the emotionally difficult task of
burying their mother. It fit into a long pattern of denial: the refusal to
attend his father's funeral; not dealing with his mother's irrational spite
for his sister; not recognizing, let alone helping to get treatment for, his
mother's drug addiction. He ignored Zeil's pleas to do something more
than just send money every time the Demerol sent their mother reeling
to the floor. By inventing a past of enormous wealth, he denied that
those family problems ever existed. And on the day his mother died, he
couldn't grapple with the toughest issue of all: the extent to which,
because of his denial, he may have been partially responsible.

Zeil knew that Jimmy Jacobs well. She assumed the emotional
burdens in their family that he would not. She resented him for it, as
she did every time he railroaded someone to get what he wanted. But
she loved him, too. It was that love which prevented Zeil from ever
suspecting that Jacobs could also be devious with her emotions. That
she never thought possible.

"That was the first time in my entire life when Jimmy admitted that I
knew how to handle something. I'm the older sister, but he always acted
like the big brother, and I should always ask, 'Jimmy, may I this or
should I that?' I realize now that he may not have wanted to make the
arrangements but he knew how. He did it with Cus D'Amato. It took
me a year to realize that he just wanted to make sure I knew what to do
and watch me do it."

Zeil paused to collect herself. "He knew at the moment of our
mother's death that I'd have some role in doing it again with him soon.
Our mother died and Jimmy decided, after thirty-five years, to get close
to me again. He spent the whole year of 1987 taking time to see me,
calling me every week like he called Mother, inviting me and my
children to Mike's fights, doing things for me that he hadn't done in
years."

Her eyes welled up with tears again, the voice rising with difficulty
into a strained shrillness. "I never understood why, what it all really

meant, until the day he died. I never knew he had leukemia. I never knew that he was dying. I believed he wanted to use the time as a chance for us to be brother and sister again for the first time since we were kids. But the Jimmy that was devoted to power, a man I never knew until he was dead, the Jimmy that could hurt people, was also setting me up for the part I had to play to make it seem to Mike Tyson and the whole world like his death was a sudden shock. Everything to him, in the end, had to do with business."

For seven years, Jacobs lived with the knowledge that chronic lymphoid leukemia could at any time kill him. His existential posture was to compete with death as if it were a handball opponent. Moreover, he wanted to deny the angst of the inevitable. But with his mother's death, Jacobs gave in to his flawed mortality. A small, whispering voice in the core of his being said that the struggle to live was coming to an end. It was the voice of fear. As D'Amato had demonstrated in his own lifetime, there are some fears that just cannot be controlled.

By all appearances, the indomitable Jimmy Jacobs looked as if he would live forever. As manager of Iron Mike Tyson, it seemed certain that he, and Cayton, would probably retain control of the heavyweight division for a decade or more. No one would have suspected that Jacobs harbored deep fears, the biggest being that he would die before his mother. He revealed that fear to only one person, childhood friend Nick Beck. "When Jimmy came home for Christmas in 1985, he told me that he had leukemia and that he could die within a few years," Beck recalled. "When that happened, he asked me to take care of his mother. He also insisted that I not tell anyone that he had leukemia."

In practical terms, Jacobs wasn't there for his mother. What he really may have feared was that she wouldn't be there for him. Without his mother, Jacob's beloved "Doll," at the other end of the phone, life may not have seemed worth fighting for anymore.

Yet to Jacobs, giving in didn't mean giving up. That was the crowning paradox of his life. He knew on one level that the battle with leukemia was probably lost, but on another he wasn't quite prepared to stop denying and to relinquish control. Quite the opposite. He would seek to control his life, and everyone in it, even more. In fact, he would overcompensate for his flawed mortality; he would connive and manipulate with greater intensity. Jacobs had always decided things for the people in his life. Now he had to decide on how each person would fit into his plans for death. Zeil, Cayton, indeed everyone in his life, would play a role—and that included Tyson.

*    *    *

Whether it was the day his mother died, or a day, week, or month later, at some point in early 1987 Jacobs devised a secret agenda. First, he wanted to make sure that upon his death Bill Cayton would become manager. It was not that he felt any great friendship or obligation to Cayton. Rather, he deemed him the man most capable of running Tyson's business affairs. Second, Cayton was the only person in boxing whom Jacobs trusted enough and could rely on to make sure his wife, Loraine, inherited his share of Tyson's ring earnings. He couldn't, after all, leave any portion of the income from licensing of his fight film collection to her. The films belonged to Big Fights Inc., an entity owned wholly by Cayton. Jacobs could only leave what he had saved or invested, and that paled in comparison to what Tyson stood to earn in the coming years. Only Cayton could make sure Loraine got a share.

The utmost secrecy was required to achieve those goals. He was too obsessed with control, with deciding for others, to have it be otherwise. More important, there was an intrinsic defect in his contractual relationship with Tyson. By revealing his plans for succession, Jacobs risked exposing that defect and ruining everything.

The New York State Athletic Commission's Rule 206.3 is subtitled "Filing of contract between managers and boxers." It states, "A boxer is permitted to have one manager only. . . . " The rule contains a simple logic. Since the early days of prizefighting, boxers have always been susceptible to the threats or illicit promises of others. If only one person is officially empowered to negotiate and sign for a bout on a boxer's behalf, and thus claim a share of his purse, there is less chance of chicanery. It's not an airtight measure, but it helps.

Despite their efforts to tell everyone at every opportunity that they were co-managers, only Jacobs held the status of manager. That in itself didn't pose a problem. The difficulties began when Jacobs died. No standard commission contract existed to engineer the transition of managership to Cayton. By the commission's rules, upon Jacobs's death Tyson would be without a manager; he would become a free agent able to sign with whomever he chose. Cayton didn't even have a New York State manager's license.

Aware of his partner's leukemia, Cayton tried early on in their business plan to prepare for the inevitable. The Reel Sports contract of September 1984 appeared merely to appoint Cayton as a personal manager to solicit, negotiate, and profit from Tyson's nonboxing activities. But clause five went one step further. It empowered Cayton to "designate a boxing manager(s) for Tyson with his consent, which shall not be unreasonably withheld." The point was repeated in a different context later in the same paragraph: "If JACOBS ceases to be a boxing manager. . ." then Tyson "shall enter into a standard boxing manager's contract(s) with another manager (designated by REEL SPORTS, with TYSON'S consent, which shall not be unreasonably withheld)." Cayton, to be sure, would appoint himself Tyson's new manager.

Jacobs knew that the Reel Sports contract wouldn't quite do it. In the wider business world, and in the general law of contracts, it was undoubtedly an effective legal device. Still, there was some question whether the Athletic Commission would allow the agreement to overrule its own regulations permitting Tyson to become a free agent. Moreover, in boxing, contracts sometimes matter less than personal relationships. The ties that kept Tyson with Jacobs were primarily emotional. No such bond existed between him and Cayton. Given their vastly different personalities and interests, none was likely to form. The Reel Sports contract couldn't, therefore, create a bond where none was likely to ever exist. And if Tyson didn't immediately grasp that, Don King certainly would. Once the door to Tyson's free agency opened up, King would barge through to try and claim the champion for himself.

Free agency, then, remained Jacobs's biggest problem. There was one other obvious way to deal with it, though it was the least likely option for Jacobs, given his will to control. He could present Tyson with a new personal services contract similar to Reel Sports. In the event of his dismissal or death, it would commit Tyson to Cayton. In other words, Tyson would willingly give up his right to free agency.

Jacobs may have insisted on full disclosure from others with whom he signed contracts, but no way was he prepared to place that obligation on himself when it came to Tyson. For such a contract raised a question that Jacobs didn't want to answer: Given that their personal relationship precluded Tyson from firing his mentor-manager, did Jacobs plan to die anytime soon?

Having never told Tyson about his leukemia, Jacobs wasn't about to reveal his subjective, and irrational, prognosis on survival. So much work had to be done to get Tyson through the remainder of the HBO series. He had two more heavyweight titles to capture before unifying the division. Nothing could distract Tyson from fulfilling the business plan.

How much Cayton should know, and when he should know it, were among the imponderables haunting Jacobs. Who else he would involve in the succession plan, when and how much he'd reveal of the ultimate goal, he wasn't yet sure. He didn't know how fast the leukemia would advance into the fatal stages. He didn't know if he would be well enough in six, eight, or twelve months to conduct important business. What if Cayton, with his heart condition, died first? Jacobs would have to find someone else to take over. He had to take it step by step and keep focused on the ultimate end: avoiding free agency for Tyson, making Cayton manager, getting Loraine his share of Tyson's future purses.

# Chapter Nine

With Tyson as heavyweight champion, Jacobs and Cayton could no longer maintain his public image within the simplistic terms of Cus and the Kid. As narrative, the fable was a useful marketing device in bringing initial interest and attention to the aspirations of the ghetto man-child. But Tyson had fulfilled his promise to D'Amato. Jacobs and Cayton now had to go beyond the fable, add new elements to the narrative, inaugurate the Tyson Era. That required delivering him into the hearts and minds of mass-market America and then the world. A whole new campaign was needed.

Jacobs contacted John Martin, the president of Ohlmeyer Communications, a multimedia communications company based in New York. Jacobs wanted Ohlmeyer to assist in the broader marketing of Tyson. Jay Rosenstein, an Ohlmeyer vice president, took up the task. "Since late 1986, they were getting besieged with offers," said Rosenstein, who fielded the offers and made recommendations. "There were cartoon books, T-shirts, pajamas, and movie deals. The list was endless. We were looking for quality."

Rosenstein advised that Tyson's first commercial should be for Signet Bank, based in North Carolina. "We wanted Mike to get a feel for what doing a commercial was like," said Rosenstein. "It was a good laboratory vehicle, and a commercial that aired in only a regional market in case it didn't come off that well."

The commercial aired in late February. The concept required certain highly accomplished people to speak directly into the camera and reveal what drove them to excellence. There was no set script, but several hours were spent in coaching until the right message, the one that sold the bank, was evoked. After each monologue a tag line came up on the screen. Actress Tess Harper got "Taking pride in what you do." For Nadja Salerno-Sonnenberg, a concert violinist: "Hard Work. Patience."

Tyson's monologue played to classic Hemingwayesque macho values (for the male market), yet with a sensitivity and insight (for the female) that tried to put the violence of both the boxer and the sport in a more acceptable light. Such cross-gender marketing was considered important with Tyson. HBO had discovered that 20 percent of the audience watching Tyson's fights was female. "When I started fighting," said Tyson softly, reflectively, in the commercial, "I started boxing, and I loved my first fight. I loved it. I loved the idea of competition. I loved the challenge. I was looking forward to a great challenge from another great individual and I liked these two great figures to clash, and then you're the best." Even for a coached utterance, it was simple and sincere, certainly a more subtle revelation of inner drives than most boxers with Tyson's background could have mustered. The producers of the commercial then chose a tag line that ignored this exploration of motive. It reduced Tyson from a reflective to a robotic being: "Action. Not words. That's how you make a name for yourself."

As a fight historian, Jacobs respected Muhammad Ali's abilities in the ring, especially the quality of character that enabled him to win against tremendous odds. But as a fight manager, Jacobs disapproved of Ali's public antics. It made him far too difficult to control. Still, there was one aspect of the Ali experience that Jacobs wanted to duplicate. Ali had the kind of larger-than-life personality that by itself generated considerable publicity. He was also interpreted for the mainstream American audience by a generation of writers eager to define Ali's larger social significance. As author Gary Wills noted in a November 30, 1975, article for the *New York Review of Books*, by the end of the 1960s, "Ali was the intellectual's catnip."

Jacobs knew that author Joyce Carol Oates was about to publish a nonfiction book called *On Boxing*, a personal meditation on the sport. He invited her to profile Tyson and run the piece to promote the book. Oates sold the assignment to *Life* magazine. It appeared in the March 1987 issue. The title, "Kid Dynamite," was old. The subtitle, "Mike Tyson Is the Most Exciting Heavyweight Fighter Since Muhammad Ali," took the hype to levels Jacobs relished.

Oates began by parroting the Cus and the Kid fable, then wandered into the darker reaches of what Tyson seemed to signify. Oates called Ali, when he was Cassius Clay, "Establishment approved," to set up the contrast with Tyson as "the outsider, the psychic outlaw, the young black contender hungry for all that white America can give." That was a bit romantic, but it did get through the hype. She went further, noting that Tyson was "trained, managed, and surrounded by white men." The implication was that somehow he was out of place and that he would one day realize it and perhaps seek out the company of people with his background. It was an astute and prescient observation. She tried it out on Jacobs and was met with a terse reply: "I doubt that Mike thinks in those terms."

Oates let the subject drop. At one point she depicted Tyson as "happy in the ring," which was difficult to reconcile with the rage and viciousness he could unleash on an opponent. She then contradicted that happy portrayal in her final thoughts. Oates sensed something deeply disquieting in Tyson, an unresolved tension. As she watched him defeat Berbick, she brooded: "The triumphant boxer is Satan transmogrified as Christ... he has become the latest in a particular lineage of athletic heroes—a bearer of inchoate, indescribable emotion—a savior, of sorts, covered in sweat and ready for war. But then, most saviors, sacred or secular, are qualified by a thoughtful 'of sorts.' In any case, it's Tyson's turn. A terrible beauty is born."

\* \* \*

The "terrible beauty" met James ("Bonecrusher") Smith on March 7 in Las Vegas for the W.B.A. version of the heavyweight crown. A billboard across the street from the Hilton displayed a bust of Tyson that looked as if it had been shaped out of hardened steel. The copy beneath read: "Your grandfather wished he'd seen Dempsey. Your father wished he'd seen Marciano. Don't you miss Iron Mike Tyson, March 7, at the Las Vegas Hilton."

The boxing press, and HBO, billed it as Tyson's first real test. The simple facts were being ignored. True, Smith had been knocked down only once in his career. But he had serious shortcomings: a late start in the sport, advanced age (thirty-three) for a boxer, and a spotty record. There were also indications that the hype about Tyson's inevitable rise had intimidated him. As Smith said at a prefight press conference: "I got an opportunity to find out if the media made Mike Tyson or not."

HBO's prefight segment on Tyson added to the new packaging Jacobs and Cayton had been working on since the Berbick fight. It began with Tyson lecturing high school students against drugs ("I love myself too much") and then made a blatant stab at gender marketing. Ross Greenberg, HBO Sports executive producer, explained: "The slant on that one was the fascination among women for Tyson. What was it that appealed to them about him? Jacobs suggested we talk to Joyce Carol Oates."

"He's just himself," Oates had responded in her squeaky voice and diminutive manner. "I think that's one of the reasons people find him so oddly charismatic—because he's not trying."

The segment then differentiated along racial lines. Oates, representing white women, spoke from mere cultural-scientific rather than sexual interest. Two models, one black, the other with traces of black ethnicity in her features, were permitted to reveal sexual stirrings. "I want to watch him fight. ... I just don't see him as a boxer," said the lighter of the two, Sabrina Barnett. "I see him as somebody else, as a little bit more sincerity [sic]. Not someone who's going out there to kill somebody."

The segment climaxed with Tyson sitting on the edge of Cayton's office desk musing humbly on his growing fame. He began by repeating the D'Amato-Jacobs gospel. "It's coming the time that everyone is going to know me. I have to deal with it. That's my responsibility.... I'm so far away from being a great fighter...people don't know what great is. ...Anybody can keep knocking out [sic]. It's when you lose, how you handle it, then it shows your personality. Then it shows what kind of man you really are."

Then, in a sudden shift, the other Tyson, the disquieting one, poked through to resist both the packaging and the purchase. Not since his remark about driving an opponent's "nose back into his brain" had Tyson so starkly bucked his image-makers. This time, he gave us all a preview of a drama to come. "Let me give you something to call me great. Let me give you a reason to call me great. You know what I mean, people call me great, you're the greatest, you're going to be champion for twenty years. People don't know how your mind works. Suppose I decide I want to get married and give up boxing. Suppose my only goal was to just want to win the title, then give it up. Or to be the greatest champion."

HBO's segment on Smith fell back into familiar territory. Without the facts to build suspense about the outcome of the match, HBO relied on racial stereotypes. It took Smith back to his childhood farm in North Carolina and had him chop wood and talk about plowing the fields, picking okra, and tending to the chickens. "I'm the only heavyweight champion in history with a college degree," recalled Smith, who still lives in North Carolina, speculates in real estate, and now has an honorary Ph.D. from Shaw University. "Having me walk through the fields was a put-down. Everything was geared toward making Tyson look good. It affected me."

In the ring, Smith, clearly psyched out by the mystique of Tyson the Ring Destroyer, decided not to put up much of a fight. He ran, grabbed, pawed, and got a few shots off when he could. If he had a fight plan, it wasn't apparent. The HBO commentators tried to hide their embarrassment with sarcasm. "Seven-hundred-fifty-dollar ringside seats for this?" Larry Merchant asked incredulously during the seventh round. Then they turned on Tyson. From the Tillis fight, they knew that Tyson was capable of passivity, but at this level of competition, he was expected to impose his will. Shortly after the seventh round began, Merchant realized that Tyson had almost no will to impose. "Mike Tyson is not dealing with it right," Merchant said. "Tyson is not going about it professionally to break him down in some way."

The dreaded flaw struck again, but this time more severely. When he had failed to knock out Tillis with an initial burst of energy, Tyson had panicked, forgotten his boxing skills, and been gripped by the fear of losing. But he had still tried to punch. Against Smith, when the first barrage failed, Tyson lost all desire to win. Instead of punching out of Smith's clinches with his shattering uppercut, Tyson let himself be held. Worse, he held on. "I got criticized for grabbing, but he was doing a lot of it, too," Smith recalled. When Tyson did punch, he seemed out of control, as if consumed by a desperate desire just to get it all over with. Near the end of the seventh round, as he threw a wild left hook to Smith's body, he fell back and down like a drunk. In his corner between the seventh and eighth rounds, Tyson muttered to trainer Kevin Rooney, "I don't want to fight."

The later rounds dragged on. Tyson all but ignored Smith's body, didn't use his trademark combinations, and kept looking for one shot to the head. After the tenth, Rooney mistakenly told Tyson there was only one round to go—in fact, there were two more rounds. In the last ten seconds of the twelfth, Smith suddenly turned it on and landed a hard right to Tyson's head. In his passivity, all of Tyson's other shortcomings in the ring were exposed. He'd gotten inside, but had stopped moving. Merchant uttered the taboo words: "He's not as good as Ali and Frazier. In truth, he's not as good as they are. He doesn't have the record to show it yet..."

The three judges deemed Smith's grabbing and inactivity a far greater sin than Tyson's inability to find a way to combat it. They gave Tyson a unanimous decision. Back in the dressing room, alone with Rooney and Lott, Tyson reacted. Lott said: "Mike was so relieved for it just to be over. He hugged Kevin Rooney and he wouldn't let him go. I'd never seen him do that so intensely before, or since."

Jacobs wouldn't tolerate any suggestion that a gap might have reappeared between the image and the man. The drawn-out struggle, the lumbering, the clinching, and the clumsiness made for a lukewarm, soupy mess. For the "cool medium" of television, it was pathetic. "That was the only time we had a tussle," HBO's Greenberg remembered. "He didn't appreciate what our announcers said. Anything that hurt the image of Tyson angered Jimmy tremendously."

Most of the press fell into place behind the party line and blamed only Smith. Those who didn't—and they were few—met with Jacob's customary evasions. Newsday's Matthews recalled: "Against Smith he didn't fight a lick. When I criticized Tyson for it, Jacobs said, 'Hey, he's only twenty!' He always wanted it both ways."

The deepest cut came from Jim Murray, the veteran sports columnist of the Los Angeles Times and one of the few journalists Jacobs considered a friend. The day after the fight, Murray wrote, "You can tell Jack Dempsey and Tunney and Ali they don't have to move over just yet... your reputations are safe from Mike Tyson."

For Jacobs, a man not given to emotional labor, they had gone too far, and were too close to winning it all, to have to rebuild the machine from the emotional core outward. Nick Beck recalled Jacobs's bottom-line lesson from the fight: "He said to me, 'We got to work on maintaining Tyson's intensity in the ring.'"

Always the same answer: "Get Tyson back in the ring."

If Jacobs ever did consider telling Tyson about the fatal progress of his leukemia, he certainly couldn't after the Smith fight. Any hope that Tyson's emotional instability had perhaps been brought under control by the Berbick fight was lost. There was no telling how he might react to news of the leukemia. Would the pending loss of a second mentor—the only one remaining who could articulate the D'Amato gospel so well— irretrievably expose the flaw and make him falter in the ring and fail to unify the heavyweight division? If Tyson leaked it to the press, would Jacobs's negotiating position for future fights, as he always feared it would, be undermined? Would King move in on Tyson?

The risks of telling him about the leukemia seemed too great. Tyson couldn't know. Jacobs's plans to make Cayton his successor would be kept secret. "I guess if anyone could figure out what was wrong with Jimmy, he and Loraine thought it would be me," Zeil said of those early months in 1987. "Jimmy invited me to see Mike fight Smith. When I got there, both he and Loraine said to me repeatedly, 'Don't talk to any reporters!'"

Jacobs also invited Randy Ziegler, the funeral director who had buried his mother. "He insisted I come, got me tickets, reserved a hotel room, took care of me—and did it for four of Tyson's Las Vegas fights," Ziegler said. Thinking back, Ziegler now realizes Jacobs wasn't so much trying to make a new friend as to get to know his own undertaker. "He knew he was going to die, and he knew in his heart and his mind that if he befriended me, I would take care of him."

According to Ziegler, Loraine may well have realized what was going on. "When I first arrived, I went to his hotel room and Loraine came to the door. We'd never met before, but when I introduced myself, she gave me a big hug and a kiss."

By March, Jacobs had also enlisted José Torres. "In early 1987, Jimmy told me he would like to make some amendments to the contracts. He said if anything happened to him, Tyson would be free. In the State of New York, you can only have one manager. If anything happened to him, he said, he wanted a contract to be effective between Mike and Cayton. I said I'd talk to the commission's lawyers."

From Jacobs's point of view, José Torres came suited for his plans. As a "Cus fighter," like Rooney, he was basically trusted by Tyson. As Athletic Commission chairman he carried the imprimatur of state office. But perhaps most relevantly, he seemed willing to bend the rules for them. Not once did Torres object to Jacobs and Cayton's calling themselves co-managers.

The only problem was Torres's occasional displays of bad judgment. It wasn't just his cheering at Tyson's fights, an act that compromised Torres's official impartiality. Torres had started to do things that made him seem an unreliable ally: he appeared to be interested in serving the special interests of Don King.

The incident at the Tyson-Green bout back in late May was a borderline case. By ordering Green to fight despite his grievances over the cut in purse, Torres had helped both Jacobs and King. In December 1986, he had helped King again. Due to the drug test that found traces of marijuana in Witherspoon's urine after his January 1986 bout with Tony Tubbs, a rematch had been ordered by the W.B.A. for December 12. A few days before the bout, Tubbs pulled out of the fight, complaining of a shoulder injury. In fact, he was owed money by King, who refused to pay. King substituted "Bonecrusher" Smith. Witherspoon didn't want to fight Smith. He had trained technically and psychologically to fight Tubbs. He had also signed an agreement to defend his title for $1 million against Tyson in March 1987. He didn't want to risk that payday.

Torres told Witherspoon that if he didn't fight Smith, he'd have his boxer's license suspended. For his part, Smith had also been manipulated into the bout. At the time, he was suing King. In exchange for dropping the suit, King gave him a shot at Witherspoon's W.B.A. title. Smith knocked him out in the first round.

That wasn't the end of it. Witherspoon had been guaranteed a $300,000 purse plus $100,000 in training expenses. After an accounting by King and his son, manager Carl, he ended up with $99,000. The elder King had charged Witherspoon $28,000, at $1,000 a day, to train at his facility in Orwell, Ohio. The indignities continued. Witherspoon was given a standard drug test prior to the fight. It showed negative for marijuana and other narcotics. But there was a slight elevation in the amphetamine tests. Eva Rivera, the commission's medical technician, believed that was probably due to aspirin or eye or nose drops. At first, she typed an $N$ on the report, indicating a negative test for actual narcotics. Then, in an effort at technical accuracy that was more like bureaucratic bungling, she typed a $P$ for positive over the $N$ to show the presence of the aspirin or the eye or nose drops.

When Torres saw the report, he assumed it was a positive test. Had he read it, he would have seen that Rivera had made an error—the commission is interested only in narcotics, not aspirin. Torres called the press and said Witherspoon tested positive for marijuana and would be suspended. Later, he realized his mistake and called the press again to retract.

On December 20, Governor Mario Cuomo ordered Joseph Spinelli, now state inspector general, to investigate the incident. Spinelli, the one-time crusader for justice in boxing when he headed the "Crown Royal" FBI investigation, produced an insipid censure. Besides forcing Witherspoon to fight, and bungling the drug test, Torres permitted Carl King to manage both fighters (against the commission's rules unless special permission is given) and allowed the fighters, and Carl King, to work even though their respective licenses had expired years earlier. Spinelli acknowledged those infractions but merely slapped Torres's wrist by chastising him for a "failure to oversee the commission." Torres was also advised to focus his efforts less on "future travel" (he had billed the commission for his trips to Tyson's Las Vegas fights) and more on "managing the commission." Clearly, there was a deeper level of incompetence—or even complicity—which wasn't being explored.

That can perhaps be explained as the state government bureaucracy protecting itself. Torres, after all, was appointed to his post by Cuomo. But, not to be ignored, Spinelli was a close personal friend of Torres. He had lobbied hard for Torres to get the posting, and he was the godfather to Torres's daughter.

James Dupree, one of the two commissioners appointed by Cuomo to serve under Torres, had his own opinions about Torres's motives: "He was under pressure because he had forced Witherspoon to fight. Why, I don't know. It seemed to me he was being manipulated by outside influences."

\* \* \*

According to the original HBO schedule, Tyson's next bout was supposed to be in Las Vegas against I.B.F. champion Michael Spinks for unification. For Butch Lewis, Tyson's victory over Berbick was all he needed to know in order to make the most crucial decision of his, and Spinks's, career. "I wasn't going to kiss Tyson's ass because everyone else did," said Lewis.

When Abraham insisted on bringing Tyson into the series, Lewis believed that he had changed the intent and letter of the original deal to suit his own interests and, as Lewis later learned, those of King as well. Back in late August, when the memorandum of agreement to include Tyson was signed, Lewis felt entitled to do the same. As a condition for

letting Tyson into the HBO series, Lewis insisted on the right to pull
Spinks out if he could get a closed-circuit pay-per-view deal to fight
Gerry Cooney. Abraham, and the others, agreed. In return, HBO got
the delayed broadcast rights.

Lewis demanded the right to fight Cooney for one simple reason.
Before Tyson's entry, his fighter had had a shot at winning all three belts.
Securing the right to fight Cooney was Lewis's compensation for the
undermining of that prospect. It was also a more equal sharing of the
new risks posed by Tyson's entry. He had to accept the greater risk of his
fighter being beaten by Tyson; Abraham, Jacobs, and Cayton, therefore,
had to accept the risk that Spinks might beat Cooney. If he did, fine,
Spinks got an extra, and originally unplanned for, payday, then returned
to the series to fight Tyson. If he didn't beat Cooney, it was up to
Abraham and the rest to deal with the problem of getting Cooney into
the series. That was the price they had to pay for Tyson's belated entry.

That, at least, was the understanding upon which Lewis proceeded
all through the fall of 1986. He had every reason to bring Spinks back
into the series to fight Tyson. Lewis wasn't happy about the purse—$4
million—but that could be dealt with later. Abraham had thrown an
extra $5.5 million at Jacobs and Cayton to bring Tyson in and given them
and King more money in fees as well. When it came time for Spinks to
fight Tyson, they would sit down like reasonable men once again and
renegotiate the purse. "Shit, even Berbick got three times what he'd
been first promised," Lewis said.

He soon found out that Abraham, King, and Jacobs and Cayton were
not interested in being reasonable. "Everything was Tyson, Tyson,
Tyson. Bow down to Tyson," Lewis said. The first warning sign came
from King. "In September, King said to me, 'Butch, we got to get Tyson
away from Jacobs and Cayton.' 'Don,' I said, 'I'm not in the business of
stealing anybody's guy.' So King takes it on himself and I'm on the outs."

According to Lewis, King waged a covert campaign to divide and
conquer. The August memorandum had to be succeeded by a formal
contract between Jacobs and Cayton and Dynamic Duo Inc. King
muddied the waters of the negotiations. "He'd tell me that Jacobs and
Cayton had problems with the contract, then he's telling them that I
don't like the contract," Lewis griped. "King's saying that they don't
want me at the negotiating table. Jacobs would be asking me why I'm
causing so much trouble, and I wasn't. It's King working his magic,
playing one big con game. King was romancing them to get inside so he
can steal Tyson."

In early December 1986, they finally all sat down to finish the agreement. "I sensed all this hostility toward me. King's all buddy-buddy with Jacobs and Cayton, Abraham is talking about Tyson like he's God, so I get this feeling that I'm supposed to be glad I'm even here. They don't want to talk about more money for Michael Spinks to fight Tyson. So I said let's go to war."

Undaunted by HBO's court action, on February 20, Lewis signed Spinks to fight Gerry Cooney outside the series on closed-circuit pay-per-view. The alliance of Abraham et al. moved swiftly to pressure him to throw his fighter back into the series. The I.B.F., under considerable pressure from Jacobs and King, threatened to strip Spinks of his title. HBO moved to enjoin the bout in the New York courts. The I.B.F. then made an apparent move to compromise. Before he fought Cooney, Spinks could satisfy his mandatory defense obligation in an HBO series bout against Tony Tucker. It was a thinly veiled attempt to keep Spinks's I.B.F. crown within grasp of Tyson on the hope that Tucker would win. Maybe he would, maybe not. Lewis declined the bout. The I.B.F. stripped Spinks and vacated the title on February 26.

In the end, Lewis won out. His contract with HBO specified terms that obligated Spinks only as a recognized champion. By stripping Spinks of his title, the I.B.F. took away his champion's status. By the terms of the contract with HBO, Spinks was thus permitted to leave the series and fight who he pleased. In early March, the New York courts threw out the injunction against the Spinks-Cooney fight. The bout was scheduled for June 15, 1987, in Atlantic City. Lewis said: "I didn't win that decision because I'm some sort of slickster; I won because I was right. They did it to themselves."

Lewis ended up with the strongest cards. As long as Spinks remained undefeated, Tyson's status as the new undisputed champion would be questioned. Whether Jacobs liked it or not, Tyson-Spinks would become a far more significant bout than Tyson against the remaining I.B.F. champion, or even Larry Holmes. It would establish who had the rightful claim to the line of great heavyweights.

"They were all listening to each other and not thinking for themselves," said Lewis of the alliance. "Jacobs always said that Cooney would beat Michael, so that became law. King was telling them whatever they wanted to hear because he wants to steal Tyson. King told Abraham that Rappaport [Cooney's promoter] would never do a deal with me and Abraham bought that bullshit. Believe me, he was pissed off at King when we announced the deal. Abraham then figured that when HBO and Time Inc. jumped on me in the courts, I'd back off. It's incredible—these guys, they're believing their own bullshit and bull-shitting each other and they didn't even know it. I got to tell you: I didn't leave the series—they forced me out for not kissing their asses."

Jacobs and Cayton had to scramble to set up a title defense bout to keep Tyson busy until the I.B.F. could muster up a replacement champion. In late March, they announced that Tyson would make his first W.B.A./W.B.C. defense against Pinklon Thomas on May 30. The bout provoked little interest. Thomas lost to Berbick early on in the series. He was mere filler. Boxing insiders were more curious to see what Tyson would do to reverse the damage to his ring image caused by the Smith fight.

The prefight HBO segment was considerably toned down. Titled "The True Champion," it dealt only with Tyson's charity work for the mentally retarded. The piece on Pinklon Thomas mentioned his one-time heroin addiction, among other personal problems. A 6-to-1 underdog, and twenty-nine years old, he had all the signs of a shot fighter. As Tyson came into the ring in his black shorts and sockless black shoes, Merchant scaled back on the hype: "There he is, Mister Primitive." No one expected it to be much of a fight.

Tyson had something to prove. Punch more, box the man, dictate the pace, impose his will and his fight plan. For the first time ever, Tyson sought help in superstition. He put a twenty-five-cent piece in the laces of his right shoe. In the first round, he came out with an energetic barrage. He threw every punch in his arsenal: jabs, uppercuts, and combinations to the body and head. Thomas didn't go down. In the second round, an emboldened Thomas started poking with his jab. It appeared enough to break Tyson's relentless offensive rhythm. By the third, Tyson was clinching more, and losing his intensity. At the end of the round, Rooney realized that he was again trying to win on one big punch, the same mistake he had made with Smith and Tillis. "You need the jab, you need the body, Michael," Rooney yelled into his face between rounds. Tyson tried his jab in the fourth, but it didn't have much effect.

For the fifth, Rooney applied stronger medicine. "Are we going to fight or are we going to bullshit? Uh? Fight or bullshit?" he barked at Tyson. That had little effect; he performed just as poorly. On the stool before the sixth, unable to look Rooney in the eye, Tyson muttered: "I'm getting tired." Rooney disregarded him. "Where's the right hand?" he demanded. "Bad intentions! Where's the right hand? This guy has balls and he's fighting you!" In the sixth, Tyson finally found the right hand—namely, a right uppercut. With a barrage of punches displaying textbook finishing abilities—a quick left hook, two right uppercuts, a left, a right, then another left—he sent Thomas to the floor. It wasn't pretty boxing, but it got the job done. The referee saw enough and called a halt at the count of nine. At the postfight press conference, Tyson spoke as if he knew the fight was his from the outset—which it certainly wasn't. "I knew he wouldn't be getting up, but I hoped he did get up," said Tyson. "I wanted to hit him a shot that would keep him down." It was the utterance of someone who seemed to be always rediscovering himself in the ring.

Given the quality of the opponent, Tyson proved little with the victory. He threw an average of forty-one punches per round. That was better than the twenty-six per round against Smith, but a far cry from the fifty-seven he had sent at Berbick. As heavyweight champion, he had yet to meet an opponent who, unlike Smith, stood in there and actually boxed and who, unlike Thomas, took Tyson's best punches, remained standing, and hit back—hard.

Tyson's next fight was in early August against Tony Tucker, who had filled the vacant I.B.F. title. Jacobs was thinking far beyond that, however, to a future title defense against Larry Holmes. But Holmes remained elusive. He wouldn't return Jacobs's repeated phone calls. Jacobs and Cayton tried a pressure tactic. They always knew that the flip side of having Tyson fight so frequently was that he'd get overexposed. Dedicated fight fans would always want to see him in the ring, but the mainstream audience, the source of the big dollar volumes, needed a fresh story angle, a hook. That would be even more important after Tyson unified the title. The answer was a world tour. The idea behind going overseas was to create spectacle rather than to find challenging athletic competition. It would give the American audience their story—"Tyson Conquers the World"—and tap into new global markets. There was nothing original to it. Muhammad Ali had done it in the 1970s.

The tour was also designed to snub Butch Lewis. Even if Spinks beat Cooney, the message said there would be no fight with Tyson for over a year. That was Lewis's punishment for leaving the HBO series.

Jacobs and Cayton decided to announce the tour early, hoping that Holmes would get on board rather than risk being left behind. There would be four fights over nine months. It would begin stateside in October 1987 against Tyrell Biggs, the 1984 Olympic gold medalist who

was having a lot of difficulty rising in the professional ranks. Jacobs and
Cayton wanted Holmes next, but if he didn't relent, it was off to Italy to
fight Francesco Damiani, another Olympic finalist, in January 1988. The
venue would likely be one of Italy's 70,000-plus capacity soccer stadiums, which they expected to fill. Then there was an as-yet-unselected
opponent to open the massive new Tokyo Dome in March. The last fight
would be against Frank Bruno, an early loser in the HBO series to James
("Bonecrusher") Smith. That was scheduled for June 1988 in London's
Wembley Stadium.

Holmes didn't have time to respond. Events beyond everyone's
control overcame them all. On June 15, in the Atlantic City Convention
Center before a crowd of fifteen thousand. Spinks defeated Cooney with
a fifth-round technical knockout. No title was at stake, but that didn't
matter. Spinks had polished off the last remaining name heavyweight.
Leaving the HBO series, and fending off HBO's litigation, had earned
him the underdog's status; beating Cooney had confirmed his claim to
the historic lineage. The press dubbed him the "People's Champion."

Jacobs gambled wrong. He had predicted a Cooney victory in the
third round. With the gathering momentum of public support behind
Spinks, Jacobs realized that he and Cayton would have to sit down with
Lewis and do a deal. Until Tyson beat Spinks, he wouldn't achieve true,
undisputed status.

The postunification picture suddenly became uncertain. If Spinks
had lost, a victory over Holmes by itself would have secured Tyson's
claim to the title. But now the lineage had split off in two directions.
Both Holmes and Spinks could claim to be heavyweight kings. For
Jacobs and Cayton, that meant having to do not one but two difficult
deals. Lewis, they could be sure, would be ten times the trouble of
Holmes. He'd returned to make their lives miserable. Until both deals
were done, they had to shelve plans for the world tour.

Jacobs and Cayton stepped back to rethink the big picture. Could
they pressure Holmes into fighting sooner? Could they somehow
diminish Spinks's claim to the lineage and thus recapture the deal
momentum? Would the alliance with Abraham and King have to be
altered? Would it even hold up? And for Jacobs, there was always the
most pressing question of all: Would he live long enough to get it all
done?

Altering the overall strategic plan brought back a familiar choice—
take Tyson into the open market, or sign a new, exclusive deal with

HBO? The open-market route meant the end of the alliance. Breaking with King was always in their plans, but Jacobs and Cayton were less comfortable about alienating Abraham. Among television networks, he paid top dollar. Several other factors also had to be weighed. The open market required a lot more work. They would have to tailor each fight to its appropriate market. That meant deciding which fights were suited for the smaller HBO audience and which for the mass audience of closed-circuit pay-per-view. The difference in revenues was enormous: $4 million, maximum, that HBO was prepared to pay for a single fight as compared to tens of millions of dollars from closed-circuit pay-per-view. Tactically, the open market could be a valuable weapon against Lewis, but only if Holmes could be made as a closed-circuit pay-per-view fight in early 1988. The hype surrounding such a megabuck promotion just might convince the buying public that Tyson didn't need Spinks in order to claim the lineage.

The open market, though, posed difficulties. Jacobs and Cayton knew little to nothing about the closed-circuit pay-per-view business. That meant taking on an experienced closed-circuit pay-per-view promoter. One day that would be inevitable. At the moment, it seemed premature. They weren't powerful enough yet to dictate their own terms to such a promoter. They decided to stick with the status quo. After all, the alliance was a good cover. As long as they worked with King and Abraham, they could always deflect criticisms and head off any legal action accusing them of acting like promoters—which, of course, is almost exactly how Jacobs and Cayton handled Tyson's career from the beginning.

In July, Jacobs and Cayton entered into negotiations with Abraham for a new multifight deal. "I was vacationing with my family on Fire Island," Abraham said. "They had me on the phone every day. They were considering the open market for Tyson. My argument was for continuity with Tyson, that we could make him a bigger attraction and that the deal would be the foundation for their larger battle plan."

Within a week the basic outlines of the deal were drawn. Abraham agreed to pay $26.5 million for seven fights plus the delayed broadcast rights to one closed-circuit pay-per-view event. It would be the largest sum of money ever paid to a fighter by a television network. Jacobs and Cayton agreed not to make any announcements until all the details were ironed out—primarily Don King's role. They wanted to use him on an optional basis. Abraham strongly objected.

The seven-fight deal required trade-offs. It meant abandoning hopes
to do Tyson-Holmes on closed-circuit pay-per-view. "For that kind of
money, I wanted the Holmes fight for HBO, and made that very clear,"
Abraham said. At the same time, the deal strengthened the alliance by
keeping the three centers of self-interest working for mutual benefit. If
Jacobs and Cayton couldn't get Holmes, maybe Abraham could with the
deep pockets of corporate parent Time Inc.

That still left Butch Lewis to contend with. The alliance, even when
renewed, would remain useless against Lewis. Without the business
leverage to work on Lewis, they decided to use PR. Jacobs headed up
the effort. He tried to convince the public that Tyson didn't need the
fight and that Spinks didn't deserve it. He assumed the public would
agree that Lewis deserved punishment for leaving the HBO series. It
was a bit of self-important myopia that would eventually backfire.

Lewis recalled his conversations with them over that summer. "I had
the fighter they wanted. My man beat Holmes twice; he had the true
lineage. Tyson just beat the has-beens. When I first talked to Jacobs I
laid it out: I promote or copromote and get a fifty-fifty spilt of the
revenues. No way, he said. He stayed with that pompous, arrogant
attitude." Lewis mimicked Jacobs. " 'Well, Butch, we'—he always
included Bill—'we don't feel... you must understand... you broke the
contract and that's not the way to do business.' I'm looking at this guy
and I don't believe it. Tyson-Spinks was his only big-money closed-
circuit pay-per-view fight and he was still jerking me around. It was all
ego."

Jacobs's tactics didn't work. Lewis was well aware that less than a year
before, he and Cayton had been prepared to share revenues fifty-fifty
with Dennis Rappaport on Tyson-Cooney. He believed he deserved the
same deal and nothing less. He waged his own PR campaign. "They
didn't realize it, but I was always negotiating with them through the
media," Lewis said of his tactics. "I had the classic underdog story: they
sicked HBO on me, the courts, the sanctioning guys, Don King, too,
who's talking about America this and America that, but now I want the
fight, me and my little one-hundred-and-ninety-pound guy, and it's
starting to look like they're running from me. That's how I'm putting it
to the press now: Tyson the big bad guy and Michael [Spinks] the
people's champion. I'm sticking it to them all the time, and you know,
eventually, Michael and me would be walking into arenas and get
standing ovations. The public loved Michael. They wanted the fight."

The more support Lewis acquired, the more vindictive Jacobs and Cayton became. Even those who knew Jacobs best didn't quite understand his vendetta approach. Nick Beck said: "He told me that he was going to make Lewis and Spinks pay for pulling out of the series. I pointed out to Jim that it wasn't Spinks's fault, he's just a guy doing what he's told. Jim said, 'So what?'"

They had gotten their way for so long—with the help of Abraham and King—that they had forgotten what it was like to negotiate with someone else as an equal. Lewis continued: "Jacobs and Cayton started on this shit that I pulled out of the series so no way in hell would Michael get to fight for the title. They thought they were punishing me, like everyone had to be on their side because they had Tyson."

Together, Jacobs and Cayton remained stalwart against Lewis. Alone, Jacobs had a different agenda. For all the reasons he wanted the fight, he felt compelled to get the deal done before he was either too sick to participate or dead. He also knew, far better than did Cayton, that public pressure for the fight would eventually get to Tyson. And that's what Lewis homed in on. "Jacobs had the fighter's heart, the power over him," Lewis said. "Mike would end up desperately wanting the fight just to shut everybody up and prove that he was the best. Jacobs had to respect that. Cayton didn't know how to. So I realized that in the end it was Jacobs who would get this deal done with me; he wouldn't have any choice."

The fight exposed a fundamental rift between Jacobs and Cayton. Jacobs understood all the broader reasons why the fight had to be made. Cayton only focused on the money and power issues. Jacobs couldn't risk not getting the deal made in time just because of Cayton's narrow concerns. He took safety measures against his partner. In late June, he enlisted his friend Shelly Finkel to intervene as a mediator.

Finkel had cut his teeth in the business world selling copy machines while still a student at New York University. He went on to set up a computer-dating service, and from there to manage a dance club in Long Island and then to promote pop concerts. With a partner, Finkel formed Cross-Country Concert Corporation, which went on to promote hundreds of concerts, including the legendary 1973 Watkins Glen Summer Jam, the largest ever. In 1980, Finkel started managing fighters. At the 1984 Olympics, he persuaded some of the top American entrants to sign with him and another manager, Lou Duva, and to be promoted by Duva's son, Dan. Short, with a large, bald, rectangular

head and an understated manner, Finkel made an unlikely fight
manager. "He comes off charming and reasonable, but he's slippery and
cunning," one promoter said.

"Finkel came to me right after the Cooney fight," Lewis remarked.
"Calls me up and says, 'Hello, Butch, how's the family?' I rarely talk to
this guy and all of a sudden he's concerned about my family. I knew
Jacobs sent him to me. Like I'm some kind of schmuck. He starts
'advising' me to make a deal, that Michael Spinks won't be around
forever. These guys thought I was stupid."

All summer, according to Lewis, Jacobs kept up the charade of
ignorance about Finkel. "Jacobs would read some barb of mine in the
press then call me up. 'Butch, I didn't appreciate your comments in the
newspaper. Wouldn't you agree, Bill?' he'd say. Cayton would be on the
phone. Both of them were talking down to me. 'We suggest you forget
about Michael ever fighting for the title.' I'd just laugh, because after
that Finkel always called me saying boxing is based on 'relationships'—
you know, playing the good cop. I told him I didn't give a fuck how they
felt about me. I wanted to promote or copromote the fight and get a
fifty-fifty split."

Lewis was the only problem that had arisen in the development of
Tyson's career that Jacobs and Cayton couldn't solve. The public, for the
first time ever, began to doubt the hype and to reconsider Tyson's
prowess on the most basic level. Was he afraid to fight Spinks? It was all
an ego issue, but that's not how Tyson saw it. He wanted the fight and he
wanted to know why it wasn't being made. Jacobs could only blame
Lewis. "Jacobs called me in the summer, said, 'Stop going to my
fighter.' I hadn't said word one to Tyson, but I knew he started to bug
Jacobs about it. That sent a loud-and-clear message to me: I had them by
the balls."

# Chapter Ten

Tyson had performed poorly against "Bonecrusher" Smith. He'd put up a workmanlike defense against Pinklon Thomas. As long as Holmes and Spinks kept standing, his dominance remained questionable. Still, the corporate world wanted a piece of the fable.

Of all the offers fielded by Jay Rosenstein at Ohlmeyer Communications, only one met his test of "quality." The international ad agency J. Walter Thompson suggested matching up Tyson with Kodak. The agency's new campaign stressed "family relationships." Jacobs and Cayton jumped at the offer. Rosenstein negotiated a flat fee of $175,975.94. It was filmed on April 20 and 21.

The Kodak commercial would for the first time identify Tyson with the products of a major, national, indeed global, corporation. It elevated the fable of Cus and the Kid to new heights of artifice. It began with a montage of color and black-and-white still photographs of Tyson with D'Amato. Some were in a boxing gym, others in front of the Catskill house. Tyson's soft, sweet voice-over covered the first set of images: "I met Cus when I was thirteen years old. . ." Then the mournful theme song laid over the remainder:

> Knock-down rounds, drag-out fights
> Endless days and sleepless nights
> And one memory that still shines bright
> You were there for me
> You were there to keep me strong
> Help me find where I belong
> In my corner right along
> You were there for me. . .

Tyson's voice came back over the last photo, which showed him embracing D'Amato. "Thanks, Cus," it said.

The message as the agency intended, was not about boxing. It portrayed a close relationship, and more—a unique, interracial bond. It was Tyson's image, through D'Amato, reduced to the simplest human terms: love, family, and intimacy. Although by industry standards the ad didn't run all that frequently, it was a tremendous success. It received awards from five different industry organizations, including the International Film & TV Festival and *Ad Week* magazine.

Tyson's next major commercial tapped into the dark side of his image, the one so effectively exploited in psyching out his opponents. Rosenstein was approached by a then little-known Japanese home entertainment video company, Nintendo. They wanted to use Tyson for Punch Out, a new game to be released for the 1987 U.S. Christmas retail season.

Nintendo wanted the vicious side of the Tyson persona. Even though that presented a contrary, and conflicting, image from the one in the Kodak ad, Jacobs and Cayton were won over by something other than "quality": Rosenstein secured a fee of $749,991, plus royalties on the volume of sales. The commercial assembled a montage of workout shots in which Tyson punched a heavy bag, sweated, grunted, snarled, and, in the last sequence of images, played the game himself before a wall of television screens. In the final shot, he swung around, joystick in hand, and laughed demonically.

Tyson the loving son versus Tyson the primal destructive force: two distinct and irreconcilable personas. Jacobs and Cayton needed a synthesis, some other angle on his overall image that went beyond Cus and the Kid. They hoped that exploiting Tyson's interest in boxing history would do it.

In April 1987, for a fee of $20,000, Tyson taped a one-hour show with an old and reliable booster of the fable, ABC's Alex Wallau. "Mike Tyson and the Great Heavyweights" was broadcast as a special segment in ABC's "Wide World of Sports" on May 30—the same day Tyson fought Pinklon Thomas. The feature began with a documentary feel. It recapped the basic fable ("When I was thirteen I met a fight trainer named Cus D'Amato and within six months he adopted me"), then turned to the subject of Tyson's place in history. Wallau showed him fight films of the great heavyweights in action, after which Tyson was asked to comment.

"I don't think I deserve to be mentioned in the same sentence with the legendary fighters of the past," Tyson said in a voice-over. "Perhaps if I could beat the fighters of my day, and conquer the imagination of the world, perhaps in two years from now I could be mentioned as one of the all-time-great fighters."

The segment then shifted to Wallau and Tyson standing in a boxing ring. Tyson wore civilian clothes as he responded to Wallau's questions.

On how much of his success he owes to studying the greats: "...they gave me courage, gave me the admiration to start at a young age..."

On copying from former champions: "Well, not really, Alex, because I was trying to be the best that Mike Tyson could be..."

On Joe Louis "(...an all-around great fighter...")," on Rocky Marciano ("I'm happy to be mentioned in the same breath..."), and on what made Ali so special ("...the most heart and the most confidence...").

Wallau finished by asking Tyson who was the greatest of the five heavyweights they'd examined.

"...Joe Louis stands alone," Tyson said.

Tyson's marketing mirrored the Joe Louis campaign. Jacobs and Cayton had contrived much of his public image, and had concealed just as much of his private life. Manipulation of the news media, marketing gimmicks, and commercial endorsements sanitized Tyson in the same way patriotism had Louis. ABC Sports was only too happy to comply. "That show with Wallau was something that Jacobs had pushed us to do for years," admitted David Downs, then the director of programming for ABC Sports. Downs denied being an unwitting tool of the campaign. "We weren't trying to make him appear to be a great heavyweight, just put a rising star in better historical context." In the words of author and essayist E. B. White, for television, telling and selling are sometimes indistinguishable.

Jacobs and Cayton tried to go beyond the basic narrative of Cus and the Kid, but it wasn't easy. They were stuck with the same opposing images of Tyson. The Kodak commercial pushed the persona of a sweet, humble, loving surrogate son to a surrogate father. The Nintendo commercial used the persona from the hype—Tyson as a primal, unstoppable, inevitable, destructive force certain to reign over the ring. Both treatments reached for the mythical, but they ended up with the maudlin and grotesque.

Behind it all, of course, remained Mike Tyson. He had played the roles as best he could. There were times that he felt the impulse to reject everything and everyone and to fall back into the state in which he began and feared he would always end up: alone. But he fought through those feelings of resignation and passivity. He lived out the strange drama of the unloved boy from Brownsville who became heavyweight champion of the world. An impulse arose to author something solely of his own making. He had been given, and had accepted, a version of himself from D'Amato and Jacobs. Now he wanted to make some of his own choices. He wanted romantic love with a woman.

Despite Jacobs's effort to control press access to Tyson, some reporters slipped through unvetted. Jay Price, a sports columnist for the *Staten Island Advance*, a New York newspaper, had known D'Amato since the late 1960s and had met Tyson in 1982. He wrote a free-lance piece for the May issue of *Sport* magazine taking stock of the boy who had become heavyweight champion.

Tyson stressed how fortunate he felt being "handled by Jimmy Jacobs" and added that he trusted him immensely. But Price knew that Jacobs did not duplicate D'Amato as a father figure.

"Do you have anybody you can talk to about things, the way you did with Cus?" Price asked.

"No," Tyson responded. "I used to keep a lot of things inside and Cus and I would talk about them. Now, when those things come up... I just keep them inside."

It didn't take long for Price to find out what those "things" were.

"C'mon, you mean there aren't a ton of girls after the heavyweight champion of the world?" Price asked.

"They don't want me," Tyson said. "They want the cash.... I look in the mirror every day, and I know I'm not Clark Gable. I wish I could find a girl who knew me when I was broke, and thought I was a nice guy."

Tyson then revealed just how isolated he'd become.

"Cus never told me it would be like this. He told me I'd make a lot of money and I'd have a lot of girls and I was gonna be happy. But he never told me life would be like this."

There were other forces pushing Tyson toward love with a woman. D'Amato wasn't the only sexually repressed, self-denying person he'd been raised around. Prior to marrying at the age of fifty-one, Jacobs's primary relationships were with an overbearing mother and with other men, like Steve Lott, who shared his passion for boxing. From the outside, those relationships appeared to be suffused with machismo. And yet there were times when a shared devotion to the sport mixed with a love of manliness verging on the erotic. For Tyson, a young man whose sexuality was still in its developing stages, that may have sent a lot of confusing signals.

D'Amato set the tone early on. In a 1985 interview with CBS's Charles Kuralt, he described his feelings when he first saw thirteen-year-old Tyson in the ring: "I got excited. I see a fighter, you know, physically I get excited just like a guy who's no longer capable of any sexual involvement and then all of a sudden he becomes sexually interested again, you know, after he hasn't been that way for twenty years."

There had been rumors for years about a possible homosexual relationship between D'Amato and Jacobs when they lived together in the 1960s. The only camp member to speak on the subject was Matt Baranski, Tyson's cornerman. He rejected the notion of D'Amato's homosexuality. He did believe, however, that Steve Lott's behavior around Tyson was sometimes inappropriate. "I've seen Steve staring at Mike in the shower in ways a man doesn't do. Once we were in a restaurant near the offices of the Athletic Commission waiting for José Torres. Steve is sitting beside Mike with his hand on Mike's lap. When José comes in, Steve takes his hand away. When José leaves, he puts it back."

Still, the getting of love for Tyson would not be easy. The urge tapped into the chaotic swirl of his dark side. "I never understood where his head was at about women" Wally Matthews of *Newsday* has said. "Once he told me, 'I just want the love,' and I believed him, I guess. He can be that sweet little guy and something inside tells you he means it. Then he

told me this story about taking three women up to his room after the
Berbick fight. He fucked the first, then fucked the second and got on
top of the third, but couldn't get it up. She started taunting him, saying
he was the heavyweight champ and couldn't get hard. He got angry and
told them all to get out of the room."

ABC's Wallau recalled a dinner with Tyson in early 1987 during which
the subject of AIDS came up. "I told him that his problem was likely to
be finding a woman who cared more about him as a person than a
celebrity," Wallau said. "He leaned in close and said, 'Alex, you don't
understand. I just want to fuck them.'"

People closer to Tyson claimed to see the middle ground. Steve Lott
said: "When it came down to it, he didn't care about looks. If he liked
someone, he'd be with them, whether she was attractive or not, white
or black. There were some knockout women that he saw once then told
me he didn't want to have anything to do with because of some
comment they'd made, or how they treated him. He screwed around a
lot, but I always felt that what was inside someone counted to him."

Opposite extremes in the ring. Opposite extremes with women.
Tyson couldn't resolve in himself the things that caused the bouncing
between rage-filled and passive states when battling an opponent. He
would have no easier a time finding some middle ground in his feelings
on which to connect intimately with a woman. But a woman, he hoped,
might be able to help him do that. The problem was that Tyson had yet
to meet one who understood his emotional turmoil and was still willing
to venture into a love relationship. No one, that is, until Robin Givens
came along. Or so he thought.

Tyson had first seen Givens on television in her role as Darlene, a
precocious high school student on the ABC series "Head of the Class."
Givens had long, flowing, thick, raven-black hair, high cheekbones, and
full lips set in a sensual pout. She was a beauty, although no more so
than any of the dozens of women who were readily available to him. The
difference was what she represented, at least on the television screen.
Clearly, it was a persona that had Tyson smitten. Her character excelled
in speech and debating. She evoked a cultivated, superior demeanor. It
made her sexy in a cool, controlled, patrician way. Unlike the women he
was used to, Givens seemed someone who gave out sex on her own
terms to whom she wanted and when she pleased. She was unobtain-
able, like some high priestess in possession of powerful secrets.

Tyson the fragile, unloved boy figured that a woman like that would
have no interest in an ugly guy from Brownsville with a high voice and a

lisp. But Tyson the heavyweight champion living the drama of celebrity wanted to claim her as his due, the victorious gladiator's prize. Both parts of him went after her. She learned how to divide and conquer.

In mid-March of 1987, Tyson asked John Horne, a friend from Albany who had moved to Los Angeles, to get Givens's phone number. Within a few days, Horne dug it up. Her telephone number was in a lot of address books. It took Tyson days just to get up the courage to cold-call Givens. When he finally did, from a hotel room in London, England, where he'd gone to do a promotional appearance for a future fight, he hung up at the first sound of her voice.

When he got back to New York, Tyson called her again. They arranged to have dinner in Los Angeles at Le Dome, a restaurant in Beverly Hills. Tyson missed his flight and arrived several hours late. Givens was still there—and so were her mother, Ruth Roper; her older sister, Stephanie; her publicist; and three other girlfriends.

One of the girlfriends recalled that ominous first meeting: "Picture this. Tyson shows up with his pal Rory Holloway and they're laughing about being so late. Robin was angry but kept it hidden. While we were waiting, her mother said to her repeatedly, 'We'll stay. He'll come.' It was like a business meeting to her. So Robin's acting all cute and sweet, and he is, too, except I keep seeing him paw Stephanie.

"I'm thinking what a farce this is. I'm sure Tyson doesn't know that Robin's been on the hunt for a black celebrity since college. It's a long list. She's been practicing her manipulations on very sophisticated, worldly men. And her mother helped her do it all. They had this master plan to marry her off to some big black star. So what I'm seeing is Robin and her mother just licking their chops at this 'boy' Tyson who thought being late was so naughty. That's just what Robin wanted. She could use it to get to him."

This was one woman—or rather, two—whom Tyson should have done his homework on. In 1985, while she was a student at Sarah Lawrence College in Bronxville, New York, Givens had bragged about her love affair with Eddie Murphy. On a few occasions Murphy had sent a limo to the campus to bring her back to his New Jersey house. Love, it wasn't.

"It was her birthday, and in the morning, when they got out of bed, she pointed that out to Eddie," said one person familiar with their affair. "She said, 'I'd like something.' Eddie recalled, 'What did you have in mind?' She asked him for a gold-and-diamond watch she'd been looking at in the window of Tiffany's. Eddie has gone on record for hating gold diggers. He's almost rabid about conniving women. He picked up the phone, dialed Given's mother, and said, 'Come over here and get your bitch daughter!' Well, Roper, who was always involved in setting up these liaisons for Givens, started berating Eddie, saying he couldn't treat her daughter like a slut and so on. Eddie said, 'I don't believe it— two bitches! Your daughter is the worst lay I've ever had, and if she wasn't black, I wouldn't even touch her.'"

Givens and her mother were no more subtle with other men they targeted. Not long after graduating from Sarah Lawrence, Givens moved to Los Angeles. Roper soon followed to function as her social secretary. In no time, Givens had the part on "Head of the Class." And in no time it was as if she and Roper were working their way down a hit list of black celebrities. "I'll only say this," snapped a former assistant to one of her agents. "Robin and her mother treated our office like an escort service sometimes."

NBA basketball superstar Michael Jordan was high on the list. Givens sent photos of herself to his agents, and Roper even contacted Jordan's parents in North Carolina. She talked glowingly about her daughter and said how nice it would be if Robin and Michael could have dinner. They did eventually meet, but Jordan got wise to Givens's designs and stopped seeing her.

By early 1987, Givens and Roper were getting a reputation in Hollywood as women to be avoided by smart men with money. Tyson came along just in time to salvage their hopes of effecting a profitable union. Givens played her role perfectly. It was as if she knew that the more Tyson could be made to hunger for something, the more infatuation and desire could be converted into desperate need.

On the night of their first meeting at Le Dome, Tyson ended up back at her apartment. Givens refused to get into bed with him. Tyson dropped asleep on her lap and drooled down her leg. Givens told him that she found it "cute." Days later he appeared at her door in the middle of the night professing love. When he returned to New York, she went to Aspen, Colorado, to make a promotional appearance. On an impulse, Tyson flew out to meet her. He followed her back in Los Angeles, bought her expensive gifts, drove her around in rented limousines, continued to call, and kept wanting to be with her every hour of the day. Givens, true to her character Darlene, played hard to get.

The boy in Tyson played along. The emerging man realized that love

The nine-year-old Mike Tyson.

Mike Tyson at age thirteen,
late 1981, in a Catskill gym.

Cus D'Amato instructing his charge, late 1981.

D'Amato and his three champions: Tyson, José Torres, and Floyd Patterson.

Bill Cayton, Tyson, and Steve Lott in November, 1985.

Jim Jacobs and Bill Cayton:
the manager and his partner,
August, 1985.

Tyson and Jacobs at an HBO
press conference to announce
entry into the championship
unification series, mid-1986.

Tyson knocks out Mark Young in the first round, December 27, 1985.

Tyson versus James Tillis in 1986.

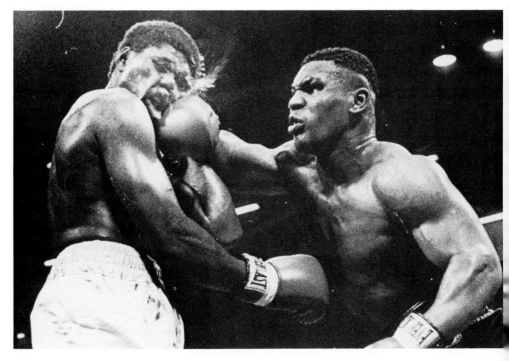

The group around Tyson on July 11, 1985: D'Amato, Kevin Rooney, Bill Cayton, and Jim Jacobs.

Knocking out John Alderson in the third round, July 11, 1985.

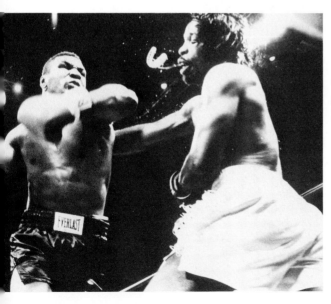

The Tyson left hook . . . against Mitch Green, May 20, 1985.

Tyson and Bill Cayton after the victory over Trevor Berbick, November 22, 1986.

Kevin Rooney and Bobby Stewart with Tyson.

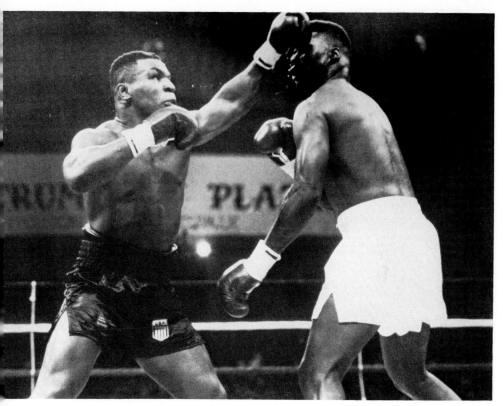

Fighting Tyrell Biggs, October 26, 1987.

A punishing body punch to Larry Holmes, January 22, 1988.

Tyson and actress Robin Givens in 1987, before their marriage.

Robin and Mike in Las Vegas, 1987.

wasn't supposed to be all one-sided. Her manipulations were maddening. To his friends it was like watching someone slide into a bottomless vortex. "Mike knew that she was trying to control him," said Jonet Sellers, a Los Angeles coed who met Tyson at the Berbick fight in late 1986 and had kept up a friendship. "He also hated how Givens and her mother talked down to him all the time. He gave in, I think, because he felt that she would make him better somehow, more acceptable to people. I don't know. Mike never understood love. He had a lot of insecurities about women then. Maybe he thought that agony was true love."

Their first high-profile stepping out as a couple was at a New York press conference announcing Tyson's fight against Pinklon Thomas. It was a highly symbolic act. He had never before paraded a girlfriend at such a boxing ritual, and certainly not one as attractive and accomplished. Tyson usually made no effort to hide his lack of interest with the proceedings. Most reporters thought that he was just bored, that his enthusiasm for boxing began and ended in the ring. They were right, partially. It was also a matter of not feeling confident in playing any other public role. By bringing Givens it was as if he was asking everyone to consider him in wholly different terms, not as the silent and deadly fighter, but as the whole man, a regular human being. With Givens at his side, Tyson was smiling, chatty, by all accounts happy. The press gobbled it up. The next day photos of the incongruous couple ran in several newspapers. The public relations office at ABC Television sent out a résumé claiming that Givens had attended Harvard Medical School and modeled for the prestigious Ford Agency in New York. The Frog Prince had finally found his Princess. Tyson may have been going through a private hell with Givens, but he was also reaping public rewards, however illusory.

The contrast between appearance and reality in their relationship became stark. After the Pinklon Thomas fight in May, he kept pursuing Givens in Los Angeles. Sellers described the general pattern: "He'd call me at night, at really late hours, to complain about her. She'd make dates, then be late. She wanted expensive jewelry. She wasn't giving him sex. I just said, 'Mike, leave her.' I knew he wouldn't."

In early June, at a New York press conference to announce his unification bout against Tony Tucker, Tyson showed up sans Givens. He seemed depressed. Again, Sellers: "Givens just told him to get out of her life. She was sick of him doggin' her about getting sex. He was really torn up about it." Tyson returned to Los Angeles to patch things up with Givens. She continued to put him off. That ignited the first of many violent outbursts.

It had been almost two years since Tyson's last attack on a civilian. Givens's manipulations agitated that inner rage. On June 21, while leaving a rap music concert at the Greek Theater in Hollywood, he wrapped his arms around the waist of a female parking attendant and demanded a kiss. When she resisted, a man who worked with her stepped in to help and was met with an open-fist smack. Both people retained lawyers to file suit. Jacobs and Cayton, in contrast to the many incidents in Catskill and Albany, couldn't keep this one away from the news media or the police. They—or rather Tyson—ended up paying $105,000 in an out-of-court settlement.

A week later, as Tyson went into training for the August fight with Tucker, Givens visited him at the Catskill gym. When he moved the camp to Las Vegas in July, Givens again showed up. As usual, Tyson was edgy in the weeks leading up to a fight, and for the third and final step toward unification he was even more so. The presence of Givens didn't help. Two weeks before the fight, after a particularly grueling sparring session, Tyson pulled Steve Lott aside and blurted, "I'm going to retire." Lott had heard him say that before. He let it pass. Back at his hotel room that night, Lott got a call from Givens. "She told me that they'd had an argument and Mike left. I had no idea what was going on between them and took her call as sincere concern for Mike," Lott said. Tyson called the following day from Albany, where he'd gone to see his friend, Rory Holloway. He didn't mention the argument. He said he'd fly back the next day.

The view in the camp was that Tyson may have finally found someone to settle down with. Givens was good for him, because it meant he would focus more on boxing. No one, not even the meticulous and controlling Jacobs, bothered to check into Givens's past, let alone her mother's. "She was pretty, well mannered, and successful. This was a woman who could be taken seriously," Lott said of the collective view at the time. "Mike liked her. He fooled around with other women, but she seemed special to him. Jimmy thought, well, okay, if he marries her, he'll settle down; it'll be good for his boxing. We didn't know. Robin was a master at mind control. She did the job on him and I didn't know it was happening until it was too late."

Only José Torres got a glimpse of the real Givens. That summer he mentioned to her some of his "concerns" about Mike's outburst in Los Angeles. Givens lashed out. "She said, 'they don't understand him at all. They don't have the slightest idea what's really bothering Mike. They will never know how to deal with him,'" Torres recalled, quoting the conversation as he recorded it in his 1989 biography on Tyson, *Fire & Fear: The Inside Story of Mike Tyson.*

Torres took the comment to mean that because they were white, Jacobs and Cayton could never understand Tyson. No doubt that is what she wanted to imply. But she had other motives too. Givens recognized the gap between the image of Mike Tyson and the reality. To her, this primal destroyer, this historic heavyweight champion was reducible to a little boy drooling down her leg, groping for love. To Tyson she was an opportunity to create something he could call his own, the means by which he could break free from the prison of "Cus and the Kid." That Tyson, Robin Givens intended to do everything she could to manipulate and, ultimately, control.

# Chapter Eleven

**"I** was in Jim's suite in Las Vegas," Nick Beck recalled. "It was the Smith fight. I saw a woman there who had to be Jim's sister: they looked so much alike. I said to Jim, 'All these years I've known you and this is the first time I've met Dorothy.' He said, 'It's about time I put that right.'" Beck had known about the leukemia since 1985 and abided by Jacobs's request not to bring it up. "He always looked healthy to me, so I didn't say anything," said Beck. He paused, then added: "Even if he didn't look good, I doubt I'd comment to him. Jimmy was the kind of person that when he asked you to do something, you did it."

Jacobs tried hard to build a new relationship with his sister. He gave her his share of the inheritance from their mother's estate. It wasn't a large amount of money, yet enough, said Dorothy Zeil, "so that I didn't have to worry about eating or making the six-hundred-and-fifty-dollar-a-month rent on my little apartment." Jacobs invited her to both the Smith and the Thomas fights. He insisted that she bring her daughter, Heidi, and husband, Irving. He paid for their suites at the Las Vegas Hilton and invited them to lavish dinners and to the postfight room parties. Through the first half of the year, Zeil didn't notice any deterioration in her brother's health. Nor did she ask questions about the presence of a quiet, unassuming man at Jacobs's side at each of Tyson's fights. It was Dr. Gene Brody, his hematologist. Jacobs kept that little detail a secret. "He introduced him to me as his friend," Zeil said. "Jimmy had a lot of different types of friends."

At the Thomas fight on May 30, Jacobs narrowly escaped being found out. The day after the fight, just as Jacobs was about to leave his room in the Las Vegas Hilton and go to the airport, he grew suddenly weak, was struck by a fever, then started to sweat profusely. By that time, Dr. Brody had already gone back to New York. Jacobs's wife Loraine waited until he stabilized. She then guided him down to a taxi, trying not to be spotted by any reporters. Jacobs slept most of the way back to New York. When they arrived, the attack subsided.

The attack could have resulted from a bacterial infection of some kind, one that people with normal cells could get through without extreme reactions. For Jacobs, however, it signified that the disease had perhaps begun to accelerate toward the advanced stages. In July, Dr. Brody ordered Jacobs to enter the hospital for a bone marrow biopsy. The results showed no transformation yet of the disease. The attack in Las Vegas had been a false alarm.

It wasn't until later in the summer of 1987 that Zeil noticed anything which, as she realized later, might have given away his secret. "It was the night before Mike fought Tucker in August," she said. "I was sitting on the couch with Jimmy. There were two men there I didn't know. Loraine came in and sat near us. One of the men commented on how similar Jimmy and I looked. When people said that, Jimmy always came back with, 'Yes, but she's got so much more hair.' That's what got me started on his eyelashes. Jimmy had long, dark eyelashes. They were the kind that in the old days movie people would spend fourteen hours putting on one by one. When we were teenagers, every girl would look at them and swoon.

"Anyway, when Jimmy made the comment about my hair, I said, 'And he's got those beautiful, gorgeous eyelashes,' I looked at Jimmy and he turned away and gave a quick look up at Loraine. I mean it was like ice suddenly. He got up and moved away from me. Loraine took over the conversation and changed the subject."

Jacobs didn't have those eyelashes anymore because of the side effects of one of the two drugs he'd been taking in chemotherapy that year, Cytoxan. "Jimmy always had a heavy beard as well," Zeil said. "Even when he shaved, he had that shadow. But even that was gone." At the time, however, Zeil let it pass. She didn't know to look for signs of cancer treatment. She believed in her brother, and if he acted oddly, it must have been her fault. That had always been the emotional equation of their relationship. "When Jimmy walked away like that, I felt like I'd said something wrong, not that I was getting at their secret," she admitted.

Torres also noticed the odd behavior of Jacobs that summer, but he didn't question it either. Ever since their first conversation early in the year, Jacobs had kept after Torres about the new contracts. "I didn't take Jimmy seriously when he said 'if anything happened to me' he'd need the contracts," Torres recalled. "I never thought anything would happen to him." Jacobs persisted with Torres on several occasions in the first half of the year. "Every time I saw him after the first meeting, he insisted I draft the contracts," Torres said. "Jimmy was not being subtle. He was very open. He kept insisting that it was 'just in case.'"

The manager of the heavyweight champion wanted to redraft important contracts, and Torres, although expected to function as the frontline watchdog in the sport, did not seem concerned about his motive for doing so. That was exactly what Jacobs expected. For how long Torres would be so compliant, he couldn't be certain. He hoped that Torres, like Zeil, would play his assigned role in the unfolding plan to make Cayton manager and enable Loraine to inherit his share of Tyson's purses.

Jacobs kept up a front as best he could that summer. The bout against Tony Tucker on August 1 was in some ways Tyson's most important. Victory would earn him the I.B.F. crown and unify the division. Everything had to go smoothly.

Tucker was a twenty-eight-year-old, six-foot-five, 220-odd-pounder from Grand Rapids, Michigan, the type of heavyweight Tyson had been chopping down for over two years. His record of 35–0, with thirty knockouts masked a multitude of problems, the first being with management. He started out in 1980 under a partnership between the veteran trainer Lou Duva and Shelly Finkel, but his father, Robert, who used to box, interfered so much in business decisions that Duva and Finkel bailed out. In 1982, a knee injury kept Tucker out of the ring for more than a year. In 1985, he broke a hand and left boxing for another nine months.

Tucker was considered a finished fighter until his surprise victory over James Broad earned him a shot at the vacant I.B.F. title. The opportunity came on the undercard of Tyson-Thomas. He matched up against a lackluster contender named James ("Buster") Douglas. The bout was an uninspired wrangle, with neither fighter showing much energy or interest. In the tenth round Tucker hit Douglas with a clean but hardly overwhelming punch. Douglas unraveled, and within seconds the fight was over. No one at the time ever expected to hear from James ("Buster") Douglas again.

In the first round against Tyson, Tucker moved laterally to avoid punches, used his greater height and longer reach to send in jabs, then stopped, planted, and delivered a right or an uppercut. In other words, unlike Smith, he boxed. Tyson relentlessly pursued, hoping to make Tucker miss so he could then pop up with a thundering counterpunch hook to the head. But this time something different, and shocking, happened. Tucker threw a right cross that Tyson artfully dipped away from. He should have then countered with the trademark combination left hook to Tucker's exposed right side: once to the body and quickly up to the head. For whatever reason, Tyson didn't do that. He froze on the inside with his gloves down. Tucker took advantage of the moment and followed with a right uppercut that caught Tyson square on the chin. Most fighters would have dropped half conscious from the hit. Tyson, with his massive nineteen-and-a-half-inch neck and first-round adrenaline, hopped back a few steps, then continued the pursuit.

In the corner after the round, Rooney knew exactly what Tyson had done wrong. He was looking for that one big punch to end the fight, and that made him forget about defensive movement. "Go to the body first, then up to the head. Don't look for the one shot to the head!" Rooney instructed. In the second and third rounds, Tucker kept catching an exposed Tyson with right hands. He was giving Tyson's future opponents a clinic, the basic tenets of which were, move constantly, don't make yourself an easy target, and get your punches in first.

Rooney kept ordering Tyson to use his jab, to box more, and to throw combinations. In the fourth, Tucker still dominated the pace. Then Tyson finally connected with two big left hooks. Tucker moved back, but kept boxing. Rooney repeated, "Jabs! Jabs!" Before Tyson went out for the fifth, Rooney said, "Do something different! Throw a punch with bad intentions!" Tyson did nothing different. In the sixth, he went after Tucker again straight on. Tyson followed one of his jabs with a right that caught his opponent flush on the side of his jaw. Tucker shook his head to say it didn't hurt—but of course it did. For Tucker, the fight was all but over.

"I sat next to Jacobs that night," said *Newsday's* Wally Matthews. "He was always so confident about Tyson in the ring, so unemotional. For the first five rounds he was mortified. He watched without saying a word, didn't take his eyes out of the ring. By the sixth or seventh round, when he realized Tyson would win, he was yelling and screaming, 'Kill him, Mike! Rip him apart!' He pounded the table so hard our computers were shaking. The press guys had to tell him to settle down."

From the sixth round on, Tucker all but stopped punching. Tyson kept working in his newfound jab. In the tenth round, he threw twenty-two jabs, sixteen of which landed. (Usually he threw ten jabs in any one round, with only five landing.) In the twelfth and final round, Tucker threw a desperation left hook that hit Tyson on the chin. It was too little, too late. Tyson won a unanimous decision, took the third and final title of the division, and became undisputed heavyweight champion of the world.

The victory confirmed that Tyson had one of the hardest chins in the history of boxing—so hard that early in the fight Tucker aggravated a fracture in his right hand. Moreover, Tyson had matured enough to realize that when he couldn't knock a man out in the first round, he had to use boxing skills. "He initiated something in the middle of the fight, he improvised, and to do that at twenty-one years old is a major achievement, the mark of a true professional," Steve Lott remarked. It was even more significant given that early in the fight Tyson had jammed his big toe and ripped off the nail. "In the dressing room, we took off his shoe and found a bloody mess. If he felt the pain during the fight, he never told Kevin or me."

Tyson was the first undisputed heavyweight champion since Leon Spinks defeated Muhammad Ali in 1978. Don King arranged an elaborate "coronation" ceremony later that night. It took the hype about Tyson to the fringes of farce. King hired six mock-Beefeater trumpeters and dressed them in blue velvet and sequins. Some of Tyson's hapless opponents, dubbed "Sir Bonecrusher," "Sir Pinky," and the like, were paraded down a red carpet. Tyson appeared in street clothes. King threw a chinchilla robe over the boxer's shoulders, thrust a jeweled scepter into his hands, and sat him down in a garish red-velvet throne. The crowd called for a speech. Tyson blurted in a deadpan voice: "Does this mean I'm going to get paid bigger purses?"

Now that Tyson had unified the division, Jacobs tried to revive negotiations with Larry Holmes. "Jimmy tried everything he could to make the deal with Holmes, but nothing worked," said HBO's Seth Abraham. "Every time he got close to an agreement, Holmes would stop answering his phone calls. The simple fact was that Larry didn't trust Jimmy and he didn't like Bill."

More than anything else, Holmes resented Jacobs's arrogance. Every time Jacobs made an offer, Holmes continued to counter by raising his price. Jacobs's ego prevented him from meeting it. Moreover, his deteriorating health precluded him from pursing Holmes as aggressively as he would have done in the past. The negotiations froze.

That posed an opportunity for Abraham. The last major sticking point in the new $26.5 million, multifight deal he'd negotiated with Jacobs and Cayton over the summer of 1987 was the role of Don King. He wanted King to promote all seven fights in the new deal; Jacobs and Cayton didn't. Abraham used the impasse with Holmes to serve his, and King's, interests.

"Jacobs and Cayton told me when we started negotiating the new multifight deal that they would make Don the promoter of the fights, but they didn't want to commit to it in a contract," Abraham recalled. "Jimmy gave me a whole dissertation about how Cus D'Amato always told him never sign a champion to a multifight agreement with a promoter. I didn't agree. I was spending twenty-six-and-a-half million dollars and I deserved a professional, top-notch promoter who knew what he was doing. Why should I risk their bringing in some amateur?"

All through September and early October, Jacobs and Cayton argued back and forth with Abraham over King's future in the multifight deal. Abraham then pulled what was obviously an astute tactical move, although perhaps a tad devious, too. He suggested that King try and sign Holmes. Jacobs and Cayton reluctantly agreed. Without informing them, Abraham then told King that he would kick in an extra $1 million for Holmes's purse if that was what it took to get his signature on a bout agreement. With that much more money on the table, Jacobs might have signed Holmes himself. King went to Easton, Pennsylvania, stayed up all night with Holmes, and by dawn had a deal. Not surprisingly, King called Abraham first with the news. "I was at a West Virginia resort for an HBO convention. He called at six A.M. and woke me up. He was very happy, to say the least. He'd earned the right to promote Tyson's fights," Abraham said.

In late October, Jacobs and Cayton agreed to let King promote Tyson-Holmes. For the remaining six fights in the new deal, he was also "preapproved" by all parties as the promoter. Any other promoter had to be approved in writing by HBO. "I'm not saying Abraham and King had it all worked out, like some scheme," Butch Lewis said. "But hey, you know, you got to wonder how they always ended up moving together on everything. King wanted Tyson. He was just waiting to make a play for him. He was pissed off about being pushed out of the deals by Jacobs and Cayton. He needed to get back in with Tyson. Abraham made that possible."

Abraham had also seen enough of boxing to know that the bond between fighter and manager is not all that strong. Time and again King ended up with the leading heavyweight in his grasp. Abraham thus kept King in the alliance as a kind of investment. If for any reason Tyson broke away from Jacobs and Cayton, he'd be free game for any number of managers and promoters. With King in close proximity, however, Tyson wouldn't get any farther than the front door.

*   *   *

Tyson's next fight was against Tyrell Biggs on October 16 in Atlantic City. In the weeks leading up to the bout, the New York boxing reporters, along with several leading boxing experts, had a collective change of heart about Tyson. In the Tucker fight, even though Tyson had matured significantly, some reporters had finally realized he could be beaten. For the first time since Jacobs and Cayton had launched their marketing campaign, the hype about Tyson came under serious review.

In a September 27 two-page feature spread, *Newsday's* Matthews said bluntly, "There are doubts about how good Mike Tyson really is." He questioned whether Tyson's taste for the nightclub life, fast cars, and expensive clothing and jewelry would distract him from improving his ring skills. The conclusion was that Tyson had a long way to go before he could live up to the hype. Ray Arcel, who had trained some of the greatest boxers of the century, said, "He has yet to prove he's great, and he may never do that."

Jacobs came back with a not-so-credible response. "Why can't he just be Mike Tyson, a good young fighter?" he said in reaction to a similar but less extensive critique by Phil Berger of the *New York Times*. "Why is everybody on video fast-forward, comparing him in onerous fashion to Marciano, Joe Frazier, Jack Dempsey, Joe Louis? Mike Tyson just turned twenty-one." Jacobs was conveniently forgetting that he and Cayton had been the first ones to make the historic comparisons.

The change in attitude about Tyson stripped away much of the pumped-up artifice that usually surrounded his fights. Jacobs and Cayton were emerging as hypocrites. Since June, Butch Lewis had wanted to get his "People's Champion" in the ring with Tyson, but to the press, at least, Jacobs kept saying no. Biggs, on the other hand, had no trouble at all getting a deal. Although a 1984 super heavyweight Olympic gold medalist, Biggs had hardly distinguished himself as a professional boxer. Soon after the Olympics he had entered a drug clinic to recover from a severe cocaine addiction. Since then Biggs had a record of fifteen wins, no losses. But none of his opponents was of any great quality. Not one of them had taken part in any of the main events of the HBO Unification Series.

At six-foot-four-and-three-quarter inches and with a typical tall heavyweight's lazy defense, Biggs would also be easy prey for Tyson. Offensively, Biggs had still not abandoned an amateur style that emphasized scoring points with frequent but light-hitting punches. He hadn't earned the right to fight Tyson, and he wasn't anywhere near capable of winning. Why was he getting a fight when Spinks couldn't?

On the surface it appeared as if Jacobs was ducking Spinks. That was not the case. Jacobs wanted the Spinks fight, but only on his terms.

Then why Biggs? It had nothing to do with what was best for Biggs's career. Biggs was being managed by Shelly Finkel. Finkel felt he had a favor coming. He'd been mediating on Jacobs's behalf with Lewis all through the summer. He hadn't achieved much, but at least the deal was still warm. And Finkel had also kept quiet about it. Now he wanted a last, big payday on which to wrap up his role in Biggs's career.

There were precedents for such dealings. Twice over the last year, Finkel had experienced trouble making viable matches for Biggs. He could get him on HBO but had difficulty finding opponents who were easy to beat yet also acceptable to Abraham as competitive. In both cases he had asked Jacobs to intervene. Abraham had promptly approved matchups with Renaldo Snipes and David Bey—two over-the-hill former contenders, whom Biggs barely defeated. Now Finkel wanted Jacobs to intervene again, this time with both HBO and the Trump Plaza in order to get a fat good-bye purse. Jacobs complied. He would, after all, continue to need Finkel in the difficult negotiations with Lewis. Finkel secured a $1.25 million guaranteed purse for Biggs. That was three times the money he had earned in fifteen fights over almost three years.

Tyson came to the fight with his proverbial bad intentions. He said to a reporter a week before the match: "I never really hated anybody. I think I hate Tyrell Biggs. I want to give him a good lesson. I want to hurt him real bad." Many boxing reporters interpreted that as revenge for the emotional slight of having been denied the chance to fight in the

1984 Olympic Games. Perhaps so, but it also dovetailed with his resentment over the new doubt about his abilities. Tyson had a low threshold for criticism. He lacked the self-esteem to take it in stride, like a champion. The hype masked that tendency in Tyson, just as it did his flaws as a boxer. Now that the hype was no longer working as well on the press, he was having a lot more trouble living with his celebrity.

In the first round, Tyson didn't attack in a flurry to score a quick knockout, but instead patiently stalked his prey. In the second round, he landed a thunderous left hook that slowed Biggs down and made him an even easier target. The rest of the fight, which went seven rounds, was a brutal display of near-heartless punishment. Tyson scored with left hooks, doubled up his jabs, and landed enough rights to the body to crack the trunk of an oak tree. For good measure he also stabbed elbows into Biggs's face, landed three low blows, and punched after the bell.

Biggs finished with a split lower lip, a reopened deep cut over his left eyebrow, and a swollen left cheek. Interviewed afterward, Tyson made no effort to hide his sadistic glee: "I could have knocked him out in the third round. But I did it very slowly. I wanted him to remember it for a long time." Tyson added: "When I was hitting him in the body, he was making noises... like a woman screaming." It was the first time Tyson had ever "carried" an opponent for the sheer pleasure of making, then watching, him suffer.

Joyce Carol Oates, who was at the fight, tried once again to get a handle on Tyson. Her "outlaw" and "savior" and "terrible beauty" returned, she wrote in an October 25 *New York Times* feature, with an "impassive death's-head face..." His violence, wrote Oates, "is somehow just, that some hurt, some wound, some insult in his past, personal or ancestral, will be redressed in the ring; some mysterious imbalance righted... his grievance has the force of a natural catastrophe."

# Chapter Twelve

In its final stages, chronic lymphoid leukemia is about the body simply falling apart. For many patients, physical disintegration and the prospect of an end to close relationships produce a feeling of resignation. Ultimately, a profound sense of hopelessness and despair takes over. The initial and common reaction is primitive but workable: denial. Eventually, however, reality sets in. That makes the patient prone to what cancer specialists term "emotional lability," or mood swings. At profound highs he feels omnipotent, as if by controlling others he can control, and beat, the disease. It's the make-believe of immortality. At the lows, the despair and resignation return.

Drug therapy also affects emotional behavior. Long-term use and increased dosages contribute to the mood swings. Shortened attention span, loss of memory, and confusion are not uncommon. At that point someone close to the patient, usually the spouse, is needed to help out with daily tasks.

It is also not uncommon for a patient with a particularly strong ego, and abilities of self-denial, to psychologically induce the attending specialist into seeing things from his point of view—in other words, into believing that he, the patient, is not really that sick, that he can beat the disease. Given that cancer is so often an unpredictable disease where the force of will can seem to put off death for weeks or months at a time, it is no surprise that a doctor can succumb to such a fantasy.

*     *     *

After the Biggs fight, Jacobs tried his best to conduct business as usual, even though the leukemia accelerated. "All through October and November when he came up to meetings in our offices, he would walk in and be sweating intensely. To me he looked thin," said HBO's Ross Greenburg. In late November, Jacobs went to Las Vegas to see his lightweight fighter, Edwin Rosario, match up against the Mexican titleholder, Julio Cesar Chavez. Hiding the disease from friends and family was becoming far more difficult. "The night before the fight, he must have known he would never see me again," said Zeil. "Loraine called me and said he wanted to have just the family for dinner, no one else. He had never done that before in all the times we had been there; it was always wall-to-wall parties. At dinner he tried to be himself—you know, in command—but he looked weak and sounded raspy."

The fight was held outdoors behind the Las Vegas Hilton on a crisp, Southwest desert night. Jacobs, suffering from an upper respiratory infection, bundled up for arctic weather. Beside him sat the ever-present Dr. Gene Brody. Wally Matthews would never forget Jacobs's appearance that night: "He looked terrible. He'd lost weight, was pale, and looked weak. It was a cool night; everyone had on a sweater, but he had on a heavy jacket, scarf, earmuffs—and even then he seemed to be shivering."

Rosario lost the fight on a close decision. With different judges, Rosario might well have won. Jacobs, as he often had in the past, was expected to argue the decision, to explain with fervent energy why his fighter should have won. Instead, he seemed resigned, almost fatalistic, about the outcome. Larry Merchant said, "He used to get angry about those kinds of fights. This time he was philosophical." In Jacobs's room later that night, Zeil remembered his reaction: "He kept saying things like, 'It's just a sport. You win some and you lose some. You can't take it to heart, it's just a business.' That was not like Jimmy. I just thought he had the flu. Everyone in my family went home with the flu after that weekend."

Nick Beck, who spoke to Jacobs briefly at ringside after the fight, tried to see him before he returned to New York. Loraine refused to let him come up to the room. "Loraine said he had laryngitis and couldn't talk to anyone. That was the last time I ever saw him."

There were people Jacobs had to see. He had made a habit of having lunch with Larry Merchant a few days after one of his fighters won, or lost, a bout, to discuss future plans for that fighter. Jacobs always came alone. "This time Jimmy brought Bill Cayton," Merchant said. "Bill had never joined us before, and frankly I never thought he was interested in the things Jimmy and I talked about. But there he was."

By early December, Jacobs's emotional fluctuations were beginning to affect business. Several details had yet to be worked out in the multifight deal with HBO. After Biggs, moreover, Tyson still owed HBO a title defense under the existing series contract. Uncertain about how long he would live, Jacobs was anxious to advance the schedule. He persuaded Abraham to overlap the two deals. Tyson-Holmes was thus made both the last fight of the series and the first one in the new deal. They scheduled it for January 22.

Abraham didn't mind making the change. It saved him money. With Jacobs and Cayton, that was a rare occurrence. He had noticed, however, that Jacobs had become more dour and humorless than usual about negotiating sticky points of the deal. "We were going over some details of the new seven-fight deal in my office. Jimmy sat at my desk; Bill and I were on the couches. They wanted bank letters of credit for each fight. They insisted that HBO pay the bank charges, which came to eighty thousand dollars in all. I refused to pay the charges. They wouldn't budge. I said, 'Let God decide; we'll flip a coin and, Jimmy, you can call it.' Jimmy looked at me with a blank stare. He was stunned. They went outside into the hall and talked about it for five minutes. They actually had to talk about it. They came back and agreed. Jimmy won the toss. That was it. No reaction from him; no happiness, no sense of humor about it."

Zeil expected Jacobs to come home for Christmas. Just as her mother had every year since 1960, she set the table days in advance of his arrival. The Christmas visit was important to her, an affirmation of the new intimacy, such as it was, with her brother. "I never expected him to start getting close to me after our mother died, but he did. He did it," she said. "I set a place for me, for Jimmy, and even one for Mike."

Jacobs called to say he wouldn't return to Los Angeles for Christmas. Instead, he and Loraine went to Jacksonville, Florida, to see her family.

"He told me they were going to Paris after that and then he'd 'definitely' be in Los Angeles in February to get his California driver's license renewed," Zeil said. "I remember asking, 'Jimmy, are you ever going to come home?' He said, 'Didn't I tell you to leave my name on the mailbox? I'll be home.'"

Jacobs felt too weak to make the Paris trip. He returned to New York on December 26. He was starting to have trouble finishing meals. He'd eat a little, then feel full. Within a few days, he began to lose weight.

On January 4, Jacobs and Cayton signed the HBO deal in Abraham's office. "He arrived late. He took off his sports jacket, and his shirt was drenched in sweat," Abraham recalled. The next day Jacobs went to see Dr. Brody, who determined that his loss of appetite had resulted from an enlarging of his spleen, which was pressing against his stomach and reducing its capacity. His spleen was also "hemolyzing"—that is, trapping and destroying red blood cells. "I determined that he had become anemic," Brody said.

Jacobs entered the hospital on January 7. He instructed Cayton to tell the news media that he needed colon surgery. The truth was quite different. On January 8, Jacobs had his spleen surgically removed. Just before the operation, he called Zeil to say he was sending $450 so she could buy a new Sony television, and a VCR, because he wanted to send her some tapes. "It was another of his good-bye gestures," Zeil said.

A few days after the operation, it was determined that Jacobs had undergone what was called Richter's Transformation. That was a potentially fatal change in the course of the leukemia. Dr. Brody decided that as soon as the incision from the splenectomy healed, Jacobs would have to enter the hospital for a new and far more intensive regimen of chemotherapy. If the chemotherapy failed to control the Richter's, then Jacobs would perhaps die. "If you don't treat it vigorously it carries a very bad prognosis," Dr. Brody said.

At the same time, intensive chemotherapy can in itself undermine the immune system, making patients increasingly prone to opportunistic infections such as pneumonia. In Jacobs's weakened state, Dr. Brody realized, pneumonia might prove fatal. Indeed, most people in the late stages of chronic lymphoid leukemia ultimately die from such complications of treatment.

The other decision that had to be made after the splenectomy was whether Jacobs should be released from the hospital at all prior to the new regimen of chemotherapy. It's not uncommon for splenectomy patients to remain in the hospital for a month or longer after the operation. In Dr. Brody's opinion, Jacobs was healthy enough to leave within a week. But his opinion may have been shaped in part by Jacobs's determination to finish important business before risking the consequences of the chemotherapy. On January 16, Jacobs went home to his apartment on East Fortieth street. He had a lot left to do before going back into the hospital. His drive to deny, and control, hit high gear. In five days Tyson would fight Larry Holmes at the Atlantic City Convention Center, and Jacobs decided he had to be there.

Prior to going into the hospital for intensive chemotherapy and risking death, Jacobs had to tie up a lot of loose ends—first, and foremost, the plan for Cayton to take over as Tyson's manager. Torres had still not completed drafting the new contracts that would, in the event of Jacobs's death, affect that transition of control and thereby prevent Tyson from becoming a free agent. Torres also hadn't finished the set of documents that would enable Loraine to inherit Jacobs's cut of Tyson's future fight purses.

Jacobs knew that he could push Torres only so far. If he suspected that Jacobs was going to die soon, he might, through a sense of personal obligation to Tyson, feel compelled to tell him the truth about the contracts. It wouldn't take long before Tyson would realize that free agency, rather than transfer to Cayton, was a real, and even preferable, career option. If that happened, Loraine wouldn't see a dime. And who knew, Jacobs wondered: perhaps Torres would also inform King of his suspicions.

There was also the deal with Butch Lewis to complete. Jacobs and Cayton had agreed with HBO to try and make Tyson-Spinks the closed-circuit pay-per-view fight of the new multifight agreement. Jacobs asked Shelly Finkel to arrange a meeting with Lewis in Atlantic City. It would be their first meeting since June, and quite possibly one of the few remaining chances for Jacobs to bang heads with Lewis on the deal. Finally, he had to keep a close eye on his sister. Zeil's medical knowledge might enable her to take the smallest bit of evidence about his deteriorating health to its conclusion.

\*    \*    \*

Jacobs arrived in Atlantic City on January 20. He had given himself only four out-of-hospital days to recover from the splenectomy. He stayed in his room at the Trump Plaza as much as possible and kept to a minimum all the prefight business he usually conducted in meetings with HBO executives, other managers, and the press. Cayton suddenly took on a higher profile in their business dealings at fights. For the first time ever, he started to function as the frontline manager of Tyson. Greenberg recalled: "You could see the transition taking place before your eyes. Bill started to assert himself more." That didn't startle people as much as the relish with which he played the new role. Ed Schuyler, boxing reporter for the Associated Press, put it this way: "Bill was mostly in the background until Jimmy started going in and out of the hospital. And to tell you the truth, being in charge of Mike Tyson went straight to his head." Bernie Birnbaum, a television producer with CBS News, was in Atlantic City to do a segment on the fight. He had known Cayton for some years and recalled the change in his demeanor: "He walked around like his Grey Eminence."

Jacobs managed to attend the final prefight press conference and the weigh-in. Anyone who could get close enough to inspect his condition knew there was something very wrong. His health became a hot subject among the press corps but, surprisingly, remained at the level of gossip—not one reporter mentioned his obvious decline in the prefight coverage. "Oh, yeah, I heard the rumors, like AIDS," Schuyler said. "I didn't believe it. Jimmy was sick, that's all."

When Butch Lewis arrived for their meeting on the twenty-first, he was astounded by Jacobs's appearance. "It looked like he had been made up like one of those guys on that movie *The Living Dead*," Lewis said. "His skin was pale, his eyes were all sunk in, with bags under them, and he'd lost all that weight. He looked scary." As with everyone else who knew anything about Jacobs, Lewis didn't for one moment suspect anything fatal. Jacobs had always been such an imposing figure. It was too much of a psychological leap to think he might die. "His health didn't affect my approach to business we had to do," Lewis added. "You didn't deal with Jacobs that way. He was always tough, even when he looked horrible."

Normally, Jacobs would lead such face-to-face negotiations with Lewis—leaving Cayton to do the contract review and detail work back in the office over the phone. Not this time. Jacobs was too weak. Cayton the consummate numbers cruncher laid out the projected figures for a closed-circuit pay-per-view fight. The gate was likely to reach $7 million and so surpass the record of $6 million Sugar Ray Leonard and Marvin Hagler had set the previous April. Total revenues would reach $30 million from all sources, and Jacobs and Cayton were prepared to guarantee Lewis $10 million, to split with Spinks as he saw fit. In return, Lewis had to forfeit to Don King all rights as promoter. King's fee would be $3 million. That left $17 million for Tyson, Jacobs, and Cayton. Lewis said he'd think about it and they could meet again in a few days.

That twenty-one-year-old Mike Tyson would defeat thirty-eight-year-old Larry Holmes, no one doubted—especially not the Tyson camp. "Our biggest concern was that Mike would hurt Larry," Steve Lott said. They were seventeen years apart in age, the second widest gap ever between heavyweight opponents in a title fight. The widest had been when Archie Moore, at forty-two, fought Floyd Patterson, also twenty-one, in 1956. Patterson won. Since losing to Michael Spinks, for the second time, on April 19, 1986, Holmes had been in retirement for 642 days. "I'm going down in history, not Mike Tyson," the perennially cranky Holmes said at a prefight press conference. "He's going down in history as an SOB. If he do happen to win the fight, down the line he'll destroy himself."

Ticket sales for the fifteen-thousand-capacity convention center reached $4 million, a record for Tyson fight. It was the dead of winter in the place cynics called Babylon-by-the-Sea, and yet more celebrities poured in than ever before to see Tyson pummel an opponent. In his final prefight comments, HBO's Larry Merchant summed up the seeming significance of the event: "...we're all here for a ceremony... this passing of the torch. From the old king to the new king."

Holmes didn't want to rush his demise. As the challenger he had to enter first, but he delayed a full ten minutes, for no other reason than to annoy Tyson. Perhaps he'd heard about Tyson's recurring dream. "I always dream that I'm going to lose. It's very scary," Tyson had said to some HBO staffers a few weeks before the fight. Or maybe Holmes had been told that just an hour earlier someone had called in a death threat against Tyson. Whatever the case, Tyson wasn't happy about having to wait. "He was pretty wound up," Lott said. "He punched a hole in the wall of his dressing room." HBO's cameras killed time focusing on celebrities—Jack Nicholson, Barbra Streisand, Don Johnson, and Kirk Douglas, among others. Not shown were the two women Tyson had invited—Suzzette Charles, a former Miss America whom he'd been seeing while in New York, and Robin Givens, his Los Angeles obsession.

Holmes arrived shrouded in a white satin robe that said "Shock the World" on the back. The crowd offered only polite applause. Tyson followed, but this time without music. He almost jogged to the ring; sweat beaded his face, shoulders, and chest. He had a tense, scowling, expression.

Holmes came into the ring at 225¾ pounds of not-so-firm flesh spread over a six-foot-three frame. Holmes knew that if he punched, or moved, too much he would quickly tire out. In the first round, he shuffled around the ring and used his ten-inch reach advantage to block Tyson's punches. When Tyson got in close, Holmes took a page from the tactics of James ("Bonecrusher") Smith and tied him up.

At the start of the second round, Holmes threw a few of his once-deadly missilelike jabs. Tyson easily slipped away and tried to counter. Holmes shuffled and blocked well enough to avoid getting hit by a solid shot. By the third, Tyson decided to start throwing a few jabs of his own. Holmes used his longer reach to catch him with a few straight rights. It was beginning to seem like a boring fight. Holmes mostly wouldn't throw punches, and Tyson couldn't land any. Just before the bell rang, Tyson finally connected with a big right, and then after the bell with another. But Holmes appeared unhurt.

Holmes came into the fourth trying to dance and jab as in days of old. That was his mistake. The experts were always saying that movement and jabbing could keep Tyson at bay, but that was true only if a fighter was quick and powerful enough to exploit his occasional laxity on the inside. It also helped to be able to survive more than just a few of Tyson's punches. As Tyson began to catch him with left hooks, it was clear Holmes couldn't withstand the punishment. Mid-round, he had his gloves up around his face to guard against the hook. Tyson threw a left jab instead and then, in a blur of motion, followed with a self-styled hook–straight right that snuck in between Holmes's gloves and caught him flush on the side of his face. He reeled over and hit the canvas, then got up. Seconds later another right sent him down again. Pride alone brought Holmes to his feet.

Tyson let loose a barrage, and all Holmes could do was try and protect himself. Tyson drove him against the ropes and landed one punch after another until Holmes buckled left and down onto the canvas for the last time. The fight was over. Tyson marched to the center of the ring, then stood with his legs apart and his gloves resting victoriously on his hips, mimicking the victory pose of an early-twentieth-century Danish lightweight champion, Battling Nelson.

It was a patiently executed victory. From the outset, Tyson didn't allow himself to get frustrated. He showed calm and waited for the opportunity to play his strength and exploit Holmes's greatest weakness—old age—then took complete advantage of it. Afterward, in the ring interview, Tyson showed both respectful aplomb ("If he was at his best, I couldn't have stood a chance") and, in response to how he'd dealt with Holmes's tactics, self-confidence ("I'm too seasoned a fighter in this stage of my life to be frustrated").

Jacobs didn't scurry into the ring this time to congratulate Tyson. Instead, he remained in his seat with Loraine and Dr. Brody. Cayton went into the ring and later, in another first for him, was interviewed by Merchant on the state of the negotiations with Lewis: "In a nutshell, Butch Lewis cannot be the promoter or copromoter of a Mike Tyson fight. It's not a money fight in any way." That was only half the truth. Lewis intended to give up promoting the fight—for a price.

The three men convened again in Cayton's hotel room on the day after the fight, a Saturday. Lewis asked for $3 million plus the live gate, a total figure that would probably amount to $10 million based on Cayton's numbers. If the gate did better than the $7 million projection, Lewis made more; if it did less, Lewis took the cut. It was a classic boxing promoter's risk. Jacobs and Cayton—who had always eschewed such risks—refused. They insisted he take the $10 million flat fee, nothing more or less. "As always, they wanted it both ways," Lewis said. "If they believed the gate would do seven million, then I was asking for the same thing. It was obvious to me that there was more money in the fight and they didn't want to share it."

Lewis played his wild card. He was willing to take a risk on the gate even though it meant he had to rely on an honest ticket count from Don King, a man he had never trusted. But now that they weren't going to let him have the gate, Lewis decided to get vindictive. "I stood up and said, 'Either you give me the gate plus three million dollars or fifteen million guaranteed.'" Jacobs and Cayton asked him where he thought the additional millions would come from? Lewis told them to take it out of Don King's $3 million cut. "I'm bringing Spinks, you got Tyson— what's Don doing to earn three million dollars?" he yelled at them. It was a scorched-earth tactic intended to shock Jacobs and Cayton into agreeing now before Lewis did something crazier. They stuck to the $10 million.

Lewis had a valid point about King. For the $3 million he would do little in the promotion besides assemble the undercard fights and make television talk-show appearances. Jacobs and Cayton functioned as the real promoters in the deal. They negotiated the purses, the site, and television licensing fees; they would also sell other advertising for the fight, and most of the foreign television rights, plus would assign someone to handle the closed-circuit pay-per-view broadcast.

"As I headed for the door, Jacobs said, 'You'll never have Michael Spinks fight for the heavyweight championship,' Lewis remembered. 'Guys,' I told them, 'you know the old cliché—never say never.'"

Lewis's lawyer, Milt Chawsky, was waiting by the elevators. As they rode down to the lobby, Chawsky told Lewis he'd been crazy to walk out. "'Milt, I had them by the balls in June, and I still got them,' I told Chawsky. They desperately wanted the fight. It was their biggest money out there. Without me, no fight, and the longer I kept them waiting, the more the greed factor would make them up the figure."

Lewis assumed, quite reasonably, that Jacobs and Cayton were of one mind about the deal; that, as always, they were fighting for the lion's share of the money and the control. He was right to a degree. They wanted all that, but they were also desperate to punish him for leaving the HBO series. They couldn't stand to see him gamble again and win, as he had when Spinks beat Cooney. Their egos dictated against it. Beyond that, Jacobs and Cayton were deeply divided.

In what was likely to be his last months of life, Jacobs didn't care as much anymore about who got a million dollars more or less or whether some control over the fight had to be given away. He wanted victory for Tyson, for what it would do to historically verify Tyson's dominance as undisputed champion, and more important for what it did for Jacobs's legacy as a fight manager. Jacobs felt pressured to get the basic outlines of the deal in place before going back into the hospital. He was willing to compromise on the money.

Money and power mattered to Cayton, and when it came to boxing that's about all that did. He felt he had the leverage to make Lewis relent and accept the $10 million. The world tour they had sketched out for Tyson the previous summer—worth $50 million in gross revenues over a year—was a viable alternative to a fight with Spinks, who, he believed, would always be there when they wanted him.

Jacobs didn't have the strength left to outmaneuver Cayton and battle Lewis. He activated his safety measure: Shelly Finkel. "Finkel called me a few days after Atlantic City," Lewis recalled. "'Butch, how's your family...'—you know, he started that bullshit again. We met the next day at the Friars Club in New York. Jacobs showed up, but he seemed spaced out. I repeated my demand. Finkel said I could get hurt at the gate, like he's really concerned about my family and my bank account. 'Shelly,' I told him, 'let me make my own mistakes.'"

No agreement was reached. Lewis never saw Jacobs again. He met with Finkel over the new few days and on February 3 lowered his figure to $14 million, guaranteed and up front thirty days before the fight. For that figure, Lewis would hand the promotion over to King. "Butch, no opponent without a title has ever made that much money," Finkel intoned, stating the obvious. Lewis, once called a "fool" for walking away from $4 million for Spinks to fight Tyson in the HBO series, snapped back: "Yeah, that's right."

Jacobs telephoned the next day and got Lewis to lower his price to $13.5 million. The deal, in rough form at last, was done. Cayton had no say. "It was Jacobs's deal the whole time, and he did it for Tyson," Lewis said.

He also, apparently, did it for Finkel. It was time to return the favor. Without telling Cayton, Jacobs verbally promised Finkel the right to manage the closed-circuit pay-per-view broadcast—or at least that's what Finkel would claim after Jacobs died. "Jim and Loraine and I had dinner one night in a restaurant, and that's where he promised me the rights," Finkel said. His "verbally" guaranteed fee: $1.5 million.

Finkel, former salesman of copy machines, onetime huckster of a computer-dating service, and a sometime concert promoter, had hit paydirt. In seven years of managing boxers, not one had ever become a major money machine, and Finkel had never handled a large-scale closed-circuit pay-per-view boxing event. With one utterance—if, in fact, anything was promised—Jacobs not only got him the biggest payday of his career in boxing to date, but made Finkel an overnight force in closed-circuit pay-per-view presentation of major bouts. It was money for services rendered, past and future, but also, perhaps, a good-bye gesture to a friend. Cayton would never have understood.

Whereas Jacobs merely hid the truth from Cayton, he actually lied to his sister. She'd been calling every day since he went into the hospital for the spleen operation. Jacobs couldn't distract her with boxing or business issues. He told Zeil that the surgery was required to remove a rectal abscess. "He had to lie to me about the splenectomy," Zeil said. "I'm a trained nurse. I worked for a doctor for twenty-five years. If I had known that, I would have realized that he had a fatal blood disease. That was the time he and Loraine started keeping me busy so that I wouldn't discover the truth."

Jacobs had no choice but to enlist his wife both to fill in where his concentration lapsed and to hide the truth. "I spoke to Loraine almost every day to find out how he was. On January 20, I got a letter from her asking me to renew his California driver's license. That was the first time I'd ever been asked to do that. It expired on February 18, his birthday. He never mentioned it to me; Loraine had to take these things over."

As Zeil watched the HBO broadcast of Tyson-Holmes, she noticed that Jacobs didn't get into the ring after the fight. "I called him to ask why," she said. "He said that he was there, that I just didn't see him." Jacobs then told her that he had bought two tickets for her to go see the NFL Super Bowl game in San Diego on Sunday the 24. On Monday, Zeil had to deliver Jacobs's license-renewal form, by hand, to the California Department of Motor Vehicles. "I noticed that Loraine filled in the entire form and Jimmy had signed it. Jimmy usually did these things himself. I asked him about it, and he said, 'I don't know, I've kind of been out of it. Ask Loraine.'"

In the weeks before going back into the hospital again, Jacobs tried his best to keep control of all the players in his life, and he appeared to succeed. The denial had worked; the will to control had overcome the apparent obstacles. Now all that remained was for José Torres to deliver the new contracts. Jacobs had been calling Torres every week about the contracts, and each time Torres assured him they'd be ready soon. Tyson had to sign them before he left for Tokyo to begin training for his next fight. He was scheduled to depart on February 17. Once the contracts were signed, Jacobs could enter the hospital. Those were the final steps in a yearlong plan. It must have all seemed so simple to Jacobs next to the battle with Lewis, so easy compared with the emotionally painful task of hiding his fatal illness from family, friends, and business colleagues.

And then the unexpected happened. Jacobs could help Tyson win in the ring, he could make him millions of dollars, but Tyson, the young man itching to author a life away from boxing, was playing out his own drama.

*     *     *

Tyson returned to New York after the Holmes fight and dropped by unannounced to see Jacobs at his office. Jacobs wasn't there. Cayton sat Tyson down to discuss the upcoming Tokyo fight on March 21 against Tony Tubbs. Cayton said the gross take—$8.5 million—was their biggest yet. He told Tyson where all the money was coming from and explained that after all fees and expenses, including the management cut, Tyson's net purse would be $3.8 million, his richest ever. Cayton laid it all out as if he were reading names aloud from the phone book. He was oblivious to the fact that Tyson couldn't have cared less. He'd only stopped by to tell Jacobs that he was going to Los Angeles to see Robin Givens. In many ways, it was a trip from which he would never return. Cayton asked Tyson if he was "serious" about Givens. "No way," Tyson apparently responded. "I know what she's about."

Not much had changed in the pattern of their relationship. Tyson continued to do the pursuing; Givens kept vying for the upper hand by reminding him of her superior social status. To Tyson it was the same old battle, maddening yet somehow perversely seductive. As Tyson admitted in January to a reporter for the *Amsterdam News*, a New York newspaper geared to black readers: "At twenty-one, I'm the heavyweight champion of the world, but she never lets me forget she was going to medical school and only dropped out to become a TV star and make lots of money."

When Tyson arrived in Los Angeles, Givens added another manipulation: she told him she was pregnant. What was left of Tyson's clear-sightedness vanished. Jonet Sellers, his occasional Los Angeles confidante, remembered the day: "Mike was obsessed with the idea of loving a woman like Robin. When she told him about the baby, it was the idea of becoming a father that hooked him." Tyson was always far more captivated by the illusion of Robin Givens than by the reality. Now pregnancy meant marriage, and in that marriage he saw himself uniting with a beautiful, educated, charming woman.

Tyson was supposed to join Jacobs, Cayton, Lott, and trainer Kevin Rooney in Atlantic City on Friday, February 5, to see his friend Mark Breland fight Juan Alonso Villa in a welterweight bout. Instead, without letting anyone know, he and Givens went to Chicago for the weekend on a whim. On Sunday afternoon, they appeared courtside at the NBA All-Star basketball game. There he recognized Father George Clements, a close friend of Jacobs's when he lived in Chicago. The previous November, Tyson had fought an exhibition match in Chicago that raised $50,000 to help rebuild Father Clements's church, which had been destroyed in a 1986 fire. Tyson proposed to Givens during the basketball game, then asked Clements to marry them. He did, later that afternoon, in a religious ceremony at the Holy Angels rectory.

On Sunday night, February 7, 1988, Tyson called Steve Lott. "He asked me, 'What would you think if I married Robin?' I said that if he loved her, it was a great idea. Mike said, 'I'm glad you feel that way. I married her already.'"

In fact, the bond had yet to be legally sanctioned. The couple still needed a marriage license. On Monday morning, the eighth, Jacobs got a call from Givens's mother, Ruth Roper. She reared up for the first time as the not-so-invisible hand beginning to shape Tyson's life. "Roper told Jim that Mike and Robin had just had their wedding blessed by Father Clements in Chicago and that we either agreed immediately to have him legally married in New York or she was going to have them flown to Las Vegas for the license. She said Givens was three months pregnant," Cayton said.

Roper and Givens had backed Jacobs up against the wall. Whether or not she was in fact pregnant didn't matter; Tyson obviously believed it. Roper had no idea of the potency of her threat. Everything Jacobs had planned was suddenly at risk. If Tyson was kept away from New York, there'd be less time, possibly none, to get him to sign the new contracts before he left for Tokyo, and before Jacobs went into the hospital for chemotherapy. He needed Tyson back in New York right away. He called Roper and guaranteed his support for the marriage.

Suddenly, what had been minor inconveniences turned into pressing problems. Jacobs had been pushing Torres for months to get the contracts done, but they still weren't drafted. In early January, Jacobs had found out that Governor Cuomo's office had asked Torres to resign as commission chairman. The Witherspoon-Smith mess, among several other incidents, had finally convinced Albany that Torres couldn't handle the job. All through January, Inspector General Spinelli had been reviewing the new candidates for the commission's office. Jacobs had to make sure Torres came up with, approved, and processed the new contracts before leaving office.

Jacobs acted quickly. The same day Roper called, he reached Torres in his office and asked about the contracts. Torres told him that they could be ready at the end of the week. "I told Jimmy that I'd discussed the contracts with the commission's lawyer, Carl DeSantis, and with Governor Cuomo's counsel, Fabian Palomino. They got together and made the contracts," Torres said.

According to Athletic Commission rule 206.5, for a boxer-manager contract to be valid "both parties must appear at the same time before the commission." But that rule didn't specify precisely where the appearance had to take place or the type and number of commission officials who had to be present. Generally, the rule was interpreted to mean at the commission's offices, on lower Broadway across from City Hall. But there was a loophole, and Jacobs knew it. He requested that they sign the new contracts in his office on West Fortieth Street. Torres agreed. They scheduled the signing for the morning of Friday the twelfth.

Jacobs also told Torres that Cayton was going to messenger down that afternoon an application to become a licensed New York State boxing manager. He would need it approved right away. The customary procedure for issuing a manager's license requires first an oral or written examination, then payment of a fee. The whole process can take weeks. Torres promised it the next day. He waived the examination and deferred payment of the thirty dollar fee.

Tyson was due back to New York sometime that Monday evening. Jacobs knew it was unlikely he'd have a chance to talk to him about Givens. He especially wanted Tyson to consider drafting a prenuptial agreement. "We knew that there was a twenty-four hour waiting period in which anyone can back out of the marriage," Cayton said. "Jim hoped to talk to Mike during this period." That afternoon Jacobs was interviewed about the wedding by New York *Daily News* boxing writer Michael Katz. Jacobs strained to maintain the appearance of camp harmony and managerial control: "I'm not surprised," Jacobs was quoted as claiming in the next day's paper. "I know Mike has been contemplating this for a while. She's an exquisite girl."

On the morning of Tuesday, February 9, Steve Lott arranged for a limousine to take the three of them to the Municipal Building near City Hall. Givens wore sunglasses indoors. There was a long line of people there, all huddled in their winter coats because of the lack of heat in the hallway. Tyson was quickly recognized and spirited up to the front of the line. He and Robin found out about the twenty-four-hour waiting period before the license could be issued and made binding, and the need to take a blood test. Only a court order from a judge could waive those requirements. "Mike was impatient," Lott said. "He wanted the license right away. We went to a courthouse down the street and got the waiver."

That evening, Jacobs and Cayton held a press conference for Tyson's Tokyo fight against Tony Tubbs. Jacobs had gained back some of his weight but was still pale. Tyson showed up with Givens. The fight was discussed, as was the marriage. One Japanese reporter asked which part of his wife Tyson liked most. "A set of legs that's awesome," he said, eliciting laughter. Givens was asked the same question about Tyson. "I love his mind." The room fell into a stunned silence.

The real news, however, went undisclosed. For years, Jacobs and Cayton had claimed to be co-managers, yet earlier that day Cayton had received his first-ever New York State manager's license.

After the press conference, Jacobs asked Tyson about his plans over the next week prior to leaving for Tokyo. Tyson said that Givens was going back to Los Angeles for a few days and that he planned to go up to the Catskill house, visit surrogate mother Camille Ewald, and relax. Givens would then be back on the weekend for a wedding celebration her mother had planned on the fourteenth—Saint Valentine's Day. Jacobs told Tyson about the new contracts—although he didn't specify their purpose—and asked him to come into his office and sign them on Friday morning. Tyson promised to show up.

On Wednesday, February 10, the Athletic Commission, in a meeting presided over by José Torres, approved a set of new boxer-manager contracts to be signed by Tyson.

With the commission's approval on the contracts, Jacobs had passed the final hurdle. Sound planning, and good luck, seemed to be on his side. Givens's return to Los Angeles was also fortuitous. Now all that Jacobs had to do was wait, and hope, that nothing, and no one, interfered with the signing on February 12. He was concerned, as always, what Nick Beck and his sister might discover. Later in the day on Wednesday the tenth, Loraine Jacobs sent Nick Beck a brief note, or rather, put up a smokescreen. "We are fine; I hope you are the same; we are pleased and excited about Mike's (or Robin's?) conquest."

# Chapter Thirteen

"It's not what a man says, but what he does at the end. That is what he
intended to do all along."

Cus D'Amato

In the wintry gray dawn of February 12, 1988, Mike Tyson was exactly
where he wanted to be: asleep in his third-floor bedroom at the Catskill
house.

At around eight o'clock he went downstairs to make himself breakfast.
Ewald was in the living room watching television. When she heard the
rattle of dishes, she went into the kitchen to say good morning. She
wasn't surprised that Tyson had come back to the house for a few days'
rest. "His life was changing so much," Ewald recalled, "and this was the
only place that remained the same. It was his home."

It was not only Tyson's home, but his refuge, a place where he could
feel the almost tangible presence of D'Amato. His boxing books were
still on the shelves, as was *Zen and the Art of Archery*, which Tyson had
still never read. Above a covered fireplace in the study was a painting
that showed Tyson snapping back Mitch Green's head with a right hook,

213

and in the background, as if suspended in air, was D'Amato looking on with that perennially skeptical expression.

There was one reminder in the house that D'Amato didn't always look so grim. A small, wood-framed photo of D'Amato sat on a table in the corner of the living room. It was one of the few photos of him smiling. It showed the spontaneous side of a simple man who, despite a rigidly Spartan life and a pervading paranoia, every now and then felt the same joys as everyone else. That was the D'Amato Tyson liked most to remember. That D'Amato he felt sure must have loved him.

The activities of recent weeks had been exhausting. Tyson needed to catch his breath. Ever since pummeling Larry Holmes in Atlantic City, he'd been on an unrelenting emotional high. When Holmes had hit the canvas, with him had fallen a generation of heavyweights. The next era belonged to him—D'Amato had said it would be that way. He had also said that being heavyweight champ would cast Tyson, as if irretrievably at times, into a circus of easy pleasures and big promises of quick money. He'd have to be committed to his training. He'd have to rely on people he could trust to guide him through it all. D'Amato had said Tyson could trust Jacobs, and he'd learned to do that.

His first significant act after the fight took place not in the ring, but outside of it. He was no longer the Frog Prince. He hated the way Robin and her mother talked down to him sometimes, and yet what problems could a woman pose that the heavyweight champion, with the help of a man like Jimmy Jacobs, couldn't solve?

Tyson looked out the kitchen window and saw that a thick blanket of snow had fallen during the night. The fifty yards or so of snow-covered driveway would have to be contended with. Then there was at least a quarter mile of gravel road before he could get to anything that was both paved and possibly plowed. He would not make it in time to catch the train to New York.

Tyson called to tell Jacobs he couldn't make it into the city to sign the new contracts. Cayton took over the conversation.

"Sit tight, Mike," Cayton ordered. "I'll take care of this."

A few minutes later, Cayton called back.

"The police are coming to pick you up," he said.

Cayton had phoned the commissioner of police in Albany, whom he had relied on before to help keep quiet some of Tyson's run-ins with the law. A marked police car arrived at Tyson's door less than two hours later. Tyson had spent so much of his short life avoiding the law; now they were here to deliver him. There was an irony in that which miffed him, one that he didn't expect Cayton to grasp.

What had begun as a lazy day to be punctuated only by a friendly contract signing of apparently no great consequence suddenly took on an unexpected urgency.

For Jacobs, Friday the twelfth began to seem like Friday the thirteenth. So much careful planning, and now the climax to a year's work was threatened because snow had fallen in Catskill. Dark, threatening scenarios loomed over the tidy perfection of his succession plan. Maybe Tyson wouldn't make it out. Maybe the police car would skid on an icy road and crash. Tyson might pull a tantrum about having to ride with the police, call back, and refuse to come in. With Givens due back that night, Jacobs couldn't risk delaying the signing of the contracts. And what of Torres, who had the contracts—he always came late to meetings. How long would Tyson hang around for Torres?

Tyson arrived in the afternoon.

The chill of Cayton's penthouse office—those battleship-gray walls— was all the more uninviting in the winter. You didn't come in from the cold here, you returned to it. Cayton sat behind his desk in his high-backed, cushiony leather chair, the only comfortable one in the room. Tyson never did fit easily into the narrow, cuplike, molded-plastic chairs in front of Cayton's desk. He plopped down on the couch. On the opposite wall was a poster-size black-and-white aerial photo of midtown Manhattan. It was like a World War II bomber pilot's view of the city. Look long enough and it almost created a feeling of vertigo.

There were two people there whom Tyson had never seen before. He was told they were from the law office on the thirteenth floor of the building. As usual with his contracts, Tyson had no independent lawyer there to represent him. The only legal opinions Jacobs and Cayton let into these sessions were the ones they'd handpicked and paid for.

While they waited for Torres, Jacobs put the time to use. "Mike, I want you to understand what we're going to do here..." and as Jacobs began to explain, Tyson interrupted him. "I know, Jimmy, you don't have to tell me..." He didn't see why this all had to be explained in such detail. He trusted Jacobs, whatever the subject. If Jacobs said new contracts had to be signed, Tyson signed them. Hadn't Jacobs always acted in his best interests in the past?

Jacobs persisted. "Now, Mike, this will also make sure that if anything happens to me, Bill will take care of Loraine, and if anything happens to Bill, I'll be able to take care of Doris…"

"I'm only too happy to do this, Jimmy," Tyson interjected, borrowing, as he sometimes did, Jacobs's formal speech. "I'm delighted. It's the first chance I've had to do something for you. I'm so pleased I can do this."

Jacobs let it go. He had said all that he was prepared to say. Jacobs did not add what was perhaps the most pertinent information: that the contracts were being signed because within days he would have to enter the hospital for a series of potentially fatal chemotherapy treatments.

When Torres finally showed up, he tried to explain it all to Tyson again. "Cut the bullshit," Tyson blurted impatiently. He held a different kind of trust in Torres, but one just as confirming. Torres knew the circus life of the champion fighter, and as a black boxer who had become chairman of the Athletic Commission he had "crossed over" into an institution of white power. If there was any problem here, Tyson assumed, wouldn't Torres smell it out?

Tyson's impatience started to call attention to their labored efforts at explanation. They had never gone to such lengths before. Jacobs didn't want to take the chance that impatience would convert into suspicion. He told Torres to lay out the contracts.

Torres indicated the first contract to Tyson. He had seen this document twice before. It was the standard, one-page, New York State Athletic Commission boxer-manager contract. Although Tyson never had read it word for word—all eleven boilerplate clauses—he understood the basics.

There was, however, a wrinkle, and one Tyson had seen before. In the first clause, on the term of the agreement, no date was filled in. Instead, under the form language a freshly typed-in sentence said: "The prior contract between the parties dated October 14, 1986 is hereby terminated." It was the same legal device for extending the term of Jacobs's management that they had used in the last boxer-manager agreement, signed in October 1986 just before the Berbick fight. But there was one small and important difference: the October 1986 agreement specified a new term of four years. The contract before Tyson specified no new term at all. Everything else about the contract seemed in order, especially the clause on the boxer-manager purse split, which remained the same: 66⅔ percent for Tyson and 33⅓ percent for Jacobs. Tyson signed several copies.

Torres then set out the second contract. It was exactly like the first, a standard boxer-manager agreement. But it differed from any other Tyson had seen before. In the clause on the term, the following was typed in under the standard language: "This agreement shall be binding on all parties for *the* period from the date *Jim Jacobs shall be deceased, if William Cayton is not deceased, to the expiration date of boxer/manager contract with Jacobs and Tyson dated February 12, 1988"* (my italics).

Tyson signed several copies of the second contract. His signature was large, bold, sweeping, and almost illegible. His was by far the most imposing on the page. It contrasted sharply with the signature he had penned on the first boxer-manager contract in late 1984. He had written small and carefully back then, in an obvious effort to make each letter readable. It was as if he had wanted no one to mistake that "Mike Tyson" had entered into the agreement. He was just eighteen at the time, and still four months away from his pro fight, and perhaps he had the fears of a young man who couldn't quite believe that he had gotten this far in life. He had better state who he was, and state it clearly, to affirm that it all wasn't some dream.

There were no such fears anymore. The Tyson who came to extend his relationship with the most trusted man in his life wrote with confidence, optimism, and happiness. On the way out, he stopped to chat with Steve Lott. "I'm happy I could do something for Loraine," he said, then left.

Jacobs signed the first contract terminating the October 1986 agreement. Then Cayton signed the second contract, which automatically made him Tyson's new manager when Jacobs died. With that transaction, they prevented Tyson from becoming a free agent. He had, for all intents and purposes, been willed by Jacobs to Cayton.

A lot of other business had still to be done. The first two contracts enabled only transition of management control over Tyson. Now Jacobs wanted to will his interest in Tyson's income to Loraine.

Torres pulled out the three remaining documents, each titled "Assignment of Manager's Contract." The assignment contract, another standard commission form, was primarily intended to protect the fighter by establishing who had a right to a cut of his purse earnings. Jacobs had again found a way to make standard contracts suit his extraordinary needs.

In the first contract, Jacobs, as manager, assigned to Cayton 50 percent of his interest in "any and all proceeds and moneys" to which he was entitled. That merely reaffirmed how in the past they had split Tyson's boxing purses. The second contract appeared the same except for two key differences. Jacobs, as manager, assigned 50 percent of his interest to "Mrs. William Cayton." That would occur under only one condition, which had been freshly typed in: "This assignment shall only be effective if William Cayton is deceased and I, Jim Jacobs, have not pre-deceased him."

The third contract reversed things. Cayton, this time listed as manager, assigned 50 percent of his share to "Mrs. Jim Jacobs." Of course, he wasn't named Tyson's manager yet; that wouldn't occur until Jacobs died. Jacobs took care of that by having the following typed in: "This assignment shall only be effective if Jim Jacobs is deceased and I, William Cayton, have not pre-deceased him."

Certain key signatures were still needed for all five contracts to be complete and legally binding. Neither Loraine Jacobs nor Doris Cayton was there to sign. Cayton claimed to have power of attorney for his wife and signed her name. Jacobs, who didn't have such powers for Loraine, did not sign on her behalf. After some discussion, they agreed that Torres would bring the contracts to Tyson's wedding reception on Sunday in order for Loraine to sign. Torres then approved, in his capacity as commission chairman, all five agreements. One of the two people who have come up from the law office on the thirteenth floor, Theresa De Meo, also notarized the three assignment agreements.

*     *     *

The five documents were the most unusual series of contracts ever drafted by the New York State Athletic Commission. No other boxer in the history of the sport in New York had, using any type of commission contract, been willed from one manager to another. And no financial interest in a boxer had ever been willed to a manager's wife in the same way either. At the same time the contracts were also, on ethical if not legal grounds, highly suspect.

The material fact of Jacobs's fatal illness had been intentionally withheld from Tyson. Moreover, no mention was made of the risks to Jacobs from his upcoming hospitalization. They had explained the basics of what the contracts did, but Tyson was not making an informed choice. Without the knowledge of Jacobs's illness, the fact that Cayton would become his manager and Loraine would profit from his fights seemed only a distant possibility—and, to Tyson, an unthinkable one. As Tyson later said: "I had no idea Jimmy was sick."

The contracts were also structured to raise all parties above suspicion in the event that the agreements were later contested. Jacobs was the only one whose life might soon end. The assignment of interest to Doris Cayton, then, was just window dressing. It created a symmetry which suggested that the concern here was not one man's death, but the possible demise of either. The whole idea, it seemed, was to create the conditions for plausible deniability. Nothing could be allowed to focus attention on the medical fact that Jacobs might soon die.

The denial, however, was not so plausible. Jacobs had planned the contracts well in advance, and knew his prognosis. Precisely what the others knew, and when they knew it, is uncertain. Still, much can be gleaned both from their actions at the time and from later interviews. Several unresolved contradictions arise.

First, José Torres. Jacobs approached him about the contracts in early 1987, and it was only after repeated requests that Torres finally got them done. He denied knowing in 1987 that Jacobs was sick, let alone that he might die. "I once noticed that he had swollen glands in his neck," Torres said, "and Jimmy told me it was something he got in Korea when he was in the Army." Torres maintained that it was only in the few weeks before the contracts were signed that he figured it out. "I realized that he must have been sick," Torres recalled. "He was calling me up all the time, pushing me. When I saw him in January, he looked so bad."

The question, then, is why Torres didn't tell Tyson that Jacobs was sick. Wasn't it his obligation, as commission chairman, to inform Tyson fully on every aspect of the decision he was about to make? According to Athletic Commission member James Dupree, it was, and by not doing so, Torres failed in his duties. "The role of the commission is to protect the fighter from those kinds of contracts," Dupree argued. "If I had suspected anything, there's no way I would have allowed them to be signed."

As chairman, Torres was the only full-time commissioner. Dupree and the third commissioner, Rose Trentman, both had other full-time jobs. They worked for the commission on a part-time, per diem basis when they were needed to discuss and vote on policy issues. They could not, nor were they expected to, keep up on the daily activities of either Torres or the commission.

Dupree lived in Syracuse in upstate New York, where he taught American history at Onondaga Community College. On February 10, he had flown to New York to attend what he thought would be one of the commission's routine policy meetings. Present were Torres and his assistant, Barbara Wayne, and to Dupree's surprise, the commission's counsel, Carl DeSantis.

To Dupree, the meeting was anything but routine. Since accepting his appointment at the commission in 1983, he couldn't remember ever before seeing Carl DeSantis at a full meeting of the commission. In fact, since DeSantis was first retained on a per diem basis, also in 1983, he had rarely been asked to offer views on policy matters. Dupree couldn't recall him ever being involved in the drafting or approval of a boxer-manager contract. DeSantis was specifically retained to assist in the collection of past-due fees from promoters for which he used his own office. He didn't even have the use of a desk at the commission.

Another oddity arose at the meeting when Torres and DeSantis put on the table five new contracts concerning Mike Tyson. "They presented the contracts to us for our approval," Dupree said. "Nothing was explained in detail, just that a renewal would be signed. We didn't get to see the contracts. They were described to us by DeSantis. There was no mention of Jacobs being sick or about to enter the hospital. I don't recall anything about Cayton becoming the new manager. No one said that Cayton had gotten his manager's license only the day before."

Dupree's account is verified by the record of that meeting on file at the Athletic Commission. In the minutes of the meeting, there is no mention of Cayton becoming the new manager. The contract that effected the transition to Cayton was referred to as "a contingent boxer-manager agreement in the event that Jacobs is deceased to complete the four-year term of the first contract."

According to Dupree, it was highly irregular to have discussed boxer-manager or assignment contracts at all. "Those kinds of contracts were not brought before the full commission," he continued. "It's only when a contract was being contested that the full commission would vote on it."

Prodded by Torres and DeSantis, and believing that the contracts were not being contested, Dupree and Trentman voted their approval. "I realized months later that the reason why Torres and DeSantis did it was to give the new Tyson contracts more validity," Dupree said. "What they did was not legal. That kind of transition was highly irregular, whichever way they chose to do it. I'd never seen anything like it before.

"What they should have done was brought everybody to the commission. I would have asked why they were signing the renewal now, and what was the reason for changing managers. Then we'd make sure Mike Tyson understood what was going on. I would have explained to him, assuming they told me, that Jacobs was sick, and that's why he wanted to sign these new agreements. I would have told Tyson that Cayton was going to become his new manager. I would have told Tyson that if Jacobs died, he was free to go out and get whatever manager he wants to get. Plain and simple, that's the only legal way it could have been done."

Dupree stressed again that Tyson should have been given the legal right to choose for himself. "He should have been told about Jacobs's cancer. Then he could have said, 'Okay, I don't want to risk being without a manager—let's do a deal, Bill.' Same thing with the money to Jacobs's wife. Jacobs could have said my interest in Tyson goes to my estate, but he didn't do that. He made his wife a party to the contract. She doesn't perform any service for that money."

The question is: What motive did Torres have for making sure, in the event of Jacobs's death, that Tyson remained with Cayton? "I did it to protect Tyson," Torres claimed. "I'll let anyone use me if it helps a fighter." But what may have also been on Torres's mind was replacing Jacobs as the new manager. He had been pushed out of the chairmanship by the governor's office. He had no other job prospects besides going back to being a writer. "Jose dreamed of managing Mike," said Matt Baranski, "no doubt about it."

Second, what was the precise role of Bill Cayton? He had known about Jacobs's illness for years. In the last few months, he had watched Jacobs waste away. At the Holmes fight he'd begun to play the role of manager as if practicing for what he knew was a certain eventuality. It's not beyond reason that he'd figured out that his partner might die and that he might soon become the new manager of the biggest money machine in sports history.

And what a money machine: Tyson's gross earning power had reached incredible proportions. In this most recent phase of his career—eight fights over one year and five months, including the upcoming bout against Tony Tubbs in Tokyo—he would have grossed $23,918,991. The Spinks bout alone was expected to bring in upward of $20 million for the Tyson camp to split. Cayton had no doubt concluded that letting Tyson become a free agent wasn't such a good idea.

Cayton claimed in several interviews that he had no idea Jacobs might die. "I never even knew that he'd had treatment for the leukemia," he said. "He always looked good to me." Cayton also maintained that he had no role at all in drafting the contracts. "It was set up by Jim. Jim handled all this," he said curtly. "I really was not directly involved in this...Jim made the appointment. The whole thing was done by Jim."

That, however, was a self-serving version of events. According to several people involved in the contracts, Cayton was definitely involved. Torres said that both "Jimmy and Bill were hurrying the contracts" in the last weeks. Dupree remembered seeing Cayton speaking with Torres in the offices of the commission just minutes prior to the February 10 meeting.

But the most damning proof of all comes from commission lawyer Carl DeSantis. "The commission itself was the client. Torres told me what he wanted the contracts to achieve. Jacobs and I never met. We talked on the phone about them," DeSantis said. "I recall Cayton phoning me at least once. He went over the same things as Jacobs; he double-checked what was going in the contracts and when they can be done. I recall Cayton telling me to 'hurry up.'"

Indeed, the more the various principals have been asked to explain their role in the contracts, the more contradictions have arisen. It's as if everyone has tried to distance himself from responsibility for the agreements. Torres, for instance, said that Carl DeSantis drafted them in consultation with Governor Mario Cuomo's own lawyer, Fabian Palomino. "Carl definitely discussed it with Fabian and other lawyers in the governor's office," Torres claimed. "Carl would never make a move without the governor's lawyers being involved. The conversation is probably in DeSantis's datebook."

Palomino, however, denied being involved. "I've never had anything to do with Mike Tyson's contracts," claimed Palomino, who is still counsel to Cuomo and also head of the Jacob Javits Convention Center in New York. His denial was confirmed by DeSantis: "No attorney from the governor's office spoke to me about those contracts."

According to Dupree, Palomino did at times play a role in the commission's affairs. "He got involved every time something went wrong," Dupree said. For instance, Palomino intervened after the December 1986 Tim Witherspoon drug-test fiasco. "Torres and De-Santis appealed to Palomino on what to do after the testing mistake had been made," Dupree said. "I recall overhearing telephone conversations on the matter between DeSantis and Palomino."

Matters get even murkier. Torres had said that he took the five contracts, plus all the signed copies, back to the commission's office across from City Hall. By his account, he then realized that the boxer-manager contracts had not been witnessed. Commission rules specify that Torres was empowered to both approve and witness such agreements. He'd done it before on Tyson's first boxer-manager contract with Jacobs in 1984. For the second one in 1986, it was done by another commission official. To have two signatures endorsing an agreement was the preferred procedure. Torres approached Peter Della, a deputy commissioner in charge of selecting and approving judges and referees for fights, to sign the two agreements. "I said, 'Peter, come here. I need a witness,' and he signed. I'm the chairman; he did whatever I said," Torres recalled.

Of course, Della had not witnessed the signing of the contracts at all. To that extent, his endorsement was invalid, if not also illegal. Della had to rely on Torres's word that the parties involved—Tyson, Jacobs, and Cayton—had actually signed their names. Torres admitted that: "He signed because he trusted me."

Della, however, later suspected that his trust had been abused. On or about February 15, he went to Joseph Pezzullo, who was the commission's chief investigator. "Pete told me that he'd signed some Tyson contracts, and that he wasn't too happy about it," said Pezzullo. It made sense for Della to express those concerns to Pezzullo. Pezzullo had previously served for twenty-two years with the New York Police Department. At the commission he investigated internal problems as well as the backgrounds of boxers and managers. He was also given a copy of each boxer-manager contract to keep under lock and key. If there was any impropriety about a contract, it was likely to be spotted by Pezzullo.

Curiously, Della didn't specify to Pezzullo what was bothering him. Pezzullo can now only speculate. "Pete knew boxing, and all the regulations," he said. "If he didn't witness the signing, he would have known that wasn't right."

Pezzullo also surmised that what may have happened was that Torres misrepresented to Della what he was signing. "Pete only talked to me about one type of contract," Pezzullo recalled. "That was the extension of Jacobs's term. He wouldn't have signed anything that willed Tyson to Cayton. Pete would have known that was a violation. I am sure that nothing he signed had Cayton's name on it. What might have happened was that Torres put something in the stack of papers that Della didn't know was there, and that contract was also kept from me."

Several months later, as the real purpose behind the February 12 contracts dawned on Dupree, he confronted Della. But by that point, Della, who never again brought the matter up with Pezzullo, had decided to lie about his involvement. Dupree said: "I asked Peter Della about six times, 'Did you sign these contracts?' and he said, 'No, I had nothing to do with it.'"

Starting in late 1988, then all through 1989, Dupree tried to get to the bottom of the contracts, among other problems that later arose over Tyson's management. But he found no interest or support from either the commission or Cuomo's office. When Dupree's term came up for renewal, he was told by the governor's office that he'd be replaced. "José started out doing a pretty good job, as long as we were working together," Dupree said. "Near the end of his term, he really started listening to somebody else. When he left there was a cover-up about what happened with Tyson."

As for Peter Della, the truth of what he signed, or didn't sign, may never be known. Della, who was in his seventies and suffering from diabetes, died in September 1990.

Certainly, though, Cayton knew that Della's involvement in the contracts was problematic. When Cayton was asked about the other signatures on the boxer-manager contracts, he feigned ignorance. "I signed it, Tyson did, Jimmy and José. That's it. Why, who else signed it?" he responded, in a tone of voice suggesting his customary command of contract issues. When he was then asked about Della's signature, Cayton suddenly became flustered, and reached over to turn off a tape machine being used to record the interview. He then realized what he was about to do, and pulled back his hand. "I, uh, I don't know that name. I'd have to look at the contracts," Cayton muttered nervously. "Oh, yes, I remember now, he witnessed them. I, uh, have things to do. We should continue this conversation later."

*　　*　　*

In the early afternoon of February 12, Jacobs must have felt a great deal of relief when Torres left the office with the contracts. Tyson had forfeited his right to free agency. If Jacobs did not survive the upcoming regimen of chemotherapy, Cayton would automatically take over as manager. Jacobs's wife would inherit his purse cut. She had no formal role in Tyson's management, yet without having to lift a finger she stood to make millions of dollars over the next four years. On Tyson's upcoming bout against Spinks alone, Loraine would take in a cool $3.3 million.

Jacobs went uptown to the offices of Dr. Brody, who gave him one more examination, then called Mount Sinai Hospital. He scheduled Jacobs to enter Mount Sinai on the fifteenth, or that Monday.

Cayton decided not to catch his usual train home to Larchmont. They had all planned to celebrate at dinner that night in the city—Jacobs, Cayton, and their wives. It would be a final dinner together, as acquaintances and business associates. It had the scent of a good-bye among fellow conspirators.

Before going out to dinner that night, Jacobs called his sister in Los Angeles. "He told me that he'd be traveling the next week," Zeil said. "I asked him if he was ever going to come home. He said—and I'll never forget his words—'It's not a matter of choice, Dorothy. You know, I told you not to take my name off the mailbox.' As I found out, what he meant was that he was going to come home in a box."

Jacobs then telephoned Don King, who was at his office on East Sixty-ninth Street. Earlier that week, Tyson had mentioned to Jacobs that he wanted to do something to help out Tawana Brawley, the black high school student from Wappingers Falls, New York, who claimed to have been raped and abused by a group of white men. Black activist Rev. Al Sharpton had become Brawley's "advisor" and had counseled her not to cooperate with the police investigation. Sharpton argued that white justice was in the end just that: Justice to serve white interests. The whole mess somehow spoke to Tyson.

Jacobs decided that as a white man he was the last person who should get involved. He asked King to meet with Tyson and, according to King, "work on this thing for him." Tyson had apparently mentioned to Jacobs during the signing of the contracts that he and King were planning to drive up and visit Brawley the next day. Jacobs called King to find out what exactly had been planned. "I told him we were just going to go up and visit the girl, show support," King said.

Letting King handle so racially charged an issue appeared like the only logical approach. Clearly, though, Jacobs had other motives. The homage to Brawley would not only keep Tyson busy in the days leading up to his departure for Tokyo, but would occupy Givens too—and now also King. The less opportunity they had to find out about, and cross-examine Tyson on the new contracts, the more comfortable Jacobs felt.

Givens returned to New York that night on the red-eye flight. When she got to Tyson's apartment early Saturday morning, King was waiting outside with a limousine. The three of them, along with Sharpton, drove up to visit Brawley. The troubled teenager fawned over Tyson so much that Givens went into a jealous snit. He gave Brawley his $30,000 gold-and-diamond Rolex watch, and promised her more financial support.

Jacobs called King at home the next morning, Sunday the fourteenth. King said that Tyson wanted to make some kind of public announcement declaring his support, morally and financially, for Brawley. "Jacobs said,

'Fine, you handle it, Don, go ahead and work on it," King recalled. "Then I got a call from him that evening. He's crazy with anger. He'd never been that way with me before. 'Don, you better watch out,' he's saying to me in threatening tones. 'Don, I'm telling you, Don, don't go too far.' He said he'd just got a call from Mike Marley [boxing reporter for the *New York Post*], who'd asked him about the press conference for Tyson the next day. That he didn't authorize an announcement. I reminded him of our conversation earlier in the day. He apologized. He'd forgotten. Made a mistake. That sickness he had, that's what did it, I figured later on."

The wedding reception Ruth Roper had organized was held Sunday afternoon, Saint Valentine's Day, at the Helmsley Palace Hotel on Madison Avenue in midtown Manhattan. She'd kept the guest list down to the Tyson camp, José Torres and his wife, and a few friends. The press was not invited. Father George Clements flew in from Chicago. Jacobs, Cayton, and their wives arrived early. When Torres showed up, they all left to find some discreet location in the hotel. Loraine Jacobs put her name down on the assignment contract. Torres told Cayton that his power of attorney was inadequate. Doris Cayton signed her own name.

When they returned to the party, Jacobs pulled Father Clements aside and, as if he were in some Catholic confessional, freed himself of the mortal burden he'd been trying so long to deny and conceal. "The end is near now," Jacobs whispered solemnly to the priest. Apparently, he had also confided in Father Clements about his leukemia.

In a bizarre twist of events, while at the party Cayton was struck by another attack of his endocarditis, the inflammation of the heart and valves that he'd had been suffering from for years. He left the party immediately and that night entered a Westchester County hospital for the standard, and usually effective, treatment of large doses of antibiotics.

The next day, Monday, Tyson and King held a press conference. Tyson said he would pay Tawana Brawley's college tuition and establish a $100,000 fund for abused children in her name. That same morning, Jacobs secretly checked into Mount Sinai Hospital on Manhattan's upper East Side. On Tuesday, Tyson left for Tokyo. He had no idea that both Cayton and Jacobs were hospitalized.

While Tyson was somewhere over the Pacific, Jacobs called his sister and got her answering machine. "I had just come in with groceries and ran to the phone," Zeil recalled. "Jim heard my voice then said abruptly, 'This is Jim, I'll call you later,' and he hung up. An hour later he called back. He said he was in Texas still, alone. First, he never traveled without Loraine. Second, he had never before hung up on me like that. I asked him why he did it and he said he didn't want to talk to the answering machine. Well, he'd never not left a message before. I think what happened is that just as he called me someone walked into his hospital room. That someone was Loraine. I'm sure of it. He didn't want her to know that it was me. I think she was really controlling things by that point and by continuing to talk to me Jimmy could blow the cover-up about where he was, and what was happening to him."

On Friday the eighteenth, Jacobs turned fifty-eight years old. The next day he called his sister again. Jacobs said he was heading back to New York. It was the last time they ever spoke. From that day on, Loraine took over the relationship.

Zeil called her brother's apartment early Saturday evening, thinking he'd be home. Loraine answered the phone. She claimed that Jacobs had entered the hospital for tests. "That's it—tests," Zeil said. "Loraine didn't say where he was or what the tests were for. She did tell me to keep it quiet. That it was all 'low-key.'" Dorothy waited for five days, hoping to hear about the results of the tests. No call. Five days later she reached Loraine. "She told me that Jimmy had 'walking pneumonia... We're not telling anyone,' she said. 'We're keeping it very low-profile because we don't want the press to get it.'"

Pneumonia was the beginning of the end for Jacobs. "It was a big pneumonia," Dr. Brody said. "Really a bad one. He was in intensive care the whole time." In his weakened state, Jacobs had little or no ability to fight back. Antibiotics could do little. Releasing that to the news media was potentially disastrous. Tyson might have cancelled the Tokyo bout and returned to New York to see Jacobs before he died. Perhaps then the implications of the new contracts would have dawned on him—and if not on Tyson, certainly on Givens or King. The threat of the bout's cancellation also hit a collective nerve uniting some of the more narrow concerns of Loraine and Cayton. As Tyson's biggest-grossing fight yet, they both stood to make record sums. Cayton and, in the event of her husband's death, Loraine would both earn $870,726.

Cayton got out of the hospital on the nineteenth. Some reporters were beginning to think that Jacobs had mysteriously disappeared. "It was strange, because since the Holmes fight Jacobs kept insisting to me that he was going to Tokyo for Tyson's fight," *Newsday*'s Wally Matthews recalled. "When he dropped out of sight, Cayton and Steve Lott both said that Jacobs was in Texas buying fight films. The rumors were flying.

Don King's PR guy, Al Braverman, said that Jacobs had AIDS, that he'd gone to Mexico for a complete change of his blood. I didn't know what to believe, but I didn't print that."

By late February, while Jacobs struggled for his life, the cover-up had become more elaborate. Matthews continued, "I asked Cayton, point-blank, 'Is Jimmy in the hospital?' and he'd say, 'No, wait, I'll put him on the phone.' Then there was a silence and sounds like they were patching him in from someplace else. Cayton was trying to keep up the appearance that Jacobs was in the office working."

Nick Beck, despite being Jacobs's oldest living friend, got similar treatment. "I heard stories from guys in boxing that Jim was in the hospital," Beck recalled. "I asked Loraine and she said, 'Absolutely not true.' She lied to me."

Starting in March, Jacobs went in and out of a comatose state. Zeil called every night to see how he was progressing. On Saturday the twelfth, Loraine told her that he had woken up from a coma and seemed to be doing better. "Loraine told me he woke up and asked for ice cream. I screamed out with joy because since Jimmy was a kid, when he got sick then asked for ice cream that always meant he was better." But Jacobs was a long way from recovery.

# Chapter Fourteen

"I'm Mrs. Mike Tyson and I'm taking over."

There was a silence. Cayton started to respond, but Givens hung up the phone. She had already been to Tokyo and back and that day, March 6, she was returning to be with her husband.

Since Cayton had come out of the hospital, being Tyson's new manager had taken a nasty turn. First he'd had to lie about Jacobs being in Texas. Then he'd had to lie about him being in the office. Now Tyson's wife had started making vague threats. A pattern was starting to develop. It had begun with her mother's threats over the supposed pregnancy. Cayton had seen it coming and had made arrangements: José Torres was on the second flight with her to Tokyo.

Givens's influence on Tyson had to be countered somehow. And if Jacobs died before the Tubbs fight on the twenty-first, Cayton would need someone like Torres, with his boxer's background, in Tokyo to control the emotional fallout. Tyson had to be kept focused on winning the fight.

The Torres maneuver almost failed. He had no official business in Tokyo, and thus no way to make New York State taxpayers foot the bill.

Cayton purchased two round-trip plane tickets for Torres and his wife. When Governor Cuomo found that out, he ordered Torres to give the tickets back. He did, and then still found a way to get to Tokyo. He told a boxing reporter that he had secured an assignment from *Parade* magazine to write a feature story on "Japanese boxing, not on Tyson," implying that the magazine was paying his expenses. Perhaps that was the case, but no such story ever appeared in *Parade*.

Tyson in Tokyo was a happy warrior. He had married the woman of his illusions, had signed a new contract extending his bond with a trusted friend, and was about to earn, net, $3.8 million for fighting an overweight opponent. Steve Lott had never seen him so relaxed. "For the first time he wasn't moody before a fight," Lott said. "He usually just turned off to everyone around him. Not this time. We were sitting around talking in his hotel room and he said, 'Can you imagine that I actually went home before the Tucker fight? It was so immature.' I was stunned. Mike had really grown up, become a professional. He knew he was there to do a job; he felt good about himself. I felt he was going to be devastating in the ring. The only time I saw him get moody was when Robin came around."

The fight also launched the world tour Jacobs and Cayton had been planning since the summer of 1987. It was a market test both of how other cultures perceived Tyson and of how well he'd perform away from familiar territory. The Japanese couldn't get enough. He was the first heavyweight champion to defend his title in Tokyo since George Foreman knocked out Joe Roman there in 1973. From the moment Tyson arrived at Tokyo's Narita Airport, he was mobbed by a throng of Japanese cameramen and photographers. He did the talk-show circuit, visited handicapped children and squatted in mock-battle photo-ops against champion sumo wrestlers. He played the global superstar sports celebrity. On the first day tickets went on sale, 80 percent were sold. "It's scary," Tyson said in the HBO prefight segment. "I don't mind being the heavyweight champion of the world, but this is a different dimension." Tyson, though, relished the symbolism of it all. He viewed his fame in the big picture. "I think this is my time."

Cayton arrived in Tokyo a week before the fight. He did not tell Tyson, Lott, or Rooney that Jacobs was in the hospital. "He said nothing about Jim being in the hospital," Lott recalled. Jacobs had never before missed one of Tyson's fights. Reporters, HBO staff, everyone who knew Jacobs questioned Cayton about his absence. He claimed that Jacobs was taking care of business back in New York. Cayton knew, however, that Jacobs was almost certain to die. Recalled Jay Bright, the oldest member of the D'Amato boys camp, who, along with Camille Ewald, went to all of Tyson's fights: "I was standing near Cayton. He was talking to somebody. I distinctly overheard him say, 'It doesn't look good for Jim.'" Bright hadn't even known Jacobs was in the hospital.

Torres visited Jacobs in the hospital several times before leaving for Japan. When he arrived in Tokyo, he told Cayton he might go back and see Jacobs before the fight. Torres had obviously concluded that Jacobs was likely to die. "Cayton said, 'No, don't do that. Stay here.' Then he shocked me," Torres recalled. "'We'll give Jimmy a bigger funeral than Cus.' I thought that he was a heartless bastard." Cayton may have been heartless, but Torres still played along with his agenda of keeping Tyson in the dark about Jacobs. Torres saw Tyson several times in Tokyo, and not once did he mention Jacobs's condition.

The day of the fight, perhaps in a move to protect himself from being accused of a cover-up, Cayton revealed to HBO fight commentator Jim Lampley that Jacobs had gone into the hospital to recover from pneumonia. By that point, Monday the twenty-first, he was almost dead.

The gigantic, cavernous Tokyo Dome, dubbed "The Big Egg," had been open only five days. The Japanese crowd of 35,000, true to their cultural manners, waited patiently, almost silently, for Tyson's arrival in the ring. Not much had, or could, be said of his opponent, Tony ("TNT") Tubbs. In the mid-1980s, he was considered one of the many pretenders to the heavyweight throne, a young man with quick hand speed but a persistent weight problem. In 1985, the six-foot-three Tubbs had captured the W.B.A. crown at a workable 229 pounds. He'd defended the next year at a grossly overweight 244 and lost. His career had wavered ever since as an uninspiring sideshow (made so in part by the gouging Kings) to Tyson's career rise.

For this fight Tubbs would earn around $500,000, plus a $50,000 bonus if he came in under 235. He unrobed at 238. A fighter unwilling to get into shape, despite incentives, cannot be expected to put up much of a battle. Tubbs knew, however, the real reason he was there, a reason capable of squashing a mediocre athlete's will: no one expected him to win. "I'm just the tune-up for Tyson's fight against Spinks," Tubbs admitted at a prefight press conference.

Tubbs won the first round, barely. Tyson had come out looking to finish the fight early with a few good blows. That made him lax on defense, which gave Tubbs the opportunity to score with jabs and a type of punch that no big heavyweight had tried in any systematic way against the shorter Tyson: body shots. Tubbs's punches seemed to befuddle Tyson at first, and upset his offensive rhythm. In the second round, Tyson came out jabbing. He threw three in quick succession with the kind of hand speed that among heavyweight champions only Ali could boast. Tubbs, too overweight to keep out of Tyson's way, decided to mix it up inside. Every time he punched, Tyson hit back, twice as accurately and hard. With thirty-five seconds to go in the round, they separated. Tyson backed him up toward the ropes, threw a right hook to his body, then threaded in an uppercut that landed. The punch snapped his head up and back. Tubbs, watery-eyed, exhausted, looked over at his corner with an expression that said, "That's it, I've had enough." Seconds later Tyson landed with a left hook that grazed off one of Tubb's eyebrow's. His balance seemingly gone, Tubbs reeled, then fell to the canvas. His trainer jumped into the ring waving a white towel. Tyson disregarded him and bent down as he swung with a left. It was a cold, calculated effort to hurt an already wounded man. Had the punch connected, the referee said at the postfight press conference, Tyson might have been disqualified.

Cayton climbed into the ring. Unlike Jacobs, who would always whisper something to Tyson at that point, Cayton said nothing. He stood at his shoulder and smiled into the HBO camera. In the postfight interview, Tyson explained why Tubbs had gotten in any punches at all. He spoke with a new confidence. "He was effective because I planned for it that way. I was looking for the opening. I planned for him to run and he didn't. He kept punching and punching. . . . Then I went for his eyes. . . My mission is to go and destroy and not to let anything get involved. . . I refused to lose. . . We fight the authentic way. . . I tried to hit exactly in the eye. . . This is my world in here."

Was the flaw of passivity finally gone? No one could be sure, but at the least Tyson was showing far more patience when the fight didn't at first go his way. He was seeming less programmed, and more consciously willful. It displayed a measure of self-control that only seasoned fighters achieve. He was a young man who felt his world complete and in perfect order.

The feeling didn't last long.

Robin Givens made her move on the plane trip back to New York.

"I want to see all the paperwork," she demanded.

Cayton responded tersely. "I'll show you a typical New York State boxer-manager contract."

"I don't want to see a typical contract," Givens said. "I want to see your contract with Michael. I want to know what you're making from Michael."

Tyson noticed the scene, and spoke to Cayton himself. He was almost apologetic. It was clear that he had not yet suspected anything was amiss with the February 12 contracts. Givens, however, obviously had.

"Bill, Robin just wants to learn a bit about the business," Tyson explained. "I want her to feel part of the team."

Cayton hesitated, then agreed to send Tyson the documents—but not Givens. "I'll give it to you, Mike, and only you."

When Tyson arrived home in New York the next day, Jacobs was sixty blocks uptown at Mount Sinai Hospital losing his battle with pneumonia. Delirium struck so hard that he started to rant and required sedation. One of his last requests was for "a good cup of coffee." At 7:30 A.M. on Wednesday, March 23, 1988, James Leslie Jacobs was pronounced dead. Later in the day, while Tyson made his way through the streets of New York in the back of a limousine, his car phone rang. It was Givens: "Michael, Jimmy is dead."

*    *    *

"I was the first reporter Cayton called, and I'm sure that was only because AP reaches more people faster than anybody else," Ed Schuyler remembered. "He said that Jimmy died of pneumonia at 7:30 A.M. That's all; nothing else."

The next day, Jacobs's body was flown to Los Angeles to be buried alongside his mother. Two planeloads of invited-only guests followed. Several stretch limousines waited to ferry people around. Bill and Doris Cayton, Loraine, Tyson, and dozens of others stayed at the Beverly Hilton Hotel. Security guards were hired to keep the news media at bay. Cayton said little to the press about the death of the man with whom he had worked since 1960, but as he promised Torres in Tokyo, he intended to outdo the farewell given D'Amato. Appearances had to be kept up. Jacobs, the wizard of handball, the don of fight film collectors, and the hard-nosed manager of boxing phenomenon Mike Tyson, had, by official account, met an entirely sudden, untimely, and, at fifty-eight years old, premature death.

Of course, to Cayton, Doris, and the now-widowed Loraine, it was not the same kind of shock. They formed an exclusive club of three who for eight years had known of the leukemia and could prepare themselves for the most wrenching agony—the day of his death. And yet with the signing of the February 12 contracts they had also traded on insiders' knowledge, and had profited emotionally and financially from their intimacy with Jacobs.

Still, the transition wasn't yet complete. Jacobs's death created the inevitable power vacuum, and it would take more than a few pieces of paper to fill it. In order to battle King, Cayton would have to abandon his myopic faith in the sanctity of contracts and learn how to fight street wars. He also had to keep Robin Givens and her mother—"the women," as he began to call them—under control.

But most crucially, he had to insulate Tyson, as Jacobs so effectively had for years, and that meant duplicating the intimacy of Jacobs and Tyson's personal bond. Cayton wasn't capable of it. Tyson wouldn't have accepted him anyway. Loraine, for whatever reason, didn't even try to help out. Cayton was destined to lose this one.

"On the flight out to L.A., Mike sat alone. Givens stayed in New York. He sat there stunned, like he was in some kind of trance," recalled a friend of Jacobs's who was on the flight. "Cayton didn't make an effort to comfort him. I expected that. Cayton wasn't the comforting type. Loraine shocked me, because she didn't try either. She avoided Mike."

They had other things on their minds—like putting up smoke screens. "The first thing Loraine asked me was if I knew a funeral director," Zeil said. "She knew that I did. Randy Ziegler did our mother's funeral. Jimmy had been inviting him to Mike's fights all year."

Loraine still hadn't told Zeil about her brother's leukemia. She found that out from the newspaper obituaries that ran the day after he died. Zeil felt the deep, wrenching remorse of not having been given the chance to comfort her brother all those years—let alone his last days—but more than that, the anger, and betrayal, of having been lied to so systematically. To make it worse, they persisted with the fiction of sudden death at the funeral.

"Doris took over the arrangements," Zeil said. "Loraine just backed out of dealing with me. Doris asked me flat-out and matter-of-factly about catering a reception after the funeral at my house. House! I told her my apartment was small, I didn't know a caterer, and that I was too distraught to eat, let alone entertain. She snapped back, 'Well, if you can't do it at your house, then we will arrange to have our friends at the hotel and you do whatever you want for yours.' They weren't in shock about this. It was just a logistical task for them."

Much of that involved plugging up any news leaks. Dr. Brody had come out for the funeral, but they didn't worry about his breaking patient confidentiality. They kept a close eye on Zeil. They couldn't be sure what, in his last weeks, Jacobs might have said—or more to the point, confessed—to her.

Zeil met Cayton, Doris, and Loraine at the airport. Cayton rushed her into a waiting limousine. Given how she'd been treated concerning the leukemia and the plans for the reception, Zeil didn't expect to be included in the funeral arrangements. They insisted she go with them to the cemetery, Hillside Memorial Park in nearby Culver City.

"I didn't want to go, but they almost dragged me into a meeting with Randy Ziegler. I knew what they were doing. To keep me away from the press," Zeil said.

According to Zeil, choosing pallbearers was more like arranging place-settings at a business dinner. "There were two lists—the actual pallbearers and an honorary list. They haggled over both," she recalled. "A name would be added, then scratched, then added again. Randy and I gave each other a look like we couldn't believe what they were doing." The final list: Tyson, Don King, two other old friends of Jacobs, and of course Cayton. The process left an impression on Ziegler: "Bill was burying a friend, but it was still business to him."

On the drive to the Beverly Hilton, they sat in silence for a while; Loraine beside Zeil, Cayton and Doris sitting opposite. Loraine leaned over to say something to Zeil, then abruptly stopped herself. Zeil glimpsed Doris making a gesture for Loraine to shut up. Cayton interjected with a compliment about Zeil's appearance. "I knew I was being used by them. I really didn't care. I'm not in their business," Zeil said.

Jacobs was entombed beside his mother. At the service, it was obvious to Ziegler that some people had come to grieve and others to play boxing politics. "King and José Torres were at the back of the chapel chatting. I got the feeling that to them it was a social gathering."

Cayton staged the reception back at the Beverly Hilton. Zeil overheard him repeatedly tell Doris and Loraine, "We have to keep the press away." He buttressed the security staff from thirty to forty-five.

At one point Tyson pulled Zeil aside. They had met only a few times, but at the moment he felt a deeper empathy with her than with Loraine. "He was devastated," said Zeil. "He hugged me, put his head down on my shoulder, and cried, tears streaming down my dress. He muttered, 'It couldn't be, it's not real, I can't believe it, I can't believe it.'"

Tyson then gathered himself and stepped back. Mixed with the grief was a growing confusion. Everyone claimed Jacobs had died of pneumonia, yet in Phil Berger's obituary in the *New York Times*, Cayton had said that he'd suffered from leukemia for eight years. Which was it? Why hadn't Jacobs told him about the leukemia? Why hadn't Cayton said something in Tokyo so that he could at least have called Jacobs in the hospital?

"Did you know that Jimmy had leukemia?" he asked Zeil.

"No, Mike," she said. "They kept that a secret from all of us."

The obituaries held several other surprises for Tyson. He learned for the first time that Jacobs had never finished high school. He discovered that Jacobs had told childhood friend Nick Beck about the leukemia in 1985. How many other people also knew? Did D'Amato? Torres? Lott? King? What else had been hidden from Tyson by or about the man whom he thought he could trust so deeply?

Meanwhile, back in New York, "the women" had been busy. While Tyson was in Tokyo over the previous few months, Ruth Roper had been combing the back roads of exclusive New Jersey in search of a suitable home for the celebrity couple. She chose a turn-of-the-century, neo-Gothic stone mansion in the town of Bernardsville, an Episcopal enclave of seven thousand residents thirty miles west of New York. The house had once been the residence of Sumner Welles, a blue-blooded undersecretary of state for Franklin Roosevelt. Givens agreed readily to the asking price—$4.2 million.

Tyson didn't have the time or interest to see the house or to get involved in the finances of the purchase. Roper and Givens decided that he would pay cash, so there'd be no mortgage, and thus no tax benefit from the interest expense. Before Tyson got on the plane to Los Angeles, Roper got him to sign papers giving power of attorney to Givens so that she could transfer the needed money out of his Merrill Lynch accounts.

Some $5 million of Tyson's 1987 ring earnings were in a variety of short-term instruments, including cash accounts, CDs, and New York State tax anticipation notes. The notes, triple tax free, came due on April 14. The accrued interest would have paid much of Tyson's 1988 tax bill. Jacobs and Cayton had taken precautions against anyone fleecing him for the money. When he wanted to withdraw any sum at all, he first had to sign for it to be transferred to a separate checking account in his name. Even then he had to wait twenty-four hours before getting the cash. That enabled Merrill executives to notify Jacobs and Cayton about the withdrawal—and let them check into it.

The situation came to a head the morning of the funeral. Incredibly, Givens called Tyson from the Pan Am Building offices of Merrill Lynch. She and Roper had shown up and demanded that the anticipation notes be cashed so that they could write a check for the house. The Merrill executive refused, saying he would continue to do so until instructed differently by Tyson. Givens, egged on by Roper, launched into a tirade. The executive, who hadn't ever before been called a "motherfucker" in his own office, still wouldn't budge.

"Michael, he won't give me the money!" Givens griped. "Tell him I'm your wife. I have a right to it."

The Merrill executive got on the phone and tried to explain the tax implications. Tyson cut him off. "She signs my checks; give her the money," he snapped. Givens exploited the moment. What had been financial controls to Cayton, and paternalism to anyone else, she turned into chicanery. "Michael, Cayton must be hiding something," she later complained to Tyson. Of course, whether he was or not, Roper had already decided to try and find out. That same day, her lawyer delivered a formal, written request to Cayton's office demanding that all financial records and contracts be handed over immediately.

Originally, Cayton had not invited Don King to the funeral. King had found out about the flight to Los Angeles from Torres, and had then showed up to join the funeral party. Once they all arrived, Cayton had to include King in the services or risk an embarrassing scene. In Los Angeles, King spent several hours lobbying with José Torres. "He told me I should become Tyson's next manager," Torres recalled. "He was making his move already."

After the funeral service, King cornered Tyson in the lobby of the hotel. He started in with how tragic the loss of Jacobs was for all of them, then got down to business. In later press reports about the conversation, King supposedly told Tyson that he didn't have to fight Michael Spinks that summer. But that's not what transpired. King knew better than to try and cancel a fight that was part of a deal with ally Seth Abraham at HBO. What he said to Tyson was that he didn't understand why there was such a rush to make the Spinks fight next. "I told Mike that he could do four or five fights for five million dollars apiece before Spinks," King recalled. "He'd make a lot more money and build up a crescendo for Spinks."

King had a point, of course. The Spinks fight was being pushed in part because Tyson wanted it badly, in order to quell the public's doubts about his prowess. But long before Tyson had wanted the fight, Jacobs had determined to get it done before he died.

Before King walked away, he put a hook in Tyson's race consciousness: "We're just niggers, Mike, you and me."

Tyson didn't understand King's pitch on Spinks fight. "Niggers," though, was a word, a concept, a way of being, that he well knew. This company of people—the managers, the promoters, the deal-makers—didn't use that word. Jacobs had not uttered it once in eight years. Hearing it from King was like remembering some seminal event in his childhood that he'd long forgotten. It was like being reminded about a part of himself that he'd left behind. Maybe that was a good thing. Maybe it wasn't... All he knew was what D'Amato and Jacobs had said so many times about King: don't trust him. Right now it was easier to believe that than confront the feelings that King evoked.

Shelly Finkel watched from across the room. He signaled Tyson over and asked about the conversation. Tyson said it was nothing important. Finkel leaned in and spoke softly to effect an intimacy between them. He tried to behave with Tyson as Jacobs would have: the trusted friend and confidant. "People will be making moves on you now, Michael," Finkel said in a near whisper. "Be careful."

Tyson went back up to his hotel room. An hour later, Gene Kilroy, once a camp manager for Muhammad Ali and a longtime friend of D'Amato and Jacobs, stopped by. Enough people had seen Tyson and King together to start a furious rumor mill. King had so often seduced fighters away from their management, it was assumed that he'd make a play for Tyson. But no one expected it to happen just hours after Jacobs was entombed.

Kilroy asked what had gone on between them. Tyson paused a moment. "The shit's starting already. They're all jostling for a piece of me," he snapped, and the remark included Finkel.

Kilroy said: "You can trust Bill Cayton. He's honest and he's a good businessman."

Tyson didn't know who to believe. Maybe Kilroy was right about Cayton. And yet besides not liking Cayton, he didn't really know him. Tyson's life was moving so quickly he could barely concentrate on the subject of trust. His marriage, the coming baby, the new contracts, Tokyo, the Tubbs victory, Robin and her mother wanting to see the accounting books, and Jimmy... why hadn't Jimmy told him about the leukemia? Why hadn't Cayton said something?

On the flight back to New York, Tyson noticed Dr. Brody in a nearby seat. "He asked me what happened," Dr. Brody recalled. "If Jimmy knew he was that sick. I told him I didn't want to discuss it there. Everybody was piled around on the plane talking to each other. I told him to feel free to call me at the office anytime, to meet, and I'd give him the details of it. He never called."

Tyson didn't call because he got the answer, for better or worse, from Givens and Roper.

# Chapter Fifteen

"You can sweat out beer and you can sweat out whiskey. But you can't sweat out women."

Attributed to Sam Langford

Ruth Newby was born in October 1946 to a middle class family in Lexington, Kentucky. While she was still a girl, her parents divorced and Ruth went with her mother to live in New York City. On a visit to her father, the teenage Ruth fell in love with Reuben Givens, a Lexington High School basketball star with professional promise. Ruth moved back to Lexington. The romance, such as it was, continued. She had a graduation present for Reuben: a daughter. They married the day after both finished high school. Five and a half months later, Robin was born.

For Ruth, her husband could never do, or be, enough. She had ambition, and it was fueled by her own mother, who was never short of advice for Reuben. They pushed him to sign up with a minor league baseball team in Buffalo, yet insisted that Robin be raised in New York in more "cultured" surroundings. Soon after she had their second daughter, Stephanie, Ruth filed for divorce. Reuben, to this day, blames

Ruth's mother for much of their troubles. "I was interfered with by her mother," Reuben complained. "I couldn't keep up to their standards."

Ruth Givens pursued a two-track plan: do what's necessary to rise up the economic ladder, and move into better neighborhoods. She left a job at Trans World Airlines as soon as she had enough knowledge to open her own travel agency. She married a successful businessman, Phil Roper, then divorced him when it became clear that he, like Reuben, suffered from limited ambition. She became an executive headhunter, then started a management consulting firm, R.L. Roper Consultants.

As she climbed, the household moved from an all-black section of the Bronx to integrated Mount Vernon, just north of New York. But that wasn't good enough, so she moved again, this time to the more upscale—and very white—New Rochelle. Robin and Stephanie went to private school, wore penny loafers and Ralph Lauren polo shirts. They had their hair straightened. Ruth bought Robin a sports car and made sure she dated the right boys.

Ruth Roper, as a single mother, seemed to be doing for her daughters what any woman would: be a strong role model and provide the best. But means and ends somehow got out of whack; ethics questionable; values too self-serving. A business partner sued Roper in state court for failing to share profits. An ex-husband also sued to recover his share from the sale of a house they jointly owned.

Roper retained her youthful looks long past her prime. She had a petite figure, high cheekbones, intensely dark eyes, fair skin, and pert lips. In the mid-1980s she had a stormy three-year affair with New York Yankee star Dave Winfield. She had borrowed several thousand dollars from Winfield to support her various business schemes. When she then pushed Winfield to marry, the baseball player retorted: "You're not the kind of woman a man marries."

Winfield had no idea who he was dealing with. Roper sued and the case made the tabloids. Givens was in college at the time. "It was all over campus," one of Givens's classmates confided. "She bragged about her mother's relationship with Winfield. Then there's this story that she sued him for giving her a venereal disease. She admitted this; she advertised it!" Roper eventually settled out of court for what was rumored to be a sizable sum of money.

More unsettling than the mother's behavior was the daughter's reaction. "I don't think Robin was ashamed," the classmate continued. "I mean, she refused to show any emotion, which was typical of her. Maybe she believed that her mother was right or being right didn't matter, it was just getting what you want at any cost. I think it was all those reasons. I know this is horrible to say, but I remember thinking that as long as her mother was around, Robin would probably do the same thing."

Had the daughter been raised in the likeness of the mother? The thought seemed cruel, yet the evidence couldn't be denied: Givens not only desired similar ends—she used similar means.

Sarah Lawrence was a small, haughty college in Bronxville near New Rochelle. It accepted Givens for enrollment in 1980 when she was fifteen. While most people make lifelong friends during their college years, Givens made enemies. She was known as smart but arrogant and, when crossed, in even the slightest way, often vicious. The enmity for her, was widely felt. When she accepted her diploma at graduation ceremonies, her classmates, almost all 129 of them, spontaneously booed.

One of the key relationships of her college years set a pattern for others to come. Holly Robinson, like Givens, was black, attractive, and ambitious. Her mother, Delores Robinson, was a major Los Angeles talent agent with clients such as Martin Sheen and Margot Kidder. Givens cultivated a friendship with Holly and together they talked for endless hours about one day becoming actresses. Then Holly made the mistake of inviting Givens home for the Christmas holidays.

Delores Robinson owned a spacious house in the exclusive Malibu, California, beach community. Givens felt that in order to impress Robinson, she had better elevate her social standing. She talked about her mother's mansion overlooking the Hudson River, about the apartment on the upper East Side of New York. Roper had Delores on the phone every other day to praise Robin's talents. At one point, Roper even said that she intended to find Robin a "rich" husband. When Delores mentioned the mansion, Roper claimed to have "sold it."

Givens was not a very subtle opportunist. She constantly pumped Delores for guidance on how to get into acting. She tried to charm one of her more famous male clients, and not so delicately. He eventually complained to Delores. Holly suggested she tone it down. Crossed, Givens lashed out. Back at school she spread the rumor that Holly and her mother had stolen money from her purse. She referred to Holly as a "slut." When a dormitory student reported money stolen from her room, Givens insinuated with professional cool that the culprit had to be the roommate—Holly Robinson. The next day, Holly cornered Givens and punched her in the face. Roper sent a car to the school to bring her daughter home.

After college, Givens stayed at home and scrambled to New York television auditions. She landed a few small, walk-on type parts. Her break was being cast as a call girl in the made-for-TV movie, *Beverly Hills Madam*. Afterwards, Givens, and Roper, moved to Hollywood to devote themselves full-time to her career. When she auditioned for "The Cosby Show," Bill Cosby himself took an interest in the budding, eager young actress. Roper told him that they were only out in Los Angeles for a season, at the end of which if her daughter didn't have a major television role, they'd return to "complete" her studies at Harvard Medical School. Cosby promised that if Givens didn't succeed in acting, he'd pay for her to finish Harvard. Months later Givens won the role on the series "Head of the Class."

The Harvard ruse fit nicely with her brainy character in "Head of the Class." Fact and fiction in her life were blurring. The highlights of her résumé turned out to be lies. Givens had never modeled for the Ford agency. Harvard had no record of her name at any of its graduate schools. She also claimed to have attended the American Academy of Dramatic Arts acting school in New York. She did, sort of: Givens was at five sessions, then never seen again.

At the time of Jacobs's death, such dirty little secrets about Givens and Roper had yet to be revealed. There were rumors about Givens and her tantrums. Roper seemed to be around far too much for even a mother-in-law. She also started to assert herself more, both in the day-to-day aspects of the marriage and in Tyson's business affairs. It became clear that daughter was not only just like mother; mother had decided to use daughter for her own ambitions.

Soon after Tyson returned from the Jacobs's funeral, Roper advised him to give up the New York apartment. Tyson moved out, but instead of giving it up, he let his older sister, Denise, who was on public assistance, and her husband, a messenger, move in.

"That was the only place he could go to be alone, or with his friends, or other women," said Steve Lott, who lived in the same building. "Isolate and conquer—that was their plan from the outset."

Roper then put a perverse twist into her role as mother-in-law. Tyson began to feel as if he'd married two women. "The three of them came up to visit one weekend," Camille Ewald remembered. "Mike and Robin could have stayed in his room on the third floor and Ruth on the couch.

Ruth wanted them all to sleep in the same room. She wouldn't let them be alone. Mike and Robin slept on the living room couch, curled up at either end, and we had to set up a bed for Ruth in the corner ten feet away."

Tyson acquiesced to Givens and Roper, but he was by no means content with the arrangement. "These women are driving me crazy," he told Gene Kilroy. "They're treating me like I'm a slave. The mother talks to me like I'm her husband."

Kilroy, who had seen Muhammad Ali go through a few wives, not to mention all the other women he enjoyed at the same time, asked impatiently: "If you were a little nigger in the ghetto and dying of thirst, do you think the mother would give you water?"

"No," Tyson said without a moment's thought.

"Then why are you letting her run you around?" Kilroy demanded.

"She's my mother-in-law," Tyson responded sheepishly.

Kilroy got Ali on the phone. Ali spoke in a low, measured whisper, as if he had to craft each word in his mind before letting it out. His Parkinson's disease had slowed the tongue, but the mind still worked. "You don't need a woman telling you what to do," Ali advised. "You need someone in your corner."

The next day Kilroy called Cayton. "I told Bill that he needed a black guy in the camp, someone other than King, if he was going to keep hold of Tyson," Kilroy recalled. "Cayton said, 'Good idea, I'll give it some consideration.' He never brought it up again."

On the morning of March 30, Tyson attended a press conference at the Plaza Hotel to promote his upcoming fight with Michael Spinks. Rumors circulated through the room that Tyson had been seen arguing with Givens on the way into the hotel. Tyson went through the motions with the news media. He was not just distracted, or in a funk—customary moods for him at those events—but almost depressed.

Cayton, who hadn't seen Tyson since Jacobs's funeral, could have asked him how he was feeling, or if there was anything he could do. Instead, he told Tyson that the financial documents and contracts that Givens had asked for on the plane back from Tokyo were available at his accountant's office to review that afternoon. "If Tyson were dying of thirst, Cayton would give him a bus route map to a fountain," one observer quipped of their relationship.

That afternoon, Tyson showed up with Givens, Roper, and Roper's attorney, Michael Winston. Winston, who was black, had a small New York practice. He had never once done any work in boxing. He now claimed to represent Tyson. Cayton sat in stony silence as Winston went over Tyson's accounts and the fight reports, pointing out all income and expenses. It would turn out to be one of Cayton's last chances to exert any influence over Tyson. The next day he left unexpectedly for Los Angeles with Givens and, of course, Roper. Within days, Don King would fly out to join them.

* * *

Cayton moved to succeed Jacobs two weeks before Jacobs was even entombed. His imperious ways, usually hidden in the back office, did not make him many allies. Cayton had trouble with the little, goodwill gestures. A business associate of Cayton's asked for two ringside tickets for the Tubbs fight. Cayton complied and the man assumed that, as with previous requests, the tickets would be free. After the fight, the man called to express thanks. Cayton instructed him to pay for the tickets, even though they were stamped "Complimentary."

In the weeks following the funeral, Cayton even began to rewrite boxing history. In casual conversations he claimed that it was he, not Jacobs, who handled all the important business dealings of Tyson's career; that he was the real manager, and Jacobs a mere front man.

Word also circulated about a boxing writer who had put Jacobs's name first when referring to the past accomplishments of Tyson's "co-managers," the term most reporters used when Jacobs was alive. But now that he was dead, Cayton insisted on reversing the order of names when it came to discussing Tyson's early management. "What comes first in the alphabet, C or J?" he asked the boxing writer in a peevish tone. "Put my name first."

But there were also signs from Cayton that he wasn't confident about his new status as the official manager of record. According to State Inspector General Spinelli, a few weeks after Jacobs died, Cayton insisted on coming by his office. After Spinelli interviewed Jacobs during his FBI investigation of boxing back in 1980, they had struck up a social acquaintance. Spinelli figured that Cayton wanted to reminisce about a mutual friend. Nothing could have been further from Cayton's mind.

"Cayton found out from Jimmy's phone log that we had spoken on the phone twice a month or so before his death," Spinelli recalled. "Cayton wanted to know what those calls were about. I told him it was none of his business. He got pissed off, and said, 'If it has to do with what may transpire in the future regarding my relationship with Mike Tyson, I want to know.' I refused to tell him. We were just talking, that's all, but I didn't like Cayton's attitude. And then I asked Cayton if he was anticipating any problems with Tyson. Cayton said: "You never know." In my mind Bill Cayton always had doubts as to his official status as the manager of Mike Tyson."

They were small incidents, but revealing ones. As Cayton's transgressions became known, more comparisons were made with Jacobs. Remarks like "Jacobs was tough, but always fair" began to resonate like conspiratorial murmurs. Of course, that smacked of a double standard. Jacobs had done his fair share of bullying to get what he wanted. But there was always something more acceptable about the way Jacobs behaved. He was an athlete and a boxing expert, and if he was intellectually brutish most of the time, he could also be charming when necessary. He was the kind of man a lot of people in boxing respected. When Cayton tried to act anywhere near the same way, he was almost hated. There was a Darwinian element to how the boxing community reacted to Cayton. It was as if people believed that a back-office contracts man, a pencil pusher with a back problem and a weak heart, was simply not strong enough to hold on to the heavyweight champion.

Such things, the intangibles of personality and subculture, suggest the inherent dubiousness about the succession. Jacobs made meticulous plans, assigned roles, and policed behavior until the February 12 contracts were signed. But he couldn't plan for everything. He hadn't foreseen the marriage with Givens, because he didn't understand those needs in Tyson. Jacobs understood Cayton, both his strengths and limitations, but he couldn't change him. That's what the succession plan ultimately required, namely, for Cayton to emerge transformed from the behind-the-scenes, impersonal contracts man to the iron-fisted, velvet-gloved, adroit boxing manager—in other words, to become a variation on Jim Jacobs. Cayton just didn't have the stuff to play the part. He'd reached, as it were, the level of his incompetence.

Don King, on the other hand, had rehearsed all his life for this one.

King could hardly believe his good fortune. On the afternoon of April 4, he sat at his desk and prepared to make one of the most important phone calls of his life—a call he, in various ways, had been preparing for since agreeing to bring Tyson into the HBO Unification Series in September 1986. He fingered the telephone message slip. It read: "Mike Tyson, L.A...." and there was a phone number. Tyson had never called King before. Nor had King ever called Tyson. In fact, not once had they ever been alone together, just the two of them.

For too long he'd pranced like a court jester before Tyson, and the world, while Jacobs and Cayton snickered, rubbed their hands and counted the money behind the velvet curtain. Now Jacobs was gone and Tyson didn't turn to Cayton—who would, after all?—but to him. King made the call.

"Don, come out to L.A.," Tyson demanded. "I want to talk."

"What you want to talk about?" King asked. It didn't take a genius to figure out that before he went he'd better have a good reason, one he could stick on Tyson—like the Tawana Brawley visit—because Cayton, and everybody else, would be watching his every move.

"Me, my business, the whole mess of shit," Tyson said. "Cayton's taking my money."

"I got to talk to Cayton first, Mike," King said.

"That motherfucker," Tyson shot back. "He has no respect for my wife."

King knew that a split between Tyson and Cayton could be the end of the alliance. He didn't care about Cayton's membership. He did, though, want to keep Seth Abraham—and the deep pockets of HBO—on his side. He called Abraham and played the innocent bystander.

"Seth, should I go?" the disingenuous King asked.

"Don, you know you're going to go; just tell Cayton," Abraham counseled.

King met with Cayton later that day. Events were moving quickly, too quickly for Cayton, who was used to the much slower pace of contract talks.

"Don't go, Don," Cayton ordered.

King could barely contain himself. Jacobs he could deal with. Jacobs he respected as someone who knew when to use a hammer and when to dangle the carrot. Cayton only hammered—no, Cayton prodded with his sharpened pencil.

"I got to go, Bill, I'm his promoter. This guy's unhappy," King bellowed.

"What's the problem?"

King couldn't help it. He relished the chance to use memorable exit lines. "You're the problem. And you better take care of it."

Cayton said he'd reach Tyson that afternoon and call King back. King waited in his office until early evening, and still no word from Cayton.

Finally, Tyson called again. "What plane you on, man?" he asked impatiently. King promised to be there that night. He called Cayton.

"I can't find him; I don't know where he is," Cayton admitted.

"He's finding me, Bill, and I'm going out there," King shot back.

The moment was too opportune. When they'd moved to exclude him from the multifight deal with HBO, Jacobs and Cayton had almost put Tyson out of reach. Only Abraham, and his own wily ways with Holmes, had kept Tyson within striking distance. King knew that Cayton would now try to banish him entirely.

During the HBO Unification Series, King had served up the necessary opponents from his own stable in order to get Tyson the three titles. He had gotten fat fees, but had given up both his equity (fighters) and much of his sovereignty (control over the purse strings of the fights). He was left with a stable of only a few unimportant heavyweights, all of them unlikely future opponents for Tyson. Cayton, he knew, wasn't interested in them. His fight schedule took Tyson overseas in matches against various national favorites. The lion's share of promotional profits would go to some local power-that-be.

King was right about Cayton's intentions. The purge began with the Tyson-Tubbs deal. As Jacobs preoccupied himself battling the leukemia, Cayton took control of structuring the promotion. Officially, the bout was a copromotion between Teiken Boxing Promotions and Don King Productions. Cayton, however, usurped all the parts. Filling in as manager, he negotiated Tyson's purse, most of which was paid by Teiken. And just like a promoter, he worked out the site fee, a split of the gate receipts, plus revenues from several foreign television markets.

King couldn't do much about the site fee negotiations. He bristled over what Cayton did with his foreign television contacts. "Cayton would find out who I was dealing with in some market, call them up, and say, 'You must cease doing business with Don King and work only with me or my agents,'" King claimed. "Then he'd smile in my face like he wasn't doing it!"

Cayton then hit King where he would hurt most. Jacobs had promised him a $2 million fee. He received a separate $1.2 million from Teiken, negotiated by Cayton, for Tubbs's purse and some promotional costs. Out of the $2 million King paid for the undercard expenses— mainly the fighters' purses—and his own costs. A few months before the fight, Cayton informed King that he wouldn't be paid the full $2 million. "Bill and Jim had one of their biggest arguments over paying me my money," King recalled with relish. "Bill didn't want to pay it, said I didn't deserve that much money. Told me himself that he 'may or may not take me on as promoter in the future.' Jacobs prevailed."

Cayton got the last word. When King arrived at Narita Airport in Tokyo, customs officials detained him with questions about prior criminal convictions. The rumor around Tokyo before the fight was that Cayton used his powerful Japanese business connections to make sure the government knew King had served time in prison for manslaughter.

Facing a purge by Cayton, King knew that it was either grab Tyson now or wait a long time for another opportunity. In the big picture, the economics of the Mike Tyson industry also conspired against him. Tyson's fight with Spinks took the promotion for the first time into the mega numbers of closed-circuit pay-per-view. Shelly Finkel, and not King, got the rights to the telecast. That, King feared, gave Finkel a foothold on future deals.

King arrived in Los Angeles on April 6, a Wednesday. By the weekend, he was seen in Las Vegas trailing along with Tyson, Givens, and Roper. "They were using each other," HBO's Abraham admitted. "The women were smart enough to see that they needed an ally in boxing, and King wanted to get Tyson's ear."

Phil Berger of the *New York Times* sat both King and Tyson down for an interview (parts of which were included in Berger's 1989 book recounting his coverage of Tyson's career, *Blood Season: Tyson & the World of Boxing*). Tyson laid out his specific grievances against Cayton. Givens and Roper had clearly done an effective job at creating suspicions. But only King knew how to fuel them with fact.

Tyson told Berger that although he didn't trust King, only he knew how to interpret Cayton's financial records. "I wanted to know what was going on with my money," Tyson stressed. He said that Spinks's purse was guaranteed and his wasn't; that Finkel was in a conflict of interest as the closed-circuit pay-per-view promoter because he also managed Evander Holyfield, then a likely future opponent; that Mickey Duff, the British promoter and friend of Jacobs, got the closed-circuit rights to the fight in Florida for $750,000 although another offer of $1 million was turned down.

King, determined to stir up trouble, had clearly taken the routine in boxing deals and made it appear sinister. Spinks was indeed bought out for a flat fee—the idea being to keep Lewis out of the promotion. Tyson's end—estimated at $20 million—came from the various revenue

sources, most of which were individually guaranteed. As to Finkel and
Duff, it seemed like back-scratching at Tyson's (minor) expense. He had
a point, but the amount was too small to make a case on.

Tyson then spewed out for Berger a litany of supporting logic, much of
which had come directly from the mouths of Givens, Roper, and King.
"When you're dealing with this kind of money, you can't trust anybody... It's my obligation to take control... Deals can't go on without
me knowing about them..." He ended the interview on a ominous
note. "I'm loyal to Bill Cayton, but I love my wife more than anything
... If she asked for every dollar in my account, I'd give it to her. No
questions asked. Bill works for me. He's not in a position to say no. Just
give her what she needs."

Cayton decided to relent—or to at least create that impression. In a
radical about-face, he told the *New York Times* that Givens was "entitled
to be interested in her husband's welfare. Anything she wants to know,
she's entitled to know." The more important work of getting down, dirty,
and personal with Tyson, he avoided.

"Bill's attitude was that Tyson should come to him as a sign of
respect," Finkel said. "The difference between me and Bill is that I
know what I don't know; he doesn't. He never realized that he could not
handle Mike or the whole situation with the women."

Finkel had lots of advice for Cayton, none of which he took. "Bill
Cayton made it easy for the women to turn Mike against him. His
aloofness alone did it." For the rest of April and May, Tyson stayed with
Givens and Roper in Los Angeles. Cayton didn't once make a trip out to
see him.

Finkel, on the other hand, lobbied hard to ingratiate himself with
Givens as the rich, benevolent uncle. When Tyson and Givens went to
New York after the funeral, Finkel invited them out for dinner with him
and his wife. He suggested that with his connections in the entertainment industry, he could help her find a "major Hollywood agent" plus
maneuver her into movie parts. Finkel's courting began to irritate
Tyson. "He calls my wife ten times a day," he complained to friends.

From Cayton's point of view, he had good reason to ignore Finkel. He
saw Finkel's schmoozing with Givens as a cynical follow-up to the claim
that he'd been "verbally" promised the closed-circuit pay-per-view
rights on Tyson-Spinks. "He took advantage of Jim when he was sick,"
Cayton said. "I never knew about his agreement with Jim, and if I'd
known I would not have approved it. Then he tried to ingratiate himself

with Tyson and the women just as they were turning him against me. I found it despicable."

(Finkel responded: "Loraine was there when Jim promised me the rights. She wouldn't confirm that to Cayton because she was afraid that he'd cut off her claim to Tyson's earnings.")

Words without deeds were not going to be enough for Cayton to keep Tyson's loyalty. As Tyson's personal life began to spin out of control, Cayton did nothing to prove that he could be relied on as a trusted friend.

On May 8, Tyson, Givens, and Roper left the Bernardsville mansion, crowded into the front seat of his $165,000 Bentley, and headed for Manhattan on a shopping spree. By the time they'd exited the Holland Tunnel, Givens and Tyson were yelling at each other. She'd slipped her hand in his pocket and found a half-dozen condoms—devices that the couple did not use. Givens started slapping Tyson. He rammed into a parked car. Two Port Authority policemen intervened and Tyson, on an impulse, threw them the keys to the Bentley. "Here, it's been bad luck for me; you keep it." The policemen drove the car to a garage in New Jersey, hoping beyond hope to keep it. The next day's newspaper account, and an angry call from Cayton, forced them to return it. Meanwhile, King went into action. He bought Tyson a new $175,000 Rolls-Royce. Cayton announced that Tyson would repay King immediately.

After the incident, the temptation for Cayton to be himself was just too much. He had shown them the accounts, and no irregularities had been found. On May 9, on Winston's demand, he also turned over copies of the February 12 contracts. While Tyson appeared to show devotion (in a May 13 television news broadcast, he said that Cayton would be his manager "to the end of my career, as long as I'm boxing"), "the women" were talking tough. Cayton feared that a good-cop, bad-cop routine was being used to stall for time until a way could be found to break his management contract. He lashed out. In an interview with Bob McNamara, an Albany sports reporter, Cayton said that if Tyson tried to break their contract he would fight it all the way to the Supreme Court, and that even then Tyson would have "to beg" him to come back. What's more, he accused Givens of having "ideas," and criticized King for using a racial pitch to win over Tyson.

Tyson struck back the next day. Whatever he had privately concluded about King's intentions, he wasn't yet saying. "Bill is just paranoid. We all know what Don King is, but if you keep a snake in a room with lights on, you can control him," he said in an interview with Mike Marley, boxing reporter for the *New York Post.*

Tyson also said he was offended by the suggestion that race alone was enough to unite him with King. His retort was intended as a sarcasm, but it came out as bigotry: "If I deal with Don King they'll slaughter me. I should only deal with Bill and Shelly because they're guys who are Jewish and good guys because they wear three-piece suits?"

Tyson went on. "I'm not going to tolerate insinuations about my wife," he said. "Imagine me begging him to come back. I've been nothing but loyal to this man." Then this about Givens and Roper: "They don't have to take advantage of me. They can have anything, any money or anything they want from me."

Meanwhile, Givens and Roper portrayed themselves as the innocents. In a May 19 story, the *Post's* Marley referred to Roper as the most "abused person" in the war of words so far, and said that she'd been "victimized" by "rumor and innuendo." Marley went further, indeed to ridiculous lengths: "It's as if she has no right to take an interest in the welfare of her daughter and her son-in-law...feel for the woman who's been thrust into the limelight merely because her daughter and a boxer fell in love."

Cayton's outburst on the Albany radio station could not have been more poorly timed. Roper's attorney, Michael Winston, had been busy since his first review of the financial records and contracts on March 30. He had not found any mishandling of monies, but did find the February 12 contracts highly suspect. The illegality of the contracts he hadn't yet figured out. Still, there was enough in the fact that they were signed just before Jacobs went into the hospital to confirm suspicions. Roper and Givens immediately told Tyson. "They [Jacobs and Cayton] told me their attorney looked it over," Tyson said in the May 19 *New York Post* interview. "Yeah, but I didn't know anything about it."

On May 20, Tyson, Givens, and Roper went to the offices of Merrill Lynch at the Pan Am Building. Tyson had already spent close to $500,000 on gifts for both women, including jewelry, clothes, furs, and a special item for Roper—a $85,000 BMW 735i coupe. Givens and Roper were also starting to buy more items for themselves. They wanted Tyson's accounts switched to another bank where they could enjoy full and unfettered check-writing privileges. Tyson ordered his account executive to move nearly $10 million to a nearby branch of the U.S. Trust Company.

Six days later, the same group, this time joined by Winston, appeared on the set of a Diet Pepsi commercial Tyson had to shoot. Cayton had secured $1.2 million from Pepsi and in exchange had given the company the use of Tyson and right to be sole sponsor of his upcoming fight with Michael Spinks. With the cameras, the extras, and the production crew ready to roll, Tyson abruptly stormed off the set. Cayton, who had also shown up, went into a closed session with Winston. Unless he agreed to cut his share of Tyson's earnings from the 33⅓ percent listed in the Reel Sports contract, Cayton was told, Tyson would refuse to do the commercial. Cayton accepted a 25 percent share and Tyson did the shoot.

\*    \*    \*

For a couple of women who were making it up as they went along, things were going fairly well. Givens and Roper hadn't started with any preconceived plan to separate Tyson from Cayton. At first they wanted only access to his money and the right to spend it as they pleased. But Roper soon came to realize that power over a multimillion-dollar money machine—Mike Tyson—was there for the taking. "I can tell you that once Ruth found out about those contracts she decided to make a play for the whole show," a former employee of Roper's said. "She got greedy."

Near the end of May, Roper directed Winston to use the February 12 contracts as the basis of a civil suit against Cayton in order to remove him as manager. About just who would handle Tyson's complex career— the six more fights in the HBO deal, the commercials, product endorsements, and other activities—Roper had only vague ideas. Formal, titular control she was prepared to assume. At the same time, she realized that she'd need an ally who understood boxing, one who would do Cayton's job plus function as a counterweight to the alliance of Don King, Seth Abraham, and wanna-be member Shelly Finkel. She worried most about King. "Both Ruth and Robin knew that there could only be one thief in the family," Steve Lott said.

The legal action against Cayton had inherent risks. She could win but not be able to exploit the opportunity. She could lose and be expelled by Tyson from his business affairs. King might meanwhile win away Tyson's loyalty. Roper needed a fallback position. She decided, as the saying goes, to play both ends against the middle. "I wouldn't say she had a plan. She had intentions, very focused ideas, about what she wanted out of the situation," revealed one woman close to Roper then. "Ruth improvised a lot. If there was one thing she couldn't get, she'd go after something else. I knew that a divorce between Mike and Robin was always a potentially lucrative option for her."

The question is whether Givens also had divorce in mind. "I'll tell you what my heart says," the woman continued. "Did they scheme to marry Robin off to a rich man? Yes. Did they entrap Tyson with the pregnancy story? I think so. Did they want a divorce to get a big chunk of Tyson's money? Ruth was capable of making a cold, calculated decision like that; Robin I wasn't sure about. Everything was so chaotic then. Every day a crisis. Maybe she could have loved him. She had feelings, you know; she's not a robot. My heart tells me that without Ruth in the picture, Robin may have stayed married to him for a lot longer than she did."

*    *    *

Emotional manipulation was something Tyson knew and understood and thought he could handle. He'd used those skills at an early age: the short con on old ladies to get food; the good-little-boy at Tryon to learn boxing; the diligent surrogate son to D'Amato in the early years. He'd practiced the art of survival in an unpredictable, unreliable, sometimes vicious world.

But ultimately he'd learned also to trust D'Amato, and then Jacobs. There were trade-offs that had to be made. They'd put their minds, hearts, and money into making him a champion fighter, and they'd profited in return. Yet Tyson had gotten the titles, the fame, the money—and the princess. With D'Amato and Jacobs it had seemed like win-win.

Then again, if that were really true, why hadn't Jacobs told him about the leukemia before he signed the February 12 contracts? Had Jacobs known he might die? Whenever he posed those questions, Tyson ended up at the only possible answer: he had been betrayed by Jacobs.

Tyson began to look at the events of February 12 in a completely different light. Didn't they trust him enough to decide for himself who his next manager would be? If, as Jacobs had explained in detail, this was a gesture to "take care" of the wives, why weren't they there to sign the contracts themselves? Had Loraine, the woman with whom he'd spent hundreds of hours in quiet conversation, not wanted to be there because she was too ashamed? If Jimmy had had so much money from his inheritance, as he was constantly implying, then why did Loraine need a share of Tyson's ring earnings?

Finally, what was the significance of Jacobs having chosen business over friendship as the last significant act of his life? Had Jacobs only ever seen him as a business proposition? Why would D'Amato have let him get involved with a man like Jacobs?

He had to find the answers, to do something, but he didn't know what. He felt helpless, and didn't know whom to trust anymore. He was confused and adrift. He had business relationships with Cayton and King, but those were suspect. He had emotional ties with Givens and her mother, albeit unsteady ones. They were an imperfect "family," but at least they'd pointed him to the answers, even before the questions had loomed up—that is, before Jacobs had died. Uncannily, they sensed, even intuited, that something was amiss. But were Givens and Roper motivated to truly help him, or only to profit themselves? If he couldn't trust Jacobs, what of two women he barely knew? Tyson couldn't be sure, and yet in the confusion that had taken over his life, it was almost as if he didn't care. He needed answers and they—with help from Don King—supplied them.

Even with his doubts about Givens and Roper, they were taking care of things, just as Bobby Stewart at Tryon and D'Amato and Jacobs had done before. It meant, therefore, one more trade-off. In exchange for the answers he was willing to put up with the problems. That was a psychic drama he understood. Adversity always drove the major changes of his life. Truth came from strangers—but so, too, did hurt.

In his hopes, or maybe his dreams, the marriage was supposed to be the stuff of a new, different, and better drama. With all the brave talk about taking control of his own business affairs, Tyson believed that he'd emerge a man. But the pernicious scheming by Roper, the obedience of Givens to her mother, and the greed of many others all dictated against that outcome.

Tom Patti, Tyson's housemate in the Catskill house in the early 1980s, put it this way: "Emotionally, he was starving to be loved, and to love, in a pure way. To have a kid, a family, to be attached, needed, wanted, and cared for. That's the angle the women got him on."

Lott added: "I'll tell you what happened to Tyson in that marriage. Roper and Givens took his heart and cut it up into little pieces."

\* \* \*

While the war of words raged, and the women schemed, Tyson prepared for his title defense against Michael Spinks. Since early May, he'd been training in the Catskill gym with Kevin Rooney. Never one to restrain his opinions, Rooney had been quoted several times in the New York papers defending Cayton. Angered, Givens insisted that Tyson leave Catskill, alone, and move his training camp to Atlantic City. Tyson did just that. Within a few days, Rooney joined him, but it was clear that Givens and Roper were looking for any opportunity to get rid of both him and Steve Lott.

They started with Lott. "They told me that their permission was required for any contact with Mike, personal or business," Lott said. "I knew already that if a friend of his called the house they didn't give him the messages. I was on their hit list."

All press interviews during training camp were handled by Lott. Givens decided to exert veto power. She told Lott that Mike could do all the interviews except *People* magazine. That one Givens wanted to be part of, and the only way to be sure Tyson didn't get all the copy was to do it after the fight at their house in Bernardsville. Lott put off the *People* reporter, who persisted with Rooney. Not aware of the arrangement, Rooney called Givens to get her approval. Givens presumed that Lott had "disobeyed" her instruction. "She got me on the phone, accused me of wanting to destroy her career, called me a motherfucker and a cocksucker, and said that Mike would punch me in the face," Lott recalled.

As he remembered the story, tears streamed down Lott's face. He kept his composure. "I loved Mike, I loved him, and his wife is telling me he's going to punch me out. I knew Mike wouldn't, but I was shaking. The bottom line was always not what I felt but what Mike felt. I didn't want him to get troubled about this."

Lott returned to the apartment that night, a three-bedroom condominium at the Ocean Club that he, Tyson, and Rooney shared during their Atlantic City fights. Tyson came in and walked right by in stony silence. Givens had obviously gotten to him first. Lott offered his side of the story. Tyson called Robin and yelled into the phone: "Fuck the magazine, just fuck it!"

"He said, 'Everything is cool, Steve, don't worry,' then gave me a kiss on the cheek and left," Lott recalled. But all the next week Tyson refused to talk to Lott. He told Rooney to fire him. Rooney wouldn't do his—or rather, Givens and Roper's—dirty work. Finally, Tyson confronted Lott.

"He wouldn't look me in the eye. He said, 'I don't want you around, you can't stay.' I asked if that's what he really wanted. 'Yes.'" Lott wiped the tears away from his face. "I miss him so much. It was so much fun, so good just being with him. Being able to touch him. He was so good. It was so rare, two people who love each other like we did."

Lott's exile put tremendous strains on Tyson. For all of Lott's fawning, as the training camp manager he took a lot of the daily pressures off Tyson, enabling him to focus solely on the boxing. Roper and Givens, for purely selfish reasons, put many of those pressures back on. The same week in early June that *Life* magazine came out with a glowing cover story on Tyson's supposedly blissful marriage to Givens, she supposedly suffered a miscarriage. Assuming that Givens was in fact three months pregnant on February 7, as Roper claimed, by June she would have been in her third trimester. Even with her petite figure, Givens would have bulged at such a late stage. Givens hadn't gained a pound.

During one interview with a reporter from the *Washington Post*, Tyson inexplicably broke down and cried. Wild rumors spread that he'd bolted camp and been seen drinking in local dives. Some reporters even claimed to have seen Givens hanging out with Donald Trump in the late hours of the night after Tyson had gone to bed. Rooney told a few newsmen that Tyson intended to retire after the Spinks fight. Finally, in a session with six boxing reporters, Tyson railed: "You ruin people's lives. I'm a sucker even to be talking to you guys. I should be ready to rip your heads off...my wife, my mother-in-law, they're being cut to pieces...When I'm in that ring, I don't have no more problems. It's easy to forget problems when people are throwing punches at your head."

Tyson then made an implicit reference to the February 12 contracts, a betrayal that he seemed prepared, publicly, to blame solely on Cayton. "The people in the fight business are so bad. I thought people where I came from were criminals, but these guys are bigger crooks than guys in my neighborhood could ever be. They're not out for my best interests. They tell me they are, but they're not. They say, 'I did this for you and that for you,' but that's not true. Whatever they did, they did for themselves. Whatever I get, they get a bigger percentage of it."

While Tyson was taping a television commercial to promote the fight, he made another comment that revealed his feelings of isolation. This time, he reverted to being the little boy. The commercial spot showed Tyson in profile standing within a few inches of a mannequin supposed to represent Spinks. Tyson had to look menacing, then say a few mean-spirited words—that is, live up to is Ring Destroyer persona. The idea was to put Spinks in later with his response through special effects. But in take after take, Tyson kept flubbing his lines. Finally, he slumped away and whined: "Why am I always the bad guy?"

Whatever Tyson said in public, he felt worse when he was alone. Late one night in mid-June, Tyson called Shelly Finkel at his home. "Shelly, I feel like I'm either going to kill Robin or Cayton," Tyson blurted. Finkel tried to throw it off with a joke. Tyson was serious, at least about being severely depressed. Finkel called Cayton the next day. "I suggested that he go down to see Mike and try and talk to Robin. He said, 'He can come to me. I'm the manager. I'm a seventy-year-old man!' I told him just to be a friend to Mike. He couldn't do it."

Cayton didn't go to Tyson. Nor did Givens and Roper. They had other things in mind: laying the groundwork for both the impending suit against Cayton and the possible divorce.

On June 13, *Newsday* reporter Wally Matthews got a cryptic call from a woman who identified herself only as "Olga," a vice president in Roper's company. Olga Rosario did in fact work for Roper's management consulting outfit; she'd done so for seven years. Rosario told Matthews that Roper and Givens were being treated unfairly by the press. The truth of it, she said, was that Tyson "physically abused" both women, and they feared for their lives.

Matthews knew when he had a hot story. But calling the heavyweight champion of the world a wife and mother-in-law beater two weeks before the most important fight of his career required that somebody with first-hand knowledge go on the record. Rosario promised to get back to him. The next day she claimed that neither Roper nor Givens would go on record. Then later that night Rosario was back with an overseas number for Matthews to call—in Portugal. Intrigued, Matthews dialed. A woman answered. She said she was Stephanie Givens, Robin's younger sister. Stephanie, a moderately successful professional tennis player, was in Portugal for a tournament.

Stephanie confirmed all of Rosario's allegations with sordid details: Tyson had hit Robin with a closed fist, had once kicked in two heavy, dead-bolt locked doors, and frequently got drunk.

"You wake up in the morning, and you wonder, how is Michael going to be today?" she told Matthews, then added, "He's like a bomb; he can just explode. [Robin's] never been alone with him. There's always someone with her, because we're afraid for her." Here was Tyson as violent, unpredictable, abusive—and it was all so believable, given his public image.

Matthews wanted more confirmation. He was suspicious about a story that had come looking for him. The next day, Roper changed her mind and asked him to come to her office. Winston sat in. He refused to let the conversation be taped. Matthews had a backup machine concealed in his jacket.

Roper offered a persuasive defense for her actions. She had become suspicious about the financial records only because of Cayton's "delaying tactics." She denied wanting to manage Tyson. Her intentions were only to make him "understand his business so he and Robin and their children will be well provided for."

Her true concerns, Roper explained, were family and love. "Truly, I have grown to love Mike," she said in a patronizing tone. "Clearly, he loves Robin and he loves me. Michael's never really had a family, and he loves it now. He calls me Mom. Being a mother at heart, I love it too."

Roper maintained that she'd become the victim of a smear campaign in the press, and that she'd received death threats and obscene phone calls. She blamed only Cayton, whom she also accused of unleashing a private investigator to dig up dirt from her past.

An hour into the session, Givens walked into the office feigning pleasant surprise to find "a member of the press" there. Givens didn't need much prompting. Almost instantly she became demure, then started to cry. "He has changed tremendously in the year and five months that I've known him," she began. "I really feel Michael has not been socialized. He's only twenty-one, and he's a young twenty-one." She said Tyson seemed to be "obsessed with his own manhood."

Matthews began to see a pattern. Rosario had also used the word "socialized" to explain Tyson's failings. So had Stephanie, and now Givens. The most important news stories, and sometimes the only really true ones, were those that people were reluctant to tell. There was a reluctance from them all at first, but it hadn't lasted long.

"My mother and sister and I, we're simple people," Givens continued. "We don't need to be rich." She finished by professing love in the same patronizing tones as her mother had. "I love Michael dearly...I think we can make a great team. I hope we can have a life together."

Had Matthews been set up? What was their motive in making all this public a little more than a week before Tyson's fight? Few people ever told reporters anything without a motive. Still, to Matthews it was big news, and he had it first. He intended to go with it, but not before getting Tyson's reaction. Matthews reached him the next day in Atlantic City. "I can't understand it," Tyson said. "Maybe I'm not the man for them, you know what I mean? Maybe I'm not man enough for them. I'll get by somehow. I always find a way to get by."

Tyson thanked Matthews for calling, then said, "You've opened my eyes to a lot of things."

When Matthews sat down on a late Friday afternoon to write the story, an anonymous caller, a woman, left a message with the switchboard: "Tell Wally Matthews to put on 'Live at Five.'" He rushed to a television set. "Live at Five" was a local New York news program. If the story they had all told Matthews had been the first shoe to drop, Givens had saved the other for the drama of live television.

"An incident happened and we noticed a discrepancy with Michael's money," she said, adding that he was supposed to have $70 million in the bank and they could only track $50 million. She talked about the private "detective" following her mother, prompting Roper to hire her own "security." "For what reason?" asked the interviewer, Sue Simmons, in one of her few attempts at divining a motive. "Well, there's so much money involved, and for some reason they consider us such a threat." Givens went on to accuse Cayton of having tried to bribe the priest who'd blessed their wedding. "He [Cayton] offered him money, fifty thousand dollars, to help us get a divorce."

Her most incredible claim put responsibility for all the foment on Tyson: "Michael has orchestrated everything," she said.

The next day, a Saturday, Givens and Roper showed up in Atlantic City. Tyson left with them immediately after his workout. They took a limousine to the Bernardsville mansion. Matthews's story came out Sunday morning. "The women didn't want him to see the *Newsday* story before they could get to him," Steve Lott said. "That way they could cover their asses."

Sunday morning, the *Post's* Mike Marley tracked them down. Marley felt scooped and slighted. He'd faithfully put in print many of Tyson's criticisms, accusations, and musings. Marley praised and defended Roper. He took Winston's word for it that the February 12 contracts were suspect, or, as he had said in a late-May story, "ethically shaky." Straining to demonstrate solidarity, he even borrowed Tyson's bigoted moniker for Cayton as a "suit." (Once, he had written that Cayton and Finkel sold regional closed-circuit rights only to white men. In the next day's edition, he'd apologized for the implied charge of racism.

Throughout the story, Marley had rarely given Cayton the chance to respond. Objectivity had not been his aim.)

For Marley, the trio suddenly changed their tune. No more mention of Tyson's violent behavior. Cayton, as always in Marley's coverage, was the sole target. If Matthews had in fact "opened" Tyson's eyes, Givens and Roper managed to refocus them. "Bill will be dead and gone in ten years, but I'll still be with my wife," Tyson said. "He's trying to embarrass us. He's trying to make it look like I can't control my wife and that they are gold diggers."

Givens jumped in: "They're trying to destroy us... They want to say who I slept with instead of asking about Mike's business... This is the day we decided about Cayton." Tyson put it crudely: "He's a snake, a ruthless guy." Givens said it with bluntness: "Bill is finished."

Roper, who was the main influence behind the manipulation of Matthews, got her own sidebar story from Marley. "I'm his surrogate mother, not his manager," she said. Next, Roper struck the pose of the grand matriarch ("I'm the glue that holds my family together. If I fall apart, we all do"), only to shift, in tears, to the defenseless, proud woman ("They're attacking my dignity and integrity as a woman... I just want to live in peace").

Tyson, as news, had always been like a sacred temple fountain for the New York boxing reporters. They had all kneeled to drink from it over the years. First it was the fable of Cus and the Kid, then the myth of Tyson's dominance in the ring and the inevitability of his reign. They parroted the hype, indulged in Tyson's dual personas of the sweet, humble man-child and the primal force of destruction. When they doubted, it was because doubt seemed to be the only newsworthy view on a stagnating story.

The marriage, and Jacobs's death, sent forth a new gush. But it was Givens and Roper, quick studies at press manipulation, and no longer Cayton, who appeared to be ladling it out. They relied on Marley for the emotional torrents. At the *New York Times*, Berger and his more sober editors were suited to pithy, hard-evidence pieces. Matthews, skeptical yet thirsty for news because he'd been kept away from Tyson for so long by Jacobs, was perfect for the long, detailed feature coverage. Michael Katz at the *Daily News* they didn't bother with; he remained loyal to Cayton.

Givens and Roper, though, were also drinking from someone else's fountain. They put up with Don King's presence to help their case against Cayton. They knew he probably had his own agenda. What they didn't realize was that they had become merely competent at the politics, emotional and psychological, of manipulation. King ranked as a master.

King let Givens and Roper do the hard work of wresting control of Tyson. Then, when he was sure that Tyson was turning his back on Cayton, King posed as the beleaguered fighter's only true friend and ally. On May 23, he persuaded Tyson to secretly sign an exclusive one-fight promotional agreement to take effect after he beat Spinks. According to the February 12 boxer-manager contract, Tyson couldn't sign such agreements without Cayton's approval. King no doubt reminded Tyson that his contract with Cayton would soon be contested in court.

Tyson would have been wiser to rely on someone else—anyone else—to get him better terms. King guaranteed him a minimum purse of $2 million, plus two-thirds of the net receipts and $125,000 in training expenses. It sounded better than it was. Should Tyson beat Spinks—and thus take away the last contender to dispute his title—he'd be entitled to a much higher guarantee than $2 million. Tyson's guarantee from HBO alone for Holmes was $3 million, plus the site fee; for Tubbs, $8.5 million! Cayton's deal for his next fight against Frank Bruno guaranteed $5.5 million.

King also shifted expense burdens. Jacobs and Cayton always made King pay for the purses of the undercard fighters; here, King deducted that from the gross receipts. In the past, Tyson always got his purse and all other monies within four months; King proposed paying his net earnings over two years, and at that from a joint account they'd both have privileges on. (King had used the joint-account device only once before, and that was with Connie Harper, his former assistant and the woman who went to prison for him in 1985 for tax evasion.)

King didn't tell Givens and Roper about the contract, and neither, apparently, did Tyson. By keeping it a secret, King retained what little trust he had been able to acquire from them. He had used them to speed up Cayton's demise. He had also fed Givens and Roper information that he knew would make them seem more caustic: it was King who had told Roper and Givens that Cayton tried to bribe Father Clements with $50,000. When asked at the time whether Cayton had tried to bribe him, Father Clements refused to confirm or deny anything, perhaps because he didn't want to get implicated in any way. Three years later, Clements finally answered the question: "No, it's not true."

The day after Tyson, Givens, and Roper ripped into Cayton, King launched his own attack. He called Cayton "an inveterate liar, a hypocrite of the first form, evil, the incarnation of Satan." He declared solidarity with the embattled trio. "I support Mike Tyson and Robin Givens and her mother. What they said is true and I will help them prove it," he bellowed, then declined to hand over the "proof." (He also didn't mention that on June 20, he'd been in court defending his claim to a $2.5 million fee for the Spinks fight. Cayton wanted to cut it in half. King won.)

Three days later, on June 24, Winston sent Cayton a letter by certified mail. "Starting now, you are to take no action on my [Tyson's] behalf as a boxing manager," it began. Winston ordered Cayton, over Tyson's signature, to direct all monies held, and due, to his office.

It wasn't ever really a matter of whether Cayton would lose the battle for "Iron" Mike Tyson, but rather how and when and to whom. The how continued to unfold. It got a lot messier before King took the prize.

# Chapter Sixteen

It didn't take long for Bill Cayton to isolate himself. The first to be shunned was José Torres. He had known since the previous January that the governor's office wanted to replace him as commissioner. Soon after Jacobs's funeral, Torres hinted to Cayton an interest in joining the Tyson camp. Torres had the position of manager in mind, even though he didn't spell it out. Cayton flatly rejected the idea. Any remaining hopes that Torres may have had were squashed when Cayton went public with his decision in an April 1 *New York Post* story. Rumors that Torres would manage Tyson he said, were "totally unfounded."

Torres now had a career decision to make. He never did like the administrative burdens of being commissioner. But he did like the pay, some $69,000 a year with an expense account. Torres knew that he'd be lucky to earn that kind of money as a free-lance writer. With the Tyson job gone, he turned to his second most lucrative option: writing a biography of "Iron" Mike Tyson.

The book project had actually begun almost four years earlier. Torres had promised D'Amato that he would write a book about how Tyson had been molded into a champion. After D'Amato died, Torres confirmed his promise to Camille Ewald. "It was about Cus and Mike, and José was supposed to share the money from the book with me," said Ewald.

But that was not the project that Torres was discussing with Warner Books, the publishing arm of corporate media giant Warner Communications. D'Amato was an important but now a small part of the every-evolving Tyson story. The marriage to Givens, and all the signs of tumult that seemed to be looming in Tyson's personal and professional life, became the new focus. Torres knew that he had the inside track with Tyson, and he exploited that in negotiations with Warner. He expected a hefty advance for the book, and retained commission lawyer Carl DeSantis—the man who drafted the February 12 contracts—to handle the negotiations.

José Torres did not have a distinguished tenure as chairman of the New York State Athletic Commission. The 1986 Witherspoon drug-testing fiasco was just one of several displays of bad judgment that climaxed with his role in the February 12 contracts. On May 9, with the book deal almost concluded, he made the hollow gesture of trying to save face before departing the commission. He talked to the sports media about all the reforms he wanted to make prior to leaving the commission: a legal advisory board to review contracts between fighters and promoters; a written test for managers and promoters; and legislation to limit the manager's share of a fighter's purse to no more than 15 percent. Not long after, DeSantis negotiated a $350,000 advance for Torres to write a biography of Mike Tyson tentatively titled *Fire & Fear.* He left the comission without making his reforms.

\*   \*   \*

Without Jacobs, and his use of Finkel as secret negotiator, the deal for Tyson-Spinks would never have been made. But now that the papers had been signed, Cayton fed on Jacobs's legacy as he pleased.

"Cayton started taking credit for the things Jimmy did to build Tyson's career, and then blaming him for all the mistakes," one hotel-casino executive said bitterly. Cayton openly criticized Jacobs and Finkel for paying Lewis $13 million. In whispering asides, he said to one Trump Plaza executive, "You must know, I could have made this fight worth millions more if I had handled Butch Lewis, and not Jim."

More than once Cayton referred to a "deathbed promise" he made Jacobs about keeping King away from Tyson. He also evoked the dictums of D'Amato against giving King any options on Tyson's future fights, as if, like Jacobs, he too had sat at the guru's feet—which he never did. Not giving King options on Tyson was of course wise; rooting that idea in a deathbed promise was maudlin. Clearly, Cayton did that in order to bring Tyson back. Instead, it gave Givens, and King, an even stronger hold on Tyson. "I think our life is being ruled by a man I never knew," Givens quipped about D'Amato. King put it more directly. He called Cayton a "necromancer."

*    *    *

Many boxing experts, including some former champions, firmly believed that the tall, awkward, and unpredictable Michael Spinks would be Tyson's undoing. Muhammed Ali in particular deemed Spinks's "stick and move" tactics sufficient to keep him out of Tyson's way and to rack up enough points to win by decision. Of course, no fighter had so far been able to do that successfully against Tyson. Such tactics only worked well against an easy-to-hit target, which he had not yet proven to be. And they only worked if the fighter had the speed, accuracy, and athleticism to do more damage than he received. That was rarely the case against Tyson. His defense was so good, and his offense so devastating, that most of his opponents soon forgot their game plans and found themselves worrying only about survival. As long as Tyson came into the ring emotionally prepared to win, the same outcome was likely for Spinks. That was the key question: whether the betrayal by Jacobs and the manipulations of Givens, Roper, and King would be enough to neutralize his will to win.

He was definitely feeling emotional pain. After one workout in a special training center set up in Trump Plaza, Tyson grudgingly sat down for a one-on-one interview with *Newsday* reporter Richard C. Firstman. He asked if Tyson felt cornered by the "clot of people that was forming around him." Tyson blurted: "I hate them all. Writers, promoters, managers, closed-circuit, everybody. They don't give a fuck about me, they don't give a fuck about my wife, they don't give a fuck about my trainer, my mother-in-law, my stepmother, my stepbrother, none of us, my pigeons, nothing. Nothing concerns me but the dollar. So I don't wanna hear anything, we're friends, nothing. That's bullshit.

"I don't want no more friends. I don't want anybody around me, know what I mean? Nobody come around. I'm saying that right now, I don't want no friends. There's no such thing as personal friendships. I can go in the street and fight. I don't need nobody to manage me, it's too late for that stage, I'm too mature. All I need is a trainer. I'll go in the street and make a million dollars in a street fight."

As if to remind himself of that newfound wisdom, during workout sessions Tyson repeatedly played "The Backstabbers" by the O'Jays.

In the closing weeks of training, Tyson seemed to use his boxing as a way to purge the pain. That became clear to the people working closely with him. "All the distractions made Mike even more determined to beat Spinks," cornerman Matt Baranski said. "He was knocking guys out in sparring. I'd never seen Mike so focused."

Tyson prepared himself emotionally not just to win, but also to become the highest expression of his persona as Ring Destroyer. It was as if Tyson, through the instinct to survive, knew that only the Ring Destroyer could get through the adversity. "I'm the best fighter in the world. No one can beat me," he said in the final prefight press conference. "My objective is to inflict as much pain as possible... Ever since I was twelve years old, I was groomed to be the heavyweight champion of the world. I've been prepared to handle the pressure... none of this bull will affect me in the ring."

Spinks was always a calmly self-confident person, but for this fight he seemed stripped of ego. In prefight interviews, he came off as unsure o his chances and even intimidated. "A little terror in your life is good," he said, as if among rational men to admit fear is all it takes to beat it.

Despite these contrasting presentations, the betting public believed that Spinks would give Tyson perhaps his biggest test yet. Tyson opened as a 5-to-1 favorite. In the days before the fight, that slid to 3-to-1.

Fight day, Monday, June 27, was filled with a series of seemingly typical moments that precede a fight of this magnitude. Considered together, they made up a blueprint of events to come.

Cayton threatened to withhold and contest $1 million of Finkel's $1.5 million fee. Badgering Finkel would prove unwise as Cayton's troubles with Tyson and King increased. He needed allies, not more enemies. Donald Trump then ordered that the fight platform be lowered several inches so that one of his guests, Frank Sinatra, would be sure to get a good view. Such caprice would haunt Trump's personal and financial future. Trump and Givens also appeared together on ABC's "Good Morning America" for reasons that no one at the time could quite figure out—until rumors circulated that they were seen up late together in the casino the night before.

The fight undercard also foreshadowed future dramas. James ("Buster") Douglas reappeared after losing his bid earlier in the year to become I.B.F. champion and fight Tyson. This time, he matched up against Mike Williams, an up-and-comer. Twice in one round he

knocked Williams down with jabs; a rare feat that testified to Douglas's
ring skills and power—when he wanted to use them. HBO's Larry
Merchant declared that Douglas was "no longer a young-hopeful
fighter"—he had demonstrated that he could box like "real
professional."

At ringside just before the fight, Givens and Roper again indulged
their taste for the melodramatic. While the ring announcer introduced
eighty-five celebrities (Sinatra didn't show up), Tyson's attorney, Michael
Winston, handed Cayton a sheaf of documents demanding that he stop
acting as manager. Also included was a summons and a copy of a
complaint alleging that Tyson was fraudulently induced to sign the
February 12 contracts.

Givens wore an electric-red, low-cut dress. Her face was heavily
made up. Over the months, as the battle with Cayton had heated up,
she'd started to look sirenlike. King sat beside her. When he heard
about the suit against Cayton, King apparently smiled like a Cheshire
cat.

Tyson entered the ring with his typical Spartan look—black trunks,
black shoes, and no socks. There were the faint outlines of a goatee
around his mouth and chin. He had come in at 218¼ pounds, his
customary fighting weight. Tyson limbered up his arms, then paced the
ring through the last-minute ceremonies. Norman Mailer, sitting
ringside, later observed in a story he wrote for *Spin* magazine that Tyson
looked "drawn." "Not afraid, not worried, but used-up in one small part
of himself, as if a problem still existed that he had not been able to
solve."

Spinks waited in his corner, covered in a white silk robe. He was
sweating profusely down the face, far more than Tyson seemed to be.
When Spinks took off his robe, he looked bigger than Tyson, which in
height he was. He had managed to get up to only 212¼ pounds. As a
natural light heavyweight, that was probably ten more pounds than he
felt comfortable with in the ring. Spinks looked nervous, as if he already
knew what the outcome of the fight would be.

When the bell rang, though, Spinks came right out into the center of
the ring to meet the advancing Tyson. Spinks had obviously decided to
make a fight of it. His punches, as befit his style, looked off-balance and
awkward. It was as if he threw them out to hit any point on Tyson's body,
instead of a specific place. They were hopeful punches; prayer punches.

Within the first thirty seconds of the fight, Tyson must have realized that this was going to be far easier than even he had imagined. It didn't take much for him to avoid Spinks's blows.

Sixty seconds into the fight, Spinks was backpedaling and covering up to avoid Tyson's punches. Tyson chased him around two sides of the ring before connecting with a short left uppercut—the first direct blow of the fight—that caught Spinks on the lower right side of his jaw and twisted his head back. Second later, Tyson followed with a right to the middle body that glanced off. Spinks dropped to one knee. The referee gave him a standing-eight count, and the fight resumed. Spinks advanced and threw a amateurish right hook directed at nothing in particular. It left him in a prone position. His entire right side was exposed. Tyson dipped away and down and sent in a chopping right that landed on the right side of Spinks's jaw. It wasn't a big punch. He didn't use any of his customary body mechanics to get leverage behind the blow; he just stood his ground, eluded, and chopped. As Spinks collapsed, his head hit the canvas under the ropes. His eyes were open, but his lights were out. It was over at 1:31 of the first round.

Tyson's first gesture as victor was not to raise his arms but to hold them out at a low angle, gloved palms up, in a gesture apparently intended to remind someone at ringside—Givens perhaps?—that an early knockout was a foregone conclusion. In the postfight interview, he acknowledged in himself what the so-called boxing experts rarely did: "I was very elusive. He didn't hit me with one punch, but no one says that, though. I'm a slugger," he said with a sarcastic smirk, then yelled a victory cry of "Brownsville!" for his old neighborhood.

At the press conference afterwards, Spinks said only "He hit me on the right spot." Tyson wasn't lacking in words. He had brought his ring persona along. "There is no fighter like me. I can beat any man in the world," he cried out to a small sea of reporters. "You tried to embarrass my family... You tried to disgrace us, and as far as I know this might be my last fight."

That night Tyson didn't sleep. The fight adrenaline continued to pump. Shelly Finkel gave him a cheesecake from Junior's, a Brooklyn deli, and he ate most of it by dawn—in between bursts of sexual release. Givens tried to keep up, but her heart wasn't in it. "Michael is a brute in bed," a haggard-looking Givens confided with exasperation the next day to a friend.

The day after the fight, a New York tabloid headline read: "The Baddest Man on Earth." Follow-up stories passed judgment on fantasy matchups. Jack Dempsey, they said, wouldn't have had a chance with Tyson; at 199 pounds, he was too small. Joe Louis had the weight, and the punching power, but a weak chin. Rocky Marciano was also too small. Sonny Liston, as Ali had proven, had no heart once he'd been hit squarely a few times. Ali would have stood a chance, but only by outpointing Tyson over twelve rounds—assuming Tyson didn't catch him with a knockout punch first. No one in times past, and by implication the present as well, was deemed able to drop Tyson, let alone knock him out. Givens and Roper would prove all the experts wrong. Tyson's victory over Spinks may have affirmed his image as indestructible in the ring, but outside of it, as they knew, he was still a little boy, and they intended to do with him as they pleased.

# Chapter Seventeen

Robin Givens and Donald Trump. At the time, few people made much of the fact that they were repeatedly popping up together in the days leading to the Spinks fight. It was business, and not personal. Trump had paid $11 million to stage the fight, and so he was entitled to spend some time with the champ's lovely wife. Even the most cynical observers refused to think that they were somehow sexually involved. "The Donald" was known for indulging his whims but so far at least, only for things material. He conquered through the art of the deal, not between the bed sheets. Trump might flirt, but he wouldn't be so stupid as to bed the wife of the heavyweight champion of the world—a man known for his volatile temper and now, supposedly, his abusive tendencies.

So much for conventional wisdom. With Trump it was always both business and personal. For his $11 million he wanted not only to flirt but to indulge, if for no other reason than that it entailed risk to his body, his social standing, and future business with Tyson. The man so devoted to the art of the deal also itched to try his hand at the art of dalliance.

"Let me tell you something about Trump that no one gets," said a former executive of one of Trump's properties. "He loved to win, he'd do anything to win, but he also got a thrill from taking risks. Robin was his biggest risk, ever."

Did they or didn't they? Not yet. Givens and Roper had their priorities. Trump could lust all he wanted. But for the women it was business first. They needed an ally in the legal suit against Cayton. If his ouster intensified the battle for control over the prize—the Mike Tyson industry—then they also needed someone on their side to counter King and HBO's Seth Abraham.

Their plan, however, never really had a chance. Trump was far craftier at getting what he wanted than were Givens and Roper. He portrayed himself as all things to all people. In the end he came out ahead on the deal—and still got the chance to indulge his lust.

"Only one joke about Trump made any sense to me," the former executive added. "Trump's alone in an elevator. A woman gets on. She starts gushing for Trump. Praising him. Then she literally gets down on her knees, licks her lips. 'Donald, please, let me do something special for you.' She points at his crotch. Trump says, 'Sure, baby, go ahead, but what's in it for me?'"

\*     \*     \*

After Givens and Roper made the first move in court, Cayton and his new passive partner, Loraine Jacobs, went for the public relations edge. "I'm very disappointed in Mike," Cayton said at a press conference in the offices of his attorney. "I thought Mike had far greater respect for Jim's memory. I'm outraged at this lawsuit." Loraine, between tears, made one of her rare public appearances since the funeral. "It's very difficult. We love Mike. We've known him since he was thirteen. Both Jim and Bill treated him as they would have treated a son. I just can't believe Mike would do this. It's distressing."

There was a cruel irony to their remarks. They were trying to make Tyson out to be the betrayer, as if he, and not Jacobs, had concealed the truth about Jacobs's mortality and schemed over the transition of control. Jacobs may have loved Tyson, but in the end it was his business interests that prevailed. Now that those interests were threatened, Cayton and Loraine wanted to create a second, and thus double, standard by which to measure right and wrong. It's love that mattered, not business, they seemed to be saying.

Meanwhile, behind the scenes, Loraine called Nick Beck and berated him for revealing to reporters that Jacobs had told him about the leukemia way back in 1985. "She blamed me for Tyson's lawsuit," Beck said sadly. Was Loraine admitting to Beck that they did in fact know he might die and that's why the contracts were signed? "That's how it seemed to me," Beck said. At around the same time, Doris Cayton told Larry Merchant that the reason they needed the money from the February 12 contracts was to help pay for the care of their retarded daughter. "It didn't make sense to me," Merchant said. "Cayton has millions of dollars."

Cayton retained Thomas Puccio for the battle. Puccio, a partner at the venerable New York firm of Milbank Tweed Hadley & McCloy, had earned his stripes prosecuting for the federal government in the Abscam case. His name had landed in the tabloids when he went on in his career to win an acquittal for Claus von Bulow, the rakish socialite charged with trying to murder his wife. Puccio was back in the tabloids now, and an eager leader of the chorus singing what King later termed the "Ghostbusters Connection." Puccio said: "Tyson maligns and does dishonor to the memory of his close friend and mentor Jim Jacobs, who, with Bill Cayton and Cus D'Amato, guided his career, which has now reached this crowning moment. Jim is no longer with us and cannot defend himself. More than anything else, that is what makes this suit a low blow."

The New York sports reporters, despite Michael Winston's allegation of fraud, chose not to take a serious look at the conditions under which the February 12 contracts had been signed.

Mike Katz of the *Daily News* wrote: "No one has accused Cayton of dishonesty before..." According to Ira Berkow of the *New York Times*, "Cayton [is] a tough businessman but an honest one." Katz went further in an interview with Bill Mazur on "Sports Extra," a local New York television show. Mazur asked a logical question: "Why didn't Jacobs leave a portion of that money to his wife and let the kid go, period...give him his freedom instead of his wife the share of Tyson?" Katz responded coldly: "When you have money, you always leave it to your family. Mike Tyson was money, in that case."

No reporter, a few if any of Jacobs's fellow members of the boxing establishment, felt that he had any obligation to inform Tyson about his leukemia, let alone obtain approval for willing his purse cut to Loraine. In October 1987, Alex Wallau, the ABC boxing analyst, was battling

throat cancer. Jacobs found out and told Wallau about his own leukemia.
"His leukemia had nothing to do with Mike or anybody else," Wallau
said peevishly. "That was a personal and not a professional decision he
made." Wallau, unlike Cayton and Loraine, was at least blunt about
Jacobs's priorities: in the end the business of Mike Tyson mattered most,
and not love for him.

Larry Merchant offered his own rationalization. The February 12
contracts, he said, were "a wrong judgment call. He should have told
Tyson, but it was not devious—just Jacobs's own craziness."

On July 11, at the Trump Plaza Hotel, Givens and Roper staged their
own press conference. Since the fight, Trump had claimed to be "a
friend and adviser" to Tyson, whom he referred to as "one hell of a good
guy." At the press conference, he spent more time with his arm around
Givens than he did chumming with Tyson. "He's got a wonderful
family," Trump said, beaming.

Tyson announced that he had formed a company, Mike Tyson
Enterprises, to handle his affairs. Roper, Winston, and Trump made up
the "board" of advisers. Tyson struck a defiant tone in regard to his
action against Cayton: "I don't want to settle. I want to fight this to the
end."

"MTE," it turned out, was just two phones on a desk in the corner of
Roper's office. It seemed a transparent effort to take control of Tyson.

The usual tactic in such struggles was for a new manager or promoter
to pop up claiming that he had a valid, enforceable contract with the
boxer. He then battled it out with whoever had the original management contract. In their ignorance about he wily ways of boxing, Givens
and Roper had blundered. Their muddled logic seemed to be that
MTE—the most important member being Trump—would manage
Tyson's career. That also included Tyson, or so he was led to believe.
"I'm calling the shots," Tyson said at the press conference. "I will
manage my own self."

But who would negotiate Tyson's purses, site fees, foreign television
rights, commercials, endorsements, video sales, fight film licensing,
and merchandising sales? Tyson didn't have the inclination, knowledge,
or time. Winston was way out of his depth. Givens and Roper weren't
even in the running. Nor was Trump.

He had bought the right to stage fights, but in no way would or could
he play any part in managing a fighter. He paid managers and promoters
to bring him fighters. If he were to take on Tyson, he would alienate the

boxing community. It would be feared that he might lure away other people's fighters as well. Managers would avoid him like the plague.

Still, Trump convinced the Tyson "family" that he was their man. And once inside as a trusted confidant, he soon realized that Givens and Roper were quite likely to enforce Tyson's retirement as leverage against Cayton. Trump doubted that they were motivated by the desire to right whatever wrong may have been committed by the February 12 contracts. The women, he surmised, had no real plan for Tyson's future. They knew only what they didn't want, and from that no one, including Tyson, would profit. "They didn't care if he fought or not. It was 'get rid of Cayton' at all costs—a scorched-earth attitude," one former Trump executive said. "They didn't know that some very powerful people wanted Tyson back in the ring."

Trump's first bit of advice to Tyson was that he go through with the bout against Frank Bruno in London in the fall. Bruno was to kick off the world tour Jacobs and Cayton had planned a year earlier. It would also get Tyson back into fulfilling his last multifight deal with HBO. As Cayton had worked it out, King would not be the promoter. Instead, two British promoters would handle the fight.

Trump couldn't have cared less about Bruno or HBO or the world tour. He wanted Tyson back in Atlantic City. His fights were good for business. On the day of the Tyson-Spinks fight alone, the gross amount—known as the "drop"—wagered at the Trump Plaza reached $11.5 million. Over the four-day weekend it topped $30 million. Casinos estimate that on average they win 20 percent of the drop.

None of that money would be his unless Tyson stayed on Cayton's fight schedule. And part of that schedule included a light heavyweight moving up the ranks named Evander Holyfield. In negotiations with Cayton on the Spinks fight, Trump had obtained the right of first refusal to stage Tyson-Holyfield. Trump's interests, then, were the exact opposite of Givens and Roper's. He needed to keep Cayton as Tyson's manager—and that was an agenda he certainly didn't share with them.

On July 14, Tyson announced that he would come out of retirement and fight Bruno on September 3 at Wembley Stadium in London. In order to make sure Tyson's career proceeded in the direction Trump wanted it to, he slyly offered the legal services of Peter Parcher, a foot soldier in the army of lawyers he sometimes called upon. Parcher did have merit, especially compared to Winston. He was a vastly more experienced trial attorney. In partnership with Stephen Hayes, he'd also done work for such clients as Bruce Springsteen and Mick Jagger. Trump also retained on Givens's behalf Dan Klores, a publicity agent at the firm he used, Howard J. Rubenstein & Associates.

Parcher took one look at Winston's suit (for a fraud allegation, a sparse eleven pages) and went to work. On July 18, over both his and Winston's name, he filed a twenty-one-page amended complaint. Parcher imported from the entertainment world a novel concept to boxing, namely, the principal-agent relationship. It assumed two things still foreign to manager-boxer relations: first, that the boxer had both a right, and the ability, to make key decisions on his own, and second, that the manager had specific obligations and even fiduciary duties to disclose all pertinent facts that could effect his client's career decisions.

Parcher zeroed in on the "common goal and scheme" of Jacobs and Cayton to deny Tyson free agency. He then labeled it "an invasion of [the] principal-agent relationship," in as much as the decision on whether to sign the contracts "should have been Tyson's to make after obtaining the benefit of his manager's advice and counsel."

The issue for Parcher boiled down to this: "Jacobs and Cayton knew that because Tyson didn't have the same intimate bond with Cayton, [he] would not have selected Cayton as his boxing manager in the event of Jacobs's death." By concealing the truth about Jacobs's chances of surviving the treatments for the leukemia, they failed in their obligations and duties to Tyson. They committed fraud, with intent.

The basic point Parcher tried to make was about the nature of choice. Informed choices are freely made; Uninformed ones—and worse, those distorted by lies—are not. Given a freely made choice, Tyson might well not have agreed to make Cayton his next manager.

Cayton's lawyers filed a response on July 19. It contained several self-serving distortions of fact. The lawyers could not be fully blamed—they based the account on affidavits supplied by Cayton and Loraine.

Cayton's name now appeared before Jacobs when they were cited together, as if he were the more important link with Tyson. Cayton also suddenly became a "boxing historian and fight film collector(s)." At no point were Jacobs and Cayton referred to as co-managers of Tyson. That little fiction was slyly skirted. After admitting that the New York State Athletic Commission prohibits a fighter from having two managers, Cayton's response asserted that both men "acted as managers" anyway.

The section on Jacobs's battle with leukemia omitted a variety of pertinent facts. Loraine said in her affidavit that in January 1988, the press reported that Jacobs underwent colon surgery. The press printed what it was told by Cayton, who got his information from Jacobs. In truth, of course, as Loraine well knew, Jacobs had a splenectomy, which was a procedure limited almost exclusively to cancer patients.

The most glaring distortion concerned the February 12 contracts. They were referred to as "standard" agreements. That's only partially correct. Standard contract forms were indeed used, but then were significantly doctored with freshly typed-in passages.

The account of Jacobs's final weeks in the hospital was also lacking in veracity. It admitted that he was first diagnosed with leukemia in 1980. But he did not, as it claimed, first receive treatment in February 1988. Dr. Gene Brody started giving Jacobs chemotherapy in 1982, and he received it off and on for the next five years. The memorandum then tried to argue that Jacobs's death was completely unexpected. "Jacobs did not believe that his death was imminent as a consequence of the leukemia... [he] had extensive notes on things to do when he was released from the hospital... In the minds of Jim and Loraine Jacobs, as well as Cayton, this was an otherwise unexceptional hospital admission." They then tried to maintain that Jacobs didn't die of leukemia, but rather of pneumonia. The fact was that Jacobs, as with so many patients in the advanced stages of leukemia, died from the complications of treating the disease. In other words, the pneumonia and the leukemia could not simply be separated as if they had nothing to do with each other in the cause of Jacobs's death.

Had the case gone to a jury trial, it would have tested Parcher's application of principal-agent relationships, as shaped in the entertainment industry, to boxing. A victory for Tyson would have created much higher standards of honesty for managers and would no doubt have also enriched both the bank accounts, and the lives, of a lot of fighters. And only by taking this case to trial could the actual facts of what happened have been separated from self-interested argument. With the extensive discovery procedures, depositions, trial testimony, and cross-examinations, the real story of just how the contracts came about, who played a role, and whether justice was served could have been determined.

The trial never happened.

On the same day Cayton's lawyers filed their account of the facts under dispute—July 19—the judge hearing the case gathered both sides in his chambers. Tyson didn't show up; he went to a sushi restaurant with Givens and Roper instead. Winston appeared on his behalf as did Peter Parcher, who, as a much more imposing legal mind and presence, was needed to wrangle with the veteran Puccio.

In the first step of the settlement, a June 29 restraining order on the Tyson-Spinks purse was lifted. Tyson got a check for $10 million and Cayton $5 million. The lawyers also agreed to try and keep the September 3 date for the Bruno fight. Early that evening, Trump met with Parcher, Winston, and Puccio. "Donald rode herd, made sure that things didn't fall apart or he'd be out a Tyson fight," said one source close to the negotiations.

It became clear that Cayton was desperate to settle, and thus open to Trump's overtures. Although Trump came out on Tyson's side, Cayton believed that their interests were actually the same: they both wanted Tyson in the ring earning them money. Trump told Cayton that he'd have to reduce his purse cut. Cayton knew that and was prepared to agree. His only concern was whether compromise would seem like weakness, and that weakness be exploited by King to steal Tyson away. "Trump gave him assurances that Tyson, despite all his bile for Cayton, knew he was the only person who could make him the big money," said a principal in the negotiations. "Trump also implied that he could keep Tyson and King in line."

Settlement talks continued through the weekend of July 22. At one point, Winston stormed out in anger at comments made by Mel Immergut, a colleague of Puccio's. Immergut compared the February 12 contracts to how racehorses are passed along by the owning family members. "It's like investing in a horse," Immergut said. "They did that and then they wanted to pass it on to their family. Happens all the time." Winston screamed "Fuck you" and left.

Trump collected the various lawyers into his office early on Monday morning. Puccio said Cayton would take $40 million in a buy-out of Tyson's boxer-manager contract, but only if the money was guaranteed by Trump in a letter of credit. Trump literally laughed. Winston, trying desperately to appear capable of playing in the big leagues, demanded that Tyson "retain the right to run his own career." Whatever that meant.

They returned to the judge's chambers and banged out the details of an agreement. The almost one hundred pages of complaint and argument were settled with a terse, two-page document of some thirteen short paragraphs.

Cayton's purse cut went from 33$\frac{1}{3}$ percent to 20 percent. His share of Tyson's income under the Reel Sports contract went from 33$\frac{1}{3}$ percent to 16$\frac{2}{3}$ percent on previously negotiated commercials. Cayton got 10 percent of any new commercials he brought in. He also retained the right to license Tyson's fight films to all foreign television markets. His share, though, went from 33⅓ percent to 20 percent. Most significantly, he would continue as Tyson's manager for the full term set down in the contracts: until February 12, 1992. The fraud allegations were dropped.

For his part, Tyson secured the right to review all fight contracts, veto any fight "that he does not want to engage in," hire and fire his own trainer and camp members, plus obtain a full accounting at any time of all financial records.

The last step in the settlement was to sign a new boxer-manager contract that reflected the revised purse split. It was presented to the New York State Athletic Commission for approval. "I still didn't know anything about the February 12 contracts," commissioner James Dupree recalled. "Had Tyson's suit against Cayton gone further maybe it would have all come out. But they settled it and brought this new contract to us. I asked Mike if he understood the new agreement, if he realized what it meant, all the conditions and everything, and he said he did. No one had any questions. As far as I was concerned, the illegality of the February 12 contracts got swept under the rug."

The next day, Trump staged a press conference for Tyson at the Plaza. "I'm making all my own decisions now," Tyson said. "If I hadn't been married to Robin, my eyes might never have been opened... Cayton is employed by me; I'm not employed by him... The main thing is, if I don't agree to anything, it doesn't have to happen... I'm walking away with a better deal than I had when I started."

Tyson's first decision shocked everyone—especially Trump. "I think I'm going to pass on the Bruno fight and take six or eight weeks off to relax," he announced to a startled audience. "I just don't feel like fighting right now." Trump turned ash white.

\* \* \*

So much for Tyson's intention to fight "to the end." Somehow, after being drilled on the injustice of the contracts by Givens, Roper, Winston, and Parcher, he was then made to believe that by reducing Cayton's share of his earnings and getting more control over his career, everything would be put right. Money and power were made the antidote to the feeling of betrayal. Tyson was persuaded to swallow it. "Tyson put on a good show for reporters, like he was in charge," said one source close to the Tyson camp. "But he didn't know. People were telling him what to think and what was best. He was too emotionally distracted to sort it all out for himself."

The antidote turned out to be snake oil. Litigation wasn't necessary to win the reductions in Cayton's share. The Pepsi commercial incident proved that he would probably have relented. Moreover, by that point in his career Tyson was entitled to demand the reductions. On the $26.5 million HBO multifight deal, Cayton's 20 percent manager's fee alone amounted to $5.3 million. That was more than a fair wage for the effort expended.

Tyson's new powers were also less than they appeared. The right to review contracts and financial statements was a right he'd always had. Moreover, there were several cases where his newly acquired right to veto fights simply couldn't be used. The opponents for voluntary title defenses, he could pick and choose. But Tyson would also meet a series of mandatory challengers endorsed by the various sanctioning bodies. He had to fight those men or suffer being stripped of the title.

In the rush to settle, and perhaps also to please Tyson by giving him the illusion of authority, potential future problems were created. Even the opponents Tyson chose for himself required, according to the boxer-manager contract, Cayton's approval. In a dispute over an opponent, they could end up in permanent stalemate.

Winston tried to put the best face on a mediocre victory. "I think we accomplished everything we wanted," he said at a subsequent press conference. "Mike's calling the shots, controlling his own destiny..."

Loraine Jacobs, who attended the final settlement talks, declined to comment. Her financial interest in Tyson's fight purses had just been cut from roughly 16⅓ percent to 10 percent. But that wasn't such a loss. She also earned half of all the other income Cayton earned on Tyson. In addition, through an arrangement between Cayton and Jacobs made in late 1987, she got 50 percent of all profits from the licensing of the vast library of fight films owned by Big Fights Inc.

Loraine also emerged as almost the sole beneficiary in Jacobs's will. The total value of the estate was never disclosed. Loraine's mother, several of her relatives, and Steve Lott also received small amounts of cash. Dorothy Zeil, her daughter, and her son, each received $5,000. Loraine took unusual steps before disbursing the money. "Her lawyer sent me a release which I was required to sign before receiving the five thousand dollars," Zeil recalled. "It said that I had received the five thousand already and would not contest the will. It was a final insult from her. I signed."

From Cayton's standpoint, the loss in future income was a small price to pay for remaining Tyson's manager over the next three and a half years. With Trump's assurances, he felt confident that Tyson, and King, would honor the contract. It soon turned out to be the wishful thinking of a man desperate to settle.

With all Trump's posturing, and despite his claims after the settlement that he and his "tiger lawyers" got the deal done, he had no lasting influence over Tyson. Tyson's decision not to fight Bruno proved that. As Cayton said with bitterness: "Donald Trump went against me because he thought he could control Tyson. He went where his interests took him, even though it betrayed me."

\* \* \*

After getting Tyson's signature on the May 23 promotional agreement, King planned his next move carefully. "Mike Tyson is my boss. When Mike speaks, I listen," he was quoted as saying at the time. Privately, however, he worked hard to turn Tyson away from Cayton.

In the settlement process, King had been displaced by Trump. That cut both ways. He knew Trump would press to retain Cayton as manager, and that made his future with Tyson uncertain. In order to have any chance of enforcing his own May 23 promotional agreement with Tyson, he had to derail the bout with Bruno on September 3. It was King, then, who probably persuaded Tyson not to go ahead with the fight.

At the same time, King also realized that the settlement posed an opportunity. Givens and Roper had grossly miscalculated. Trump couldn't fill the vacuum in Tyson's career. With their admissions in June to Wally Matthews about Tyson's violent behavior, they were also losing control over his heart and mind. They were sending too many conflicting signals about their feelings and loyalties. King had the chance to pose as Tyson's next mentor.

Seth Abraham had so far managed to stay out of the wrangling over control of Tyson. But now, with the Bruno fight threatened, HBO's interests were being undermined. He brought Cayton, King, Tyson, and HBO chief Michael Fuchs into his office. King sat in uncharacteristic silence while Abraham prodded Tyson about his plans.

Suddenly, Tyson snapped at Cayton: "I don't want to go to London." Cayton shot back: "Mike, you must honor your contract."

"You're my manager—get me out of it. I don't care what it costs."

And King, still playing the innocent, only smiled.

Tyson then flew to Los Angeles with Givens and Roper. King followed. He had to find an alternative to Bruno. King summoned the fighter José Ribalta and his manager, Luis DeCubas, to Los Angeles. As a matchup the fight made little sense. Tyson had beaten Ribalta back in August 1986. But King didn't care about the merits of the matchup. He needed to prove to Tyson that he could get him paydays. He also had to get an opponent over whom he had complete control—that is, several options on his future bouts, should he beat Tyson. He had one such option on Ribalta. For a $700,000 purse to fight Tyson in the fall, Ribalta signed away three more.

Tyson returned to New York with Givens and Roper. On August 10, without telling anyone about the Ribalta deal, he inexplicably changed his mind again and signed to fight Bruno in England. The new date: October 3. "I think King told him to sign," said one sports broadcasting executive close to the events. "That way no one got suspicious about him."

On August 12, Tyson flew—alone—to Cleveland. King had arranged for him to receive the key to the city. After the ceremony they went to King's estate, just east of Cleveland. On August 16, in an announcement to the New York boxing reporters, King dropped his bomb. "I am this guy's promoter. I'm the guy's friend. I love this guy. He was sleeping in my house. He just went back home. Does he want me to promote for him? He must, because he signed something. I don't do nothing just oral."

King didn't hand out copies of the May 23 agreement, or his contract with Ribalta, but that didn't matter. Cayton knew that King was doing everything possible to derail the Bruno fight. He immediately threatened to sue for "tortious interference." If Cayton hadn't figured it out before, he now knew with certainty that Trump's assurances meant nothing.

Givens and Roper didn't want to sue anyone again. They played one end for power but the middle held up. It must have seemed to them time to play the other end for money. A marriage license with the heavyweight champion of the world had monetary value—in a divorce.

*    *    *

Givens and Roper made sure that the news media did not lose the scent on a troubled celebrity marriage. Throughout July, Givens continued to claim in interviews that Tyson had a violent temper. When pressed, she could not provide any physical evidence that he'd actually hit her. Still, the stories about domestic violence wouldn't disappear.

They had gone to Phil Berger in April, Mike Marley in May, and Matthews in June. They had yet to find a reporter at the *News* to see the story their way, because the *News's* boxing reporter, Mike Katz, had aligned himself with Bill Cayton. In early August, Mike McAlary, who covered various subjects for the *News*, suddenly popped up with exclusive access to the chauffeur and chef who had been living with the troubled couple at the Bernardsville mansion since April.

McAlary wrote that when they were interviewed for the jobs they were told by Olga Rosario that they worked "for Ruth Roper. Anything you see this guy do, you report back to us confidentially. And if you ever cross her, you're finished." The chauffeur-chef couple saw far more than they bargained for.

McAlary reported that Tyson apparently spent more time sleeping alone on the couch of his private den than he did in bed with Givens. There were constant arguments. After one such dispute, Givens came to the kitchen and made up an ice pack for her face. During another argument in their Rolls Royce, Tyson ordered the chauffeur to "drop this bitch" off with Roper and to take him home. Givens argued and Tyson just jumped out of the car. He wasn't heard from for almost a week. Eventually, Roper fired the help, and that's when they appeared at McAlary's door.

McAlary's access wasn't, perhaps, the result of dogged reporting. His lawyer was Ed Hayes, whose brother was none other than Stephen Hayes, the law partner of Peter Parcher. The other boxing reporters surmised at the time that Roper and Givens had used that chain of relationships to feed, and manipulate, McAlary. "McAlary got used like the rest of us," one *New York Post* reporter said.

By mid-August, it became clear to Givens and Roper that Tyson was slipping from their grasp. Whenever they couldn't schedule some activity for him—mostly shopping—King did. Tyson was also spending a lot more time with old Albany friend Rory Holloway, the only confidant from his past whom they had not succeeded in purging. As it turned out, Tyson wasn't only out of their control, but also at an emotional breaking point.

At 4 A.M., on Tuesday, August 23, Tyson and a few friends drove up to Dapper Dan's, a clothing store on East 125th Street in Harlem to pick up a custom-made white leather jacket with the words "Don't Believe the Hype" across the back in bold, black letters. That was also the title of a song by the controversial New York rap group Public Enemy.

The group's music, its message, and its image spoke to Tyson. The more he fought with Givens, and the more King kept pulling him in one direction and Roper in another, the more he retreated into the persona of the Ring Destroyer, who could, after all, always solve his problems in a matter of seconds. The Ring Destroyer answered all questions, removed all doubts, and established the most certain loyalty of all—to himself. Perhaps not so coincidentally, that also seemed to be King's life credo. But whereas King lived the credo like it were the inner stuff of his being, Tyson wore it like armor. Inside, he was falling apart. "You got to have that arrogantness," Tyson told a reporter in early August. "There's nothing wrong with ego. You got to have it. I don't understand great fighters who say they don't have it. This is a hurt business. You either hurt or get hurt. I'm not a killer, but when I fight, I'd rather hurt them than have them hurt me."

As Tyson was leaving Dapper Dan's, Mitch ("Blood") Green—his twenty-first victim in the march to the title—blocked the door. Green, a former Queens gang leader who always had trouble controlling his urges, had not learned many important life lessons from his ring experiences. His boxing career was over, and he had returned to crime. That summer Green had held up a gas station and taken it over, collecting money from patrons at the pumps. Just a week earlier, while awaiting trial on the robbery charge, Green had been arrested for possession of drugs.

"You know, I really didn't fight you. You really didn't beat me, because Don King done took my money," Green yelled at Tyson.

Words were exchanged, grabbing started, then shoving, and finally punches. Green ended up on the sidewalk with a deep gash between his eyes that needed a half-dozen stitches. Tyson suffered a hairline fracture in his hand that required a cast. The date for the Bruno fight in London was delayed again, this time to October 22.

The news media jumped on the story. The heavyweight champ who had perhaps abused his wife, the "Baddest Man on Earth" who had destroyed Spinks in seconds, was running amok in the streets of New York. Despite Cayton's tinny-sounding defense ("I hope this will not affect Mike's image. . . . I will talk to Mike. . . . He's as innocent as a newborn babe in this"), reporters concluded that the real Tyson had once again emerged from the deep, dark basement.

*Newsday's* Matthews set a self-righteous tone: "As undisputed heavyweight champion of the world, a millionaire and an important athlete who strives to be a role model for youth, especially underprivileged black youth, Tyson should know better...it is just another blotch on Tyson's increasingly besmirched personal image."

So began a radical shift in perspective. A view turned inside out. It was as if the news media, after celebrating Tyson for three years, both the man and all his personas, had wiped away the rosy mist to see a monster. What made him a great boxer proved his downfall as a human being. Tyson had been mythologized for so long, and now it was time to demonize him.

In the same story, Matthews delved into the roots of Tyson's violent past to show that he had not been brought up as a "responsible member of society." A "family source" was quoted on how D'Amato and Jacobs paid off people to hush up Tyson's early outbursts, on how he was thrown out of school and promised a tutor—facts that had been laying around for years and that no reporter had bothered to dig into before.

Dempsey, Floyd Patterson, and even Sonny Liston, all former heavyweight champions, controlled their anger outside the ring, Matthews pointed out, then asked: 'Why can't Tyson?'"

Ruth Roper had asked the same question. About a week prior to the Mitch Green incident, she advised Tyson to see a psychiatrist. She had arranged an appointment with Dr. Henry McCurtis, a psychiatrist and stress expert who practiced out of New York's Harlem Hospital. Tyson refused to see him. Givens and Roper, however, persisted with McCurtis, and convinced him that Tyson needed to be medicated. Based solely on their information and opinions, McCurtis went ahead and prescribed two drugs, Eskalith CR and Thorazine. Roper herself had the prescription filled, and gave it to Tyson.

Eskalith CR is the substance lithium carbonate and is used primarily to treat manic depression. The symptoms of this disease vary widely in their severity. At the top, or manic end, a person charges into tasks with no rational goal. Delusions of grandeur—believing, for instance, that one has superhuman physical or psychological powers—are common. At the bottom end comes severe, immobilizing depression. Lithium has been found to smooth out and shorten the cycles, and in some cases to prevent their reoccurrence.

The customary procedure for prescribing lithium and Thorazine, besides a firsthand examination of the patient, includes interviews with parents, siblings, and longtime friends in order to acquire a psychological history. The patient then goes through a trial period during which he's given blood tests to determine the appropriate dosage levels. The side effects, after all, can be severe. They range from diarrhea and vomiting to muscular weakness, drowsiness, and lack of coordination. Thorazine is commonly used in combination with lithium to help control the vomiting, but mostly it is an additional curb on psychotic anxiety. Adverse reactions range from drowsiness to general motor impairment, and in the event of an overdose, agitation, convulsions, and even coma.

McCurtis appeared willing—initially, at least—to forgo all of those steps. That did not seem like sound medical judgment, particularly because as a boxer constantly in training, Tyson also required special monitoring. Lithium can have an acutely toxic effect on those who sweat a lot, causing them to become dehydrated and depleting their sodium levels. Just why McCurtis wrote the prescription, therefore, seems puzzling. It can only be presumed that he was led to believe by Givens and Roper that Tyson was in fact psychotic.

At first, Tyson resisted taking the drugs. "Mike never liked to take medication of any kind," Steve Lott recalled. "Not aspirin, penicillin, anything. Someone always had to be on him about it." Roper took an active hand in making sure he took the drugs. She instructed her brother, Michael Scott, to administer them. But Tyson, according to Rory Holloway, refused Scott several times. Roper then asked Holloway to do the job. All too aware of what she and Givens had done to get rid of Tyson's other friends, Holloway sheepishly complied. He gave Tyson two 300 mg. tablets of the lithium in the morning and two in the evening, along with one small, red Thorazine tablet. On a few occasions, Holloway said in press reports at the time, Tyson vomited. The drugs also made him drowsy and listless.

Roper would call almost every day to make sure Tyson had taken the drugs. When Holloway said he had run out, Roper herself would send new supplies—overnight by Federal Express.

On September 4, Tyson was at the Catskill house with Camille Ewald. He hadn't been spending much time recently with Givens and Roper, who were either in Los Angeles or at the Bernardsville mansion. "He'd been on those drugs for a few weeks," Ewald recalled. "When he came here he looked dopey, like he was drunk. He wasn't Mike. Usually he always joked with me. He was withdrawn."

It rained all morning. Tyson wanted to take Ewald into Albany that night for Chinese dinner and a movie. Ewald didn't want to be out driving in such bad weather. She suggested they go on another night. Tyson spent the day sitting around watching television. Late that morning, he told Ewald he was going into town to buy a magazine. Tyson decided to take his BMW 750iL.

"I went out to the porch to wave good-bye," remembered Ewald. "His car got stuck in the mud. The wheels spun around, but he didn't move. Then the car shot forward and hit the chestnut tree. I ran to the car. He had his head back and his eyes were closed. I slapped his face to see if he was okay. I thought he broke his neck. By the time the ambulance came he was still out."

Tyson was rushed to a local Catskill hospital. Later that day, Givens had him moved to Columbia-Greene Medical Center in the larger town of Hudson, just six miles away across the Rip Van Winkle Bridge. He had suffered a chest concussion and blunt head trauma from hitting the steering wheel.

Givens put security guards outside his room. Ewald, Holloway, Lott, and Rooney were barred. So was just about everybody else Tyson ever knew. Givens left a list of names "approved" to see Tyson: the lawyers Peter Parcher and Stephen Hayes, Howard Rubenstein (the PR man), and Donald and Ivana Trump. The Trumps never did visit.

The news media gave the story major play. Reporters speculated on whether Tyson would be able to meet the October 22 date with Bruno. Cayton, always with business in mind, announced that Tyson would. The New York State Athletic Commission wondered whether the concussion could be deemed a knockout; if so, Tyson couldn't fight for sixty or ninety days. Cayton tried to save the Bruno date: "I don't think a suspension is in order... the rules of boxing say the knockout has to be in the ring." Every bit of medical information that could be cleaned about Tyson got coverage. While he was in the hospital, doctors discovered an irregularity in his heartbeat. According to Cayton, that was a common condition for many athletes.

Three days later, on September 7, the *Daily News's* Mike McAlary, again enjoying unique insider's access, reported that the accident was a suicide attempt. "'I'm going to go out and kill myself. I'm going out to crash my car,'" he quoted Tyson as having told Givens. McAlary revealed, with intimate, fly-on-the-wall detail, how a week earlier Tyson had threatened to kill Givens. "Friends" were quoted as saying that Tyson had bought two shotguns in Catskill for the job. McAlary portrayed a grieving Givens at Tyson's hospital bedside. Tyson, he said, muttered: "'I told you I'd do it. And as soon as I get out of here, I'll do it again.'"

According to McAlary, Tyson had not yet seen McCurtis. Givens and Roper had been pleading for weeks that he go, but Tyson had resisted. "Sources" contended that McCurtis wanted to commit Tyson for "psychiatric evaluation." McAlary went on to describe Tyson's "chemical imbalance," for which he had taken medication as a child. The medication had been discontinued by D'Amato, and his inner "demons" were now out of control. Only Trump, his PR man Rubenstein, and lawyers Parcher and Hayes really understood his needs and were "more interested in the fighter's future than his next fight."

McAlary went on to report that the "wife-beater" Tyson had learned how to hit Givens without leaving any marks. He was also big on choking, and took every opportunity to humiliate her in public. McAlary cited, via "friends of the couple," a vacation they took to Paradise Island in the Bahamas where during which Givens suffered a black eye and swollen jaw.

Such intimate details in McAlary's coverage could only have come from Givens and Roper. They, or someone acting on their behalf, obviously used McAlary to build a mental-cruelty divorce case against Tyson. For his part, McAlary seemed, to say the least, uncritical about the motives of his sources.

By the time the suicide story broke, Tyson had released himself from the hospital but not before finally and for the first time being examined by McCurtis. He continued to take the drugs. Ewald confronted him. "I told him that lithium is a very powerful drug, you only take it if you're slightly insane," Ewald recalled. "At that moment the doctor called, McCurtis. He wanted to make sure Mike took the drugs. I asked why he was taking them. I told him that Mike should see more than one doctor about it. McCurtis said, 'Just make sure he takes it.' He told me that three times."

On September 8, Tyson and Givens left for Moscow. Givens had to film an episode of "Head of the Class." Roper and a publicist she had hired, Phyllis Polaner (a former talent coordinator for MTV), went along. Before leaving, Tyson told reporters that the suicide story was "funny" and "ridiculous," He also said this: "I love my wife. I don't beat my wife, I'm never going to leave my wife. My wife's never gonna leave me." Givens added: "Nobody, but nobody, is busting up our marriage. I'm still in this... I love Michael and I will take care of him.... Michael loves me too much to [kill himself and] leave me alone."

The car accident marked the definitive turning point in the marriage.

Tyson began to alternate between two states well known to him since boyhood: extreme passivity and violent rage. Stories of the rage came exclusively from Givens, Roper, and her employees. The news media lapped it up. Whether reporters could verify the incidents of violence with their own eyes didn't seem to matter. Every move, every utterance, was dutifully recorded with prurient interest. It was as if everyone expected Tyson one day to climb up the Empire State Building with Givens in his grasp, battle biplanes, then fall and splatter on the pavement. The Tyson Watch had become a death watch.

When they all returned from Moscow a few weeks later, the supposedly "true" story of what happened during the trip was leaked, presumably by Roper. Tyson had crawled along the railings of the hotel high above the lobby; he had poked publicist Polaner with a fork at the dinner table, then kicked her; he had thrown the pajama-clad Givens, Roper, and Polaner out of his room in the middle of the night and locked the door.

Roper hired two retired detectives from the New York police force as bodyguards. Tyson promptly fired them. Then, on September 21, the "family" all went to see Dr. McCurtis. The next day, Tyson was quoted in an interview as admitting that he suffered from manic depression. "I was born with the disease. I can't help it. Maybe that's why I'm successful at what I do. It's like going through a metamorphosis, changing from very, very depressed to very, very high strung. And the high strung period is so overwhelming... you know, like I'm anti-drugs but it's like being high and not being able to sleep for three or four days and always being on the run. You're just paranoid. It's abnormal."

Givens chimed in, sounding concerned and empathetic. "He's been like this for many years and they've been ignoring it. Michael takes a great deal of protecting... you can't put a Band Aid on it. Who cares if he fights again? This guy's got to live the rest of his life." Then, in an afterthought, she added: "We'll be in treatment together."

On September 29, Givens decided that Ewald was no longer part of the solution to Tyson's problems. "She objected to Mike giving me money to support the house," Ewald said. "He'd only starting doing it. He gave me twenty-five hundred dollars. First Ruth told me, then Robin, that if he was going to support the house, the title should be put in his name." Ewald was speechless. The next day, Robin called back. "She ordered me to stay out of Mike's life."

Tyson called a few hours later from one of his cars. For months now he'd stopped telephoning Ewald from the house, for fear of being reprimanded by Givens or Roper. "I'll take care of you, Camille," he said listlessly, then hung up.

"At that time Mike was not able to stand up for nobody," Ewald said. "He was too confused. He was just like floating."

That was certainly the impression millions of people got that Friday evening on the ABC newsmagazine program "20/20." Television personality Barbara Walters decided to get to the bottom of the story. She taped Cayton in his office, then went out to the Bernardsville mansion to interview Roper and Tyson individually. Givens, for some reason, was left out. Just as the crew was about to pack up, Givens pulled Walters aside and told her she (Walters) still didn't have the truth. Whether Walters realized it or not, Givens was about to end the marriage.

Tyson and Givens cuddled on a couch.

"It's been torture. It's been pure hell. It's been worse than anything I could possibly imagine," Givens said flatly. "He's got a side to him that's scary.... He gets out of control, throwing, screaming, he shakes, he pushes, he swings. And just recently I've become afraid, very, very much afraid. Michael is a manic-depressive."

Givens sat on the right-hand side of the screen, closest to Walters. Tyson leaned in around her shoulder, glassy-eyed, impassive, with a slight smile on his face. Givens's face was heavily made up. She'd spent several thousand dollars—of Tyson's money—for Zoli Management of New York to send out a team of stylists and makeup artists. The look was supposed to be glamorous, but it looked vampish.

Tyson, his lisping, high voice almost a whisper, cut in: "I do have many millions. My wife would just have to ask for it and she has everything I have. Just leave—she has the power to do that."

Givens quickly upstaged him. This was her moment. "I don't know what Mike Tyson would be without my mother. I mean, she's been the glue that's kept us together.... If we left Michael... and I do come with a package, that's how I am... he would be—"

Walters interjected: " 'We' is you and...?"

"My mom, my sister. He would be alone. He would undoubtedly be alone. And I don't want that to happen. He would have gotten so, so bad that I think maybe one day he would have been more deliberate and killed himself or hurt somebody else. That undoubtedly, unquestionably, would have happened."

Roper watched her daughter admiringly from behind the cameras. When Givens stopped, Roper opened champagne. "The house, everything you see here, I'm responsible for," she said, toasting herself. She meant the material things, but the comment made her seem more like a gloating Lady Macbeth.

Givens's true confession. An obsequious "Iron" Mike Tyson. It was one of those moments that made television viewers squirm. It was worse than coming upon a private, wrenching moment between a married couple; worse than witnessing by chance some lurid sexual act. Few people who watched the show felt that Givens really desired sympathy. No. she seemed to be verbally castrating her husband. And most incredible, Tyson—heavily drugged, as it turned out—sat there with that silly smile on his face as she sliced away.

The next day, Tyson started to get phone calls from outraged friends. Didn't he see now, finally, what Givens and Roper wanted? Did he believe they really loved him? Tyson didn't take the drugs that day. In between the calls, Tyson helped Roper celebrate her birthday. One person who attended said of Tyson's mood: "If a broken heart had a sound, Tyson's insides were screaming."

On Sunday, October 2, when he got up in the morning and wandered into the den, there on the couch, at least according to some sources, was an eight-by-ten envelope. "Mike Tyson" was typed across the front. He opened it to find a private detective's report. It detailed an afternoon and evening his wife had spent with Donald Trump on his private yacht that summer. Included were photographs of Givens leaning over the railing wrapped revealingly in a plush terry-cloth bath towel.

When Givens walked into the room, Tyson threw a sugar bowl at her. Chairs went through windows. Givens and Roper fled to a nearby telephone booth and called Dr. McCurtis. He advised that Tyson be committed to a hospital for examination. McCurtis also told police that he felt Givens and Roper were in serious danger being at the house. Givens ended up filing a seven-page report with the Bernardsville police. Tyson, meanwhile, drove off.

That Monday, Givens and Roper left for Los Angeles. Late in the afternoon, Tyson showed up unexpectedly at Cayton's office, embraced the estranged manager, and cried. Cayton awkwardly pulled himself away and picked up the phone. His first call went to a Dr. Abraham Halpern, director of psychiatry at United Hospital in Port Chester, New York. He wanted Tyson cleared of the manic-depression diagnosis. His next call went to London. Cayton felt a December 17 date with Bruno could now be made. Then, looking at his watch, he headed for the door to catch his customary train home. Tyson felt all the more dejected. "I

asked why he didn't go with Mike or take him to his home that night,"
Ewald said of a later conversation with Cayton. "He had to be a father to
Mike; that's what he needed. Bill said 'I can't do that.'"

The next day, Dr. Halpern examined Tyson. He spent one hour
asking him questions, then he spoke with Ewald, Lott, and Cayton.
Halpern tried to call Givens and Roper but their phone had been
disconnected. He also had a brief conversation with Dr. McCurtis, who
claimed now that he had never diagnosed Tyson as being manic-
depressive. According to McCurtis, he suffered instead from a "mood
regulatory problem." Prescribing lithium and Thorazine for such a
problem was rarely done by physicians, nor was an application of those
drugs approved by the Food and Drug Administration. McCurtis all but
admitted to Halpern that early on he had based his diagnosis on the
opinions of Givens and Roper. "Getting his information from Mrs. Tyson
and her mother, it led him to feel Mike Tyson was kind of volatile," the
*New York Times*, quoted Halpern as saying. After Halpern's examination, Tyson moped about the office. It was obvious that he wanted more
than just phone calls from Clayton. He needed someone to be with, to
reassure him, to take control of his life, and perhaps most important, to
keep Givens and Roper at bay.

Don King could do all that. Indeed, he'd been waiting for the chance.
Which is why King assembled that detective's report and made sure
Tyson got to see it—or at least so said a King confidant. Perhaps he did,
or maybe he showed it to Tyson after the visit to Cayton's office. In any
case, sometime soon after the "20/20" show, Tyson did apparently see
what was labeled as a detective's report detailing Given's time with
Trump on his yacht. If it was King who had arranged for the report, it
was a truly masterful move. King, after all, needed some device by
which to bring Tyson in from the cold—and away from Cayton.

On Thursday, October 6, between 5 and 7 P.M., King took Tyson
around to each of his bank and brokerage accounts. Any check or
transfer signed by Givens and Roper would no longer be honored. The
accounts—holding nearly $15 million—were then switched back into
Tyson's name. It turned out that they were just in time to stop payment
on a $581,812.60 check Givens had written to Robin Givens Productions
and tried to deposit in Los Angeles. The notation said: "reimbursement
on expenses."

The next day, King and Tyson appeared at Roper's offices to seize any
records, checkbooks, and receipts of Mike Tyson Enterprises. A

secretary called Givens, who got Tyson on the phone and begged him to come to Los Angeles and "stay away from King." Tyson refused. An hour later Tyson learned that Givens, early in the morning in Los Angeles, had filed for a divorce on grounds of "irreconcilable differences." She retained divorce lawyer to the stars Marvin Mitchelson.

"My husband," her divorce action stated, "has been violent and physically abusive and prone to unprovoked rages of violence and destruction." She then recounted all of Tyson's outbursts, from Moscow to the Bahamas and beyond. Less than a week later, she fired Mitchelson, or so Givens said. Mitchelson gave up the case when her retainer check for $70,000—written on Tyson's account—bounced. Givens then hired New York's version of the celebrity divorce dean, Raoul Felder. King meanwhile retained L.A. litigator Howard Weitzman to represent Tyson.

It looked as if both sides had lined up for quite a battle. Givens moved for jurisdiction in California, which is a community property state; in other words, Tyson might be required to give up half of his assets to Givens, at that time an estimated $40 million. Tyson claimed in his New Jersey countersuit (where monies are distributed equitably, according to the length of the marriage and the contribution of each partner) that he had been "the hapless victim of intentional fraud" when Givens had claimed to be pregnant. He said she was "motivated solely by personal aggrandizement and a need to enhance her level of public recognition and personal wealth."

No great battle ensued. Givens tried to rally the public behind her cause, but failed miserably. On October 14, she returned to "20/20" to defend the California filing and to apologize to Tyson and his fans. She claimed to still love Tyson. The facts, and public sentiment, went against her.

News reports surfaced that she had run up, on Tyson's tab, a $9,500 bill at the Zoli agency for a series of beauty makeovers. On the day of the "20/20" shoot at the Bernardsville mansion, Roper purchased a $85,000 Russian sable coat as a birthday gift for herself. Givens also wrote herself a check for $2 million, noting it as a "gift" from Tyson. In all, Tyson's attorney claimed that in the course of the marriage $5 million of his client's money had simply disappeared. Givens's gynecologist, Dr. Sheldon Cherry, also admitted that she had had only one miscarriage: on June 3. If she was in fact pregnant when they married, Givens would have miscarried at seven months. There were no signs of an expanding womb on Givens through the spring months. A producer from her television show said that she had not once appeared on the set with a visible bruise.

Boxing insiders also speculated on whether there was some connections between Tyson's Catskill car accident and the drugs Roper and Givens insisted he take for his supposed manic depression. "Rumors went around that the women wouldn't have been so surprised if Mike died in a car crash," Steve Lott recalled of the climate of opinion in those chaotic days. Bill Cayton added: "I heard the same thing. There was no way of knowing. I do know that Robin became a beneficiary on his annuity if anything should happen to Mike."

Cayton didn't have it exactly right. Tyson did have a $2 million "death benefit" on the annuity that Jacobs and Cayton purchased for him in 1987. Givens inquired about the policy and its features. "She called and wanted to find out what it was," said George Cohen, the insurance agent who sold the policy. "She knew she couldn't touch it. The beneficiary was never changed. If he dies, it's the estate of Mike Tyson." The question was thus whether Givens became a beneficiary in his will. Cayton admitted: "Not that I know, but Roper's lawyer handled everything then." Michael Winston did switch Tyson's bank accounts so that Givens could write checks, but there's no evidence that he also managed to get Tyson's will rewritten so that Givens became sole beneficiary.

Givens tried to settle the divorce for $8 million, then $2 million, both of which figures Tyson attorney Weitzman rejected. Felder then announced that she would agree to grant Tyson a divorce but would neither "seek nor accept" any money for herself. The statement also said that she had never "said one bad word about Michael or done anything to hurt him personally."

Clearly, Givens had been advised not to risk a trial. Instead, she first tried seduction. At a November 5 settlement meeting in Las Vegas between Givens, Tyson, and their respective attorneys, Givens tried repeatedly to kiss, stroke, hug, and sweet-talk Tyson into leaving the room with her alone. He resisted. Ten days later, she filed a $125 million libel suit against Tyson, which Weitzman called a "transparent and pathetic" effort to "shift blame for her conduct to someone else and blame them for any problems she perceives she's having... Truth is the best defense against libel." Givens had no interest in letting the truth be known. The libel suit died. The divorce plodded along. Givens was old news. The center of Tyson's life became occupied by someone else: Don King.

# PART THREE

# The Man Remade

# Chapter Eighteen

**T**yson sat sprawled across the chocolate leather sofa in the "family room," thumbing through a magazine. King was on the phone, as he had been since the moment they'd arrived. Tyson presumed that the calls were about him. He was in the middle of a divorce, and had been whisked away with Albany buddies John Horne and Rory Holloway to the protection of King's rural Ohio estate. When King hung up the phone, he went over to the bookcase, pulled out a book, and threw it onto the couch beside Tyson. "Try this, Mike. Get some educating on how Cayton treats us niggers," he said, then left the room. Tyson picked up the book: *Countering the Conspiracy to Destroy Black Boys.*

King had brought them all there after he took Tyson around to close his bank accounts. His estate was a long way from D'Amato's reverently designed late-Victorian house on the hill in Catskill. They approached in a stretch limousine through a wrought-iron gate that had "Henri" and "Don" written across the front, and a sign that read: "Beware of dogs. Stay in car and sound horn. Wait until you are met. Do not approach on foot. Danger!" There was a Rolls-Royce Silver Spur in the courtyard, a Zimmer, and a 1976 Cadillac convertible. The tall white columns of the mansion gave it the look of a Southern plantation. Between the lines of statues of Greek gods and goddesses flanking the walkway to the front door stood King's wife, Henrietta, waving. When they got out of the limousine, something off to the side caught Tyson's eye: it was a county sheriff's car. King told him that he and Henrietta were Ashtabula County deputy sheriffs.

Henrietta gave Tyson the tour: a bright, white, shiny kitchen, and outside through the window a generator to supply electricity if the power went down. Upstairs, off the master bedroom, with its massive, circular bed, was a bathroom with a black bathtub, couches, a telephone, a skylight, and hanging plants. Back downstairs, they went through the family room and out through ornate glass doors to an enclosed Olympic-size pool shaped like a boxing glove. Over the thumb stood a green miniature Statue of Liberty.

They ended up back in the family room. The sunken bar looked like it could seat twenty people. There was a beige Steinway piano (with an open Bible next to it on a pedestal), a pool table, a wall of videotapes, chairs made of cattle horns, and a collection of stuffed animals in one corner—small ones, like raccoons and squirrels, dwarfed by a lion. If Tyson had looked, he would also have seen that there were a half-dozen other copies of *Countering the Conspiracy to Destroy Black Boys* on the bookcase. It was the type of book that King gave all his young black boxers. That was King's way into Tyson's heart and mind. D'Amato had given Tyson *Zen and the Art of Archery* so that he could find spiritual resources to empower him in the ring. King wanted Tyson to attribute the motives of D'Amato, and everyone else who'd had anything to do with his life to that point, to a racial conspiracy of symbolic castration.

Now that King had Tyson, he wasn't going to let him go. The first order of business was to keep him occupied. That's where John Horne came in so handy. King gave Horne a phone number and address in Cleveland. He was to go there and bring back some women for Tyson. They were, of course, prostitutes.

King had met Horne at one of Tyson's 1987 fights in Las Vegas. As far as King could figure out back then, Tyson and Horne weren't extremely close friends. But Horne, who had moved to Los Angeles to pursue acting, clearly wanted to change that. When Tyson became champion in late 1986, Horne had sought him out to cultivate the friendship. He was ambitious, and to King that meant he could be recruited. Starting in early 1987, King put him on the payroll. When King knew that Tyson would be in Los Angeles, he'd notify Horne. Much to Tyson's surprise, when he'd arrived at the airport, there would be Horne, all smiles, ready and waiting to take Tyson on the town. Tyson was unsuspecting. "Mike once told me that every time he came to L.A., he could always be sure that he'd see two people," said former Catskill housemate Tom Patti, who also later moved to Los Angeles to become an actor. "He'd see me and John Horne. He could never figure out how Horne figured out when his plane would arrive, and then be there waiting at the gate."

The next order of business for King was to keep Tyson away from Cayton. On one level, that would be easy. Cayton wasn't about to invite Tyson to stay at his house in Larchmont. He couldn't reach out to Tyson like that. But he was still the manager, and he had made a deal for Tyson to fight Frank Bruno in London on December 17—a fight not being promoted by Don King. Cayton had also announced that he was concluding deals for the other fights in the long-planned world tour, all of which would also exclude King: Adilson Rodrigues in February in Rio de Janeiro during Carnival, then back to the United States for a title defense in April before leaving for Italy to fight Francesco Damiani. There was talk of an upcoming closed-circuit pay-per-view blockbuster promotion of Tyson against Evander Holyfield, a cruiserweight who had recently moved up in weight class.

King knew that he had to handle the subject of the Bruno fight carefully. It was a fight that HBO ally Seth Abraham wanted badly and without too much more delay. That's why at a brief meeting with Cayton in Abraham's office on Friday, October 7, King "apologized" to Cayton for having called him a "Satan in disguise" the previous June. King, of course, was just buying time until he could figure out what to do about the Bruno fight. He now realized that he couldn't displace Bruno with one of his own handpicked fighters. But he could probably keep the match stateside. The question was whether Cayton, and the British promoter of the fight, Jarvis Astaire, would accept a change in venue.

The battle with "the women" had given Cayton a lesson in the Realpolitik of being a fight manager. King had the fighter's ear now, and Cayton realized that unlike with Givens and Roper, this time he had better appear to be a team player. He didn't believe King was sorry about anything, but he played along. Over the weekend of October 7, Cayton told the New York boxing reporters that in moving Tyson's bank accounts, "Don King has been a positive force. He's proven that he's working in Mike's best interests." Cayton was hoping that the truce would last long enough for King to bring Tyson back to New York that coming Thursday for a meeting with Jarvis Astaire at which the Bruno date could be finally confirmed. King had no intention of doing that.

The same day that Cayton's conciliatory remarks were published, King informed him that Tyson had aggravated the fracture in his right hand that he'd suffered the previous August in the street fight with Mitch Green. Cayton suspected a delaying tactic, but King said that a Cleveland doctor would send X rays to confirm the diagnosis. Later in the day, rumors got back to Cayton that King was also trying to fire trainer Kevin Rooney. He had invited Richie Giachetti—former trainer of Larry Holmes, and an old adversary of King's—to his Ohio estate to meet with Tyson. That such moves were part of a scheme by King to steal Tyson away were discounted by Cayton as ridiculous. As manager, Cayton said, only he could decide who would train Tyson. "Remember, I have a contractual commitment with Mike Tyson. Don King does not," he bravely asserted to Newsday.

Realpolitik for Cayton had sunk in only so deep. Events were once again leaving him behind. Within a few days, Giachetti, who knew well King's abilities at subterfuge, was being quoted defending King. Giachetti had not touched a champion in five years, and would say just about anything for a shot at training Tyson. "This time King is not the culprit," Giachetti said in a Newsday story. "Believe me, Tyson came to him, not the other way around. He needed to go to someone for guidance. Someone he understands and listens to."

The meeting between King, Cayton, Abraham, and promoter Jarvis Astaire convened on October 13, sans Tyson. He remained in Ohio under the watchful eye of John Horne. The meeting broke up with nothing decided—except that another delay was likely. King, meanwhile, had been secretly prodding executives from both the Trump Plaza in Atlantic City and the Las Vegas Hilton to bid on the fight. They wanted the bout, but not for a late December date. That was too close to the Christmas holiday season, a time when the spirit of giving replaced that of gambling. The earliest either casino could take it was January 14, which was the only weekend in that month not dominated by football playoffs. King also played the press. He instructed Horne to leak to the New York Post's Mike Marley that Tyson was "adamant" about fighting in Las Vegas or Atlantic City. Horne added that Tyson was angry with Rooney for recent remarks he had made criticizing King.

By the weekend of October 14, Cayton and Astaire had still not relented on moving the fight. Astaire instructed Frank Bruno to come to to New York as in a publicity stunt to force King's hand. But King decided that if they didn't want to play his way, he'd take his toys someplace else. He announced that he and Tyson were going to Venezuela to attend the annual convention of the W.B.A. From there, they'd fly to Mexico City for the W.B.C. convention, and then go on to Las Vegas to watch the October 29 title bout between King's lightweight fighter Julio Cesar Chavez and José Luis Ramirez. The message was loud and clear: Tyson wouldn't start training until early or mid-November. Even a January date with Bruno—wherever the fight ended up—didn't seem likely.

Before Tyson left for Venezuela, he took a parting shot at Givens and Roper in an interview with a reporter from the *Chicago Sun-Times*. The emotions were his, but the words came directly from King. Givens and Roper, Tyson said, were "evil" and "don't like black people. They use them, but they don't like or respect black people. They want to be white so bad. The way they talk about black people, you'd think you were living with the Ku Klux Klan. They thought they were royalty. She and her mother want so much to be white, it's a shame. And they were trying to take me away from the people I grew up with and throw me into their kind of high-class world."

After the Venezuela trip, King took Tyson to the Chicago offices of his attorney to sign a new promotional agreement. It replaced the one-fight contract he had secretly signed with King the previous May. The new agreement, dated October 21, gave King exclusive promotional rights over Tyson for four years. That was not in Tyson's best interests. As undisputed champion, he could sell his services to the highest-paying promoter on a fight-by-fight basis. King could have offset that with hefty minimum guarantees—but he didn't. This time, instead of a guarantee of $2 million, as detailed in the May 23 contract, Tyson got only $1 million plus $200,000 in training expenses. King threw in a kicker of $66^2/_3$ percent of the net receipts. With any other promoter, that might have been a good deal, but with King, who was known for inflating his expenses and being otherwise creative with accounting, it wasn't. The agreement did not spell out in any detail just how the net figure would be arrived at.

The other terms in the contract blocked Tyson from taking any legal action against King in the event of a dispute. King had the right to sue Tyson for any breach, but Tyson waived his right to defend against the suit. He also agreed to hold King harmless and even to cover his legal fees if the contract was later contested.

The first eight pages were double-spaced and seemed to be written in the standard language used by King in his promotional contracts. The ninth, and last, page was single-spaced and tailored to Tyson: it contained a clause recognizing that Cayton had a legal contract with Tyson and that his approval, as manager, was required for the promotional agreement to take effect. It appeared that King's attorneys added the last page as an afterthought. What they had in mind wasn't clear. It could have been a defensive measure to deflect accusations that King was trying to steal Tyson away; that would be the obvious interpretation. But King may have had something far more devious in mind. Just as "the women" had done time and again, he was possibly setting Cayton up in Tyson's eyes as the bad guy. With Cayton, as Givens and Roper had discovered, that was easy to do.

When King announced that Tyson had signed the agreement, he also revealed that on October 5 Tyson had appointed him "adviser and counselor." Cayton demanded that the New York State Athletic Commission hold a hearing to determine if King had violated regulations and should have his promoter's license revoked. Tyson immediately lashed out. "That is a low blow," he was quoted as saying on October 24 in the *New York Post* after learning of Cayton's protest. "Every time I try to do something for Bill, he turns against us. He's not on our damn side." King chimed in: "I took less years than Mike wanted to give me," and later in the same story, "I'm not trying to be this fighter's manager, but we're inseparable. No one is going to knock us out of the box or split us up."

King had no doubt depicted the contract to Tyson as something that symbolized his right to make his own decisions; what mattered was the act of signing it, not the fairness of the specific provisions. Cayton's refusal to sign, and his protest to the commission, were thus no doubt portrayed to Tyson as a personal affront.

At that point, Cayton had two choices: sue King for tortious interference or make him the promoter of at least two or three of Tyson's fights. His experience with "the women," and his own instincts, told him to sue. There was, however, considerable pressure on him to settle, much of which came from HBO's Seth Abraham.

With the Tyson-Bruno fight still not scheduled, let alone the remaining five bouts in the multifight deal, Abraham took a far more active role in Tyson's affairs. He had tried not to get involved in King's courtship of Tyson. He didn't want to be accused of aiding and abetting King in spiriting away a fighter. For almost ten years, Abraham had managed to not get his hands dirty in his ally's affairs, and he wanted to keep it that way. But, as usual, his interests were on a parallel track with King's.

Two years earlier, Abraham and King had worked together to bring Tyson into the HBO Unification Series. When Jacobs and Cayton hadn't wanted to make King the primary promoter in the $26.5 million, seven-fight deal with HBO, Abraham and King had prevailed. And a good thing they had, Abraham no doubt now reasoned. When Tyson's life had started to fall apart, it was King's close proximity to Tyson that had enabled him to play savior. Abraham had always figured that somehow King would end up in control of the winner of the Unification Series, whoever that might be. If King were successful, Abraham could only profit.

Abraham needed Tyson on HBO, and not tied up in court. As he predicted, Tyson's victories had revived the cable company's growth. The number of subscribers had stalled in 1985 at 14.5 million. During 1986, when Tyson fought four times on HBO, they increased to 15 million. His four appearances in 1987 jacked them up to 16 million. The signs were that in 1988 Tyson's two live fights on HBO, and the delayed broadcast of the brief battle with Spinks, would increase subscriptions to 17 million or more. Tyson-Holmes, for instance, had earned a 33 rating on HBO, the highest rating for the year of any programming on the cable station, including feature films, comedy specials, and series.

After Cayton filed his protest with the Athletic Commission, Abraham pleaded with him to meet with King and Tyson to work out a truce. Cayton agreed, reluctantly. A meeting was scheduled for the morning of October 29 at the Las Vegas Hilton, the day of the Chavez-Ramirez fight. Cayton arrived with Loraine Jacobs and his personal attorney, Irving Gruber. King came with two of his attorneys, Charles Lomax and Robert Hirth. Tyson's attorney, Howard Weitzman, represented him in the discussions. Present for the Las Vegas Hilton was the president of the Hilton Nevada Corp., John Giovenco.

There were three sessions stretching over several hours in the course of the day. Tyson sat in for the first two. At the third, the outlines of a truce were agreed upon. Tyson would fight Frank Bruno at the Las Vegas Hilton. The Hilton, and not King or Jarvis Astaire, would be the compromise promoter. Cayton would remain manager through to the end of his term, or February 12, 1992. He would select opponents, determine the date and location of fights, and negotiate purses. King would be the exclusive promoter for Tyson's next four fights after Bruno, or for one year, whichever came first. For fights overseas, he could be copromoter.

The financial controls agreed upon protected everyone involved. Cayton got his manager's 20 percent, plus one-third of the monies from Tyson's fight films and videotapes. He also got to handle foreign television sales, from which he earned another 20 percent. He put in a schedule on how and precisely when he would receive his money. He even insisted that King put up as collateral a $500,000 letter of credit thirty days before each fight.

King would have to negotiate his cut of the purse directly with Tyson. Obviously, Cayton didn't want to have to haggle with King over the amount. It would be Tyson's headache. But Cayton detailed for Tyson's, and of course his own, protection, the types of expense items King was permitted to deduct from the gross receipts. Cayton also had the right to inspect all contracts entered into by King for the fight, plus his records—including all checks, invoices, faxes, and correspondence. King had never before agreed to let himself be so curtailed.

The agreement still needed Tyson's approval. Weitzman said he would present it to Tyson and they could all reconvene later in the evening. The group adjourned for dinner, then went into the Hilton's indoor arena to watch Chavez beat Ramirez by a technical knockout. When they convened again after the fight, Weitzman was late. He walked in with an expression on his face of someone at a funeral. "Gentlemen, we don't have a deal. Mike wants the four-year agreement with Don instead," Weitzman said.

Cayton, his lawyer, and Loraine Jacobs left without saying a word. Cayton was livid. He never expected King to settle. In his mind, the truce talks had been just an elaborate ploy to disguise King's influence over Tyson. "It was a trick to make it look like Mike was making the decisions," Cayton recalled bitterly. "If Mike said no to the deal, it was because King told him to in so many words." Cayton also blamed Abraham: "I was very angry with Seth, and I told him that. He led me into it."

Abraham claimed total innocence: "Don wanted the deal. It was in his best interests. He got what he was looking for. It was Tyson who killed it, not Don."

Tyson may have indeed finally come to grips with the fact that he had been betrayed twice: first by all the people involved in the February 12 contracts, and second by Givens, Roper, and Trump, when he settled with Cayton on the fraud charges. By saying no to the truce, he was striking back.

It also made sense, however, that King would want the truce. In the four fights over one year, he stood to make around $10 million, for which he didn't have to select opponents, negotiate purses, or sell foreign rights. All he had to do for his money was organize the undercard bouts and promote the fight to the public (a job that was increasingly being taken over by the site management, be it a hotel-casino, indoor arena, or stadium). The truce meant easy money for King, and without it there was likely to be nothing but litigation and expense.

Then again, it's believable that King would reject the truce. It made him guaranteed promoter for only four fights, or one year. What if Tyson decided not to renew? King's pride may have also dictated against being constricted by the financial controls—either that or his sense of larceny made him want to do with the money from the fight as he pleased.

Even if King didn't unilaterally nix the truce, he may well have greatly influenced Tyson's decision. At the least, his hectoring about racial identity and independence emboldened the boxer to decide things for himself instead of letting others lead him along—as Tyson had always done in the past. Seen in that context, the truce was highly risky for King. Here he was doing a deal with a man he'd portrayed to Tyson as "Satan in disguise." The truce made good business sense to King, but to Tyson it might have seemed like backsliding; that King didn't practice what he preached.

"I'll tell you what happened," said one insider privy to Tyson's legal team. "When Howard Weitzman presented the deal to Mike, Don watched him very carefully. When Mike took exception to something, Don jumped up and screamed bloody murder about how he'd been forced to accept the deal. Don was covering his ass. If Mike had just sat there and nodded, there would have been a truce."

In the days following, Abraham tried to revive the truce agreement. Tyson, through King, said that he wanted his October 21 four-year deal with King instead. Any hope that Tyson might have put the past behind him was perhaps forever lost when the November issue of *Vanity Fair* magazine hit the newsstands. A feature profile of Robin Givens that had been researched and written during the summer depicted her as the true hero, and innocent victim, of the marriage. The story also contained photographs showing Givens eating lunch with Donald Trump on his yacht *Trump Princess*. They were similar to the photographs contained in the detective's report that made its way into the den of Tyson's Bernardsville home on the morning of October 2.

By November, especially after the "20/20" interview with Barbara Walters and the divorce action, Givens was exposed as something of a gold digger. Clearly, the woman assigned to do the *Vanity Fair* story, contributing editor Leslie Bennetts, had gotten it all wrong. Bennetts had recently joined the magazine after ten and a half years with the *New York Times*. It was her first assignment, and in the eyes of the magazine's editor in chief, Tina Brown, a botched job. "Bennetts screwed up and Tina wasn't at all pleased about it," admitted Elise O'Shaugnessey, a *Vanity Fair* editor.

The meeting on the *Trump Princess*, as could be expected, had had an official purpose. At the time, Trump was still an "adviser" to Mike Tyson Enterprises. Givens, who had been approached by *Vanity Fair*, suggested the *Trump Princess* as a venue for the photo shoot. It was after the photographers left that whatever happened between Givens and Trump happened. Tyson was told later by associates of King that they had overheard Trump complaining about Givens's facility with oral sex. "She's got the sharpest teeth in the world," Trump apparently complained.

Whatever may have actually happened between Givens and Trump, Tyson believed the worst. In early October, Trump approached him at a social function and motioned to shake his hand. Tyson brushed him aside and muttered, "Get out of my way, you motherfucker." In November, Trump added insult to injury by demanding in a formal letter a $2 million "adviser's fee" for having helped Tyson settle with Cayton the previous summer. Tyson refused to pay.

It's no surprise that when Cayton's attorney made one more effort to reach a truce, Tyson was in no mood to forgive and forget. On November 21, his lawyer received a formal contract agreement that listed all the terms and conditions discussed the month before at the Hilton. Tyson's answer came on November 23, no doubt with King's full support. He filed a civil suit against Cayton in U.S. District Court in Manhattan.

Tyson's federal suit, like the state action filed the previous summer, sought to end Cayton's managership. The core of his case remained fundamentally the same: that he had been defrauded by the February 12 contracts. As Tyson's attorneys well knew, in the July settlement he had agreed to withdraw the fraud accusation. They had to find new grounds on which to make the same charge. They argued that Cayton had failed to abide by the terms of the July settlement, and worse, that he had intentionally misled Tyson with promises in order to induce him to settle. Cayton did that, the complaint stated, in order to exert total control over Tyson's career. Such control disregarded his rights and "sought to deprive Tyson of his dignity and manhood."

Added on were a variety of other accusations, ranging from Cayton's trying to act as both manager and promoter to his overcharging Tyson on expenses. Some of those charges had merit, and some didn't. The central issue was whether Tyson, under King's direction this time, would finally succeed in exposing, and putting right, the deception of the February 12 contracts.

From that point on, Tyson and King conducted their affairs as if Cayton were no longer manager. On December 12, Howard Weitzman finalized an agreement with the Las Vegas Hilton and Bruno promoter Jarvis Astaire. HBO's Abraham also played a key role, particularly in allaying Astaire's concerns about King. The bout was set for February 25 at the Hilton, which would pay $7 million for the right to promote, a sum of money it hoped to recoup from ticket sales and gambling revenue. As punishment for the delays, and for moving the fight from England, Tyson had to cover the costs of the undercard matches, plus pay $350,000 in sanctioning fees from his total purse of $8 million ($3 million from the Hilton's fee, $4 million from HBO, and the rest from foreign television).

Around the same time that the Hilton agreement was signed, Tyson also fired trainer Kevin Rooney. (Rooney was having other problems too: he was convicted of assault after beating up his wife's lover.) Cayton got the message: he was being squeezed out of every decision in Tyson's career. He knew that he had to respond to Tyson's federal suit. The decision was whether to respond only to Tyson, or also to King as well for interfering with his boxer-manager contract.

Cayton chose the latter tack. It turned out to be another error in judgment about the character, and emotional needs, of Mike Tyson. Cayton filed his response in late December. It denied all of Tyson's accusations, and made a few of its own, naming both Tyson and King as codefendants. In doing that, he reinforced the budding relationship between Tyson and King. Years later, Cayton realized his mistake.

"Whatever chances I had of getting Tyson away from King were lost when I did that," Cayton admitted. "Frankly, my lawyer, Tom Puccio, wanted to do it, and I was initially reluctant. But we did it nonetheless."

*  *  *

On Thursday, December 15, Tyson held a press conference in Los Angeles to kick off the promotion of the upcoming bout with Frank Bruno. He had left the public spotlight a pathetic and all but emasculated figure: the supposedly indomitable Ring Destroyer who had been cut to pieces by a scheming wife and mother-in-law. Now, after two months with King, he presented the rather paradoxical image of a young man not full of resentment, but rather of maturity and resolution.

"I'm back and I'm happy to be back," Tyson said in a tone of voice suggesting boredom rather than joy. Tyson wanted the gathering of reporters and television newsmen to believe that he'd made a full recovery from the marriage. "I've gone through a lot, had a lot of distractions recently, but I really think it's good for somebody to go through something like this.

"Actually, I've been through this before, but I didn't have any money. I've been through this pain before, too, but this time it was publicized. I know I've learned a great deal about myself and how to deal with adversity.

"My main objective now is to get back on top. It doesn't matter if I'm famous or recognizable; you can't be on top if you don't perform, and I plan on performing again and getting back on top."

When asked about Givens and the marriage, Tyson waxed philosophic: "Hey, I went through a stage, fell in love, and I might fall in love again, but not the same way."

Everywhere America looked this new and improved Tyson—albeit always in the company of Don King—was there to peruse. In a November 14 *Jet* magazine feature, Tyson claimed to be born again: "Remember this—reach for God. Don't reach for the stars. You might get a cloud, and nothing in the clouds. Reach for God. Reach to shake God's hand." The same story detailed how Tyson was giving hundreds of thousands of dollars to charities and lecturing inner-city black youths on the importance of school. For the first time in his public remarks, Tyson referred to a black hero who wasn't a boxer—scientist George Washington Carver.

Tyson had also found a new love—himself: "To be the best you have to be cocky, arrogant and conceited. Conceited is just loving yourself. If you don't love yourself, you can never achieve anything. And I love myself. When Ali said 'I'm pretty,' Ali meant it because he was so in love with himself. I love myself. I look in the mirror and say I look good. I look in the mirror and say, wow! They can't mess with him."

He wanted to make it clear that he had the inner strength to persevere: "I'm a doer. I'm not a survivor. The only thing a survivor does is live and don't care about nobody but his own self. I'm a doer. I make things happen. Take all of my money and in a few months or a year, I'll make it back again."

Those seemed to be the thoughts and feelings of an emerging young man who had learned much from the adversity of recent months. Still, it was difficult to reconcile the new Tyson with his dual personas of the past. There were no signs of the smoldering anger and macho bravado of the Ring Destroyer; no sweet, high-voiced murmurings from the man-child. Gone also were the catchphrases and affectations of speech Tyson had picked up from both D'Amato and Jacobs. Was this new and improved Tyson finally the real Tyson?

It had become almost impossible to get a fix on a "real" Mike Tyson. No doubt the urge for a renewal was there. But there was something wrong with the picture. He seemed to be reading from a mental script, and still using language and concepts completely foreign to him. There was no conviction to his insights. If he'd become the happy, ambitious, born-again, self-loving man of action, this image seemed a no more authentic Mike Tyson than those of the past.

Once again, there was someone else authoring Tyson's reality—namely, King. That had its good side. In the last weeks and days of the marriage, he had helped Tyson get back in control of his life. But at the same time, as he had demonstrated so many times with other fighters, anything King did for someone else was designed ultimately to benefit only himself. As one boxing manager said in a cynical vein: "King figured that the better he could make Tyson look, then the less people would question his intentions. I can assure you, all King wanted to do was get Tyson into the ring making money."

The important issue was how their relationship would evolve. Tyson had already embraced King as he had Tryon counselor Bobby Stewart, then D'Amato, Jacobs, and Givens and Roper—as someone who could help him survive. A pattern had developed in all of his mentor relationships. Tyson seemed caught up in a cycle of trust and betrayal. Whether he would let that happen with King had yet to be seen.

# Chapter Nineteen

**M**ike Tyson's 1989 started out with a bad omen. The thoughtful young man who had reached for God was also doing some random fondling. In early January, twenty-nine-year-old Lori Davis of Long Island, New York, filed a $1 million lawsuit against Tyson for grabbing her buttocks in Bentley's Discotheque on Manhattan's East Fortieth Street. Davis claimed that she told Tyson that if he did that again, "I'll smack the shit out of you!" Tyson, she maintained, laughed, and said, "Whoa, we have a live one here." He then allegedly approached another woman at the bar. According to newspaper reports of the incident, she informed him that she already "had a man." Tyson responded, "But I am the man." The woman stormed off, and he pursued her, grabbing at her buttocks and breasts, according to reports. Confronted by the woman's friend, he supposedly said, "Doesn't she know who I am?" Horne and Holloway reportedly had to pull him out of the bar before anything worse happened. One of Tyson's bodyguards later confirmed what had happened: "Mike was drinking in those days, a lot."

Tyson once admired the old-time boxers for their haircuts, attire, gold teeth, lack of jewelry, and victory stances. When he found out that onetime welterweight champion Roberto Duran, "The Hands of Stone," loved to drink champagne, he copied that too. During the days, King would drag him around to charity events, but at night he was consuming large quantities of champagne. By late December 1988, Tyson's weight had shot up to 255 pounds. Obviously, he hadn't been doing any serious training.

With Rooney gone, just how well Tyson's training would go for the Bruno fight came into question. Rooney was one of only two trainers (the other being Teddy Atlas) who intimately understood D'Amato's unique "system" of boxing that Tyson had used to become, and remain, champion. When he did it well, Tyson created a seamless union between defense and offense, performing a highly destructive pugilistic ballet. But like all such athletic skills, it was something that had to be practiced constantly to be done well. Without Rooney in the process, Tyson was likely to regress into a more conventional boxing style.

King replaced Rooney with Aaron Snowell, who claimed to have trained former champion Tim Witherspoon. That wasn't the case. He was trained by "Slim" Jim Robinson, for whom Snowell, barely thirty, carried the towels and the spit bucket. But Snowell suited King's purposes. When Witherspoon sued King, he switched allegiances and went on King's payroll. He wasn't now so much a "trainer" as just another person, like John Horne, employed to keep an eye on Tyson.

Tyson's training was interrupted by the fallout from the suit he had filed against Cayton the previous November. After filing his response, Cayton made efforts to settle. He put on the table the same terms that had been discussed in the October meeting at the Las Vegas Hilton, with one major difference: he no longer wanted King to have a four-fight, or one-year, term. He now proposed that King promote only on a fight-by-fight basis. It was a tougher stance that didn't play well with Tyson. Tyson wanted the deal he'd signed with King, and nothing less.

In early January, Tyson's attorney moved to have the depositions taken in private. The judge, however, ruled that in airing his accusations through the media, Tyson had opened the door of public access. The depositions started on January 9, in Ballroom C of the Desert Inn Hotel in Las Vegas. Members of the news media sat in an adjoining room, where they could watch the question-and-answer session on closed-circuit television.

Tyson was the first witness. D'Amato, he said, had told him early on that Jacobs would one day be his manager. He'd always assumed that Cayton was Jacobs's partner in the fight film business. According to

Tyson, D'Amato often referred to Cayton as "greedy." As to his own views about money, he said that he'd been promised $21 million for the Spinks fight, but couldn't recall when, or if, he'd been paid. In fact, as it was pointed out to him by Cayton's attorney, Thomas Puccio, he'd received his full share, around $12,328,937. Tyson couldn't recall what he'd done with it. He had no idea of what became of it. King, and the accountants and lawyers he hired, controlled his finances.

Although money didn't interest Tyson, the February 12 contracts did. "[I had] total trust, implicitly, totally, with every soul of my body, in Jim," he said. He had no idea that Jacobs was sick, and no specific recollection that if he died, Cayton would become his manager: "Jimmy had said something about him and about their wives getting a share of the money," Tyson recalled. He didn't read the contracts. "I just signed it because Jimmy asked me to sign it."

Puccio tried to determine whether it was explained to him that if Jacobs died, Cayton would become his manager.

Tyson: "I just signed this because Jim told me. I didn't understand anything."

Puccio: "Did anyone try to explain it to you?"

Tyson: "Jim asked me to sign it. I always trust Jimmy. I never believe, my listening to Jimmy, it would all come down to this and being here facing you."

Tyson claimed that he never "cared" for Cayton and wouldn't have wanted him to be his manager.

Puccio: "Did you understand he was your manager?"

Tyson: "No, I didn't understand. Because Jimmy, by some means, I can't understand why, Jimmy had me sign this. Like I said, I trust him and I signed it. I wanted to fight in the glory of Jim. I loved Jim. "I was so alarmed in knowing that I was caught into a trap... He could have informed me about Mr. Cayton being my manager, which he didn't. He could have done that."

Tyson was questioned again the next day. He gave thanks to King—"I handle my own business, and basically, I mean, he's helping me blossom into a man"—and had trouble believing the accusations made against King over the years by Larry Holmes and Tim Witherspoon. Then he qualified: "Well, I don't want to say I don't believe their claims. . . . It's very difficult for me to believe when someone hurts you, why would you continue to come back."

Clearly, Tyson didn't yet understand the full range of King's power over the heart and mind of a fighter. Tyson understood only his own needs, and even twisted the logic of D'Amato's teachings to justify them: "Cus was a believer in, he didn't like a fighter being with any promoter. He thinks a fighter is free. It's my choice to choose, that's what he felt." Tyson insisted that he chose King, and that he demanded the exclusive four-year promotional contract. "I was calling the shots and it was my life."

The heavyweight champion now "calling the shots" had no idea about the specific terms of his contract with King. When grilled on those terms by Puccio, he spat back, "You're stressing me out."

But not so stressed out that he couldn't make a pass at Puccio's legal associate, Joann Crispi. During the second day of questioning, Tyson told her that she had a "nice ass," then tried to catch her attention by poking his finger in and out of his fist to suggest sexual intercourse.

A few days before King's deposition, Mike Katz of the *Daily News*, quoting a "friend" of Cayton, said that he (Cayton) had taken Tyson's accusations "like a knife through the heart." Loraine Jacobs reportedly reacted with tears to the claim that her late husband had defrauded Tyson. "I'm sure she cries her eyes out at night," the friend said. Katz went so far as to argue that Cayton needed to fight for his share of Tyson's purses in order to support his retarded daughter. The Caytons, this anonymous friend said, wanted to make sure their daughter was "cared for when they are gone—and not in an institution." In fact, without Tyson's money, Cayton was already a millionaire many times over.

King's deposition took place in Puccio's New York offices on January 18. Also present at the table were Cayton and Loraine Jacobs. This session was also televised on closed-circuit for reporters. Puccio tried to expose King's less-than-ethical business practices with past fighters. "You have to understand, I am the best promoter in the world," King blared. "My record substantiates that... despite a few allegations by dissidents. My record is irrefutable."

The more Puccio tried to bring King back to the question, the greater his defiance became. "You subpoenaed me and then you got to deal with me," King bellowed. Soon, it was King's ego, and not the facts of the case, that became the issue. "Your job is to give me questions that can be answered," he lectured Puccio. Near the end of the session, he pointed at Cayton and yelled, "Mr. Cayton is an inveterate liar. He's a tyrant, a despot, a power zealot. He's an egotistical maniac. Nobody likes Bill Cayton. He's never been liked by anybody. Everybody loved

Jim. Everybody hates you. You're the most hated man in boxing." King finished with this: "I said he was Satan in disguise. The disguise is gone. He's just Satan."

King continued his deposition the next day. The bluster was gone now. He got down to what had always bothered him most about Jacobs and Cayton—namely, that they had usurped his role as promoter. "Mr. Cayton wanted to emasculate me. He took all the promotional rights and used me for a beard, he used me for a shield."

On that fact, King was right. While Jacobs actively managed Tyson, Cayton formed, and wholly owned, a number of different companies to exploit the fighter's career. There was Big Fights, Inc., which sold Tyson's fights to foreign television, plus his films and videos. Reel Sports, Inc. made 15 percent on Tyson's commercial appearances. For the Spinks fight, he created Sports of the Century, Inc. to gather in the closed-circuit pay-per-view monies, and all other revenue from ancillary rights, including radio rights, advertisers, sponsors, and merchandise sales. Sports of the Century, for all intents and purposes, was the promoting corporation of the fight.

With Jacobs gone, Cayton had become like an octopus over Tyson's career. He did the manager's job, plus many of those duties customarily relegated to the promoter, which was an infraction of the rules and regulations of the New York State Athletic Commission. He selected opponents, and negotiated their purses; he worked out site fees with the hotel-casinos; he owned, and sold, all television and video rights. Granted, when King did function as a traditional promoter, his fighters rarely made as much money as they normally could have, but Cayton too was obviously no model of propriety.

Cayton had committed two other transgressions. As president of Big Fights, he took a 20 percent commission from the sale of television rights. The remainder of the money was put into the pot of gross earnings from the fight. Then, as manager, he took another 20 percent from the gross. In other words, he took commissions twice from the same chunk of money. There was no rule or regulation in boxing against such a practice—called "double-dipping"—but it was considered highly unethical, a blatant display of plain and simple greed.

Cayton had also overcharged Tyson on expenses. But unlike the double-dipping, this was strictly against the rules and regulations of the Athletic Commission. The boxer-manager contract entitled Cayton to deduct from Tyson's purses "reasonable and necessary training and transportation expenses incurred by, or on behalf of, the Boxer." From the outset of Tyson's career, however, it's arguable that both Cayton and Jacobs deducted far more than was reasonable—to wit, $200,000 in lawyers' fees and all of Big Fights's various other expenses. Both items should have come out of Big Fights's own gross earnings. The effect was to reduce the size of the pie from which Tyson earned his $66^2/3$ percent.

Cayton was supposed to be questioned for his deposition in early February. That was put off until after the Tyson-Bruno fight.

\*   \*   \*

By the beginning of February, Tyson was ready to open up his workouts to the press. Reporters weren't startled to see that he'd gotten down from 255 pounds to around 230. Any athlete with a twenty-two-year-old's metabolism who trained hard every day for several weeks could shed excess fat. The shock was Jay Bright, one of the youths from the Catskill house. Tyson had asked him to be a cotrainer.

Bright was a pale, rosy-cheeked, corpulent, thirty-year-old with no experience in training boxers. He was born and raised in Bayside, Queens. His father worked as an electrician at the New York Stock Exchange. As a boy, Bright weighed 380 pounds. He had an interest in boxing and a deep admiration of Muhammad Ali. He had read about Jacobs's fight film collection and called him once to buy a tape of one of Ali's exhibition fights. They struck up a friendship. When Bright was quite young, his father died of a heart attack, and his mother of cancer. Jacobs arranged for him to live with D'Amato. He got his weight down to 175, and had three amateur bouts. A thumb in the eye required surgery and ended his boxing career. After D'Amato died, he stayed with Ewald, and put much of the weight back on. Bright was known as a walking, talking clone who spouted D'Amato's ideas and who, like D'Amato, was a loner and a malcontent.

"I'm familiar with Cus's terminology, and with his ideology and philosophy as well. Mike is a tremendous athlete, but he needs to have his psyche addressed too," Bright said. No doubt that was precisely what Tyson wanted him around for: to evoke the remnants of a past he'd left behind. But Bright, concerned about bringing down King's wrath, was selective in what he evoked. As Rooney later recalled: "He said he was doing it for Cus, yeah, so Mike and him was missing the whole point of what Cus was about. What does Mike need King for? Why is he letting a known thief make the money?"

The final weeks leading up to fight night carried none of the old hype that had once surrounded Tyson's fights. The billboard advertisements put up by the Las Vegas Hilton were toned down from earlier efforts. "Tyson's Welcome Home Party. Punch Served," read one billboard. "This is War," said another. No longer were there comparisons of Tyson with all the legendary fighters. No longer was he on the cover of *Life* or *People* magazine. In the popular culture he wasn't perceived anymore as some kind of machinelike menace. He was now being defined through the failure of his marriage. The February issue of the *National Lampoon* showed Tyson splayed on the canvas underneath a triumphant Givens and Roper counting, "One million, two million, three million..." *Vanity Fair* magazine, unrepentant about its botched November profile favoring Givens, decided to keep rubbing Tyson's nose in her alleged infidelities. It ran a full-page photograph of Givens leaning over the railing of the *Trump Princess* in a plush bath towel.

On February 14, St. Valentine's Day, Tyson and Givens were granted a divorce in the Dominican Republic. Considering how much of Tyson's money she had already made away with during the marriage, she did extremely well: she received $1 million in cash, and got to keep the jewelry and various other possessions she'd bought with Tyson's money. It was also apparently stipulated that Givens, and Roper, couldn't publicly discuss either the settlement or the marriage. Givens would no doubt comply. Her public image, and thus her acting career, had suffered as a result of the marriage. Roper took some of the settlement money and formed an independent film production company in New York, Never Blue Productions.

With yet another of Tyson's surrogate families gone by the wayside, King scurried to conjure up his own. He spent thousands of dollars (of Tyson's money) to have Los Angeles fashion designer Jeff Hamilton custom-make a dozen black, red, and white leather jackets that said "Team Tyson" on the back. King, Horne, Holloway, and Bright also had a new wardrobe of sweatshirts, T-shirts, and hats that said, "It's a Family Affair." But while King propped up an artifice of family values, Tyson tore them down. "People say, 'Poor guy.' That insults me," he said at the one and only prefight press conference he agreed to attend. "I despise sympathy. So I screwed up. I made some mistakes. 'Poor guy,' like I'm some victim. There's nothing poor about me."

They were a strange family indeed. Tyson had camped out at King's luxury condominium complex. Horne, Holloway, and Bright stayed in suites at the Las Vegas Hilton. According to Hilton president John Giovenco, they treated the hotel like their private banquet—again at Tyson's expense. "These guys arrived in jeans and T-shirts, and within a few weeks they were wearing gold watches and jewelry from the hotel shops," Giovenco said. "And they were stealing towels."

In the final days before the fight, Tyson confessed that he hadn't watched any films of Bruno's past fights. That used to be standard preparation, and now it would have seemed all the more necessary, given that he'd been out of the ring for eight months, his longest layoff ever. "I got no particular idea about him," Tyson told one reporter. "I really don't care. As far as the jab, I can pick it off."

In the opinion of the bookmakers, Tyson's troubles were not likely to increase Bruno's chances of winning. Tyson was favored by 7½-to-1. Bruno's number one ranking from both the W.B.C. and the W.B.A. overstated his chances. He had fought in obscurity against more than two dozen unranked opponents before meeting Tim Witherspoon on July 19, 1986. He had led on the judges' scorecards, then was suddenly knocked out. A subsequent battle with James ("Bonecrusher") Smith about a year later took a similar course. Against top-level competition, Bruno's chin was suspect.

He would have faded out of contender status had it not been for Tyson, whose victories over every other ranked contender in 1987 and 1988 moved Bruno up the ladder. Cayton selected him to kickoff Tyson's world tour, in which the matchup didn't matter so much as the need to get Tyson out of an overexposed U.S. market.

Still, as could only be expected, Frank Bruno talked bravely in his deep, cockney accent about how he would be "Kryptonite" to Tyson's "Superman." On the day before the fight at the weigh-in ceremony, he attempted a stare-down. Tyson, in an act of ghetto culture machismo, yanked open the front of his briefs and exposed tufts of pubic hair, then lifted up his entire organ with a jerk. It was a gesture of disdain for Bruno's abilities, and a tasteless one.

Tyson didn't have much to fear. Bruno, twenty-seven years old, hadn't fought in sixteen months. They had also met before. Six years earlier, they'd sparred for twenty rounds in Catskill. According to the lore, Tyson had given Bruno a sound beating. He was the kind of tall, slow fighter whom Tyson used to routinely elude, then chop down with lightning-fast combination body and head shots. Bruno's jab lazily prodded out for no other purpose than to set up his one formidable punch, a straight right. He hardly moved in the ring.

Bruno's major merit was aesthetics. His skin was the deep, rich brown of fine dark chocolate. He had the sculpted body of Michelangelo's David: broad shoulders, a narrow waist, every muscle discretely outlined. By all accounts, he was a gentleman; he was highly regarded in England, where he lived with a common-law wife and their two children. He would make $3.5 million for the fight, but that was less than he had earned over the years doing television commercials and product endorsements in England. The camera, as they say, loved him.

Tyson entered the ring covered in sweat. The Dempsey-style haircut he'd sported for the last few years looked shorter, and more severe than usual. He had managed to bring his weight down to 218 pounds. There was still something slablike about his musculature. He would have needed a few more weeks of training to hone it taut. When Bruno came into the indoor arena at the Hilton, the estimated two thousand fans from England rowdily chanted, "Bru-no, Bru-no, Bru-no," and waved Union Jacks. When Don King got up in the ring, the crowd, American and British, loudly booed.

The fighters came straight out at each other and met in the middle of the ring. For the first few seconds, Tyson put on a fine display of D'Amato's "system." He took the inside positioning so necessary to reach the taller Bruno, and he did it without getting hit. That produced early results. He caught Bruno with a short right, then a glancing shot to the top of the head that sent him down to one knee.

After that, both men changed tactics. Bruno leaned away from Tyson's punches, or blocked them. He tried to tie Tyson up, then hold him at the back of the head and pound into his ear—a standard though dirty method of upsetting an opponent's sense of balance. The Tyson of a year ago would have punched out of the clinches. But this Tyson backed off. He gave up the inside positioning, and didn't seem to have the confidence in himself to get it back with the same seamless, fluid motion of defense and offense that had made him champion. He had been trained by D'Amato to make his opponent miss and then to exploit the error by counterpunching with something the other boxer didn't see coming. And so, instead of slipping and dipping to the left or right, then sending in a body shot to set up a hook to the head—once standard stuff for Tyson—he came straight in. He seemed desperate to land the one, big, knockout punch. Without elusive movement, though, he couldn't get in close enough to connect. He started to reach with his punches, most of which missed. He began to look like any other conventionally trained fighter.

With fifty seconds to go in the first round, it dawned on Tyson that he had to get inside. He was about to make a major tactical mistake. He came straight in, winging punches and bobbing like a jack-in-the-box. Bruno timed a right hook that caught Tyson flush. He didn't try and dip out and away from Bruno's next punch, but bobbed again, then came up with a wide left—and took another punch on the side of the head.

Tyson hadn't been hit so squarely, and hard, since eating Tony Tucker's right uppercut in August 1987. This time, he didn't recover as well. He was rocked, and momentarily lost his offensive rhythm. Bruno was too surprised by his own good fortune, and handiwork, to seize the moment. With an immediate barrage of punches, he might have been able to score a knockdown. He didn't, the round ended, and Tyson recovered.

In the second round, both fighters slowed down considerably. When they weren't clinching each other, they stood straight up, like two statues with movable arms. Near round's end, Tyson found a glimmer of his old style. Bruno let a lazy jab hang out, which he slipped to the inside, then sent a straight right around Bruno's arm that landed flush on his jaw.

The punch recaptured something for Tyson. He began the third round moving more, but it didn't last. It must have become clear to him that he no longer had the ability to put even a Frank Bruno down in a few rounds. The flaw of passivity and acquiescence started to creep out. In the fourth, Tyson recovered. He came out jabbing consistently for the first time, and it paid off. Even a proficiently conventional Tyson was too much for Bruno, who just stood there taking the punches. But he didn't go down. Before going out for the fifth, Tyson looked disappointed with himself. He sat on the corner stool, shoulders slumped, his head hung low.

Tyson came out slugging in the fifth on the hope that something, anything, would connect. He landed with a short left hook from an off-balance position that hurt Bruno and backed him up. He followed with several more well-placed hooks and uppercuts, against which Bruno put up virtually no defense. The referee called it off late in the round.

In the postfight interview, Tyson made light of his technical deterioration. He had, after all, won the fight. Then he posed: "Those fellas, how dare they challenge me with their primitive skills." Tyson said of his future opponents. "They're just as good as dead."

The fact was that Tyson's own skills had also regressed to a primitive state. He still had the will to fight, but much less desire to excel in his craft. His strident egotism struggled to deny that clearly visible fact. If this was a sign of what to expect from his relationship with King, then things could only get worse.

With the Bruno fight completed, King was free to promote Tyson as he pleased—unofficially. The early signs were ominous. The day after the fight, Tyson made an appearance on the Los Angeles talk show of Arsenio Hall. He said that if he was going to be ripped off by someone, he'd prefer it be by a black man rather than a white man.

After the fight King talked about Tyson meeting José Ribalta next, or perhaps the more highly ranked Carl Williams. He mentioned taking Tyson on a tour of fights in Brazil, Italy, Japan, and Zaire. Both Ribalta and the tour were meant to usurp Cayton's role as manager. Ribalta was one of the few heavyweights King controlled. As to the tour, which of course was originally Cayton's idea, King planned to take it over.

On February 27, Cayton filed a complaint against King with the New York State Athletic Commission. On March 8, he then sued him in U.S. District Court in Manhattan, alleging antitrust violations, racketeering, fraud, and defamation. It was by far the most sweeping series of charges ever lodged against King. It detailed many of the tactics he had used over the years to take control of boxing, most of which he applied to Tyson.

Before Cayton's suit could go any further, depositions for Tyson's action had to be completed. Cayton was questioned on March 22 in New York. He claimed to have been Tyson's co-manager. When it was pointed out that no such status legally existed, he said he felt he had acquired that title by custom because he shared in Tyson's purses. When Cayton was asked if he understood the Athletic Commission rule against a fighter having two managers, his attorney, Thomas Puccio, refused to let him answer. He was cut off in the same way on the subject of functioning as both a manager and promoter.

After he gave an extremely detailed explanation of the various commercial and fight deals he'd negotiated for Tyson over the years, Cayton's memory suddenly became fuzzy on the subject of the February 12 contracts. He couldn't readily recollect where they'd been signed. As to the signature of Peter Della—the deputy commissioner whom Torres cajoled into witnessing the contracts even though he wasn't there—Cayton was unsure about whether or not he was present. He also equivocated on the issue of authorship. He claimed that the special wording which made him manager in the event of Jacobs's death was not put in at his direction. "I'm not sure whose idea it was," Cayton said.

Howard Weitzman, Tyson's attorney, then caught Cayton in a contradiction. If he already thought he was Tyson's co-manager, then what was the purpose of the February 12 contracts? Puccio refused to let him answer.

Weitzman persisted: "Sir, was there some concern that if Jim died there might be a problem with you becoming manager?"

Cayton tried to deflect the issue, make it appear that they were all doing some magnanimous gesture for the "wives." He was referring to the second series of contracts that gave each of their wives a cut of Tyson's earnings. "Essentially, the purpose of this whole series of agreements was to protect Loraine in the event of Jim's death and Doris in the event of my death," Cayton said.

As to why they selected February 12 to do the contracts, Cayton harped on about protecting the wives. Weitzman got back to why the contracts were needed if he felt he was already manager. This time Cayton was permitted to answer, and it rang false: "Just to make everything more... more binding, perhaps."

The next day's session picked up with the contracts again. Cayton admitted knowing before they were signed that Jacobs would enter the hospital immediately afterwards for chemotherapy. He confessed to not having told Tyson about either Jacobs's leukemia or the hospital visit, because it would have made Tyson "sad." He also insisted that he had no conversation with Torres about the contracts—even though he did meet with Torres two days before they were signed. He repeated several times that Jacobs's death was a total shock to him—despite how badly Jacobs looked after his spleen operation. As to the role of commission attorney Carl DeSantis in drafting the agreements, Cayton's memory became conveniently vague. He said he didn't know "anything specific" about which attorney, if any, worked on the documents with Torres— and yet he had spoken to DeSantis himself, demanding that he "hurry up." In later interviews on the subject, Cayton was even more blatant: "Jim did everything. I had nothing to do with these contracts. They were all Jim's idea."

Although this new round of litigation had advanced to the deposition stage, it would soon be derailed. As when Givens and Roper had initiated a similar suit against Cayton the previous summer, the money Tyson could make for everyone, and not justice for his grievances, took priority.

King had no interest in nailing Cayton for the alleged contract fraud or for any other infraction. The deeper Tyson got into the case, the more risk there was that a judge would enjoin him from fighting until it was resolved. "Don wanted Mike in the ring, and not in the courtroom," King ally Seth Abraham admitted.

Cayton's accusations against King removed any hope that the litigation would ever go to a jury trial. In order for Tyson to press his suit, King would also have had to defend himself. That gave him another reason to derail Tyson's case. He didn't want to risk having his career as a promoter—what with Larry Holmes, and Tim Witherspoon, and Mitch Green, among a score of other fighters, prepared to testify against him—left in the hands of a jury. In other words, by helping Tyson fight for justice, King was committing career suicide.

Cayton was just as desperate to settle Tyson's federal suit as he was the state action the previous summer. He didn't want Loraine Jacobs, José Torres, Carl DeSantis, Dr. Gene Brody, and James Dupree to take the stand and be grilled on the motives, authorship, and signing of the February 12 contracts. His action against King could thus be seen as a crafty defensive gambit. By suing King, Cayton protected himself.

HBO's Seth Abraham knew enough about King's history with litigation to surmise that he didn't want to push a trial. Abraham was still owed four more fights from the existing seven-fight deal. But now that King had the solid allegiance of Tyson, and Cayton the contract, Abraham's role would have to change. In order to keep Tyson fighting, Abraham had to make it seem as if he respected both camps equally, even though he knew it was King's bond that mattered most. He would mediate between them, albeit with an ulterior motive. Tyson could conceivably complete the seven-fight obligation within a year. Abraham had to start laying out the terms of a new and far more complex multifight deal that would go beyond Cayton's tenure as manager.

By late April, Abraham had succeeded in forging a two-fight truce. I.B.F. challenger Carl Williams would be Tyson's next opponent for a July date. (Williams had to sign away three options to King for the shot at, and payday with, Tyson.) With Tyson now under King's control, it's not surprising that he got back the traditional promoter's powers. He would negotiate every aspect of the promotion, which Cayton then had the right to approve. The only deal on which they had to work together was foreign television sales. It was Cayton who now did little for his money besides rubber-stamp another man's work. Still, he was concerned that King would hold up his 20 percent purse cut. Abraham agreed to give Cayton directly his share of the HBO licensing fee directly.

The truce didn't resolve all the outstanding business issues. King still wanted Tyson to fight José Ribalta, for no other reason than he was one of the few ranked heavyweights on whom he had a long-term contract. There were rumors that King wanted the fight because his son Carl was written in to get a manager's cut. Cayton strongly objected to Ribalta. He wanted Tyson to match up with Evander Holyfield on closed-circuit pay-per-view. On March 11, Holyfield beat the aging former W.B.A. heavyweight champion, and ex-cocaine abuser, Michael Dokes in a tenth round knockout. He'd had only two previous fights as a heavyweight, both of which he'd won, but against similarly unimpressive opponents: James Tillis and Pinklon Thomas. Still, Holyfield was a new name in the heavyweight ranks, for whom there was growing interest from both the boxing press and the public. King objected to Holyfield because his manager, Dan Duva, refused to give up any options on future fights. In other words, King didn't want an opponent he couldn't control.

Abraham turned to work on the new multifight deal. He considered it the payoff for having been a loyal ally to King over the past ten years. Now that King had control over the biggest money machine in boxing, Abraham felt entitled to crank the arm. "I like Mike Tyson for the same reason I like Don King," Abraham said in a May 1989 interview. "I've been loyal to him, and he's been loyal to us beyond the paycheck. I respect and appreciate that."

Abraham had in mind an omnibus agreement that would cover almost every revenue source, and for a term lasting the remainder of Tyson's career in the ring. He was inspired, in part, by the April announcement that Time Inc. would merge with another giant in the entertainment industry, multimedia Warner Communications: "Live fights, closed-circuit pay-per-view, and connecting Tyson to the other mediums available through the merger of our parent Time and Warner, such as advertising, books, and movies," Abraham said. "And I was prepared to spend a lot of money to get him." Abraham firmly believed that money alone solved everybody's problems. "The lifetime deal will point out to everybody how much money can be made by not arguing," he added in a reference to the recent litigation. "HBO is the bank in boxing, and it's not smart to fuck with the bank."

The first formal meeting on the lifetime deal took place at King's

Orwell, Ohio, training camp in late May. Events that day foreshadowed many future frustrations for Abraham. In the months to come he would be hit by the sobering reality of what doing business with King ultimately meant. For King, money, and more important the power to make it and take it as he pleased, came before loyalty.

King's camp would have gone unnoticed if it hadn't been for the enormous American flag King had erected in a neighboring field. He'd surrounded it with some thirty-odd other flags of nations from around the world. There was a two-story, white-clapboard farmhouse that he'd made into an office, and behind that he'd built a red-brick dining hall large enough to feed a football team. Next to that was a gym with two boxing rings and various types of training equipment. There was also a main dormitory building with a recreation room and at least twelve bedrooms. A gravel road led back to two other small, red-brick bunkhouse structures and a black-asphalt basketball court.

The camp had the feel of a once-bustling place, and in fact it had been when King built it in the early 1980s. He'd kept his stable of boxers here, charging some of them up to $1,000 a day for the privilege of using the gym and eating the food of chef "Captain Joe," a bell-shaped, bald black man in his fifties with heavy eyes and an obsequious manner who bore a resemblance to Uncle Fester from "The Addams Family." King had closed the camp two years after losing part of his stable to the HBO Unification Series and the rest, Tim Witherspoon, to litigation.

He opened it again now for Tyson's exclusive use. Captain Joe remained as private chef, plus chauffeur. Tyson moved into one of the small bunkhouses, although he had also bought a house nearby, which King's wife, Henrietta, was decorating. He kept a fleet of cars at the camp: a canary-yellow Rolls-Royce Corniche, a black Ferrari Testerossa (the plate read "VAPORS1"), a white, angular, military-looking Lamborghini ATV, and four Mercedes-Benzes, two of which had gold-plated rims. Horne and Holloway used two other Mercedeses and two customized BMW 530i M6s, both with gold-plated rims and diamonds inlaid in the name of the dealer. "It's like a banana republic and King is Papa Doc," HBO chief Michael Fuchs cracked, referring to "Papa Doc" Duvalier, the much-feared former dictator of Haiti.

Abraham and Fuchs arrived mid-morning of May 31 to discuss the new lifetime deal. Tyson didn't show up, and so they waited. Apparently, he'd spent the night before on the party circuit in Cleveland and had missed his predawn training run. No one knew exactly where he was. But Horne and Holloway were certain about one thing: they loved the champ. "We're as much of a family to him as Jimmy Jacobs and those guys," argued Holloway, who had a quiet, understated air, darkly colored skin and a shortish, pudgy-boy build. Horne was just over six feet, lean but not muscular, and far more assertive. He tended to speak in a high-pitched, complaining tone. "This camp is much more at ease for Mike," Horne said. "It's the first camp he's had where he feels at home. We give him more stability...He's happier as a person all around, not just in the ring...It's Mike's turn to be happy. We're here for him."

King also espoused the party line: "It's a family affair where togetherness, solidarity, and unity prevail," he boomed as if reading from some internal TelePrompTer. "Mike understands that he has to be better than he is. My job is to be honest with him—he's the man—to allow him to make his own mistakes. He has to grow up like everyone else. It's all about Mike growing up, and I can't wait to make him independent of me." It was all meant to be a counterpoint to how Tyson was treated by D'Amato, Jacobs, and Cayton—except for the "independence" bit, which King had cribbed from the D'Amato gospel. "I do not try and emasculate him, decide what's right and wrong for him," King continued. "He decides. I'm not his father, but the heart of the father that many kids in the ghetto don't have. I can relate to what Mike Tyson is suffering."

By lunch Tyson still hadn't shown up. Abraham and Fuchs started the meeting with King over a trayful of Captain Joe's fried chicken. King, who was dressed in a toffee-brown leather shirt and pants, ate six pieces while he listened to the pitch. "We bring money, *saichel*, and a good word," Abraham told King to start things off. The Yiddish *"saichel"* meant common sense, and was an allusion to Abraham's truce powers with Cayton. There was talk about the number of live fights on HBO, how many closed-circuit pay-per-view "windows" Tyson could use, and the term of the deal. King chomped, licked, smacked, and every now and then intoned "uh-huh" to show he was listening. He had the look of a man who believed he had all the time in the world to do this deal his way. They wrapped up with nothing decided. "Can I get you anything else, Mr. King?" Fuchs asked sarcastically.

Tyson showed up at 4 P.M. dressed in a black-and-white-striped leather Alpine lederhosen. By that time, Abraham and Fuchs had to catch a plane back to New York. Fuchs gave Tyson a present—a painting of a football locker room where the players were naked women, black and white, putting on their gear. Tyson looked tired, and puffy, as if he'd spent the night eating and drinking. There was a cranky edge to his mood. He didn't hang around to talk. He thanked Fuchs and without another word walked the painting back to his bunkhouse.

Here were a captain of the entertainment industry and his lieutenant ready to spend tens of millions of dollars on his future, and Tyson couldn't care less. A sense of pathos seemed to linger in the air as the group watched him lumber off. It was like watching two different beings: the massive, hulking body, and the lonely man inside. They didn't seem in sync with each other. It was as if a part of Tyson wanted to escape the awkward grotesqueness of his corporeal form and break free from all the artifice of his life as heavyweight champion of the world— but felt that he never could.

"He's got a King Kong walk," Fuchs said, breaking the silence of the moment.

*     *     *

The young man whom King had started to call "The Baddest Man on the Planet Earth, The Meanest Man in the Universe" was scheduled to fight Carl ("The Truth") Williams in Atlantic City on July 21, 1989. Tyson lived up to his new moniker. He gave only one prefight interview, and that was to the reporter he and King most easily controlled: Mike Marley of the *New York Post*. (Marley's exclusive access was deeply resented by the other reporters: "He's a blatant opportunist," said Phil Berger of the *New York Times*.) In the days leading up to the fight, King threatened to bar Berger, plus *Newsday's* Wally Matthews and the *Daily News's* Mike Katz, from the press conferences. Matthews responded by organizing a general media boycott of the fight, and King backed down.

Tyson had always seemed bored at press conferences, but he'd still managed to show some respect for the questions and the questioners. Not this time. He had evolved into the scowling visage of Sonny Liston. Even King was a target. King spewed out a litany of overblown adjectives to introduce Tyson, who glanced over at him with contempt. (Indeed, at a Los Angeles press conference the previous April, in the midst of one such introduction, Tyson had told King to "shut up.")

Asked if he hoped to break Rocky Marciano's record of forty-nine victories and no losses, Tyson spat, "Hey, if it happens, it happens." As to his prediction, he snorted, "Just come to the fight. I'm sure you'll enjoy it." In response to a question about his strategy against Williams, he said, "I have no idea," and later, "I just want to get it over with." One reporter wondered whether Tyson intended to quit the ring. "If I did that, I would be making a lot of people happy, and I don't want to do that," he said. The climax of his disdain came when a woman reporter for a radio station asked what message he had for children about drugs. Tyson leaned forward to bear down on her: "You're not a sportscaster, are you?" he asked in a menacing tone verging on verbal abuse. Suddenly, everyone was embarrassed, not for the reporter but for Tyson, who had apparently launched at her for no other reason than that she was female.

There was, after all, a context now in which to place his feelings about women. Just weeks before the fight, José Torres's biography, *Fire & Fear: The Inside Story of Mike Tyson*, was released. At first, Tyson had cooperated with Torres. Then, in June 1988, Roper asked Torres to testify on Tyson's behalf in the suit against Cayton. She wanted him to admit that Jacobs and Cayton had engineered a fraud with the February 12 contracts. Torres refused to do that. Tyson's lawyer sent a letter to the publisher withdrawing his cooperation. Torres had to give back a portion of his $350,000 advance.

Torres put a complete whitewash over his own role in the February 12 contracts. He also seemed more interested in Tyson's sexual nature than anything else. He portrayed Tyson as a sexual deviant who liked to hurt women during sex: "I like to hear them scream with pain, to see them bleed. It gives me pleasure," Torres quoted him as saying. There were also stories about Tyson's all-night sexual marathons with two dozen prostitutes, and of the professional pride he took in abusing Givens.

Torres was a self-righteous narrator, to say the least. Though married during and after his own boxing career, he philandered. Since the early 1980s, he had kept a mistress as well, and not so secretly. She was a former beauty queen from Puerto Rico whom he sometimes flaunted at boxing matches in Las Vegas.

Although Torres claimed to have audiotapes of Tyson's admissions, their truth was still questionable. "I was there during some of the interviews," Jay Bright claimed. "Torres would lead Mike into talking about sex, then urge him on to give details. Mike got carried away with it."

Tyson never formally denied the book's stories. He did berate its author. "He's your friend and he's hugging you and he tells you how much he loves you and he'll die for you, and 'my family is your family, but now I have to make some money so I'm going to cut your throat out and leave you to bleed to death,'" Tyson was quoted as saying. "Torres is worse than a murderer. He's a rapist."

Whether or not he suffered from a bent sexuality, there were aspects about Tyson that did seem to be warping. He had always eschewed flashy gold chains, but now on social occasions he was laden down. The music he chose for his entry into the ring on fight night was from the rap group Public Enemy. There was concern among the HBO production staff about some of the lyrics being anti-Semitic. Tyson also refused to be in the ring when the national anthem was played.

His sparring sessions were closed to the public, but word leaked that he was taking a beating, especially from sparring partner Greg Page, a former titleholder. Instead of working to make Tyson improve, cotrainers Snowell and Bright temporarily pulled Page and put in a less capable crew to bolster his confidence. That produced worse results. He got bored with them and boxed even more sloppily—and he knew it. "I just couldn't get interested," he admitted to Harold Conrad, the septuagenarian former publicist of Muhammad Ali who was there to profile Tyson for *Rolling Stone* magazine.

He also knew that Snowell and Bright weren't doing him much good. "They irritate me," Tyson told one friend. He had no respect for their knowledge about boxing, and could see easily through their transparent efforts to bolster his confidence. Tyson needed to be told the truth, but Snowell and Bright—and for that matter, King as well—were afraid to do that to this belligerent Tyson who, as he said time and again, "made all the decisions." They were treating him like some mad emperor. No one wanted to be the messenger bearing the real, let alone the bad, news.

Tyson was losing the sense of process in the honing of craft. The only convictions he could seem to muster were those of resentment. Whether he was doing it consciously or not, as Tyson banged away with his anger, he was letting slip a faint echo of the fear of failure. "A lot of them are waiting for me to self-destruct," he told Harold Conrad. "I'm aware of that, but I think I'm too smart to self-destruct."

"Self-destruct": it was a revealing choice of words. It implied not just a defeat that he alone would author, but also one resulting from an opponent who could push the right buttons; listen hard enough and that was his message. King and his new "family" obviously weren't listening. Others were. "I believe he can be manipulated in the ring," argued Carmine Graciano, the trainer of Carl Williams. "He can be manipulated outside the ring. Why not inside?"

It was a valid point. Tyson was flawed: he could let himself fall, and perhaps be pushed, into a passive, acquiescent state. He escaped only on raw ability and power. With the erosion of his interest in and commitment to boxing, and with no one to bring it back, maybe even those qualities could be neutralized. All an opponent had to do was bang long, and hard. Graciano sensed that too: "You can beat Tyson by doing what you intended to do for twelve rounds instead of four."

Carl Williams was not likely to play any part in Tyson's destruction. The Las Vegas bookmakers listed him as a 12-to-1 underdog. It was the largest such margin any Tyson challenger had had to labor under since he'd taken the title. Williams was twenty-nine years old and past his prime. He was six-foot-four, fought at 218 pounds, and had a fourteen-inch reach advantage over Tyson, but he was also prone to left hooks, by which he'd been floored seven times in a career of twenty-six fights. That also suggested he had a suspect chin.

Fight day was full of revealing little incidents of how much Tyson's life had changed and yet oddly remained the same. Jacobs and Cayton had conjured up the myth of Tyson's ring prowess to advance their commercial ambitions. But they had never lost sight of the obligation to keep him well trained and, if possible, psychologically prepared. King's ambitions for the money replaced all other considerations. He set up a 900 phone number that callers could dial for $5 in order to get "exclusive" information about the champion. That consisted of a tape recording of King asking Tyson such questions as "If you beat Carl Williams, who will you fight next?" to which he'd respond, "I don't know."

Meanwhile, Shelly Finkel, who overnight had been made into a closed-circuit pay-per-view nabob with the Spinks fight, tried again to schmooze with the new cadre of Tyson insiders. He approached Rory Holloway and, as he had with Givens and Roper, affected the role of the trusted confidant. "If you and Mike have any problems with Don, I want you to know that I'll always be there for you," Finkel whispered. Holloway shot back: "I'd rather eat shit with spikes in it than deal with you." Finkel was working with Evander Holyfield. No doubt he hoped to convince Tyson to fight Holyfield much sooner than King was planning.

The fight took place in the Atlantic City Convention Center, the site of Tyson's victories over Biggs, Holmes, and Spinks. When King got up into the ring he was booed. The various attending celebrities were introduced, but none were cheered as loudly as Holmes, Bruno, and

Holyfield. Tyson's victims, and the one man increasingly perceived as able to beat him, were becoming more well liked than both he and King. "We don't need this shit," HBO chief Michael Fuchs muttered to Seth Abraham.

Tyson chose "Fight the Power," a rap song by the group Public Enemy, for his entry music. He'd put the title of an earlier song from the same group, "Don't Believe the Hype," on the back of a custom-made jacket the previous summer. The lyrics said much about Tyson's posture of general contempt: "Got to give us what we want/ Got to give us what we need/ Our freedom of speech is freedom of death/ We got to fight the powers that be... Fight the Power."

As usual, Tyson started out looking like the fighter that had made him champion. Williams, searching for those buttons on Tyson, decided to box—not a smart thing to do for a man prone to left hooks. As Williams jabbed, he let his right arm drop. Tyson waited for the right moment to send in his counterpunch. It came ninety-three seconds into the first round; Tyson dipped down, out, and away from the jab, planted, and with textbook D'Amato-honed body mechanics, sprang up with the left hook. Williams flew back onto the canvas. At the count of eight he was up, and the referee asked if he could continue. Not satisfied with the response, the referee called it over. Williams protested, but the conclusion was foregone.

In the postfight interview, HBO's Larry Merchant tested out Tyson's claim that he was making all his own decisions. He asked about future opponents, one of whom was James ("Buster") Douglas, who had squeezed out a victory that night on the undercard. "I'll take all comers. I don't duck any man. All comers. Come one, come all. Nobody can get close to me. I'm the best fighter in the world," Tyson said.

Merchant then tried to delve into Tyson's heart.

"You've always been able to focus on fighting no matter what other stuff has gone on. Are you as content as you can be now?" he asked.

"I want to fight, fight, fight, and destruct the world. Thank you very much, Larry," Tyson snapped, abruptly ending the interview.

Afterwards, at a press conference, Tyson delivered every answer as if it were an accusation. And again, unprompted, he dangled the prospect of his defeat. "This one's for everybody who wants to see Mike Tyson discouraged or have his head [messed] up," he declared, by way of a backhanded dedication of the fight. "Someday I won't be champion and you guys will have a lot of things to write about me. You're going to have to live with the way I am now until that day happens," he spat, pointing his finger at everyone, and no one.

* * *

The shape of Tyson's relationship with King became clear. It's unlikely that he trusted King in the way that he had D'Amato, Jacobs, Givens, and Roper—either about matters of the heart, of money, or of his knowledge of boxing. But he wasn't looking for that kind of bond anymore. Indeed, Tyson didn't want intimacy with anyone. He had gone beyond all the old personas, myths, and narratives. He was posing now as the Public Enemy. If he took anything from King, it was a lesson or two on why that posture made so much sense for him.

The betrayals by Jacobs, and then by Givens and Roper, had confirmed Tyson's deepest childhood fears—he was to be used, but never loved, by others; he was, in the end, hollow. Tyson decided to brick up the hole inside rather than fill it again with faith in, or from, others. He had finally found the resolution to the paradox that had haunted him since the day he'd begun living with D'Amato: as long as he was heavyweight champion of the world he was not an "I," but an "it."

Tyson knew that King understood those things. He talked about family and love and togetherness, but he didn't really believe it; such qualities of humanity didn't exist for some people, for those who lived in a world without rules or justice where survival was all that mattered. King had elevated that realization into a religion of the black man's struggle: "It's us, the public enemies, against them. You have to do it to them first, and take what you want without reflection, doubt, or remorse." That was King's credo.

And if King "did it" to Tyson? It wouldn't be any worse, or hurt any more, than what had already happened. Or so Tyson thought. The issue was how long he could live by denial, like some unfeeling, uncaring variation on a Don King theme. Bang long and hard enough on a hollow man, and he will eventually crumble.

# Chapter Twenty

Tyson had defied the world to live with him until the day he was defeated. The world was prepared to do that. Ever since the death of Jimmy Jacobs, it had been tempted by the prospect of an early denouement to the dramatic arc of Tyson's life. He had approached, and hovered over, the brink, but he had not yet fallen. And as he remained there, growing uglier and nastier in the posture of the Public Enemy, his defeat, however impossible it seemed, became almost desired.

*Boxing Illustrated* magazine set the tone for this reversal in public opinion: a summer 1989 cover story was titled, "Is Mike Tyson Becoming the Most Unpopular Heavyweight Champion in History?" *New York Times* sports columnist Dave Anderson got more to the point. "Who's Out There to Stop Tyson?" he titled one of his columns. The sportswriters used to ask if Tyson could be beaten, but in a way that focused on the abstract concept of defeat. Now it was getting personal. They were searching for the one man who could do the job, and sooner rather than later.

Tyson's problems didn't end there. As Jacobs and Cayton had predicted two years earlier, his early-round knockouts required taking him to fresh markets around the world. The Las Vegas and Atlantic City casino-hotels made it clear to King that they weren't going to pay fat, multimillion-dollar site fees anymore for one-round knockouts. The only fight that would interest American audiences was Tyson against emerging contender Evander Holyfield. A July 15 victory over the washed-up Brazilian, Adilson Rodrigues, had earned Holyfield the number one ranking from the three major sanctioning bodies. He was now the challenger next in line to fight Tyson. The closed-circuit pay-per-view gross on the matchup was projected to be $65 million.

That Holyfield wasn't a "true" heavyweight, and that he'd cut his teeth on lackluster opponents, was being vigorously discounted. Even against the aging Michael Dokes, Holyfield had taken a lot of punches, proving that he had a good chin, but rudimentary defensive skills. The matchup with Tyson seemed like a reprise of the Spinks fight. Still, to the boxing public, none of that seemed to matter: he was perceived as the only fighter who could save us all from The Baddest Man on the Planet Earth.

The deal, however, couldn't be made. Publicly, King argued that the fight would be worth more the longer it could be delayed. But privately, he still refused to make the deal unless Holyfield and his copromoters, Dan Duva and Shelly Finkel, signed over options—which they were not prepared to do.

With the only so-called serious contender being held at bay, the various pretenders were marched forward. Tony Mandarich, a second-pick tackle in the 1989 National Football League draft, and dubbed "The Incredible Bulk" by *Sports Illustrated*, was being posited by Shelly Finkel. Said the six-foot-six, 315-pound Mandarich: "Mike Tyson isn't a boxer. He's a brawler, the best there is." That set the standard for the ridiculous, and set up the sublime. It came from candy-voiced rapper Will Smith, whose group Jazzy Jeff and the Fresh Prince did a slapstick comedy music video with the refrain, "I can beat Mike Tyson."

There was also a rash of supposedly serious foreign offers for Tyson to fight on closed-circuit pay-per-view. One Japanese promoter talked of his fighting Bam Bam Bigelow, a 400-pound American wrestler who sported tattoos on his head. Former champion George Foreman was in the early months of his comeback in 1989. A Seattle lawyer announced that he had convinced the People's Republic of China to pay $25 million the rights to stage Tyson-Foreman in Beijing. The deal died after the Chinese government brutally killed dozens of protesters in Tiananmen Square. The lawyer then claimed to have an $18 million commitment

from a group of businessmen in Taiwan. An Israeli promoter popped up
with a $10 million guarantee for Tyson to fight anyone in Tel Aviv. King
played hard to get: "I got a deal in Taiwan for forty million dollars," he
said in an interview in late July. "Eighteen million is chump money."

Before Tyson went anywhere, he still had to give HBO three more
fights. As always, King was only interested in signing up opponents he
controlled. Ribalta, though, was no longer a viable opponent. He had
fought on the undercard of Tyson-Williams, was knocked down, and
barely won the decision. King and Abraham put together a new "A" list
of opponents to get Tyson through the existing deal without much risk:
Michael Dokes, Canadian champion Donovan ("Razor") Ruddock, and
James ("Buster") Douglas. King had several options on Douglas, and
was in the process of negotiating with both Dokes and Ruddock.

As to Abraham's hope for a new lifetime deal, no progress had been
made since the meeting at the training camp in late May. Abraham
offered a firm $100 million, but King didn't bite. Ironically, the truce
he'd forged between Cayton and King had worked a little too well. He'd
positioned the lifetime deal as the best reason why both men should
keep Tyson in the ring and out of the courtroom. Although Cayton was
frustrated with King for not yet making a match with Holyfield, he
appeared content to sit back and collect his 20 percent until his contract
ran out. He readily agreed to the new "A" list of upcoming opponents.
With Cayton no longer part of the problem, Abraham's solution lost its
potency. He hoped that the lifetime deal could be used to buy Cayton
out of his management contract. In other words, Cayton would have
gotten a portion of the $100 million—around $20 million—to walk away.

After the Williams fight, Tyson also seemed to back off. "His attitude
at the time was that if Cayton just leaves him alone, he could probably
live with it," Tyson attorney Howard Weitzman said. One Tyson
confidant expanded on the point: "You know, Mike thinks the money
will be forever. Whether he decides on a fight today or tomorrow doesn't
matter to him."

For King, avoiding further litigation meant being free to play cat and
mouse with Abraham. The closer they got to completing the existing
HBO deal, the more King could raise the specter of taking Tyson on the
world tour instead of renewing with HBO. Abraham, perhaps naïvely,
didn't believe King would do that. He'd been a loyal business associate
for a decade, had turned a blind eye to King's worst infractions against
fighters, and in the ultimate gesture worthy of a return favor, had kept

King in striking range of Tyson. "I believe Don will come through on a deal," he said in August 1989.

Michael Dokes refused to fight Tyson for anything less than $3 million. King turned to Donovan Ruddock, who accepted the fight for just over $1 million. In mid-August King started looking for a site to stage the bout. The hotel-casinos weren't interested. Trump had coughed up $2 million for Tyson-Williams, and at that felt burned by the quick knockout. Trump expected Ruddock to meet the same fate, for which he was willing to pay only $1 million. The ever-resourceful King made a deal to put the fight in Edmonton, Alberta, for $2.6 million on November 18, 1989.

Almost four months would pass between bouts for Tyson. He wouldn't have to start training again until mid-October. In the meantime, he would hit the party circuit—hard. What little respect he had left for his own craft as a boxer, and for the skills of his opponents, would virtually disappear in the coming months.

\* \* \*

After the Williams fight, Tyson went to Los Angeles. He stayed in King's condominium apartment on Wilshire Boulevard, near Westwood. Rory Holloway, who had gotten married in July, was back in Albany with his new wife. From the day they arrived, Tyson and Horne went, as they called it, "tramping," which consisted of one long bacchanalian romp through the smart-set haunts of L.A. "Sometimes there's five women waiting in the lobby," said the doorman at the Wilshire condo. "They go up one at a time to the apartment all afternoon. I went in there once. He had a box of condoms—I mean like a big box—right on the coffee table."

On August 3, King held a press conference at the Beverly Hills Hotel in Los Angeles to formally announce that Tyson would do two Toyota commercials for a fee of $1 million. "I want to let the world know that his image is back," King thundered to the group of fifty-plus men and women from the local news media. What King failed to highlight was that Tyson would be plugging the Dyna 2000, a boxy, flatbed truck sold in Japan and other countries, but not the U.S. Tyson hadn't been offered a U.S. commercial since early 1988.

"He'll be doing commercials for Tyson's Chicken, and be on a Wheaties box too," King added without giving specifics. Tyson, nattily attired in a cream silk-cotton suit, white shirt, and black patterned tie, rolled his eyes in disgust. "Don't put the sage of wisdom on a man twenty years old," King said, browbeating the audience before a single question had been asked. "Now he's cleaned up himself. Look at him— he's handsome and debonair." Everyone looked. Tyson sat there sullen and uninterested in the proceedings. King tried to fill the void with discussion about upcoming opponents. A reporter cut in, "Mike, you spend a lot of time with Don King. Do you ever talk?" Tyson stared at the reporter a moment: "I got nothing to say."

Except, that is, to the female reporters. Away from the pressures of a fight, Tyson treated women a lot differently. They were his playthings. He sat down to do an interview with a local television reporter, a striking blonde with heavy makeup, and before she could get in a question, he said, "You have very beautiful, glowing eyes... and a ring on your finger."

John Horne showed up with four young black women in tow. King had arranged for Tyson to dine with representatives from Toyota that night. Tyson wanted to bring all four of the women. King talked him out of it, but Tyson got to bring two.

The commercial was being shot the next day. Tyson and King were supposed to show up early in the morning at a Westwood hotel where executives from the Japanese advertising agency were staying. From there, they'd go by limousine convoy to the location, Rancho Mirage, an expanse of desert fifty miles east of the city. By eleven o'clock, they still hadn't arrived. One of King's attorneys, Charles Lomax, was also waiting. "He has an attention span like that," Lomax was overheard saying to one of the Japanese executives as he held his fingers apart by a quarter of an inch. "When he wants to go, he goes; or sleep, he sleeps. It happened at the dinner last night with Toyota. He put his head down on a girl's lap. We were so embarrassed."

At noon, King, Tyson, and Horne pulled up in a black stretch limousine. Tyson jumped out and blurted, "Where are the girls?" Before anyone could answer, before he'd bothered to shake hands with the Japanese executives, he darted into the hotel. He had found out that a modeling agency was holding an audition in a suite on the second floor. He came back out fifteen minutes later, several phone numbers in hand.

On the drive to the location site, Tyson slumped back in his seat, ate three bananas, drank two bottles of orange juice, played a tape of rapper Quick Rick, called three different women on the cellular phone, and complained about a toothache. "I want to see a dentist—now," he moaned to no one in particular. King smiled broadly, then buried his head in the newspaper. Clearly, part of how King controlled Tyson was to let him do what he wanted, and part was to simply ignore him. Tyson fell asleep for the rest of the drive.

They arrived at Rancho Mirage just after lunch. The midday sun had driven the temperature to 105 degrees. Tyson retreated into an air-conditioned trailer. A stunning young Japanese production aide came in and explained the concept: he was to dress in his customary black shorts and shoes, put on boxing gloves, then growl a lot into the camera. "You say, 'Tyson Power!' mean and fierce," the PA said in broken English. He was fixated on her large, dark eyes and ruby-red lips. "I'm very, very crude," he told her in a whispering, high voice, adding, "I like you. Do you like children?" She giggled, then backed out the door.

Tyson grunted and growled into the camera through several takes. During a break, he walked over to one of the security guards on the set and asked for his gun. King flashed a nervous grin as the guard began to pull it out. Tyson turned away, laughing under his breath. He still had his boxing gloves on. He couldn't pull the trigger with his tongue, and that was the joke, that there are people who would do anything for him. The gloves came off and he took the gun, pointed it off into the barren distance, and blasted away. Within seconds, several men from the production crew pulled guns from their cars and trucks. Tyson, bare-chested, smiling a child's smile, took each one and shot off its load, shouting, "I'm a famous person; what a trip!" King played the chorus. "Mike Tyson wants to be a nigger! Mike Tyson is a nigger!"

Back in the trailer, he was in a pensive mood. He talked about how much he admired Jack Johnson, the original Public Enemy in American boxing: "Johnson stood up to all of white society. No other black boxer did that. He used to catch punches with his hand, and tape things to his dick to make it look bigger and intimidate white boxers," he said with a chuckle. Tyson seemed to enjoy most the part about Johnson's scare tactics. There was something curiously adolescent about how Tyson took his pleasures. He was like a little boy telling stories about other mischievous little boys. He wanted to be seen as someone who wasn't really responsible for his actions.

"Can I tell you something? I'm a complex person. I sometimes fuck my own self up. I'm so spontaneous. If I see this boy I can say, 'Let's go get some toys.' If I see a commercial on TV about starving kids in Asia, I'll go see some starving kids. I'm like that. I just do shit," he explained softly. "I got a secret for you: I can't defend myself. People don't realize that. People want things from me. I don't want to hurt people's feelings, so I give it to them."

The words seemed like his, and the feelings genuine. It was far different from the contemptuous Public Enemy of the Williams fight. If that was the dark side of his relationship with King, perhaps this was the light side. But there was something unsettling about the Mike Tyson whom King had let run amuck. His two postures shared a common denominator: he'd completely regressed to a childlike state. It was as if he had gone back to being the little boy in a small, dark apartment in Brownsville, watching cartoons on television, then going out to beat somebody up. Except this time he had millions of dollars in the bank, women to taste, and things to buy. Every now and then he also had a fight to win. Still, being the heavyweight champion of the world seemed the least of his interests or concerns. He was leading a fantasy life full of denial about responsibilities and obligations.

It was the life of a lie, and everyone around him endorsed it. "He's wiser, more careful, and more grown-up," John Horne said on the day of the Toyota shoot. "It's the press that won't let Mike grow up. We're the best people for him. I try and make Mike understand that it will take a whole lot of work for him to be the greatest fighter ever. I want him to be the best person he can be."

The biggest lie came directly from Tyson. "I train the hardest for the guy who is supposed to be the big underdog," he said on the drive back to Los Angeles.

The truth was that although he would put in time at the gym over the next few months, he wasn't at all preparing to win a fight. Little boys can't win heavyweight fights—and they know it. "He still calls me sometimes, late at night from weird places, and he just wants to talk, just have someone there who doesn't want something from him, who's not on the payroll," said onetime girlfriend Jonet Sellers.

*   *   *

After Torres left the Athletic Commission in May 1988, Governor Cuomo's office took several months to choose a successor. Torres's tenure had been one embarrassment after another. Cuomo's advisers wanted a chairman who knew boxing, but who also had a greater sense of professional responsibility; someone who could handle the administrative duties and avoid conflicts of interest. Randy Gordon, a former editor of *Ring* magazine and a boxing commentator for a sports cable station, had been lobbying hard for the job since January 1988, and eventually got the nod.

To commissioner James Dupree, however, Gordon did not seem an impartial chairman when it came to Tyson's affairs. In late 1988, Tyson filed a complaint with the commission to revoke Cayton's manager's license. Dupree examined the charges and realized that the settlement he'd approved between Tyson and Cayton had by no means resolved things. "That was when I realized Tyson had been deceived by the February 12 contracts," Dupree said. "There wasn't much we could do about it except hold a hearing and try and bring it to light." But that's not what Gordon had in mind: "It was one stall after another from Randy."

Gordon was certainly biased against King. "King wants Al Sharpton to run the hearing, not me," he complained in May 1989, then quickly added, "Wait, don't print that." After several efforts by Dupree, Gordon finally agreed to hear Cayton's complaint against King first. The hearing took place on August 28, 1989. Carl DeSantis, the author of the February 12 contracts, joined Gordon, Dupree, and the other commissioner, Rose Trentman. Tyson showed up with John Horne, Rory Holloway, King, and King's lawyer, Bob Hirth.

Shortly into the hearing, Hirth tried to shift the focus to Tyson's accusation that the February 12 contracts were "born in fraud." DeSantis flatly asserted, "This commission will be making no determinations about whether any contracts are valid or invalid, void or otherwise." DeSantis was contradicting himself. The hearing was being held in part to investigate Cayton's charges that Tyson's contracts with King were illegal.

Near the end of the session, Dupree insisted that Tyson be given a chance to discuss the deception of the February 12 contracts. Tyson went through how he didn't know Jacobs had leukemia and how he wasn't told Cayton would be his manager if Jacobs died. He unpacked all the salient events of February 12. When he finished, Gordon asked for an off-the-record recess. He then pulled Tyson aside and, referring to a recent conversation he had had with Cayton, told him that his exclusive promotional contract with King was "not going to get [him] a fair shake." King's lawyers demanded, unsuccessfully, to have Gordon removed from chairing the hearing.

Gordon refused to allow the transcripts of the hearing to be publicly released for several months. Said Dupree: "I asked him to release them several times. He said he would, but it took months. I had to instruct the transcribing company to do it. In my opinion, Gordon was involved in a cover-up over Tyson's contracts."

* * *

In late September, Tyson started to train for the upcoming bout with Donovan Ruddock. Most nights he was seen in the Las Vegas dance clubs—Sharks, Botany's, and Uptown—often with a soft drink in hand, but sometimes also a tall glass of champagne. He missed a lot of early-morning running workouts. In sparring sessions he was, to say the least, uninspired. "I was hitting Mike with a lot of straight rights," one of his sparring partners said. "I can't do that unless he's not moving like he should. He wasn't moving, and he wasn't punching with any snap."

In mid-October, the training camp moved to Edmonton, Alberta. The fight was scheduled for November 18. Ruddock didn't seem much to worry about. He had had twenty-four bouts, one of which was a loss. Fifteen of his victories were by knockout. But many of his opponents were little-known journeymen he'd pummeled in backwater Canadian cities. His first victory over a name fighter was in August 1986 against former champion Mike Weaver. That had brought Ruddock to the attention of American promoter Murad Muhammad.

The matchup with Tyson appeared to be academic. Ruddock looked like the type of tall, lazy-defense opponent Tyson could easily dispatch with. He had fought five of the same opponents as Tyson, and won each bout, but far less convincingly. Tyson knocked four of those men out within two rounds; it took Ruddock from two to ten rounds.

The fifth common opponent, James ("Bonecrusher") Smith, was the only anomaly. Tyson grappled with Smith for twelve rounds. Ruddock fought him two years later, on July 2, 1989, and in the fifth was knocked to the canvas. But he got up, came back swinging, and won the fight by knockout in the seventh. Against the tougher competition, Ruddock could muster both guts and the big punch.

Tyson, however, wasn't taking Ruddock all that seriously. "The day after he arrived, Tyson held a workout for the local media," recalled Gary Stevenson, the site promoter. "He looked terrible. The sparring partners were pushing him around in the ring. One of them, Greg Page, hit him hard, and was mocking him, and Tyson lost his temper." Stevenson suspected that as Tyson and King had started reading more about Ruddock in the local newspapers, they'd gotten worried. "They bought six televisions and VCRs. I think they saw tapes of his fights, too, and realized they'd made a mistake."

On the morning of October 26, King told Stevenson that Tyson would have to pull out of the fight. He was complaining of chest pains. Stevenson sent over a doctor from the boxing commission to examine Tyson. The doctor did only a preliminary diagnosis. He wanted Tyson to check into the hospital for tests. Tyson refused. By late in the afternoon, King announced that Tyson would not fight on November 18. The bout, King said, would be rescheduled for late January. In the meantime, Tyson's private physician, Dr. Elias Ghanem, had arrived. That evening the entire Tyson camp flew back to Las Vegas. "King didn't tell me they were leaving town," Stevenson said.

Ghanem later produced a medical certificate stating that Tyson had contracted pleurisy, a bacterial infection of the membrane around the lungs. But Tyson didn't act like a sick man. Upon returning to Las Vegas, he hit the party circuit again. "I saw him in Sharks having a drink a few days after he supposedly got sick," said *Newsday's* Wally Matthews. "I asked him about being sick and he said, 'I'm all right, I could've fought.'"

It was quite possible, of course, that Ghanem did tests in Las Vegas that revealed the pleurisy. Still, his diagnosis was at odds with the findings of the doctor in Edmonton. "At most he had a bad cold," said Ruddock promoter Murad Muhammad, who inspected the records. "The doctor said if he had to, Tyson wouldn't be able to fight that night. He didn't prevent him from fighting the next day, or the next month. He could have fought on November 18."

For the next eleven days, King didn't return any of Stevenson's phone messages to discuss rescheduling the fight. He finally surfaced, and set up a conference call with Stevenson that also included HBO's Seth Abraham and Murad Muhammad. King and Abraham played a "good guy-bad guy" routine. Stevenson, and his backers, had already handed over $500,000 of the $2.6 million purse. He had secured letters of credit for virtually all of the remainder. Money had never been an issue—until now. King asked Stevenson if he still had the remainder of the money lined up. He did, and King agreed to make a new date for late January.

That's when Abraham intervened. He claimed that within a few hours the cable television guide would go to press. He had to confirm the January date in HBO's programming schedule. He needed proof that the fight would take place—specifically, copies of financial documents. "We talked at two P.M. and Abraham said he had to see the documents by four-thirty or he couldn't agree to televise the fight," Stevenson said.

"I couldn't get to my backer's office, which was across town, then to the bank, and process the papers he was demanding in two and a half hours. It was impossible and Abraham knew it. He was being used as a goat by Don King to pull Tyson out of the fight." Stevenson asked for a full business day. Abraham stuck to his deadline. Stevenson promised to pay the costs of having to delay printing the television guide, but again Abraham said no. "It was a sham, a total farce," he concluded.

Murad Muhammad believed that Abraham was lying about the deadline. "I talked to Abraham one week before," Muhammad remembered. "He gave me his word and the 'guarantee of HBO' that Tyson would fight Ruddock within the next few months. At that time, he said that he had a publishing deadline of two weeks. Seth was working in King's interests." Muhammad sued King the next month.

And so, another believable lie. In this case, it was designed not only to avoid Ruddock, but also to get Tyson an easier matchup for a much larger payday. When King disappeared over those eleven days, he made a deal for Tyson to fight in Tokyo for $6 million. But it wasn't just the money; he matched Tyson up against the one person who he was convinced would be a bona fide pushover: James ("Buster") Douglas.

By raising the red-herring issue of the publishing deadline, Abraham enabled Tyson to fight Douglas. For that service, he was duly rewarded. In mid-December, he reached a verbal agreement with King on an extension deal with Tyson of six fights for $26 million.

The new deal with HBO brought order back to Tyson's business future. It would take him to the end of the management contract with Cayton. Included were two windows for closed-circuit pay-per-view fights. King had also settled his differences with Holyfield's promoters. The fight was scheduled for June 18, 1990, at the Trump Plaza, and Tyson would earn $25 million. Cayton grudgingly agreed to the extension deal, and gladly signed off on the Holyfield fight. The litigation appeared to be defused.

All that remained for that new order to be ushered in was for Tyson to defeat James ("Buster") Douglas. He didn't, of course, and it would cast the heavyweight division into a state of mayhem. It was a fate that King and Abraham, in all their scheming, couldn't avoid, because Tyson, in all his childlike groping, wanted to lose.

# Chapter Twenty-One

**O**n January 8, 1990, Abraham held a send-off breakfast party for Tyson and Douglas at HBO's Los Angeles offices. He had hoped to have been able to announce the formal signing of the new extension deal, but King kept delaying. In recent weeks, he'd been exploring the free-agent market for Tyson. While Abraham pleaded for a signature, King exchanged faxes with businessmen in Taiwan, Brunei, Berlin, Zaire, and Indonesia. He even held discussions with a group of Japanese investors willing to pay $50 million for Tyson to match up against wrestler Hulk Hogan. King was savvy enough not to mention those plans on HBO's own turf. At the breakfast, he and Abraham put on a good show of unity about their future together. King's tone, though, was patronizing. He referred to his faithful ally as a "fine Jewish lad."

Tyson, as usual, attracted the most attention. From the moment he arrived, he was corralled by cameras and reporters asking questions about the upcoming fight. He wore an Italian-cut, double-breast, deep-blue suit, which would have looked much better had he not put on so much weight—at least thirty pounds.

Off in the corner, James ("Buster") Douglas stood quietly nibbling on a muffin. He was well over six feet tall, and wore an ill-fitting dark blue wool suit. He had a high forehead, a round, bulbous head, a chubby face, and a wet-eyed, soulful expression that made him look both hurt and perplexed at the same time. He knew well the feeling of being ignored. The day before, a dozen friends and supporters had held a farewell party for him in a suburb of his hometown, Columbus, Ohio. The mayor was supposed to have come. He didn't.

Beside Douglas was his manager, John Johnson, also tall, but leaner, and wearing a tacky brown sports jacket over dark blue pants and cowboy boots. Johnson was white, had small, hawkish eyes, and tended to glower with simmering resentment. The smartly dressed woman who was checking off the invitees from a list approached Johnson. "Excuse me, but what is your name?" she asked politely. "I'm this guy's manager," Johnson said with hints of Appalachia in his voice. As the woman walked away, he muttered, "Motherfucking Don King didn't put my name down."

The whole group flew to Tokyo that afternoon. Once there, Tyson did everything he could to avoid the throngs of Japanese media. He'd announce that his morning run would be at 4 A.M., then would go out and run at 3 A.M. Some days, he didn't run at all. Gym workouts were almost all closed. Tyson holed up in his hotel room the rest of the time. He had brought over a collection of a hundred videos, none of which included one of Douglas's fights. He spent countless hours sitting on the floor watching martial arts movies. "His favorite character was this old guy with a long gray beard who didn't look like he could fight," said Sam Donnellon, the boxing reporter for *The National* (a daily sports newspaper, now defunct) and the only U.S. newsman granted access to Tyson. "But he turned out to be the nastiest, meanest one of them all, a real superhero. Tyson loved that."

About ten days prior to the fight, and before many of the U.S. reporters arrived, Tyson was knocked down in sparring by Greg Page. It was a simple right hook that Tyson walked straight into. He crumpled to the floor. The Japanese media gave it front-page play. They speculated that the knockdown was staged to increase ticket sales. Most U.S. reporters discounted it as unimportant. Bill Cayton, who decided to stay in New York, was quoted as saying that it had happened at least twice before in sparring. Donnellon also didn't take the knockdown too seriously—until he saw Tyson spar. "It was two days after the knockdown. His trainers were working on getting him to the spot where he could deliver a punch. He couldn't get to the spot."

A few days later, King, either oblivious or indifferent to Tyson's deterioration, opened up the sparring session to the public for $60 a head. Two hundred people watched him get pushed around by Page and respond with sloppy frustration. The session was supposed to go two rounds. Snowell and Bright stopped it after one and told everyone to leave. "King was pissed off with them," one Tyson camp insider said. "He just wanted to make a few bucks. He had no idea what was going on with Mike."

Donnellon noticed that Tyson was having trouble with his weight. "When I arrived, he was two hundred thirty pounds. All I saw him eat was fruit and chicken soup," he said. "King's cook was making chicken and beef and vegetables, a great spread, and Tyson wouldn't touch it. He felt that if he looked good, he'd feel good."

Appearances were deceiving. Tyson weighed in the day before the fight at 220½ pounds. His sparring partners, though, knew that he wasn't ready. HBO's Larry Merchant talked to Greg Page after the weigh-in. "Greg thought that Tyson could definitely be beaten in the fight," Merchant recalled.

At the final prefight press conference, the Japanese media were still fixated on the sparring-session knockdown. They tried to search Tyson's emotional state. One reporter asked whether he was seeing a psychiatrist. Tyson barked, "If you can't fight, you're fucked!" which the Japaneses translator censored as, "It difficult to fight if you do not have skill."

In the closing days before the fight, the rumor mill churned out some disturbing stories. During one session for a local camera crew, Tyson supposedly grasped a pigeon by the neck and said with sadistic glee, "Do you want to see magic?" as he began to rip its head off. One of his bodyguards stopped him before the incident could be recorded by the cameras. Other stories claimed that he had secretly flown back to New York for a weekend, that he was buying special, gourmet pears worth $15 apiece and eating them by the bushel basket, and that the night before the fight he had sex with two Japanese women. The stories were probably fabricated, but they did indicate an undeniable truth: people in Tokyo sensed something terribly out of balance about Tyson, and they were searching for explanations.

James ("Buster") Douglas's skills in the ring, and everything else about his career, were of little interest to the gathered media. He played basketball in junior college, then quit because he failed to meet academic standards. Douglas became a professional boxer in 1981 at the age of twenty. He was trained by both his father, who was an accomplished middleweight-light heavyweight in the 1950s and 1960s, and his uncle. Douglas lost his sixth fight, struggled back with victories against mostly unkowns, and in 1983 lost again. He was about to give up, and then met John Johnson.

The son of a West Virginia coal miner, Johnson was an assistant coach for the Ohio State University football team under the legendary Woody Hayes during the 1970s. He went on to coach high school football, but couldn't hold down a job. "I'm the kind of guy who two days after you hire me, you want to fire me," Johnson admitted to a reporter. He had little experience managing fighters, but he was a motivator, the kind of man who used faith in God and fiery, rebel-screaming boosterism to build up confidence.

Fundamentally, Douglas was a good athlete. He had basic skills, quick hand speed, and agile movement. But he was not a good believer in either Johnson or himself. After the 1983 defeat, he won four fights in a row, then was beaten again, this time by Jesse Ferguson. His problem in fights seemed to be much like Tyson's: he'd be overcome by a sudden passivity, and would give in to his opponent's will. At his lowest points of motivation, Douglas ate too much and trained little. For his seventeenth fight, on April 16, 1983, he hit the scales at 260 pounds.

Douglas eventually earned a shot at the vacant I.B.F. title in 1987 against Tony Tucker. He seemed to be winning the fight; then, in the tenth round, he was unraveled by a single punch, and lost. His father was so disgusted he stormed off, and later quit as trainer. Douglas plodded along, chalking up five victories. The last, on the undercard of Tyson-Williams the previous July, was a listless performance against Oliver McCall. He fought at an unwieldy 242½ pounds. But he convinced King that he was the right man for the Tokyo match. Douglas took the fight for $1.3 million, his biggest payday ever. Only one Las Vegas casino bothered to set a betting line on the fight: 40-to-1 against Douglas, the longest odds ever in a heavyweight title defense.

Those were the tangible facts. But there were also the intangibles, all of which, as it would turn out, would be factors in his victory over Tyson. In July 1989, Douglas became a born-again Christian. A few months later, his wife left him. Soon after, he found out that the mother of his eleven-year-old son, Lamar, was dying of a terminal disease. Then in early January, as he was training to fight Tyson, his mother died. Douglas didn't repress his grief. He let himself feel it, and in the process underwent a transformation.

"The night before the fight, I went to see Douglas in his hotel room," Larry Merchant remembered. "When the talk meandered around to his mother, he started to cry. I think her death could have been a motivating factor. I mean, if your mother just died, what's the worst thing that can happen to you in the ring? Douglas may have thought that he had nothing else to lose."

It seemed too simplistic, this idea of Douglas using his grief to create the single-mindedness to go into the ring and fight like he'd never fought before. And yet maybe that's what a man who lets himself feel so fully can do sometimes. If his mind can tap into and discipline the right emotion, then the feeling can rise to thought, and he can "become" the idea. In this case, the idea was to be more than just champion; it was to be The Man Who Beat Mike Tyson. Asked at the final prefight press conference how he planned to do that, Douglas responded in a low, mumbling monotone: "I'll just hit him, I guess. It seems as though nobody ever hit him hard enough to gain his respect."

Perhaps the fervent and messianic Johnson finally provided James Douglas with a more certain idea of himself. "Johnson said from the very beginning that they were 'going to go out there and kick the son of a bitch's ass,'" Merchant recalled. "He kept saying that they 'were going to hit him and keep hitting him.' No one had ever put it in those words before. They weren't afraid of Tyson. I think that kind of cheerleading from Johnson must have kicked into who Douglas is—or became, for that fight."

\*   \*   \*

The cavernous Tokyo Dome seated 63,000, but on the morning of the fight (scheduled for 9 A.M. February 11 so that it could be broadcast on Saturday night the tenth in the U.S.), only 30,000 people were sprinkled among the seats. It was impossible to heat the space evenly from the winter cold. The temperature hovered in the low seventies. The Japanese, as befit cultural custom, sat quietly. Most of the $1,000 seats on the green-carpeted floor around the ring were filled by middle-aged men in gray suits, white shirts, and black ties. It looked like a convention of undertakers. A lone banner way back in the stadium, brought by some American fight fans, read, "Say No to Don King."

Douglas entered the ring first. He wore bright white trunks. As he

awaited Tyson, he bounced around and limbered his up arms. His face
and head were beaded with sweat. Tyson headed toward the ring
covered in his customary white towel. He usually rushed to the ring,
but this time he strolled. Inside, he paced, but there wasn't the usual
twitching of the neck or darting of the eyes. There was no sense of
purpose about him, let alone menace; he seemed flaccid.

Before the bell sounded to start the first round, Douglas hopped in
place, anxious to begin. Tyson stood motionless, staring at him with his
head cocked to one side. The first round established the blueprint for
the rest of the fight. Douglas got off the first punch, a quick left jab that
missed by only inches. He anticipated the counterpunch, and bounced
back and away from Tyson's jab. Douglas didn't run. He stood his
ground, used the jab to throw off Tyson's offensive rhythm, and tied him
up to prevent being hit by his trademark body shots.

Douglas had come to slug it out, and he wasn't in the least
intimidated. Tyson's past opponents had been quickly made to pay for
their bravery. Not this time. Tyson walked straight in at Douglas,
feinted with his head infrequently, didn't slip to avoid the jab, and made
only a minimal effort to weave and dip. Nor did he follow up on
conspicuous opportunities. Douglas tended to let his gloves drop, but it
was an opening that Tyson couldn't, or perhaps wouldn't, exploit. When
he did punch, he often missed, and instead of slipping away from the
counterpunch, he stood there as though his feet were glued to the
canvas. Douglas's punches—often two or three at a time—hit their
mark.

It obviously soon dawned on Douglas that this was a vastly different
fighter from the one he'd expected to confront. He realized that a Tyson
who didn't move, or hit back, could indeed be beaten. And so he
punched, and punched, and almost every time he did, he landed, and
still Tyson didn't counter.

Tyson no longer seemed able or willing to use any part of D'Amato's
"system" to compensate for his smaller size. He was being reduced to
not just a conventional fighter, but a bad one. With every punch
Douglas landed, that fact magnified. Douglas used his longer reach to
get the jabs in from a safe distance—so safe that Tyson had to lunge to
land his own jab, which Douglas could therefore easily see coming and
avoid. Superior height and greater weight, which were once disadvan-
tages for a Tyson opponent, were now suddenly great assets. Douglas
used them to lean on, tie up, and push the once-formidable champion
away.

In his corner, Tyson looked disappointed with himself. He knew what he was doing wrong. The question was whether he could correct it. There was no sign of that in the second round. He kept walking into the punches. Douglas's straight rights sailed through almost unchallenged. When Tyson did get a punch in, Douglas immediately countered as if unaffected. With fifteen seconds to go in the round, he let go a barrage of five punches—jabs, rights, left hooks—then tied Tyson up and shoved a forearm and elbow into his face to push him back. In the second round alone, he landed fifty-two punches, versus Tyson's sixteen.

In the third, Tyson came out moving more, but within ten seconds Douglas connected with another straight right, and Tyson regressed. It was as if every punch that Douglas landed knocked out another brick, and out came this other Tyson, the child who didn't want to win, but only to acquiesce. He started to hold his gloves up around his jaw in the old peek-a-boo style, the signature of the D'Amato system, but it made him look like a little boy hiding behind something and no longer a lethal weapon ready to spring out from unexpected angles.

Curiously, Douglas was now the one using intimidation tactics: he punched after the bell, dug elbows into Tyson's face and neck, and swiped at him when the referee broke apart their clinches. While it was all happening—this remarkable display of one man's calm, patient, workmanlike advance to victory, and another's complete technical and seemingly spiritual breakdown—the Japanese spectators sat in near-total silence. An American fight crowd would have raised the roof.

After the third round, cotrainers Snowell and Bright pleaded with Tyson. "You're not closing the gap inside," Snowell whispered in his soft, nasal voice. He seemed in shock, as if he had a fighter on his hands who didn't know what to do, not even the basics, and he, Snowell, could only restate them like someone reading from the first chapter of a boxing manual. "You've got to get inside. You're flat-footed in there. You got to punch," he whined. Jay Bright, poking his head in through the ropes, tried to evoke their days with D'Amato: "Get back to what you know. Do it. Let it go!" he said plaintively. Tyson couldn't look them in the eyes. He stared down, slouched, then responded in a tone of self-disgust, "All right."

He started the fourth round trying to move again, hoping maybe that he would find what he had once known so well that, as Teddy Atlas used to say, he couldn't have done it wrong even if he'd wanted to. But the knowledge was gone. Both men continued to fight in the same way, but less intensely. Near round's end, Tyson scored with two punches, but

Douglas hit back without hesitation. The same pattern dominated the fifth. Douglas shot out two jabs at a time, then followed with rights. In one sequence, a jab glanced and the right hit flush on, then another left flattened Tyson's nose and jerked his head back. "That's when I saw his knees begin to tremble," said Earl Gutskey, who was covering the fight for the *Los Angeles Times*. "He was losing the strength in his legs."

In the fifth, Tyson's left eye began to swell from Douglas's punishing rights. Incredibly, Snowell and Bright hadn't brought an endswell, a small, rectangular piece of chilled alloy metal used to push away the fluid that collects under the skin around the eye. But someone in the corner did have a condom, which they filled with cold water. It was an ineffective substitute, and a desperate act by two men who despite the overwhelming evidence—Tyson had been hit by more punches in fifteen minutes than he had over his thirty-seven previous fights—couldn't utter the only words that might have saved him: that he was losing the fight. He had to be shocked out of his passive state and made to see the ugly reality of what he was letting happen. Tyson obviously couldn't do it to, and for, himself.

In the sixth round Douglas began to tire. So did Tyson, but more threatening than his exhaustion was the swollen left eye, which would prevent him from seeing rights coming in. Both men continued in their seemingly inexorable paths. In seven rounds, Douglas threw a total of 272 punches, 50 percent of which landed. Tyson delivered only 132, and connected with 42 percent, most of them glancing. He had thrown an average of nineteen per round—far fewer than the fifty-seven against Trevor Berbick when he'd first won the title; and fewer than the twenty-six against James ("Bonecrusher") Smith, which prior to this had been his worst fight.

The seventh could have been a turning point. Douglas was known to give up late in a fight, even when he was winning, and that looked like it might happen now. He stopped moving away from the punches. But Tyson couldn't take advantage of his exhaustion, and when he did connect—especially with two low blows—it served only to remind Douglas that he had to stay alert to win the fight. He recovered in the eighth, controlled the round, and in the last twenty seconds punished Tyson with a series of blows that wobbled his legs. Tyson groped along the ropes, and in his first inspired moment of the fight, ducked a jab and sent in a right uppercut with every ounce of his dwindling strength.

The punch rotated Douglas's head up and over his shoulder, and in that instant he seemed to explode open, then go limp as he crashed

backwards onto the canvas. Tyson craned his neck around the referee to
see if he would stay down. He wouldn't. His head hadn't even hit the
canvas, only his shoulders, and he started to rise immediately. Douglas
propped up on his elbow and pounded the canvas with his other hand,
in a sign of disappointment for having let this happen. He was lucid,
though, and attentive to the referee's count. By nine he was up and
ready. The bell sounded, ending the round.

If Tyson had fought anywhere near to his ability, and if he wasn't
being beaten by a man deemed so dismal an opponent, then what was
about to happen might have gone down in boxing history as legendary:
the brave champion who fought with all his heart. Instead, given how
badly Tyson had fought from the opening bell, the punishment he was
about to take made it seem that he wanted to lose the fight; to have
something literally beaten out of him. It looked like a bizarre form of
religious flagellation in which, contrary to the rules of the sport, there
existed some unspoken agreement between the two men that this was
all just a ritual for driving out demons. It was like a pugilistic exorcism.

Tyson came out slugging away with the vague hope that the
knockdown had taken the stuff out of Douglas. Quite the contrary.
Douglas responded with a sequence of eight punches, four of which hit
their mark. Tyson receded, then came back with another desperation
punch, which landed. Douglas fought through it, and found the energy
to keep retaliating. Both men were now exhausted. Douglas was clearly
arm-weary, and Tyson on some kind of instinctual energy that ebbed and
flowed. Then, suddenly, Douglas lunged at him with the same tactics
he'd used from the outset. A combination sent Tyson to the ropes. The
strength in his legs gone, he leaned back for support, then threaded in
another uppercut that missed. This time Douglas knew better than to
give him the room to punch. He leaned in with his elbow, and followed
with a left and right that snapped Tyson's head back. There were still
fifty-seven seconds left in the round.

Without the ropes, Tyson would have fallen. Exhausted, Douglas
backed off. Tyson used the room to send in a right uppercut. It missed.
In the last thirty seconds, Douglas connected with five punches in a
row, and Tyson stood there like a punching bag. When the round ended,
the referee had to give Tyson a push-start to get him moving back to his
corner.

His last significant act as champion was a straight right that hit
Douglas square on the jaw the moment they met to start the tenth
round. It must have felt like a blow from a baseball bat, but Douglas

fought on. In the final sequence, he probed away at Tyson's peek-a-boo with his jabs, trying to open enough space to drive through the winning punch. Tyson tried to cover up his swollen eye. Douglas changed tactics, and sent in a right uppercut instead that twisted Tyson's head back and to the right. That punch alone probably knocked him out, but he didn't fall; he teetered back, and as he did Douglas let go with two glancing blows, then moved in closer with a third, a punishing straight left that hit Tyson like a battering ram.

When Tyson's head hit the canvas his mouthpiece popped out. He reached up to his mouth, but was too late to catch it. He lay there no more than a second, then slowly rose onto his right elbow, his mouth agape, his face slack, and his one good eye glassy and unfocused as the referee counted. He turned over onto his hands and knees to look for the mouthpiece. The first sweep with his glove missed it. He tried again, got it this time, and stuffed a corner of the mouthpiece between his teeth. It hung there dangling. On nothing but the instinct to survive, Tyson struggled to his feet. He made it up, but his knees were bent. He hunched forward into the referee's chest and clutched his arm for support. The referee waved it over, then wrapped Tyson in a bear hug to spare him the humiliation of falling again.

As Douglas's cornermen swarmed around him, the new champion lifted his arms up in a single gesture of victory.

Tyson was surrounded by his "family." Punched nearly senseless, he didn't even know that the fight was over. "Mike, you were counted out. KO," Snowell said softly.

Tyson wouldn't give a postfight interview. Douglas did.

"Why did it happen, James?" HBO's Merchant asked.

"Because I wanted it," he answered with no more enthusiasm than he had put behind his stated intention before the fight to just "hit" Tyson.

Merchant pressed with the same question, until Douglas stopped him. "My mother. Mother. Mother, God bless her heart," he said, then began to cry.

*   *   *

Don King had no doubt done all the important calculations in his mind even before Tyson rose from the canvas. He had three options on Douglas's future fights. If the victory was a fluke, then Tyson was likely to get back his crown in an immediate rematch. If it wasn't, and he lost again, proved washed up, then King would control the new champion.

The point was that without the rematch, Douglas would go on to fight Evander Holyfield, a boxer over whom King had no control. Therein loomed his worst nightmare: if Holyfield beat Douglas, then for only the second time in more than fifteen years, he would be without a heavyweight champion.

Within minutes of Douglas's victory, King conspired to withhold official recognition. He sequestered the heads of the W.B.C., the W.B.A., and officials from the Japanese Boxing Commission, and convinced them that Douglas had been counted out in the eighth round. The mistake, he argued, was referee Octavio Meyran's, who had failed to pick up the "official" count from the ringside timekeeper. Douglas, King argued, rose at Meyran's count of nine, when in fact it had reached thirteen. His conclusion: Tyson won the fight first.

As believable lies go, this was his most brazen. A discrepancy did in fact exist between the two counts. But the rule, and the common practice, in boxing is that the referee controls the fight. And it is only the referee whom the fighter is obliged to watch and listen to. Which was precisely what Douglas did.

*The National*'s Sam Donnellon and a few other reporters happened to see King and the others emerge from the meeting. "It is a fact that Mike Tyson knocked out James ('Buster') Douglas," King screamed into Donnellon's tape recorder. "It will be a grave injustice here if it holds that Mike Tyson was knocked out." José Sulaiman, president of the W.B.C., and long considered King's minion, seemed distraught. Donnellon said: "He muttered, 'This is the worst day of my career, what I am about to do.' There's no question in my mind that Sulaiman felt he was being coerced into doing something he regretted."

King called an impromptu press conference that excluded Tyson, Douglas, and John Johnson. "The first knockout obliterated the second knockout," he screamed almost uncontrollably. Most reporters were still filing their stories, and weren't there to get the news. King went off to meet for three more hours with officials, then held another press conference at 6:30 P.M. for the full gathering of the news media.

By that point, Sulaiman had been sufficiently bullied, or coached, to speak for himself. He claimed that the referee should have taken the count from the timekeeper. That rule, he implied, held sway over the fighter's obligation to the referee. "At the moment I am suspending the recognition of anybody as champion," Sulaiman announced. W.B.A. president Gilberto Mendoza, sitting beside him, nodded agreement. So did referee Meyran, who admitted having made a mistake. (The Japanese officials bowed out of the dispute.) Sulaiman said that a decision on who won the fight would be made at a W.B.C. meeting on February 20.

Sulaiman had perverted both the rules and the customs of boxing, for no other reason than to justify an immediate rematch, an agenda seemingly dictated by King. "A rematch is absolutely necessary," Sulaiman told the gathered reporters. Some of them pointed out that there have been numerous similar cases throughout boxing history where the referee's count lagged behind the timekeeper's, and that in no case was the victor ever penalized. No precedent existed for withholding recognition from Douglas. Sulaiman knew that, but wouldn't admit it.

Tyson was vague on the subject of recognition. Part of him obviously wanted to do the right thing. "You guys have known me for years. I never gripe or bitch," he said behind sunglasses while holding a white handkerchief to the swollen side of his face. But he had also gotten an earful from King, and was convinced that he'd been wronged. "I knocked him out before he had me knocked out," Tyson added in a griping tone. The strutting Public Enemy was gone now. He seemed to want understanding, and empathy; he was almost beseeching the reporters—many of whom had closely followed his career since 1985—to see him as he once was, the little boy in the fable of Cus and the Kid: "I want to be champion of the world. That's what all young boys want."

The only reporter who sided with Tyson was Mike Marley of the *New York Post*, which surprised no one. "Shouldn't it be declared that Mike Tyson is still the heavyweight champion of the world?" Marley asked Sulaiman, to the groans and guffaws of the other reporters. Even Sulaiman wouldn't go that far. He didn't answer.

King had many times gone far beyond the bounds of ethical, and perhaps legal, conduct, but there was something different about this transgression. He seemed mentally unprepared for Tyson's defeat, and emotionally incapable of accepting it. "King saw the power and the money fizzle away and he panicked, he made a huge mistake," said Ed Schuyler, who was at the fight for the Associated Press.

For the boxing reporters who had never been able to prove his past rip-offs, who were frustrated by all the times King had wriggled out of a legal action, or who were told by editors that the public didn't care about the dirty world of boxing, this was poetic justice. Hubris had caught up with Don "Only in America" King. He had forgotten that the whole world was watching, and the boxing reporters were going to make sure he paid this transgression. "It's so easy to get cynical about guys like King and what they do to boxing, and to let the bullshit pass. This time we weren't going to that. We were going to do the right thing," admitted one reporter from a New York newspaper.

On Monday, February 12, all the major newspapers roared with indignation over King's scheme to withhold recognition from Douglas. As those views were picked up by the television networks, public opinion galvanized in agreement. Meanwhile, King and Tyson were flying back to New York unaware of the reception they were about to get. They were greeted at Kennedy Airport with accusations from a rabble of print and television reporters. But it was Sulaiman, who had gone to Los Angeles, who retracted first. He called AP reporter Ed Schuyler, who by Monday evening had returned to his home in New York. "He wanted to recant," Schuyler said. Sulaiman's remarks appeared in newspapers around the country the next day. "The W.B.C. never stated that we would not recognize Buster Douglas as champion of the world," Sulaiman was quoted as saying. He "officially" recognized Douglas.

King had been foiled by one of his own allies. And this time there was nothing HBO's Seth Abraham could do to save him. On Tuesday morning, King and Tyson held a press conference in the Grand Hyatt Hotel in New York. It was their turn to recant. "There's never been a question from my side as to who the heavyweight champion was," King said. "No one had designs to overturn the decision." Tyson added: "I wouldn't want the title on a changed decision. All I'm asking for is a rematch, simple as that."

Whether or not a rematch would take place, at least larceny had been removed from the equation. With it went King's scheme to regain total control over the division. He could now only hope that Holyfield, as the mandatory challenger to the new champion, would agree to step aside—for a hefty fee—and let a rematch take place. If Tyson beat Douglas, he'd then be clear to fight Holyfield, and after that perhaps match up against the aging but increasingly popular George Foreman.

King had much to gain from an immediate rematch. But others had just as much to gain from preventing it from taking place. Holyfield's promoters, Shelly Finkel and Dan Duva, knew that if their fighter beat Douglas, King would be halfway out of the division. Without a champion in his stable, he'd have to accept their terms on fight purses. They pushed for Douglas to meet Holyfield in June, after which he'd fight Tyson—or perhaps George Foreman instead.

Despite public utterances about working out with King "a deal that makes sense," Finkel and Duva were giddy with the prospect of his purge. And they weren't the only ones ready to jump at such an opportunity, which is what ushered in the mayhem. On the Monday after the fight, Trump announced that he had an agreement with King to stage Douglas-Tyson in June. That turned out to be an empty deal. King had options on Douglas, but he still needed his and manager John Johnson's signature on a bout contract. Those signatures had to be obtained even before Holyfield could be paid to step aside. Johnson wasn't in any hurry to do a deal with King. Within days, he'd been contacted with competing offers from promoter Bob Arum (who was looking for an eventual matchup with his fighter, George Foreman), John Giovenco of the Las Vegas Hilton, and Steve Wynn, head of the newest, and most extravagant, hotel-casino in Las Vegas, The Mirage. Although Johnson told reporters that he wanted "respect" from King in the negotiations on the rematch, it was money that his heart desired most.

Among all the men anxious to get rid of King, Steve Wynn had the most money with which to do it, and Bob Arum had the best brains. They joined forces on February 12. The next day, Arum met with Johnson in New York and suggested a deal with Wynn.

On February 13, he sent as his personal calling card promoter Arum to meet with Johnson and Douglas in New York. The idea was to lure them to Las Vegas, where Wynn would make an offer for the new champion to defend his crown in bouts staged at The Mirage. In return for Arum's efforts, Wynn promised him the opportunity to promote the bouts. They arrived February 18 on a flight from Columbus, Ohio, via Wynn's private jet.

A cocky Johnson demanded $60 million, plus one hundred thousand shares of stock in Wynn's company, for two title defenses. Surprisingly, Wynn didn't haggle. But he did propose something radical: He, and not Arum or King, would promote the fights. Even more incredible, Wynn wouldn't take the standard one-third promoter's fee. Instead, his return would come from the ticket sales and gambling revenue.

It was the first time that a hotel-casino had set out to become both the site and promoter of a major heavyweight bout. And it was also the most money a champion would ever be paid for two title defenses. Wynn's only proviso was that Douglas's contract with King had to be broken.

On February 20, King met with Douglas and Johnson in their garden bungalow at The Mirage to discuss a future together. King got bushwacked. In marched Wynn with an offer to King: $2 million to rip up his contract with Douglas, and a flat fee of $3 million to copromote with him two title defenses, the first of which would be against Holyfield. In other words, he proposed to send King back to the kind of arrangement Jacobs and Cayton had tried to impose years earlier. "It's nothing personal, Don, just business," Wynn said, obviously pleased with his bold foray into the brass-knuckle art of the deal in boxing. King boomed, "It's personal to me," then headed for the door. He always relished good exit lines: "I like this hotel—I think I'll take it from you."

Wynn had grossly miscalculated, and he knew it. He chased out after King and suggested they meet the next day to talk it over. But he was just buying time. He had no choice now but to sue. King showed up for the meeting, but not Wynn. That afternoon, King went for a checkup at his doctor's office, where he got a phone call with the news that he had just been sued by Douglas and Johnson for breach of contract. Wynn was also named as a plaintiff. In fact, it was his idea, money, and lawyers who filed the suit.

The following day King sued Wynn et al. for tortious interference. Within two weeks three other lawsuits were filed: Trump sued Wynn in New York State for interfering with his right to stage Douglas-Tyson; Shelly Finkel and Dan Duva filed against everyone, including the W.B.C. and the W.B.A., to enforce Holyfield's right as mandatory challenger; and then King sued the sanctioning bodies as well to block Douglas-Holyfield on the grounds that by virtue of the so-called long count Tyson deserved an immediate rematch.

While the bickering and money-lust dragged on, and Douglas enjoyed his sudden celebrity, there remained the fallen figure of Mike Tyson. He was the youngest heavyweight champion in history. He had successfully defended his crown nine times. Over a career of thirty-seven victories, he had taken fewer punches than perhaps any other titleholder in the division, and he had delivered more effective and decisive punishment. But with Tokyo, Tyson had earned the added distinction of being the only heavyweight champion considered still in his prime to have lost to an opponent of Douglas's undistinguished stature.

# Chapter Twenty-Two

"I'm just a normal guy with heart."

Mike Tyson, October 1990

For the sports news media, Tyson's defeat presented a rare opportunity both to affirm an ethical duty and to achieve personal liberation. It had exposed King's scheme to withhold recognition from James Douglas, and now that Tyson had been defeated, it felt free of both the myth it had helped perpetuate and the man it had grown to despise. He wasn't, as it turned out, indestructible.

But moral victory and liberation from Tyson weren't enough for some sports columnists. These were the men who most desired Tyson's fall, because they felt he deserved it. Mike Lupica of *The National* was by far the most vitriolic. For him, Douglas was a Cinderella Man, and Tyson two shades short of evil. Lupica, in a February 12 piece, called Tyson's loss just desserts for someone who "bounces women around, and gives it in the back to his friends, and turns his back on people who helped make him champion: making it seem as if dogs have more loyalty than he does."

By "friends" he meant Jacobs and Cayton. Those "friends," of course, had deceived Tyson into signing the February 12 contracts, an event documented to some degree in two separate legal actions. Lupica wasn't interested in factoring that into his diatribe. It wasn't enough for him to be free of Tyson's scowling visage; Tyson had to pay for his sins. Lupica speculated ominously on what the final price was likely to be should he ever again become champion. "Because there are certain terrible headlines that when you finally see them, you feel as if you have already looked at them in a newspaper before. Billy Martin was one. Mike Tyson, believe me, would be another."

The reference was to the recent death in a car accident of baseball manager Billy Martin, another violent man, and a drinker. It was an old theme about Tyson originally evoked in 1986 by author Joyce Carol Oates, who once referred to his "impassive death-head's face." For Oates, and Lupica, Tyson was the victim of his own primal urges, the most prevalent being a death wish. That was a stereotype, of course, and a common one imposed on black boxers: Tyson as some kind of savage on whom the culture bestows all that is noble, only for him to reject the gifts, and the givers, and revert to life on the instinctual level. The only end for such men is death.

With that, Lupica probably felt he had an explanation for why Tyson lost in Tokyo: he was merely getting in some practice for the final gesture of self-destruction.

Lupica was wrong.

While only a boy, Tyson had chosen boxing over self-annihilation on the streets of Brownsville: renewal over death. What happened in Tokyo was the result of that same inner drive. The survivor in him knew that he had to start over.

*   *   *

A few days after returning to New York, Tyson went up to stay with Camille Ewald in Catskill. It was almost two years ago to the day that he had stood in her kitchen looking out at the freshly fallen snow, wanting to remain there in the warmth rather than go to New York and sign new contracts. But now he didn't have to go anywhere. It was up to him what to do next with his life.

"I asked Mike what happened," Ewald said. "All he could say was, 'I don't know. I really don't know.' And I believe it. To me it was like he was walking, but not there in his body. I was sitting in a front-row seat. I saw him walk to the ring like in a daze. Like somebody gave him something. He stood there and didn't fight. He didn't throw any punches, no vicious punches. I don't think he was drugged. He looked like he wanted to lose. Maybe he got tired of it all. He might have wanted to lose just to get hungry again."

That Mike Tyson—the one behind the Public Enemy and all the other personas—rarely appeared in public. He did, on occasion, peek through his packaging. The largest portions of that person were known best by Cus D'Amato. With his death, and under the tutelage of Jacobs and Cayton, that Tyson had gone underground. He had kept many of his deepest thoughts and feelings—particularly his fears—sealed up.

But he had always wanted to be humanized. That's what the marriage to Givens was all about. The inner self, with all its fears and faults, struggling to be loved the hollowness to be filled. He wanted to create a life for himself rather than subsist within the strictures of the fable of Cus and the Kid and the artifice of his persona as Ring Destroyer; and he also wanted to escape the fawning jock-worship of D'Amato, Jacobs, and Steve Lott.

Tyson had been mythologized by a marketing plan, then demonized by the media circus that took over his marriage. His deepest urge was to be human. That's not how things turned out. Jacobs's betrayal involving the February 12 contracts, then the greed and second betrayal by Givens and Roper, perverted the whole process. And despite the perniciously inspired reports that the August car crash was a suicide attempt, even in the depths of a failing marriage he had struggled to survive. He had done that by attaching himself to a stronger ego with a more certain identity: Don King.

Whatever good King served in helping Tyson through the turmoil of the two betrayals didn't last long. He believed that letting Tyson do, and be, as he pleased was the best means by which to control him, and through that, to acquire money and power. This turned out to be the last step in the perversion that Tyson could live with. He had gone back to being the little boy taking his pleasures, just as he had once stolen fruit from grocery stores. Just as he had used boxing to be renewed at that time, he used it again now to kill all the personas and postures, to get back to the struggle to become human. He entered the ring against Douglas not to win, but to achieve catharsis. To that extent, the loss was an act of courage. "It's like people didn't treat me like a human being," he told cornerman Jay Bright after Tokyo. "They thought all I had to do was look at an opponent and he'd be paralyzed."

The question is to what extent he actually succeeded in being renewed. And more important, renewed into what?

Three weeks after his return, Tyson agreed to see Earl Gutskey of the *Los Angeles Times*. He kept Gutskey waiting in an Albany hotel for four days, then abruptly rescheduled the meeting at the nearby house of Rory Holloway.

Tyson admitted that he hadn't trained properly, that he had let his weight reach 245 pounds, then starved himself in the weeks before the fight. Those were the obvious explanations for the loss. But it was clear now that he felt newly empowered to deal with the future. "People are coming up to me and saying: 'Get the title back, Mike.' They mean well, but no one has to tell me that. I will. I'll be ready. Can I tell you something? If I had to psych myself up for this, for what I have to do, I'd be an insecure person."

In defeat he had found a purpose, and it was grounded in an authentic sense of self shorn of all artifice. And even if he was now what he always feared he'd be—alone, and unloved—he had finally faced it. The death ten days after the Douglas fight of his sister Denise, who was grossly overweight and suffered a heart attack, only underlined that discovery. "People think I'm going to have to come back like this," he said to Gutskey, contorting his face and growling. "I'm supposed to get all pumped up, all hostile and going for revenge, right? Can I tell you something? It won't be like that, not at all. It'll be just another fight. Except this time I will be prepared properly. I won't be in some kind of pressure cooker."

The paradox that had nagged Tyson since his first days with Cus D'Amato was thus resolved. As he instinctively knew he would, through boxing he had found the "I." What he hadn't bargained for was undergoing the cruel dialectic of faith in, then betrayal by, the people he had learned to trust along the way to self-discovery. But that was all behind him now. He was resolved within himself, and with his situation. While talking with Gutskey, he stroked his new dog, a 110 pound blond mastiff he had named Warlock. People project their identities onto their pets. D'Amato did it with the banged-up boxer he called Cus. Tyson was no different. "Isn't he beautiful?" he asked rhetorically.

Still, the ultimate act of courage, the most humanizing renewal, would have been for Tyson to leave boxing. He knew that too. "I was going to quit, at least for a couple of years... maybe after the Holyfield fight," he told Gutskey of his plans before losing in Tokyo. But what he hadn't banked on was being caught in an anomaly. By losing he had found a self, and yet this new Mike Tyson was a captive. "But now I can't," he went on. "Now I'm a whore to the game. Now I have to prove something. In fact, now I wonder sometimes if I'm not bigger than I was before, because I lost."

The next stage in Tyson's life was to be framed by a single question: Would he win back the heavyweight championship of the world?

This new, resolved Tyson wouldn't necessarily return to being the same devastating, dominant boxer of the Spinks fight and before. This new Mike Tyson, by definition, had to become a different type of boxer. The flaw of passivity and acquiescence would probably be gone, but with it also much of the psychic energy and rage. Those were, after all, qualities that had built up from an inner paradox now resolved. There was no more doubt over whether the belief in him by others was based on love or self-interest, because he now could start to believe in himself.

A Tyson with a sense of identity also didn't need mentors anymore, living or dead. Out, then, went D'Amato's arcane religion of the fists, and his "system." For Tyson, D'Amato's teachings had made him into a ring robot. No wonder that from the Bruno fight on he had started to shed those unique skills and look more like a conventional boxer. It must have been a liberating experience: he could go into the ring and create the moment for himself, feel the rush of emotion from being in physical jeopardy and finding a way out. That became a preferable ring strategy to executing some instilled program.

A conventional Tyson, and one beaten so decisively by Douglas, was also liberating for his opponents. They no longer had to enter the ring with intense feelings of dread and intimidation. Tyson could be hit. His punches, though fast, could at least be seen coming. He was beatable. Of course, not all of his opponents would believe that. He still had power and hand speed. He was still far better at being conventional than most of the top-ranked boxers. Whether he had the same will and drive and determination to win remained to be seen.

But Tyson's ring skills weren't going to be enough to get the title back. His ascent had resulted from a combination of factors that came together at the right time, in the right place, for the right fighter. Besides the bond with D'Amato as son to father, student to teacher, there was the money, marketing, and business acumen of Jacobs and Cayton. Add to that a pliable boxing official, José Torres, and a news media searching for an heir to Muhammad Ali, a Prince of the Ring who could unify and restore meaning and order to the heavyweight division.

Finally, there was a television executive (Seth Abraham) willing to spend any sum of money to create the forum for that unified champion, and a promoter (King) desperate to steal him away.

Only three of those factors remained, and by no means in the same form. There was Tyson, a contender again, and of more questionable abilities. The alliance among Jacobs, Cayton, Abraham, and King was mostly gone. Only Abraham and King remained bound, but even their decade-long union looked as if it might lose its purpose now that Tyson was no longer champion. As for King, he had a tenuous grip on the new champion, and if he lost the legal war with Steve Wynn perhaps no grip at all. In the post-Tokyo era of heavyweight boxing, power had become fractured again. It wouldn't be as easy this time around to get Tyson a shot at the title.

To Tyson, though, none of those Machiavellian subtleties mattered. The new narrative of his life, and one that he could author alone, was to become champion again. That's all he saw in his future, and all he wanted from it. If, in order to do that, he had to become a "whore to the game," then he'd need a pimp; and there was no better pimp in the business of boxing than Don King.

It's no surprise, then, that King remained part of his life after Tokyo, as did cotrainers Aaron Snowell and Jay Bright, plus his two-man entourage, John Horne and Rory Holloway. So many people blamed the loss on King or on his inept cornermen, but he wasn't willing to do that. "For me to fire them would be blaming someone else for what was my fault," Tyson told Gutskey. On a special HBO broadcast a week after the fight, Larry Merchant asked him about the failure of his corner to take proper care of his swollen eye. "You have another one—use that one. You fight to finish...my heart was still beating," he responded defensively.

Perhaps for Tyson, such twisted logic made sense. He may have felt that if he blamed the others for Tokyo, he would somehow denigrate the value of his newfound sense of self. Maybe the survivor in him knew that he needed King to get a title shot, and couldn't afford to alienate him. Or maybe it was just an act of taking responsibility: he chose them, he'll stick with them and make it work. Whatever it was that bound him to King, the bond persisted—as it would turn out, to Tyson's detriment.

\* \* \*

Bill Cayton grasped at the opportunity to use Tokyo as a nail in the coffin of King's career. He reactivated his federal suit against Tyson and

King with an amended complaint filed on March 14, 1990. "They owe me six hundred thousand dollars," Cayton said in an April 1990 interview. "My lawyers and I have been asking for a complete audit of King's and Tyson's books for over a year. This case won't be settled. I knew I'd be the only one to stand up to King because I have the money."

Cayton's chest-beating was ignored by the news media. The dispute between him and Tyson was ancient history. Not much was even made of the claim by commissioner James Dupree that Tyson had been a victim of a cover-up at the New York State Athletic Commission. Ever since the hearing the previous August, Dupree had been prodding new Athletic Commission Chairman Randy Gordon to take up Tyson's complaint against Cayton of contract fraud. He sent Gordon four separate memos, all of which were ignored. Finally, in a February 14 letter, Dupree formally accused Gordon of being "deeply involved in a cover-up." He sent copies to Governor Cuomo, two state senators, and a state assemblyman. Two weeks later, Dupree was notified by the governor's office that his term as commissioner would not be renewed. Tyson, in fact, had also sent a letter to Governor Cuomo, in which he complained about how he was "tricked" by Jacobs into signing the contracts. That one, too, was ignored.

Dupree left office on March 1, 1990, and on that day held a press conference in New York to announce that he believed there was a cover-up at the commission. Five reporters appeared, but coverage was limited to a single paragraph in most newspapers the next day. "I think the boxing reporters felt that because they hadn't made a big deal out of the fraud before, they didn't want to now. It would have made them look ridiculous," Dupree said.

Tyson made no comment on Dupree's charges. He was holed up in Catskill, where he'd decided to base his new training camp. He put Jay Bright in charge of building a gym above a children's clothing store on the main street of town, kitty-corner to where he had been trained by D'Amato, Teddy Atlas, and Kevin Rooney. The street had changed little over the years. The only addition was Cars of Distinction. In its window display was a 1990 Mercedes going for $100,000, and a red Porsche Targa priced at $48,100. It looked oddly out of place amid the mom-and-pop dime stores and pizza shops. Some entrepreneur was apparently aware of Tyson's passion for buying luxury cars on a whim.

Kevin Rooney was also still in the area. He had started training professional fighters in the old gym, which had been named after Cus

D'Amato. He'd separated from his wife, and in April 1990, declared bankruptcy. Rooney showed no assets, and debts of $1.4 million—most of which were gambling losses owed the casinos.

Tyson insulated himself from his past. Both Robin Givens and Ruth Roper called Ewald's house all through February, but he wouldn't talk to them. Brian Hamill, a friend of Rooney's and Tyson's, also called several times, then eventually gave up. "I called the house and some guy answered, and wouldn't let me talk to Mike," Hamill said. "And he wouldn't even tell me his name. He was a goon."

As for Tyson and King, there seemed to be an unspoken agreement to avoid each other in the weeks after the Tokyo bout. It was as if both men wanted to repress the impulse to cast blame. Said one source in the Tyson camp: "Mike wanted another fight. He didn't care who it was, just a body he could beat to prove he was back. Don knew that without even asking him."

King was indeed busy. He fought the battle to promote Douglas's next fight on two fronts: in the courts against Mirage owner Steve Wynn, and in Douglas's hometown. Throughout March, while his lawyers filed and responded to a variety of court motions, King rolled into Columbus, Ohio, and as he done so many times in the past, made a play for the fighter's heart. He used the issue of race to convince Douglas's father, his friends, and the entire black community that John Johnson, as a white man, could not do the new champion justice. He held press conferences, spoke on radio and television, and preached in the local black Baptist churches. "He went all the way back to when whites were enslaving blacks," Johnson said in press reports of King's race-baiting. The ploy didn't work. King left town without the fighter's heart because this time, unlike with so many other young men he'd bullied into contracts, Douglas had an alternative: Steve Wynn and his promise of $60 million.

In battling to promote Douglas's next two title defenses, Wynn took a page out of King's own tactical handbook. But the challenge wasn't only posed to King and other promoters. Wynn announced his intention of turning all the Douglas, Holyfield, and Tyson fights into closed-circuit pay-per-view events, the sales of which he would control. With that move, he alienated two other major players in the complex equation of the boxing deal: the closed-circuit pay-per-view businessmen, and Seth Abraham. It's no surprise that while King fought Wynn in court, Abraham, and others, maneuvered against him outside of it. Friends who had become enemies were now becoming friends again. The business of boxing started to regurgitate upon itself.

"Wynn is an amateur in boxing," Abraham declared in March 1990. "He's trying to be a one-stop shopper, and lock up all the rights." In early April, Abraham suggested to King and Bob Arum, who had been sworn enemies for a decade, that they join up to oppose Wynn. They happily agreed. "We decided to carve Steve Wynn a new asshole," Arum said.

King huddled with Abraham to select an opponent for Tyson's first comeback fight, which was scheduled for mid-June. Abraham opted for Renaldo Snipes, who was ranked in the top 10. But King was looking for the safest fight possible. He lobbied for an unknown Argentine named Walter Armando Masseroni, whom Abraham promptly rejected. They settled on Henry Tillman, who had twice beat Tyson in the 1984 Olympic trials but whose professional career had since fizzled.

Abraham paid Bob Arum $1 million for George Foreman to fight Brazil's Adilson Rodrigues on the undercard. Rodrigues's tenth-place ranking in by the W.B.A. overstated his credentials. He had recently been knocked out in the second round by the soft-punching Holyfield.

King and Arum sold the doubleheader to Caesars Palace for $3 million. King's last fight at Caesars had been Larry Holmes-Gerry Cooney in 1981, and he had vowed then that it would be his last. Bob Halloran, at that time director of sports at Caesars, had apparently treated Holmes and King like sharecroppers on his desert plantation. "King goes on about race, but this time he had a beef," Larry Merchant said. "Holmes was the champion, but Caesars gave Cooney far better treatment. Then Halloran made a play for some of King's other fighters. He wanted Caesars to become a promoter. King vowed never to go back."

Two other interesting figures popped out from King's past. Richie Giachetti, who had worked with King in developing Holmes, then sued him over purse splits, was hired to be Tyson's new trainer. Aaron Snowell and Jay Bright were demoted to towel-and-bucket carriers. Giachetti, in fact, wasn't so much hired as assigned. It turned out that he had been on King's payroll for several years as a gofer and watchdog over his other fighters.

The second disgorged figure was Henry Groomes, whose claim to fame as a boxing manager was established during the aborted 1977 ABC boxing tournament. Five of the seven fighters Groomes had entered into that tournament, a Don King promotion, had been given fictitious records. Groomes was now managing Henry Tillman. "Groomes kept his mouth shut over the ABC thing, so this was King paying off an old debt," said one insider to King's affairs.

For that matter, Tillman had been spat back up too. He had learned his trade in the California Men's Correctional Facility in Chino. Defeating Tyson in the Olympic trials, then taking a gold medal in Los Angeles, would turn out to be the high point of his boxing career. He started as a professional in the cruiserweight division, won a minor title, then lost it in his first defense. In his second title bid, against cruiserweight champion Holyfield in February 1987, he was knocked out in the seventh round. Cayton then wanted Tillman to fight Tyson in Japan in March 1988. But he was beaten again by a journeyman opponent in November 1987, and again the next year by the unknown Willie deWit. Tillman fought only three times in 1989 and 1990, all against dim prospects. He was more interested in a budding real estate career, acting, his wife (the granddaughter of black track and field legend Jesse Owens), and organizing a boxing program for inner-city Los Angeles children, than in becoming a champion. He was, in other words, precisely the right opponent for Tyson's first comeback fight. He also came at the right price: $250,000. "Tillman's a shot fighter who can't punch," said trainer Joey Fariello, who worked Tillman's corner in 1987. "What kind of challenge could he be?"

In Tyson's early press conferences for the fight, he was refreshingly lighthearted, introspective, and charming. "I took the championship for granted," he told a group of reporters in New York on April 30. "I lost respect for the championship. I was abusing myself, taking advantage of my body, gaining weight. I got out of my system. You have to realize, from the age of twelve to twenty-one all I did was fight and be a part-time husband."

Several days later in Los Angeles, he elicited laughter from another group of reporters with a story about his reaction to watching a tape of the Tokyo fight: "I sit there and I tell myself, 'Hey, man, duck!' But on screen, I don't duck. I scream, 'Duck, you dummy!' But the dummy don't listen to me." When one brave reporter asked whether Tyson felt suicidal after the loss, he brushed it off with aplomb. "Hey! I got lots of money to spend before I kill myself. You have to deal with things like this every day. Did I cry? I wish I could cry! The last time I cried was when I got my divorce. That's when you cry. Actually, can I tell you something? It was a relief, is what it was. It was a relief of a lot of pressure."

Tyson also talked about his new son, who'd been born on May 2 and whose mother was Natalie Fears of Los Angeles. He named the boy D'Amato Kilrain Tyson after Cus D'Amato and Jake Kilrain, who fought John L. Sullivan in the last bare-knuckle heavyweight championship fight, on July 8, 1889. "You know, if I was, like half the fighter I am and I lost the title to someone, and I knew I could never beat this guy, that might, you know, tend to dishearten me," he continued. "But this is something you know isn't going to last forever."

Tyson started his training early. He arrived in Las Vegas in mid-April, which gave him eight weeks of preparation, compared to his customary four to six. He used to set up in Johnny Tocco's gym, a small, dirty, and cramped relic from the 1950s just off the Strip. Now he relocated to Golden Gloves, a much larger, newer, and more modern facility located on the edge of a park in a residential district.

Tyson arose every morning at 4 A.M., ran three miles by himself, returned to King's condo, worked out in a gym set up there, ate, then slept the rest of the morning. In the afternoons, he went to Golden Gloves for several hours. "He punched the heavybag right off the ceiling," demoted cornerman Jay Bright said. Most evenings he'd show up at the Las Vegas Sports Club to ride an exercise bicycle for two hours. From there it was back to the condo to watch a video, then get into bed early. King had hired a special chef to cook low-fat, protein-rich, high-carbohydrate meals. By the end of April, Tyson's weight was already down to 220 pounds.

In the final weeks, Tyson barred reporters from all but three of his workouts. There was much speculation about that, ranging from conflicts with trainer Giachetti to his poor performance in sparring. He did, in fact, have one shouting match with Giachetti, which climaxed with Tyson screaming "get out of my face," then marching off in a huff to the Sports Club. He also worked with a new group of sparring partners. (After knocking down Tyson in Tokyo, then boasting about it, partner Greg Page lost his slot.) Most of the new members in the sparring group were mere punching bags compared to former champions like Page, bodies whose purpose was to build Tyson's confidence.

The news media seemed to understand, and respect, his decision to train in private and fight whom he pleased. A fallen man, after all, should have the right to dictate the early course of his comeback. Besides, as fight promotions go, George Foreman was sufficient entertainment. Foreman had first won the title in 1973. He had not been a well-liked champion. In an era of boxing dominated by the expansive and poetic Ali, Foreman's quiet, simmering, bad-humored public profile had cast him in the role of an angry grouch. He reigned for nearly two years before being defeated by Ali via a late-round knockout in the infamous "Rumble in the Jungle."

After Zaire, Foreman won five fights in a row, then lost a 1976 decision to contender Jimmy Young. In the dressing room afterwards, he claimed to have had a "religious experience." He retired, became an evangelical preacher in his Texas hometown, built an athletic center for the local children, and in the subsequent ten years mellowed considerably.

In 1987, at the age of thirty-six, he started a comeback, and built a new winning record with early-round victories over men with names like Ladislas Mijangos in places like Fort Myers, Florida, and Marshall, Texas. By 1990, he'd honed a crowd-pleasing shtick to back up both his title dreams and his growing physical proportions. "I've developed a 'pork-chop-and-gravy punch.' Anybody who doesn't eat pork chops and gravy can't beat me," the bald Foreman quipped from what seemed like a prepared list of borscht-belt jokes. In Las Vegas, where such humor passes for high entertainment, he was at home. "I've been sticking to my diet," he said at the final prefight press conference. "It's a see-food diet: everything I see, I eat."

Foreman spoke in more serious, and thoughtful, terms about what it was like to lose the title. "You are ashamed to see everybody, especially the skycaps at the airport; you don't want to see the taxi drivers; 'cause everyone is going to say something in your mind. And you have to build yourself up, so you start spending billions of dollars on cars, suits, and anything you can to make yourself look like the best in the world. Mike Tyson will never sleep again until he gets a chance to fight for the title again, and win it. He'll never sleep again until he redeems himself. I hate to see a young man go through that, but that's the way it is."

On fight night, June 16, everyone played his expected role. Lumbering "Big George" Foreman planted himself in the ring like a boulder with arms. A left hook to Rodrigues's jaw ended the bout in the second round, earning Foreman comeback victory number twenty-two. Tillman also cooperated with his destiny. From the opening bell, he backpedaled away so fast that twice he almost stepped out of the ring, and fell. Tyson pursued patiently, but when he finally caught up with the fleeing former Olympian, he was tied up. A few minutes into the round, Tillman decided to try a punch or two. One of them, a straight right, hit Tyson square. He hardly flinched. A few seconds later, Tyson planted and let go a wide, looping right hook that caught Tillman on the side of the head and sent him to the canvas. He was counted out.

The fight showed that Tyson could pursue an opponent for two minutes and forty-seven seconds, and that he still had a knockout punch—but didn't prove much more than that. He looked like a hungry, well-conditioned, conventional fighter, but then again, he didn't have the opportunity to seem like anything else. For ticket buyers, and Tyson-watchers, it was a nearly pointless exercise. But King elevated it into a major moment in boxing history. "He's back! He's Mighty Mike Tyson, no longer Iron Mike Tyson," he blared at the postfight press conference.

As King ran off at the mouth, Tyson yanked at his arm and said, "Shut up." King talked through it, "You know you're back!" he said, but did shut up because it was obvious that Tyson wanted to keep the victory in perspective. "Thank you. I'm glad to be back," Tyson began on a formal, and respectful, note. "Henry is a good fighter, and my friend. I'm an experienced fighter, and I'm happy to get the win. I prepared to fight all night." There was not much to ask about the fight, so some reporters turned to his personal life. "My baby, he's so gorgeous. He's five, no, six weeks old, and twelve pounds. Fighting don't have anything to do with him. He can already sit. I live for my son."

Late in the press conference, a reporter asked what he had proved with the victory, and in so doing pushed a button in the former champion that emitted an old, and sour, note. "I know I'm the best fighter in the universe," he said matter-of-factly. A few reporters rolled their eyes, and others cursed under their breath ("same old fucking Tyson," said one). Clearly, they wanted this new Tyson to be sputtering nothing but humble pie. But that's not how Tyson decided he was going to win back the title. He might not be the same style of boxer anymore, and as a result, at least when up against a quality opponent, not as dominant either. Still, he was determined to believe in himself, and nothing could take that away.

King announced that Tyson's next fight would be on September 8 against Alex Stewart. He was only marginally better than Tillman, and his selection confirmed that King intended to keep Tyson in reserve until he fought again for the title. The only shock was the date. It was twelve days prior to the bout Steve Wynn had scheduled between James Douglas and Evander Holyfield at The Mirage.

\* \* \*

In the early 1970s, Steve Wynn was a Las Vegas liquor distributor itching to get into the casino business. He bought up enough shares of the ailing Golden Nugget, Inc. to join the company's board, then staged a palace coup to become chairman, president, and chief executive officer. Wynn turned the Nugget around, and set up a new property in Atlantic City. The success didn't last. In 1981, New Jersey gaming authorities investigated him for cocaine use. He beat the charges. Within a few years he had to sell the Atlantic City property, at a considerable loss. Wynn's hotel-casino cash cow—the Golden Nugget in downtown Las Vegas—also fell into a slump.

He had to try something new. In the mid-1980s, he borrowed $900 million to refurbish the Golden Nugget and build The Mirage. The Nugget remained a dismal performer. Wynn's future, therefore, hinged on the success of The Mirage. He saw boxing as a central component in that success.

Hotel-casinos stage boxing matches as a magnet to attract big-time gamblers. The event in itself isn't a profit center. Ticket sales are expected to cover the site fee paid to the promoter. Wynn's foray into boxing turned that concept on its ear. He provided the site, and functioned as both the promoter and the television licensee. He expected to profit from all of those sources, plus bring in added revenue from the surge in gambling.

All through the spring months, King and Wynn waged legal war. Wynn's lawyers, who also represented Douglas and Johnson, moved to have their suit tried in Nevada. They contended that King's contract with Douglas was illegal under the Nevada Athletic Commission rule prohibiting exclusive, multioption promotional contracts. King's side argued that the contracts were legal under general contract law, and that venue should be in New York, where King maintained his principal place of business. On May 21, a Nevada judge ruled in King's favor; the trial would take place in New York. Meanwhile, a New York judge gutted Wynn's case of all arguments except one: whether King's actions in Tokyo constituted a breach of contract.

Even before stepping into the courtroom, King won two important battles. First, he managed once again to prevent the specific terms of one of his promotional contracts from being challenged in a jury trial. Such a judicial contest might have finally been determined as a point of law that exclusivity and multioption clauses in boxing amounted to legalized slavery.

Second, although King usually tried to settle out of court, this time a trial was worth the risk. It would be difficult for Wynn's lawyers to prove King had done anything wrong in Tokyo. His public statements alone seemed damning, but their meaning could be easily blurred under testimony. Ultimately there would have to be a smoking gun; someone to come forward and declare that King conspired to deny Douglas the title. The only person in a position to do that was one of his most loyal allies: José Sulaiman. King had no incentive to settle this one. "Don smelled blood, and he was going to get it," Seth Abraham said.

On June 10, the W.B.A. held a "purse bid" to select the promoter of Douglas-Holyfield. Purse bids are a type of auction used when promoters and fighters can't agree on a price for a fight. Wynn's $32 million—$24 million for Douglas and $8 million for Holyfield—won. King didn't bother entering a bid.

Such competitive bidding was the other route Wynn could have taken to becoming a promoter, and one without the legal fees and headaches. But in an effort to seem like a selfless hero to Douglas and Johnson and so lure them to The Mirage, he stumbled into a trial. For their part, Douglas and Johnson were ecstatic that they finally had a chance to expose King's scheme to withhold recognition. Wynn felt nothing but dread. He had no intention of risking defeat at the hands of a jury. "At the first sign that they were losing the jury, Wynn planned to settle with King, whatever the price," said one insider to the trial.

The trial began in early July in U.S. District Court in Manhattan. Bob Arum testified on behalf of King. He revealed the plan to break King's contract, and quoted Wynn as saying, "We'll buy him off, give him a piece of pie, and let him take a walk." Wynn's lawyer was a senior partner from a Los Angeles firm who had no prior experience in boxing cases and had been hired shortly before the trial. Arum led him around by the nose. "If you asked better questions, you'd get somewhere," Arum scoffed. The jury seemed amused. That afternoon, Wynn's attorney's offered King a $3.5 million buyout. King declined.

Sulaiman testified as expected. A short, portly man in his late fifties, he affected a gentleman's charm and a continental worldliness. He maintained that King didn't lodge a protest about the long count, and that neither did he try and have the decision overturned. As to withholding recognition from Douglas, Sulaiman pleaded to be forgiven. "In the bottom of my heart, I did not withdraw recognition," he muttered imploringly. "I made a terrible mistake. I came back to the U.S. and had the courage to say so."

In his testimony, King justified his actions in Tokyo as normal for a promoter trying to "seize the time and grasp the opportunity" for a rematch. "I'm stirring things. It was a fait accompli that Tyson had been knocked out. The only remedy was a rematch. I was trying to box them in," King said, clearly contradicting himself but at the same time blurring the meaning of his words and actions in Tokyo. When he spoke to reporters in Tokyo of a "grave injustice," he now said, he meant that it would have been unjust only if the decision had held "without a rematch." As to his other statements in Tokyo, King admitted that he routinely lied to reporters when it helped a promotion. Said Douglas: "If he lies to the press, he lies to everyone. He comes down to any level he has to to get what he wants."

After two weeks of testimony, in which Douglas took the stand only once, and Johnson and Wynn not at all, settlement talks hit high gear. On July 17, Wynn arrived in New York to personally strike the deal. He paid King $4.5 million for the right to promote Douglas-Holyfield. He also forked over $2.5 million to Donald Trump for displacing his claim to stage the rematch. King retained the right to promote Douglas's second and third defenses—assuming he beat Holyfield.

In one sense, Wynn was wise to settle. He probably would have lost the jury decision. "Some of us were totally on King's side," one female juror later admitted. "While we hadn't heard the other side, King's case was presented very well. I found King believable." Another juror approached King afterwards and said, "God bless you and always keep the faith." King invited all six jurors to Tyson's next fight.

For all the litigants, however, it was a bittersweet outcome. Douglas and Johnson were free of King for only one fight, and it cost them $7 million: Wynn deducted the settlement payment from the $24 million promised to Douglas for his first defense. As for Wynn's bold foray into boxing, if Douglas lost to Holyfield, he'd be without a champion, and out of the promoting business. He would have been wiser to attempt a copromotion with either Arum or King, rather than a purge.

King walked away with a chunk of money, but he lost the first, and most important, battle to maintain his power over the heavyweight division. His ability to get Tyson a shot at the title was thus severely undermined. If Douglas lost to Holyfield, King would have no claim over the new champion, who might, or might not, decide to fight Tyson next. Holyfield's victory could put the title a year or more out of Tyson's reach.

*　　*　　*

In the weeks following his victory, James ("Buster") Douglas reveled in his celebrity as the Black Knight who had slain the dragon. It started with his triumphant return home to a crowd of 10,000 cheering supporters. This time the mayor of Columbus showed up, and he announced plans for a parade in the new champion's honor. Douglas went off to make appearances on the morning talk shows, the evening talk shows, and the late-night talk shows. He "took" meetings with television producers (Bill Cosby) and feature film makers (Clint Eastwood). He refereed a wrestling match between Hulk Hogan and Randy ("Macho Man") Savage, in which he pretended to hit Savage and knock him out. He was formally honored by the mayors of Duluth, Minnesota; Kansas City, Missouri; and Kansas City, Kansas. He participated in the Easter Seals Telethon, visited homeless families, and cuddled babies with AIDS. He set up a 900 number on which callers could hear Douglas muse about being champion. He even reunited with his wife, Bertha.

There were, however, cracks starting to appear. Douglas made The Mirage his second home, and all through the spring months he was seen spending more time in the bars and restaurants than anywhere near the hotel's training gym. Wynn didn't seem to care. He covered the cost of the $900-a-day bungalow Douglas stayed in, plus his meals, bar tab, and the limousine that ferried him around town. And Douglas reveled in that too. "I pulled him out of one club so drunk he couldn't walk," one Mirage chauffeur recalled.

On a trip back home to Columbus, Douglas rammed his 1970 Cadillac into the rear end of a car waiting to turn left. His mother's death had been motivation for his victory in Tokyo, and now he used it to explain his distractions. "It's Mother's Day," he told manager John Johnson when asked about the accident.

As time passed, Douglas didn't want to explain himself to Johnson anymore. In late May he was seen in Las Vegas with promoter Butch Lewis, the savvy engineer of Michael Spinks's record 1988 purse. Then, in July, there were rumors that he was angry at Johnson over the settlement with King. "He was promised by Johnson that the deal would free him from King, and instead he only got a one-fight reprieve, and that cost him seven million dollars," said a member of the Douglas camp. "John Johnson isn't smart enough to deal with guys like Wynn and King."

By August, Johnson was halfway out the door. Immediately after the Tokyo fight, he had set up James Buster Douglas, Inc., to handle the champion's new fortunes. Douglas asked him to leave the company, and informed him that COACH, Inc., Johnson's management firm, would no longer be handling any of his affairs. He then pulled out of a Columbus boxing promotion that Johnson's son was setting up to raise money for a new youth education center. It was supposed to be named after Douglas's mother. He elevated two of his closest friends, who had no experience in boxing, to the positions of executive assistant and accountant. Johnson tried to be philosophical about it all. "Everybody has wings," he told one reporter. "And they got to spread them. James is just spreading his wings." He reminded the reporter that he was still getting his 23 percent cut of Douglas's purse.

Privately, Johnson was not so calm about the changes. He berated Douglas for letting money and fame change him. Anyone who argued with Johnson about the wisdom of the deal with Steve Wynn was accused of being "a King man." In a business where alliances are crucial, Johnson's rebel-screaming, emotional diatribes made him a lot of enemies. "Some people in boxing use anger as a business tactic. John Johnson was just an angry man," Seth Abraham said. "In a past life he must have been Cotton Mather."

Douglas, meanwhile, started to lose his fan club. In early August, he and Holyfield started a tour to promote their upcoming fight, which had been put off to October 25. At such events, the fighters were expected to snipe at each other. Douglas stepped over the line. Holyfield, a quiet, soft-spoken, unprepossessing type, spoke earnestly about how he felt he'd earned his title shot. "Cakewalks! Cakewalks every one of them. He didn't fight anybody!" Douglas spat, and in doing so called attention to his own record of easy opponents—many of whom he'd ended up having trouble with. "It'll be a cakewalk when I beat you," Holyfield retorted.

By early October, the old doubts that had swirled around Douglas prior to Tokyo were back. He'd been training for several weeks in Las

Vegas, but wouldn't permit John Johnson into the gym. He wasn't training all that hard. By October 4, or three weeks prior to the fight, he still weighed 250 pounds. Rumors circulated that he wouldn't tolerate any criticism from his trainers. It became apparent why the fight was put off to October 25, hardly a desirable date given that it could conflict with baseball's World Series if just one of the games were rained out: Douglas needed more time to get in shape. The betting line in the casinos made Holyfield a 2-to-1 favorite.

Away from the theater of press conferences and in situations where Douglas got the chance to be more thoughtful, he still came off as somehow false. The simplicity of "I'll just hit him," his statement in Tokyo, was now gone. He spoke volumes about himself, about his drives and motivations, and about how he would again overcome the doubters. But it was as though he had to convince himself of something he didn't quite believe this time. The idea of victory was there, but not the core feeling that he would actually achieve it. And that, perhaps, was the ultimate fate of a boxer so controlled by his emotions: they can't always be relied upon.

The day before the fight, Douglas weighed in at 246—14½ pounds heavier than his fighting weight against Tyson. Only three other heavyweights in history had ever won titles, or defended them, above 235 pounds, and it was not an illustrious club: Primo Carnera, Greg Page, and John Tate. As champions, Foreman, Ali, and Holmes were all in the low- to mid-220s. When Douglas's weight was announced at The Mirage, a stampede of gamblers rushed to the casino and bet a total of $200,000 on Holyfield.

In the third round, James ("Buster") Douglas joined the list of twelve past Cinderella champions, men like Max Baer, Ingemar Johansson, and Leon Spinks, all of whom lost their titles in the first defense. After two rounds of uninspiring boxing, Douglas dropped his right shoulder in a motion that telegraphed the coming punch, a right uppercut that sailed off harmlessly into the air. It was so overtly set up, slowly delivered, and poorly aimed, and left Douglas in such an exposed position, that even Holyfield, who was no speed demon, simply rocked back out of harm's way, loaded, and returned with a short right to the chin. It wasn't a blow like Tyson's uppercut in Tokyo, but it was enough for this James Douglas. He landed on his side and rolled over. His eyes were open and, in the opinion expressed afterward by referee Miles Lane, he seemed lucid enough. But as Lane counted, not once did Douglas make an effort to get up.

The crowd booed and hissed in disgust. In his dressing room, Douglas cried. Later that night, one of his trainers was asked why so pathetic a defeat, and answered, "James Douglas is the boss," implying that it was he who had decided not to train and that his trainers and other camp members could do nothing but wait for the paychecks. One of Douglas's cornermen climbed out onto the roof of The Mirage that night and sat on the edge, feet dangling, tears streaming down his face, the light from the flames of the mock-volcano out front flickering across his face. He was talked down by Mirage security officials.

Steve Wynn, the man whose money had tried to make Douglas into something more than he could ever really be, said only this: "We need to do something to give these guys more incentive to win."

And after the fight, at a press conference, Douglas seemed to return to his own, simple self. It was perhaps where he belonged. "Sometimes it goes your way, sometimes it doesn't," he said flatly. The next day, he flew back to Columbus, Ohio, $17 million richer.

# Chapter Twenty-Three

**O**n the night of his victory over Douglas, it was announced that Holyfield's first defense would be against George Foreman in April 1991. That meant Tyson would have to wait at least half a year, perhaps longer, before he could fight for the title. "He'll have to get in line, like everyone else," said Dan Duva, Holyfield's promoter.

King's worst nightmare had come true. Just hours earlier, the three sanctioning bodies had mandated that if Douglas won he had to defend against Tyson within 120 days. His victory would have restored King's control over the heavyweight division. Whether or not Tyson then took back the title, King would end up with the champion. Now, for the first time since 1973, he'd have no part whatsoever of a heavyweight championship fight. All he could hope for was to use Tyson's number two ranking to pry open the door of the division and get back in. Dan Duva and his partner, Shelly Finkel, would do everything possible to prevent that from happening.

The day after the fight, King feebly argued that Holyfield had to respect the 120-day mandate. He knew that wouldn't happen. By the rules of all three sanctioning bodies, Holyfield had a year to fight Tyson.

In the meantime, he could step into the ring with whomever he pleased. Over the next several months, King ranted and raved about how Tyson deserved a shot at the title by virtue of the grave injustice done to him in Tokyo over the so-called "long count." At times it seemed possible that José Sulaiman of the W.B.C. might do his bidding. There were rumors that the W.B.C. would strip Holyfield if he went ahead with the Foreman fight. But even Sulaiman wouldn't have gone that far, not after the upbraiding he'd suffered over Tokyo.

Without the power he once enjoyed, King reverted to using theatrics. They were intended solely for Tyson's benefit. "In Tokyo, King promised Tyson a title shot within six months," one HBO executive said. "With every passing day, his promise looked emptier. King was turning out to be a toothless lion. He had to make some noise to keep Tyson happy."

The difference between what Tyson was told by King and the truth of his situation was first made evident at a July 1990 New York press conference on his upcoming bout with Alex Stewart. Tyson believed that he would get first crack at the winner of Douglas-Holyfield. "I don't care who wins. Regardless of the situation, I was ordered a rematch by the contract. I'm going to get a rematch no matter who wins," he declared. That, of course, was not the case, as Tyson found out in due time.

Tyson-Stewart was scheduled for September 22 in Atlantic City. On August 31, Tyson apparently suffered a cut over his eye in sparring that required forty-eight stitches. The fight was postponed to December. He made no public appearances to reveal the cut, nor did he allow Stewart's managers to verify it with their own doctor. One fight manager speculated: "King was gambling that Douglas would beat Holyfield, then fight Tyson next, and he wanted Tyson fresh and fit for the bout." There were also rumors that Tyson had discovered he didn't have a "contract" that guaranteed him a rematch, and after confronting King pulled out of the fight in a fit of anger.

Tyson's title hopes took another blow in early October when King's oldest, and most useful, alliance fell apart. Since Tokyo, King and Seth Abraham had continued their negotiations on an extension deal. The picture had become more complex. In January 1990, Abraham secured the approval of HBO's parent, Time Warner, to set up a pay-per-view company to telecast championship boxing. "I can look on the horizon and see what's coming," Abraham said in August 1990, by way of congratulating himself. "I don't know how I do it, but I do. Boxing is only the start of what I have in mind. Don't be surprised if one day you see the World Series on pay television."

The economics of pay television posed an enormous opportunity. Of the 60 million homes hooked up for cable, 15 million could receive a pay-per-view feed. If only 10 percent of those homes paid to see a championship fight at an average of $40 each, the gross revenue would be $60 million. As a source of revenue, that dwarfed monies from closed-circuit telecasting. By 1995, the number of homes in the pay-television universe is expected to reach 40 million. That put the gross return from a single event into the hundreds of millions of dollars—in the U.S. market alone. By the end of the 1990s, most of the industrialized world could be hooked up.

Through the spring and summer of 1990, Abraham tried to get King and Bob Arum to join him in the new boxing pay-television venture, which he called TVKO. The idea was to do a series of monthly championship fights in the various weight classes. Some would be major events, for which the charge would be around $40 a household. Others would involve lesser known fighters at $15 to $20.

Arum was anxious to do it, but not King. His legal battle with Steve Wynn, and the struggle to find Tyson easy opponents for his comeback fights, distracted him from the negotiations. By late summer, Abraham and King finally agreed to do two separate and interlocking deals: a new series of Tyson fights on HBO, and an agreement for TVKO to handle his pay-per-view events. At the time, Abraham was optimistic: "Don gave me a number, a big gigantic number, and if I meet it we can close the deal in thirty seconds."

But by the first week of September, it had all started to unravel. King demanded an up-front signing fee of $20 million to bring Tyson into TVKO. Abraham refused, and the deal died. They returned to work on the HBO fights, and by mid-October had reached a verbal agreement. Tyson would get $85 million for ten appearances. There was one window to do a pay-per-view event. King got a $5 million up-front signing fee, plus another $5 million when all ten fights had been fulfilled.

It was a rich deal for everyone involved. Tyson would earn $8.5 million per fight, or double what he got paid under the previous multifight agreement. He would also get a sizable share of both foreign television rights and, presuming King followed past practices, site fees. No other television network, cable or otherwise, would have given him that kind of money.

For King, it meant an easy $10 million, plus at least $20 million in site fees, 10 percent of foreign television rights, and all the revenue from ring mat advertising. All King had to do was deliver Tyson. That was the reward Abraham expected for the services he'd rendered to King over the past decade.

But King saw it differently. He chose to satisfy Tyson's whims instead of fulfilling the implicit mission of his tie with Abraham. "He said that Tyson didn't like Larry Merchant doing the broadcasts. So Merchant had to go, or no deal. I wouldn't do it. I wasn't going to let King and Tyson tell me how to run the network," Abraham said.

Two days later, King set up a conference call with Abraham that included Tyson and John Horne. "It was cordial at first. Tyson seemed happy with the deal. Then King said, 'And it's a good thing Merchant ain't going to be involved.' I was shocked. I corrected him. 'That's not right, Don—Larry will be doing the broadcasts.'"

Tyson blew up at Abraham for "reneging" on the deal. "What probably happened was that Mike complained about Larry, and Don promised to rid of him. He couldn't make good on the promise, so he put the blame on me," Abraham explained.

Abraham and King met later in the week to try and save the deal. By that time, King had changed the agenda. He had found out that Holyfield had signed to fight Foreman when, and if, he beat Douglas. King's only recourse was to get the W.B.C. to mandate that Holyfield fight Tyson or be stripped, leaving him with only the W.B.A. and I.B.F. crowns. The plan was for Tyson to then fight for the vacant W.B.C. title. He asked Abraham to support the maneuver. "I spent twenty-six and a half million dollars of my company's money to unify the heavyweight title. I was not about to start taking it apart," Abraham said. "I told Don to forget it, he's on his own."

Within a few days, King formally rejected the HBO deal, and their eleven-year alliance was over. Within weeks, Abraham signed multifight agreements with King's adversaries: promoters Shelly Finkel and Dan Duva. He also did a deal with Bob Arum. That left King without a television ally. "I can imagine that King ran to Tyson and told him the split happened because I still refused to get rid of Larry Merchant," Abraham cracked. "And then he said, 'See, Mike, I threw away eighty-five million dollars for you. It's you and me, Mike. You and me.'"

For Tyson, self-discovery was turning out to be a bittersweet experience. After shedding all the old postures, and resolving the central emotional paradox that had nagged him since boyhood, he was desperate to prove he could be champion again on his own terms. Now it looked like he might not get the chance to do that for a long time. That was the added price he had to pay for losing to Douglas. But at the same

time, he'd never expected King to turn out to be a toothless lion. That
was the final, and cruelest, of all the ironies that had plagued his life.

D'Amato, Jacobs, and Cayton were powerful forces in boxing, but in
the end betrayers. Tyson kept an emotional distance from King in order
not to be betrayed again, and then he turned out to be powerless. The
worst part, and the source of a fresh tide of frustration, anger, and
resentment that began to well up in Tyson, was that he felt cornered.
"Mike has a lot of pride," former friend and cornerman Steve Lott said.
"He chose Don King. He made a big deal out of how important it is for
black men to stick together. He'd look like a fool if he had to admit that
King was a mistake."

A few days before the Douglas-Holyfield fight, Tyson was interviewed
on a conference call by a group of reporters. He was asked about the
state of his relationship with King. "None of your business," he snapped.
"What do you like about your wife? Most of you guys write this and that.
Well, Bill Cayton is everything you think Don King is. Cayton is a piece
of shit. He's got you in his fucking hand. Bill, with his pompous attitude.
I'm no slouch. If not for me, you'd have never heard of Cayton. He
couldn't hold a bag of shit compared to me." Incredibly, one of the
reporters pressed the question. "Is Don King family?" Tyson was asked.
"I'm not looking for any motherfucking family! I'm not a homeless guy.
I'm not starving for a family," Tyson screamed into the phone, then hung
up.

All through the fall, there were more rumors of his growing
estrangement from King. "He came out of the limousine screaming,"
said a doorman at the Trump Taj Majal in Atlantic City. " 'I want my
money!' he yelled, and King came out after him like a big puppy dog
saying, 'Mike, Mike, hold on.'"

The first evidence that something was amiss in Tyson's finances
appeared on November 1, 1990. He had been convicted of battery for
fondling a woman in a Manhattan disco in December 1988. In order to
assess damages, Tyson was required to file a statement of his assets. That
was done by Bob Hirth, who in fact wasn't Tyson's attorney, but King's.
The implication was that King controlled Tyson's finances. The statement revealed that King still owed him $2,097,000 from the Tokyo fight.
Tyson had trouble explaining his finances to the court. "I don't know,"
he responded when asked if the Tokyo money had been paid. "It's been
a long time since Tokyo."

His other assets included $2.3 million in cash; the Bernardsville mansion, which was valued at $6.2 million; a 27,000-square-foot, six-bedroom house in Southington, Ohio, not far from King's estate; $645,058 of personal effects, mostly jewelry and furs; and cars worth $843,688. Over the previous year alone he'd bought a $90,000 Porsche and three Ferraris: a $150,000 328; a $150,000 Mondial Cabriolet; and a 12-cylinder, $220,000 Testarossa. He also planned to purchase, for $1 million, the last car Enzo Ferrari had designed before dying in 1988.

In total, the statement claimed assets of $15 million. If that was the case, then Tyson, and King, had a few questions to answer. Up to and including the Spinks fight in June 1988, Tyson's net earnings from all sources of income, before taxes, reached around $34 million. That figure was derived from financial documents included in the litigation with Cayton. Since June 1988, his net purses should have been an additional $19 million. No records have been made public to prove that Tyson actually received all of that money. But it was clear that from total net earnings of an estimated $53 million, he had little left. Subtract taxes, and that figure is cut to around $35 million. If in fact Tyson's assets were actually worth $15 million (the real estate market had soured since Tyson had bought his houses), then in his six years as a professional boxer he'd spent $20 million—and he had nothing to show for it. No doubt, some of that money had ended up with Givens and Roper, and other large portions went to legal fees in the battle with Cayton. A few more million went to a retirement annuity. Still, there were several million dollars unaccounted for, and unless Tyson was ready to say that he'd spent it all on limousines and women, the finger pointed in the direction of Don King.

The jury awarded the plaintiff $100 in damages. Tyson stood up in the courtroom, pulled out a $100 bill, and smacked it onto his forehead. It stuck.

\* \* \*

Atlantic City in December was usually cold, wet, and uninviting. In the days leading up to Tyson's bout with Alex Stewart, the sun broke through the cloud cover and a warm, moist wind blew in from the ocean. On the day before the fight, a Friday, the weekend crowds arrived and began to jam the boardwalk. There was an air of expectancy, and it surrounded the former champion. The rumors about the cut over his eye in training, about the arguments with King over money, and about his frustration over not getting a title shot until late 1991 created a new curiosity about Tyson. It might be hard, the speculation went, for a fighter to get motivated when the object of his desire was so far away.

Alex Stewart didn't have the credentials to be a spoiler. He was ranked 7 by the W.B.C. and 5 and 4, respectively, by the W.B.A. and the I.B.F. Born in England and raised in Jamaica, he later moved to Brooklyn, New York, to become a boxer, and in September 1986 turned professional. He was called "The Destroyer," but in twenty-six matches had fought only one ranked opponent: Evander Holyfield, on November 4, 1989. Stewart wasn't given much of a chance in that bout, but he'd managed to rock Holyfield in the fifth round before losing by a technical knockout in the eighth after being cut above the eye. He became a credible opponent, though not a contender.

At the prefight press conference, Tyson dismissed Stewart in far more subtle terms than he'd used for past opponents. "I'm a champion. Being a champion is a frame of mind. I'm always going to be champion," he said as though stating the obvious. He put the match in the larger context of fighting for the title, a pursuit that he admitted had its price. "Being happy is just a feeling," Tyson said. "Like when you're hungry or thirsty. When people say you're happy, it's just a word someone gave you to describe a feeling. When I decided to accomplish my goals, I gave up all means of even thinking of being happy."

For his part, Stewart tried to contest the prevailing wisdom (Las Vegas considered him a 9½-to-1 underdog) with a sober assessment of the new Tyson. "He's going to come straight ahead. He's not going to take no side routes," Stewart said. "Tyson's style seems to be a lot more simplified. I know what he's going to do...I figure he's going to hit me, of course he's going to hit me. But knock me out? I don't think so."

In seventeen bouts over five years, HBO's staff had always filmed the prefight segments profiling Tyson. Since the Bruno fight, he and King had complained that they'd become biased, unfair portrayals. This being Tyson's last fight for HBO, it decided to let someone else handle the job. Feature film director Spike Lee was paid $50,000 to do the segment. Lee had earned a reputation for grappling head-on with highly charged racial issues. His documentary sensibilities would confirm this reputation.

Lee insisted on complete editorial control. His seven-minute, black-and-white minidocumentary was delivered to HBO the day before the fight. No changes were made. As could only have been expected, he made the film a blunt racial statement. "Everything's totally against us,"

Tyson said. "We're two black guys from the ghetto and we hustle and they don't like what we're saying. We're not, like, prejudiced antiwhite. We're just pro-black." King endorsed the theme. "They always change the rules when black folks come into success. Black success is unacceptable."

The validity of the issues couldn't be denied. Prejudice exists. Successful blacks are often held up to a double standard. Black pride isn't by definition antiwhite. It was a distinctly black man's view of Tyson, and one that HBO's audience had never gotten before. But what did it mean? At a screening for the news media the afternoon before the fight, some reporters walked out of the room in disgust. To them, and to many other boxing people, Lee enabled Tyson, and King, to imply that it was racism that was preventing them from getting a shot at the title. Lee came to make a statement, but he ended up being used to confuse the facts.

Tyson entered the ring to the sounds of Public Enemy's "Welcome to the Terrordome." That's precisely what it turned out to be for Stewart. Tyson launched at him like a windmill, and four seconds into the round, a looping right caught Stewart on the temple, sending him to the canvas. He got up, but instead of running, he tried to counterpunch. It was no use. Tyson swarmed in with a frenzied and illogical sequence of hooks and head shots. He was so out of control, and off balance, that at one point a punch missed and he stumbled and fell forward. Suppressed laughter could be heard in the cheaper seats.

Stewart did connect once, which was no surprise given how exposed Tyson was leaving himself. But it didn't matter. Stewart went down two more times, and the referee called it over. When he got up, Tyson put his arm around the beaten boxer's shoulder. "Don't be discouraged. You're a good fighter. Remember, I got beat by a bum," he said, meaning James Douglas. It was patronizing, but well meant.

The Tillman and Stewart fights removed any doubt over whether Tyson had the appetite to become champion again. King now knew that with each passing day, Tyson would blame him for not getting a title shot. He had compounded his problems by letting Tyson walk away from the $85 million HBO deal. That had been a big mistake. For catering to his petty whims, King had set himself up to be accused of also failing to bring in the money. Tyson training for a championship fight wouldn't care about his bank account. But a bored, frustrated, and angry Tyson was likely to start questioning King's handling of the books.

Tyson needed distractions, and the ever-resourceful King found them. He dragged out an old whipping horse: Bill Cayton. King revived the legal battle with Cayton over the alleged fraud of the February 12 contracts. He retained Vince Fuller from the Washington, D.C., firm of Williams & Connelly to amend Tyson's suit with fresh evidence. Meanwhile, King tried desperately to avoid going to trial over Cayton's suit against him.

King also put together a new television deal. In December 1990, he announced "KingVision," which for all intents and purposes was a rip-off of Abraham's concept for TVKO. He planned to promote a series of weekly fights that would be shown on the Showtime basic cable station. He would then do monthly events, and at least four "blockbuster" bouts, on Showtime Event Television, the pay-per-view service. Tyson would fight in the first two so-called blockbusters.

King claimed that the deal guaranteed Tyson $120 million. That was later contradicted by Showtime executives, who disclosed that he could earn $120 million based on the "upside" potential built into the agreement. The actual deal obligated Showtime to put up front money of only $1 million to cover some of the promotional costs of each fight. It then paid another $1 million to $3 million for the delay broadcast rights. In return, Showtime got a share of the net pay-per-view profits, around 10 to 15 percent. Tyson's money principally came from the gross receipts. His minimum purse guarantee from King, plus King's own cut, were not revealed. King also announced that Tyson's next few fights would be staged at The Mirage. One-time enemy Steve Wynn was now an ally. Wynn had lost $3 million on the Douglas-Holyfield fight, and had decided that the risks of being a promoter were just too great.

As King's deals go, this one was a classic. A lot more money was promised than was likely to be produced and the terms and conditions for the fighter were fuzzy. But it was enough to placate Tyson. "Don told Mike he was getting a hundred and twenty million, and that it was a much better deal than ours, and I'm sure Tyson believed him," Abraham said cynically. King also structured the agreement to give himself total control of all the gross receipts. With both the HBO and TVKO deals, he had had to relinquish much of that control to others. Now he had his own pay-per-view company, owned all the rights, collected and counted all the money. Showtime was just a distributor. "It's a license to steal," one sports television executive quipped.

The only good part of the deal for Tyson was the first opponent: Donovan ("Razor") Ruddock. "I'll give Don credit for matching Tyson up with the only available fighter out there who could give him a challenge," Abraham said. Indeed, it was more than a challenge. Tyson believed that he had only two dark spots on his record: dropping out of the first matchup with Ruddock in October 1989, and the defeat in Tokyo. James Douglas had gone into seclusion since his loss. They would probably never fight again. But now he could disprove the speculation that he was afraid of Ruddock. It was the first true test for the new Mike Tyson.

The fight was scheduled for March 18, 1991. Tyson started training in early January. He was vigilant about his morning run, about keeping his weight down, working hard in gym, and getting plenty of rest. Said Tom Patti, the Catskill housemate who had spent time with Tyson in camp: "We were watching TV one night and one of Ruddock's fights came on. Mike saw something, like a weakness, or flaw, in Ruddock, and said, 'I'm going to kill this guy!' He was happy, really, really happy."

Only a man with supreme confidence would be "happy" to get into the ring with Ruddock. After Tyson backed out of their first meeting, Ruddock had a lot of trouble getting fights. "It sent an arctic chill through the heavyweight ranks," promoter Murad Muhammad said. "Guys were afraid of him, and they should be. He's tough, and confident like I've never seen."

On April 4, 1990, Ruddock had defeated former titleholder Michael Dokes in a fourth-round barrage that left the ex-champ unconscious on the canvas for fifteen minutes. After that, Ruddock's career stopped in its tracks. The title was locked up for at least two years by Douglas, Holyfield, Tyson, and Foreman. No top-10-ranked opponent would risk fighting Ruddock and lose status on the heavyweight totem pole; not the has-beens hoping for one last, big payday (Tim Witherspoon, Tony Tubbs, Tony Tucker) or the new generation (Riddick Bowe, Ray Mercer, Lennox Lewis). Ruddock took the fights that he could—Kimmuel Odom and Mike Rouse, both of whom he dumped within three rounds.

Ruddock's apparent prowess (Dokes, after all, was over the hill, and the others were mere journeymen) also got the attention of King. He did not make the match merely in order to satiate Tyson's hunger and give him a distracting challenge. Without a champion in his grasp, King needed as much leverage as he could get in the division. He offered

Ruddock the only bout against a name opponent that he could get, and did it for a price. Ruddock had to make King the copromoter of his next six fights.

\* \* \*

"If he's not dead, it doesn't count. It doesn't count."

Tyson uttered those words with deadpan earnestness just days before the fight. They weren't said to hype the fight so people would buy more tickets. Nor was it the Ring Destroyer, or the Public Enemy. It was Tyson taking self-confidence up and beyond machismo. He spit out the idea of death, and with spine-tingling matter-of-factness let it sit there for everyone to regard. And that, finally, was the real Mike Tyson: a young man who knew death from his days in Brownsville, and who could with ease yank up the memory of the feeling and live it for the moment, then stuff it back. He was like a Method actor who had learned how to use all of his past experiences to inform the present; he had that kind of reach into all the contents in the many rooms of his psyche. He could just as easily be thoughtful and introspective, or crude and obnoxious. He didn't care anymore about how his behavior or utterances would be construed by the news media. He had no interest in what the American public thought about him. Through wrenching life experience he had acquired a knowledge of self, and though that self had an ugly side, it was the real and only person he felt he could be. That such a view would also get him into trouble in, and possibly out, of the ring seemed likely. But then again, Tyson was used to trouble. It's when he was supposed to be happy with his life that he always ended up paying the highest price.

\* \* \*

A crowd of 16,000 filled the outdoor stadium on a parking lot in back of The Mirage. People huddled for warmth from the March chill that had crept into the desert night air. Tyson came out in a ski cap and black-and-white-striped cloth robe that resembled an Arab gown. His cornermen sported black leather baseball caps with "Kick Ass" written across the front in bold white letters.

When Tyson's robe came off, there was no sweat on his body. He looked relaxed, as if he felt at home. Ruddock, on the other hand, hopped up and down in place, limbering up his arms, all the time focused on Tyson. He was hyperventilating from nervousness. Much of the muscle on his six-foot-three frame seemed to be packed into his deep, wide chest and massive shoulders. He looked fit and, despite rumors about an injured right biceps muscle that had stopped him from sparring two weeks earlier, ready to mix it up.

Seconds into the first round, Ruddock fired off a left uppercut that missed with such spent force that his whole upper body arched up and backwards. Tyson unleashed his customary and impatient first-round barrage, all of it aimed for the head. Ruddock blocked most of the punches, or moved back and away, and a few times countered. Two of his rights connected easily, and they seemed sufficient to convince Tyson that this wasn't going to end quickly.

In order to have any chance of winning, Ruddock would have had to come out in the second, and as James Douglas had done in Tokyo, bring to bear a full range of boxing skills. But he didn't do that. Until the sixth round, he let himself be chopped apart by Tyson.

If Ruddock did have a fight plan beyond hoping to survive into the later rounds where, he probably assumed, his chances would improve, it wasn't evident. He had no mobility, threw few combinations, and held his arms low, which made him prone to Tyson's trademark hooks. He used no left jab at all, and no head movement. Ruddock just lumbered in, then took a punch or two before countering. When he did, it was invariably a left uppercut, and sometimes an odd hybrid of uppercut and hook. They were big punches, big enough to make a career against unranked opponents. However, against Tyson they had little noticeable effect; many he bobbed under, most he walked through unfazed. So ended the mystery about Donovan ("Razor") Ruddock. Fighters ranked in the top 10 had valid reasons to avoid him. And though he might have been able to beat the Tyson of 1989, he was no match for a well-trained, fast, and hard-punching Tyson the hungry new contender.

Near the end of the sixth round, Ruddock tried to turn the tide of the fight. He landed a crushing left hook to Tyson's head, then followed with right uppercuts and more lefts. Amazingly, Tyson didn't back off, but stood in harm's way for more, and shook his head to say that no damage had been done. Ruddock hit him again, this time with a straight right, and still he didn't move. Tyson shook his head and tapped his jaw, daring Ruddock to hit him again, which he did with another right that also seemed to have no effect.

Tyson strutted back to his corner, sat down on the stool, and cleared his nose with a snort. New trainer Richie Giachetti was so shocked by what he'd seen, he could barely talk. He knew little about his fighter, and no doubt Tyson preferred it that way. Tyson hadn't intended to get hit by the first series of blows, but then the idea of creating a moment of jeopardy had taken over. It was as though he wanted to authenticate himself by reenacting some of Tokyo. For the moment to be affirming he had to take Ruddock's best, and come back twice as hard.

Ruddock's whole fight went into the sixth. Tyson chewed it up, and in the seventh round spit it back. His first left hook caught Ruddock flush on the side of the jaw. As he stumbled back toward the ropes, Tyson drove in four more hooks, most of which glanced. Yet it was enough for the referee, Richard Steele, to declare a technical knockout. It was a hasty call. Ruddock had taken a lot of punishment, and was losing the fight, but he was still standing, and appeared able to continue. Steele, by common practice, should have taken him by the gloves, looked into his eyes, and asked a question or two to determine his condition before calling the fight. Instead, he held Tyson back and only glanced over at Ruddock to make the decision.

Ruddock's corner jumped into the ring in protest. In the ensuing melee his promoter, Murad Muhammad, kicked repeatedly at Richie Giachetti, who had fallen to the canvas. Muhammad would later complain that he had never wanted Steele to referee the fight. Steele, it turned out, worked in one of Mirage owner Steve Wynn's casinos as a pit boss. To the extent that Tyson's victory benefited Wynn, his working the fight appeared to be a conflict of interest. Responded Steele, one of boxing's most experienced and respected referees, "I saved Ruddock's life."

That exaggerated the point. What he did do, in his squeamishness, was create enough uncertainty about the outcome for Don King to be able to set up an immediate rematch. Putting them in the ring again made little sense. Ruddock was tough, had pride, and was seemingly fearless, but lacked a full package of basic skills. Still, his toughness made him a difficult opponent for the conventionally styled Tyson, as he would have been for anyone else in the top 10 rankings—including champion Evander Holyfield. Tyson would no doubt beat Ruddock again, but not without risk.

Compared to what Tyson could once do in the ring, he had greatly deteriorated. He fought with determination, but rarely moved his head, and didn't slip, weave, or dip to capture the inside positioning. He fought standing straight up on the outside, which—as even the one-punch-at-a-time Ruddock proved—made him vulnerable to a quick punch from someone with longer arms. Tyson's punches, though still the fastest and most powerful in the division, came in one at a time, or twice at most. He didn't create punching opportunities anymore, but rather took them as they came. Tyson's determination, and conditioning, gave him the toughest chin in boxing, but it was now possible to rack up enough points on him to win by decision. Unless Ruddock came back in the rematch with radically improved boxing skills and a new set of more mobile legs, he was not likely to do that. But he might get close on points, and that would only serve as a blueprint for future opponents on how to best fight Tyson.

In what was perhaps an effort to hype the rematch and improve pay-per-view sales, Tyson took his Method acting beyond the bounds of good taste—even for boxing. "I'll make you my girlfriend," he lisped at Ruddock during one of their television appearances. It was a vocabulary drawn from the jailhouse, which of course was part of his life experience. "I'll make you kiss me with those big lips," he added. The sports news media, quoting psychiatrists, speculated about the state of his sexual identity, among other possible mental problems. For Tyson, though, it was just his brand of crude humor, and an aspect of his personality he no longer wanted to repress. It didn't make him all that likeable to mainstream America, but he didn't care.

Ruddock promised to use a jab this time around and to more frequently deploy his right hand. That seemed belied by his weighing in at 238, a gain of ten pounds likely to slow down his punches and tire him out. He said that the gain was intentional, muscle put on from doing more gym work and less running. If so, then he was only trying to improve on a strategy that had already failed—namely, to take Tyson into the later rounds and hope for a knockout from one of his big left hands. The extra muscle-weight would supposedly enable Ruddock to absorb the punishment he'd surely take trying to get there.

Many boxing experts predicted Tyson would win in three to five rounds. It went the distance of twelve. Tyson won by unanimous decision. For brief moments in the first round, he revealed shades of his old boxing style. Over the remainder of the fight he competently worked away at Ruddock, and took a lot of punishment in the process. A pattern started to emerge in Tyson's offense: he would walk in, punch once, sometimes twice, take a few counterblows, then let himself get tied up until the referee broke the clinch. As styles go, it was a rough, brawling, blood-and-sweat ring stomp evocative of the men and the era of boxing Tyson has most closely identified with—Jack Dempsey, Gene

Tunney, and Jack Sharkey of the 1920s. It was no pugilistic ballet, but effective nonetheless.

Ruddock again relied almost solely on his left hook and uppercut. His jab pawed out, and he moved even less than before, no doubt because of the added weight. He was knocked down in the second and fourth rounds. When he did deliver right hands or combinations, they usually connected, though they did little to stop Tyson's relentless forward movement. Ruddock won the third, seventh, and eleventh rounds, when he decided to box. Tyson had points deducted in the ninth and tenth for low blows. If Ruddock had been only marginally more active in those two rounds—as it was, 53 percent of his 198 power punches landed—he could have won them. That would have given him five rounds to Tyson's seven: not a victory, but certainly an achievement. He would have surpassed the record of James ("Quick") Tillis, who in May 1986 took four rounds from Tyson.

*     *     *

On April 19, at the Trump Plaza in Atlantic City, Evander Holyfield put up an unimpressive defense against George Foreman. He won a decision, but it took the full twelve rounds. He appeared unable to hurt the forty-two-year-old Foreman, let alone knock him down, and in the process Holyfield received considerable punishment from Foreman's slow but powerful punches. Foreman surprised the experts, not so much with his ring skills but with an indomitable presence and unexpected stamina; not once did he sit down on the stool between rounds. Holyfield, on the other hand, looked like a beefed-up cruiser-weight who through shrewd management, hard work, and weight lifting was able to rise in the heavyweight ranks and then take full advantage of Douglas's Tokyo fluke to luck into the crown. The question now was whether he was a credible champion, that is, willing to fight and able to beat the leading contender—Mike Tyson.

Tyson, of course, was desperate for the fight. But King had other priorities. Due to the ever-expanding base of pay-per-view homes and the enormous audience appeal of Tyson's long-awaited second shot at the title, the match was expected to break all revenue records by earning as much as $100 million. King relished the chance of raking in and controlling such a sum through his own pay service, KingVision. But that wasn't likely, and he knew it. The champion's management—Shelly Finkel and Dan Duva—traditionally dictated the terms of the deal. They were now aligned with Seth Abraham, which meant televising the fight on TVKO pay-per-view.

King nonetheless made a bid to do the deal on his terms. He demanded $25 million for Tyson's services and the right to televise the fight on KingVision. Finkel and Duva offered $15 million, and as expected, opted for TVKO. They also imposed one more condition: that King sign over options on Tyson's future fights. That was a monopolistically inspired device King had imposed countless times on every opponent who matched up with his champions—when he used to have them.

Attached to the options was a rider entitling TVKO to do the pay-per-view of Tyson's fight. That seemed like a tweak of King's ego by the spurned former ally Seth Abraham, a power play to remind him that in the end he would get what he wanted. In fact, it was a desperation move. TVKO began to sputter. Abraham's concept required both the occasional major title bout involving marquee names and monthly cards of lesser-known fighters. Holyfield-Foreman, by grossing around $51 million from pay-television sales alone, was a resounding success. But Abraham's two other, smaller cards, shown in May and June, lost money. TVKO's future hinged on the megafights. Abraham had Holyfield under contract, and George Foreman, but he needed marquee heavyweight opponents, and King controlled them both: Tyson and Ruddock.

Because the rival promoters couldn't reach an agreement, the fight went to purse bids. Finkel and Duva won with an offer of $51.1 million, of which Tyson would still get $15 million, for a November 8 date at Caesars Palace, Las Vegas. King again rejected the offer. By late June, both parties were trying to use the prospect of a match with George Foreman to force their respective terms. Finkel and Duva offered him $12.5 million—the same amount he earned in his first battle with Holyfield—for a rematch. King came in with a $20 million offer. Within hours of the second Tyson-Ruddock fight, he gave Foreman's brother a $1 million check as an enticement.

Foreman preferred to fight Holyfield. The faster, more powerful Tyson would not only beat him, but do it far more decisively, and Foreman knew that would diminish his aura as a contender and thus limit the size of his purses in future fights. The smaller, slower, lighter-punching Holyfield he could keep at bay into the late rounds, and with luck quite possibly defeat.

Foreman, though, made the mistake of playing hard to get, and lost a $12.5 million payday. He used King's offer to bid up the money from Finkel and Duva, but they wouldn't budge. A smug Foreman decided to wait it out. He assumed, and was told by his promoter, Bob Arum, and adviser, Ron Weathers, that the deal for Holyfield-Tyson couldn't be made. He believed that King would never give up control of a $100 million title fight. He also speculated that King preferred to make the bout after February 12, 1992. That's when Bill Cayton's contract as Tyson's manager expired. King didn't want Cayton to get his 20 percent cut.

In the end, all the assumptions, advice, and speculation proved wrong. In June, rumors circulated about how angry and disillusioned Tyson had become with King for not getting him the promised title shot sooner. He had also apparently accused King of bilking his purses and delaying payments, which led to a public shoving match. Then, in early July, reports surfaced that Tyson had accepted an invitation from Harold Smith, a onetime boxing promoter who served time for a $21 million bank fraud, to meet in Los Angeles and discuss his future. When King got wind of it, he immediately flew in from New York and spirited Tyson away.

King flew to Foreman's home in Houston to make one last effort at closing a deal. It failed. A few days later, Tuesday, July 9, Foreman's promoter, Bob Arum, met with Finkel and Duva in New York to negotiate a rematch for the fall. By mid-afternoon an agreement in principal was reached, and Arum returned to his hotel expecting to sign a formal contract the next day. Meanwhile, King arrived in town with W.B.C. president José Sulaiman. Early that evening, they too met with Finkel and Duva. King was offered $15 million for a November match, or $20 million for an April 1992 date. King agreed to accept the $15 million, but he insisted on a share of the profits above $45 million. Everyone adjourned to consider the terms. King returned to his townhouse on the East Side, where Tyson was anxiously awaiting news of the outcome. "Forget the money," Tyson snapped at King. "I want Holyfield in November." The deal was made the next morning. Tyson got his title shot for November 8 at Caesars Palace, Las Vegas, for a purse of $15 million. King gave up all control of the promotion to Finkel and Duva, meaning that the fight would be televised by Seth Abraham's TVKO. King managed to secure 40 percent of the profits above $48 million. He also didn't have to sign away options to TVKO on Tyson's future rights. Although Bob Arum claimed to have been double-crossed by Finkel and Duva ("It's Machiavellian!" he said, claiming that his deal was made first), Foreman will still end up getting his second title shot. Holyfield, in a moment of empathy, demanded that a clause be put in the contract obligating the winner to make "best efforts" to fight Foreman by mid-1992.

Holyfield's credibility as champion was thus confirmed, partially at least. He will take on the leading contender. But can he beat him? It doesn't seem likely.

Holyfield uses a bigger arsenal of punches than Ruddock and has a respectably strong chin and a solid will. He doesn't, however, have a heavyweight's punching power. But that won't be his biggest problem: Holyfield, like Ruddock and so many of Tyson's opponents over the years, has always had a tendency to stand his ground and trade punches. His basic instinct is to brawl rather than box. That has made him easy to hit. Tyson's own defensive shortcomings will make him an easy target as well. But for every punch he takes, he will give back twice as hard. The simple fact is that Holyfield has never been hit by a punch as fast and brutal as Tyson's. If he can stand up to the punishment as well as Ruddock did, and still maintain his punching accuracy, stamina, and heart, as Douglas was able to do in Tokyo, then he might be able to win a narrow decision. But that means he will have to fight with the qualities of three men, which he cannot do. He will only be himself, and unless there's an Evander Holyfield in there whom no one has yet seen, he will lose the fight, and his title, and Mike Tyson will once again reign.

This second era of Tyson as champion may not last long. At the moment, he is hungry to get the title back. When that's accomplished, his determination to keep winning will slowly drain away. He will have put the crown on his new, resolved self. Much of Tyson's unique defensive ability is, of course, long gone. Within a year of winning the title, his offense will probably start to diminish as well. Tyson's punches will be less devastating. He won't be able to walk through as many of his opponent's blows. And with that his transformation into an ordinary boxer will be complete. That will put him, for the first time in his career, on an equal footing with his opponents. His margins of victory will get narrower. Then one day an extraordinary young contender will come along dreaming a champion's dreams. In order to survive, or for the want of love, he, too, may let himself be made into something that no man ultimately could or would want to be. But that's the price he will pay to beat Tyson. And after being champion for a while, he, too, will want to seek out his humanity, and so he will lose, all of which is the inexorable march known as championship boxing.

# Epilogue

**O**n February 26, 1989, a plaque was placed on the crypt of James Leslie Jacobs. At the ceremony, his widow, Loraine, handed out a poem. It was given to Jacobs by his mother years ago, and began with a question: "Is anybody happier because you passed his way?"

Within a few days of Tyson's Tokyo defeat, the New York tabloids revealed that Donald Trump was having an affair with Marla Maples, a former model from a small town in Georgia. His marriage subsequently fell apart. Soon afterwards, so did his real estate empire. Trump had built it on an estimated $2.3 billion of debt, of which $600 million was personally secured. He fell upon the mercy of his many creditors. By July 1991, he and Maples were planning a marriage.

After struggling through a slump in her career, Robin Givens landed her first starring role in a feature film, *A Rage in Harlem*. "To me, she functions as the ideal woman," said Givens of her character in a May 30, 1991 *Us* magazine profile. "Someone who could be your lover or your friend. But she's also a villain—a bad girl gone good. Initially, she is subservient to men in the story. And then I turn the tables on them; I show them all up."

James ("Buster") Douglas was seen on the streets of Columbus, Ohio, weighing, according to an eyewitness, "at least three hundred pounds."

There have been many rumors about how Don King has pilfered Tyson's money. Until King opens up his accounting books—which he has never done—or Tyson brings suit, nothing can be proven either way. The only shreds of evidence have come from his handling of the monies earned through Tyson's fights on KingVision, particularly the first bout with Donovan Ruddock.

Not surprisingly, the "upside" for Tyson of the KingVision/Showtime venture was limited. The fight brought in around $28 million from pay-television sales. Add in all other sources of revenue, and the gross reached an estimated $41 million. King got to keep only 50 percent of the pay-television money, plus he had to pay Showtime a percentage, and he had basic expenses promoting the fight.

But the deductions didn't stop there. He used the money left over to build up, and keep happy, his dwindling stable of fighters. King put Mexican lightweight Julio Cesar Chavez on the undercard and paid him $2.5 million—an enormous sum for a match that would do little to bring in more pay-television sales in the U.S. market. Welterweight Simon Brown also got on the undercard for $1.5 million, which was more money than he'd ever seen. And then there was Ruddock: for the match, plus the six options, King paid him $5 million. Given King's other expenses, he was left with a net of $8.5 million. King then deducted his one-third promoter's fee. Tyson ended up with $5.7 million.

That's not a bad purse for an evening's work (assuming King ever paid Tyson the money), but it was still less than the $8.5 million Tyson would have netted, as a guarantee, in the new multifight HBO deal that King scuttled.

Said one Tyson confidant: "At the moment, Mike believes that Don can get him the best deal. If Don can't, Mike will do what's best for himself."

One can only hope that he will indeed do that.

# Postscript

**A**s this book was going to press, Mike Tyson was indicted for rape. The charges were handed down by an Indianapolis grand jury on September 9, 1991, and included two counts of criminal deviate conduct and one count of confinement. The indictment stemmed from his alleged sexual assault on an eighteen-year-old beauty pageant contestant whom Tyson had met the previous July 18 at the Indiana Black Expo. The alleged rape, and other acts, were said to have occurred in the early morning hours of July 19 in Tyson's Indianapolis hotel room.

Tyson's trial is scheduled to begin in early 1992. That means he will go ahead with his effort to regain the heavyweight title in a November 8, 1991, bout with champion Evander Holyfield. As of the week of the indictment, Tyson had the full support of all the principals involved in the promotion. It still remained to be seen to what extent public opinion, the state boxing regulators, and the sport's sanctioning bodies, would endorse his decision.

Until the trial begins, and the facts of the case are known, no one is in a position to pass judgment on Mike Tyson. But as a biographer of his life to date, I do feel informed enough to remark on the significance of the indictment as it relates to the various themes, and facts, in this book.

We are all products of the ongoing interplay between basic character and life experience. For Mike Tyson, that mix, that churning, has brought to the surface a darkness of heart. Most of us never have to contend with the dark side of our natures. Tyson has been moving in and out of its shadow since childhood. More important, almost every time he has tried to step fully into the light of faith in another way of being, he has been betrayed. I don't believe he has ever given up trying to escape the darkness. And I am sure that when he does try, he has no interest anymore in letting us know.

Just where Tyson stood existentially on that morning in Indianapolis is now a matter for a jury to decide. A verdict of innocent would not surprise me. A verdict of guilty I would consider tragic.

| 1985 | Mar. | 6 | HECTOR MERCEDES, Albany, NY | KO | 1 |
|---|---|---|---|---|---|
| | Apr. | 10 | TRENT SINGLETON, Albany, NY | TKO | 1 |
| | May | 23 | DON HALPIN, Albany, NY | KO | 4 |
| | June | 20 | RICARDO SPAIN, Atlantic City, NJ | KO | 1 |
| | July | 11 | JOHN ALDERSON, Atlantic City | TKO | 2 |
| | July | 19 | LARRY SIMS, Poughkeepsie, NY | KO | 3 |
| | Aug. | 15 | LORENZO CANADY, Atlantic City, NJ | TKO | 1 |
| | Sept. | 5 | MIKE JOHNSON, Atlantic City, NJ | KO | 1 |
| | Oct. | 9 | DONNIE LONG, Atlantic City, NJ | KO | 1 |
| | Oct. | 25 | ROBERT COLAY, Atlantic City, NJ | KO | 1 |
| | Nov. | 1 | STERLING BENJAMIN, Latham, NY | TKO | 1 |
| | Nov. | 13 | EDDIE RICHARDSON, Houston, TX | KO | 1 |
| | Nov. | 22 | CONROY NELSON, Latham, NY | KO | 2 |
| | Dec. | 6 | SAM SCAFF, New York, NY | KO | 1 |
| | Dec. | 27 | MARK YOUNG, Latham, NY | KO | 1 |
| 1986 | Jan. | 11 | DAVID JACO, Albany, NY | TKO | 1 |
| | Jan. | 24 | MIKE JAMESON, Atlantic City, NJ | TKO | 5 |
| | Feb. | 16 | JESSE FERGUSON, Troy, NY | TKO | 6 |
| | Mar. | 10 | STEVE ZOUSKI, Uniondale, NY | KO | 3 |
| | May | 3 | JAMES TILLIS, Glens Falls, NY | W | 10 |
| | May | 20 | MITCH GREEN, New York, NY | W | 10 |
| | June | 13 | REGGIE GROSS, New York, NY | TKO | 1 |
| | June | 28 | WILLIAM HOSEA, Troy, NY | KO | 1 |
| | July | 11 | LORENZO BOYD, Swan Lake, NY | KO | 2 |
| | July | 26 | MARVIS FRAZIER, Glens Falls, NY | KO | 1 |
| | Aug. | 17 | JOSE RIBALTA, Atlantic City, NJ | TKO | 10 |
| | Sept. | 6 | ALFONZO RATLIFF, Las Vegas, NV | KO | 2 |
| | Nov. | 22 | TREVOR BERBICK, Las Vegas, NV | KO | 2 |
| | | | (Won WBC Heavyweight Title) | | |
| 1987 | Mar. | 7 | JAMES SMITH, Las Vegas, NV | W | 12 |
| | | | (Won WBA Heavyweight Title/ | | |
| | | | Retained WBC Heavyweight Title) | | |
| | May | 30 | PINKLON THOMAS, Las Vegas, NV | TKO | 6 |
| | | | (Retained WBC/WBA Heavyweight Titles) | | |
| | Aug. | 1 | TONY TUCKER, Las Vegas, NV | W | 12 |
| | | | (Won IBF Heavyweight Title/ | | |
| | | | Retained WBC/WBA Heavyweight Titles/ | | |
| | | | Became Undisputed World Heavyweight Champion) | | |
| | Oct. | 16 | TYRELL BIGGS, Atlantic City, NJ | TKO | 7 |
| | | | (Retained World Heavyweight Title) | | |
| 1988 | Jan. | 22 | LARRY HOLMES, Atlantic City, NJ | KO | 4 |
| | | | (Retained World Heavyweight Title) | | |
| | Mar. | 21 | TONY TUBBS, Tokyo, Japan | TKO | 2 |
| | | | (Retained World Heavyweight Title) | | |
| | June. | 27 | MICHAEL SPINKS, Atlantic City, NJ | KO | 1 |
| | | | (Retained World Heavyweight Title) | | |
| 1989 | Feb. | 25 | FRANK BRUNO, Las Vegas, NV | TKO | 5 |
| | | | (Retained World Heavyweight Title) | | |
| | Jul. | 21 | CARL WILLIAMS, Atlantic City, NJ | TKO | 1 |
| | | | (Retained World Heavytweight Title) | | |
| 1990 | Feb. | 11 | JAMES DOUGLAS, Tokyo, Japan | KO | by 10 |
| | | | (Lost World Heavyweight Title) | | |
| | June | 16 | HENRY TILLMAN, Las Vegas, NV | KO | 1 |
| | Dec. | 8 | ALEX STEWART, Atlantic City, NJ | TKO | 1 |
| 1991 | Mar. | 18 | DONOVAN RUDDOCK, Las Vegas, NV | TKO | 7 |
| | June | 28 | DONOVAN RUDDOCK, Las Vegas, NV | W | 12 |

Fights: 42    Wins: 41    Losses: 1    Draws: 0    KO's: 36

# Index